Teach me how to live when...

my faith is weak . . . my mate and
I have drifted apart . . . my self-
esteem is gone . . . I fall into sin
. . . I'm alone and afraid . . . I am
overwhelmed by urgent de-
mands . . . my dreams have
been shattered. . . .

Teach Me How to Live is a
unique devotional. It amplifies
what Scripture says about problems, emotions, and attitudes—
and teaches you how to
develop biblical character day
by day. It takes you by the hand
and guides your steps in the
Christian walk, giving you practical experience in godly living.
Monthly themes concentrate on
specific areas, including:

- **Faith**
- **Self-esteem**
- **Oneness**
- **Commitment**
- **Leadership**
- **Fruitfulness**
  - **Knowing God**

Teach Me How To Live

*A Second Devotional Journey
with Kay Arthur*

Fleming H. Revell Company
Tarrytown, New York

Permission to quote from the following is gratefully acknowledged:

Love Life for Every Married Couple by Dr. Ed Wheat. Copyright © 1980 by Ed Wheat, M.D. Published by The Zondervan Corporation.

Run for the West by Bernard Palmer. Copyright © 1979 by Bernard Palmer. Published by David C. Cook Publishing Co., Elgin, Illinois.

The Cross of Christ, The Throne of God by F. J. Huegel, Copyright © 1965 by Bethany House Publishers.

"The Christian Life: A Marathon We Mean to Win?" in *Christianity Today,* 1981.

Unless otherwise identified, all Scripture quotations in this book are taken from the New American Standard Bible, Copyright © THE LOCKMAN FOUNDATION 1960, 1962, 1963, 1968, 1971, 1972, 1973, 1975 and are used by permission.

Scripture quotations identified KJV are from the King James Version of the Bible.

Scripture quotations identified NEB are from The New English Bible. © The Delegates of the Oxford University Press 1961 and 1970. Reprinted by permission.

Scripture quotations identified NIV are from the HOLY BIBLE New International Version, copyright ©, New York International Bible Society, 1978. Used by permission.

Library of Congress Cataloging in Publication Data

Arthur, Kay, date
  Teach me how to live.

  "Power books."
  Bibliography: p.
  1. Devotional calendars. I. Title.
BV4811.A78 1984   242'.2   83-13782
ISBN 0-8007-5125-6 (pbk.)

To my Lord Jesus Christ . . .
   God's answer to my prayers for peace.
And to my earthly lord, Jack . . .
   God's answer to my prayers for a husband.

CONTENTS

Do You Know God?

"The people that do know their God shall be strong, and do exploits," says the prophet Daniel. This month begins a two-part meditation on God's sovereignty. We will ask, "Should a Christian expect adversity?" For the next two months I'll share some of my life experiences and how God has used them in His loving sovereignty to mold my life.

When We Ask "Why?"

If I were permitted to share only one truth with you, I would choose to teach you the character and sovereignty of our God, for this truth anchors my soul when I do not understand the circumstances of life. In this truth I find peace, security, and rest that makes me a conqueror over doubt and distress.

Listen to Me!

God's message for this month's meditations in Malachi is not an easy word, but it is a very necessary one! Look around you at those who profess Christ. How many do you see that are totally sold out to Him, committed to His will no matter what the cost? I pray that you will listen. If I speak truth, follow it . . . live it . . . preach it. Our time is short. He is coming.

Do You Like Yourself?

I have held them in my arms, and they have said through flooding tears—"I can't believe God loves me" . . . "I can't believe I am worth anything" . . . "I can't believe anyone loves me." Attractive, capable, intelligent, personable people have been rendered inopera-

CONTENTS

tive due to low self-esteem. This is for these dear ones, and for those of you who love those who "can't believe."

Oneness

Oneness—it is laying hold of that for which He laid hold of you. There are three major earthly relationships that God uses to achieve oneness with Him—family, marriage, and the church. Learning oneness in these relationships plays an integral part in learning oneness with God.

Make Oneness Your Goal

How confession and forgiveness figure in oneness. God's design for marriage is oneness, and oneness involves commitment—total, complete, unconditional commitment. For better or for worse, for richer or for poorer, in sickness and in health until death do us part! This is God's commitment to us—except that even death does not end our relationship with Him.

What Does It Mean to Live by Faith?

Faith that moves mountains finds its ability to do so not in itself, but in God. The warrant of faith is always found in what God says, and this in turn rests on who God is. And if we have trouble believing, we can change our unbelief to belief. This comes as we get to know our God; it is difficult to trust someone you do not know.

Why Are You in Despair, O My Soul?

The church is lulled into apathy because we have become caught in the things of this world. And I tremble, for we are not rooted or grounded in the Word of God. We are too busy; it takes too much time, too much discipline. What will we do in the day of calamity that is on the horizon? How will the just live by faith then, when we are not living by faith now?

CONTENTS

When the Leaders Lead, the People Follow

Part one of a two-part study on leadership. From Judges, the life of Abraham, and the example of Joseph, we will consider the price and responsibilities of leadership.

Leadership Is . . .

Leadership is knowing the Deliverer . . . being taught by God . . . expecting to be challenged . . . being brought to impassable, impossible waters . . . a life of petition and intercession . . . deciding whose glory—yours or God's . . . doing God's work God's way.

Taking the Bitter, Making It Sweet

The cross is the identification mark of a Christian, first because of what it effects in our lives . . . and second because of our constant identification with its work. The cross works deliverance from sin's dominion, sin's penalty, and Satan's power.

Following in His Steps

Unjust suffering is so hard to understand, isn't it? You wonder where God is and, if He is sovereign, how He can allow it. Sometimes the questions seem overwhelming. And sometimes the suffering seems unbearable. How do you handle it? I pray that God will use the teaching, and your meditation, to speak to you far beyond the power of these feeble words.

Preface

"And He humbled you and let you be hungry, and fed you with manna which you did not know, nor did your fathers know, that He might make you understand that man does not live by bread alone, but man lives by everything that proceeds out of the mouth of the Lord" (Deuteronomy 8:3)

Beloved, it is my prayer that this book will give you an even greater appetite for His Word so that God Himself might teach you how to live.

Teach Me
How To Live

JANUARY

Do You Know God?

January 1

I will never forget the first time I really saw Daniel 11:32b. I had begun to read J. I. Packer's outstanding book, *Knowing God*. When I came across his quote of the Daniel passage—"but the people that do know their God shall be strong, and do exploits"—it was as if my Divine Guide had taken me into a magnificent museum of truth. On the walls hung exquisite pieces of art—each one a portrait of my God. Awestruck, I fell to my knees as I knew the presence of the Sovereign God. The realization of the fact that God did according to His will in the army of heaven and among the inhabitants of the earth and that no one could say to Him, "What doest Thou?" hit me like a bolt of lightning, throwing me from my knees face down before His throne (Daniel 4:34, 35). "He rules!" Incredulously, the reality of the words throbbed in my head. Nothing happens by happenstance. I am not in the hands of fate, nor am I the victim of man's whims or the devil's ploys. One sits above man, above Satan, and above all heavenly hosts, as the supreme and ultimate authority of all the universe. That One is my God and my Father!

As suddenly as I had entered that museum of truth, my mind raced back to my first days as His child. Once again I could see Dave Pantzer standing in my living room. He had taken off his ring, placed it in his palm and then tightly wrapped his fingers around it. "Kay, you are just like this ring now that you belong to God. God has you in His hand, and no one can touch you, peek at you, or say anything to you without God's permission." I will never forget how Dave's other hand tried to pry open those whitened knuckles, nor shall I forget how his head bent down to peep at the ring, but it was all in vain. The hand held fast to the ring so that nothing could touch it or even look at it until the hand permitted it!

Now, as I lay prostrate in that museum of truth, I understood what Dave had been teaching me. My God is sovereign! When I walked out I knew that I would know my God better and that, knowing Him, I would be able to stand firm and do exploits for His glory.

This month, Beloved, God wants me to take you into this museum of truth so that you, too, might behold your God and, knowing Him, stand firm and do exploits. I do not pretend to know all or to have plumbed the depths of the wisdom or the knowledge of God, but, as we stand before each portrait of His character, I will share with you some of what He has taught me. Together we will grow to know Him more intimately.

January 2

I never read any more of *Knowing God.* Yet Dr. Packer's book served its purpose, for it drove me immediately into God's Word to search out all I could learn about the sovereignty and the character of this One who sits on His throne, supreme over all. In that magnificent museum of truth, my eyes widened in wonder as they fell on engraved plates of gold. Omniscience . . . Omnipotence . . . Omnipresence . . . Mercy . . . Justice . . . Righteousness . . . on and on I walked. As I read each inscription, the swell of a great orchestration of violins, harps, trumpets, cymbals, and other magnificent instruments provided the background for multitudes of heavenly choruses singing, "Holy, Holy, Holy, is the Lord God, the Almighty, who was and who is and who is to come" (Revelation 4:8). Yet, although caught in this stereophonic orchestration of praise, I could hear the Spirit's whisper, "Behold your God . . . and live." Suddenly lost in reverence and awe of Him, concerns about myself—my well-being, my security, my loved ones, my needs, my hopes, my dreams, my ambitions—fell into insignificance. Standing in the knowledge and the presence of One far greater than man or angels or Satan, I was enveloped in a security I had never experienced before. I had found my dwelling.

He who dwells in the shelter of the Most High will abide in the shadow of the Almighty. I will say to the Lord, "My refuge and my fortress, my God, in whom I trust!" For it is He who delivers you from the snare of the trapper, and from the deadly pestilence. He will cover you with His pinions, and under His wings you may seek refuge; His faithfulness is a shield and bulwark (Psalms 91:1-4).

Then I knew, as never before, "Lord, Thou hast been our dwelling place in all generations. Before the mountains were born, or Thou didst give birth to the earth and the world, even from everlasting to everlasting, Thou art God" (Psalms 90:1, 2).

January 3

If we are to know God we must have correct definitions of those terms which describe His being. When I say that God is sovereign, I mean that He rules over all, that nothing can happen in God's universe without His permission. Now, those who do not like this teaching or who cannot reason this out fully in their minds will oppose the idea of God's sovereignty with rebuttals about the free will of man. "But if God rules over all, then that makes man a puppet!" Or, "If God is sovereign and nothing can happen without His permission, then man cannot be accountable to God. He has to do whatever God wants!" Yet in defining God's sovereignty I would also say that although God is sovereign, man still retains his free will and is totally responsible and accountable to God.

Man has been given a free will and stands answerable to God for all his actions, but God so rules and overrules that no man or angel, demon or devil—nor any circumstance of life—can thwart God's desire or God's plan. Neither necessity, nor chance, nor Satan's malice controls the sequence of events or their causes. Rather, God rules supremely over all.

Now you need to stop and meditate upon all of this. Think it through and talk to God about it. Ask the Holy Spirit to guide you into all truth. When it comes to having total peace of mind, I honestly do not believe that there is a more reassuring doctrine in all of Scripture than the sovereignty of God. I know of so many people who have been able to pass through trials as truly more than conquerors because they realized that God is sovereign and rested in that truth.

So meditate upon what I have said. The doctrine does not originate with me. It has been the mainstay of saints down through all of the ages. Write down your questions, your "ifs," your "buts." Seek His face and trust Him by His Spirit and through His Word to guide you into all truth.

January 4

Have you ever read the book of Daniel? It's quite a book! Liberals deny its authenticity. They join many historians in saying that it could never have been written by Daniel, for it is far too accurate historically and, therefore, must have been written after the fact. Neither can they contend with its miracles; there is too much of the supernatural! However, students of eschatology (future things) find it to be one of their main texts. Those who accept the Bible as the verbal, plenary, inspired

Word of God would remind you that the prophet Ezekiel referred to Daniel three times and that Jesus warned His own to take heed when they would "see the ABOMINATION OF DESOLATION which was spoken of through Daniel the prophet" (Matthew 24:15). The enemy would seek to destroy its veracity. The father of lies once again hisses his age-old "yea, hath God said?" But we will not fall captive to the philosophies and empty deceptions of higher criticism; rather we will believe our Lord Jesus Christ who constantly attested to the veracity of the Old Testament during His sojourn here on earth.

Remember, Daniel declares that "the people who know their God will display strength and take action. And those who have insight among the people will give understanding to the many" (11:32b, 33a). God will use not only the knowledge of His character to strengthen your life, but He will also use you to give understanding to others, to those who will listen.

Listen, Beloved, listen.

As you read through Daniel, you will notice that at Chapter 4, Daniel stops writing! Another takes up his pen and adds a personal word of testimony. I can see it all. Apparently Daniel, led by God, began writing a chronological account of the events in his life after he was taken captive by the Babylonians, when Nebuchadnezzar was king. In Daniel's diary, he recorded the various dreams and decrees of Nebuchadnezzar in abject honesty. However, when Daniel comes to the story of the king's humiliation by God, Nebuchadnezzar must tell his own story! He had finally recognized that as for the King of heaven, "all His works are true and His ways just, and He is able to humble those who walk in pride" (4:37).

We will read his story tomorrow.

January 5

As Nebuchadnezzar takes up his pen to give his testimony, he gives his reason for writing: "It has seemed good to me to declare the signs and wonders which the Most High God has done for me. How great are His signs, and how mighty are His wonders! His kingdom is an everlasting kingdom, and His dominion is from generation to generation" (Daniel 4:2, 3).

Obviously, Nebuchadnezzar is concerned that all who live upon the earth should recognize God's sovereignty (4:1). But did King Nebuchadnezzar always feel this way? No! Not until after God visited him through a prophetic dream which was interpreted by Daniel and then came to pass in Nebuchadnezzar's life. As humbling as it was, the king needed to see **"that it is Heaven that rules"** (4:26). Thus the interpretation of his dream and the decree of the Most High came upon the king "that you be driven away from mankind, and your dwelling place be with the beasts of the field, and you be given grass to eat like cattle and be drenched with the dew of heaven; and seven periods of time will pass over you, until you recognize that the Most High is ruler over the realm of mankind, and bestows it on whomever He wishes" (4:25).

Twelve months later, the dream was fulfilled. As you read Nebuchadnezzar's account, note why he had to be humbled. Then tomorrow we will look at the end result of it all.

"He [Nebuchadnezzar] was walking on the roof of the royal palace of Babylon. The king reflected and said, 'Is this not Babylon the great, which I myself have built as a royal residence by the might of my power and for the glory of my majesty?' While the word was in the king's mouth, a voice came from heaven, saying, 'King Nebuchadnezzar, to you it is declared: sovereignty has been removed from you, and you will be driven away from mankind, and your dwelling place will be with the beasts of the field. You will be given grass to eat like cattle, and seven periods of time will pass over you, until you recognize that the Most High is ruler over the realm of mankind, and bestows it on whomever He wishes.' Immediately the word concerning Nebuchadnezzar was fulfilled; and he was driven away from mankind and began eating grass like cattle, and his body was drenched with the dew of heaven, until his hair had grown like eagles' feathers and his nails like birds' claws" (Daniel 4:29–33).

January 6

Humanism. It has come to the forefront lately in our vocabulary, and yet it is as old as Satan's enticement, "you will be like God" (Genesis 3:5). We find the first public declaration of humanism in God's Word at the Tower of Babel. "And they said, 'Come, let us build for ourselves a city, and a tower whose top will reach into heaven, and **let us make for ourselves a name;** lest we be scattered abroad over the face of the whole earth' " (Genesis 11:4). God's word to man after the flood had been to "be fruitful and multiply, and fill the earth" (9:1). At Babel, Nimrod instigated a rebellion in direct opposition to that command. No, they would not obey. Instead, they would make a name for themselves and maintain their human unity. Man, not God, would be supreme. And that is exactly what humanism purports. It makes man the measure of all things and puts man at the center of the universe rather than God.

Man does not want to acknowledge that there is a God in heaven who has a direct role in his affairs. Rather, he prefers to attribute the occurrences of nature and the destiny of man either to the nebulous hands of fate or the caprice of men with power. In this way, man would deny that God has any role in our world at all. Humanism is an insidious doctrine that, like leaven, has spread into the theology of the church, puffing it up into a heady, higher criticism of God's Word. Beware of the leaven of humanism.

It greatly affected King Nebuchadnezzar, who became caught up in his own importance. He had built Babylon by his own power, for his own glory (Daniel 4:30)! Yet, when brought face to face with his own impotence before God, he honored God as God. " 'For His dominion is an everlasting dominion, and His kingdom endures from generation to generation. And all the inhabitants of the earth are accounted as nothing, but He does according to His will in the host of heaven and among the inhabitants of earth; and no one can ward off His hand or say to Him, "What hast Thou done?" ' " (4:34, 35).

O Beloved, who is at the center of your universe? Do you imagine that you are the captain of your own destiny? Do you imagine yourself in the hands of some fickle power called fate? Or have you in total humility bowed your knee to the Sovereign Ruler of the universe and said, "My Lord and my God, I recognize that I exist because of Thy will and that I was created for Thy pleasure. I humble myself before Thee, my King."

January 7

Do you read the newspapers and tremble? It seems as if the news serves only as a prophet of doom. If you do not become the victim of some atrocious crime, then surely unemployment or inflation will price you right out of a decent life. If you manage to escape becoming one of those statistics, perhaps you will find yourself devastated by flood, earthquake, or tornado. If not, it is still possible that a routine examination will proclaim the frightening news, "Cancer." Yet, supposing you remain untouched by "all of the above," is there not the possibility of suddenly finding yourself a statistic of divorce or a broken home? Yet escaping this, is there not talk about a global war within the next two to four years, at the most? And what about your loved ones? If you should escape, will they also?

Is it any wonder that multitudes are committing suicide while others escape into the oblivion of drugs or alcohol, and still others live in the darkness of depression? Psychiatrists, psychologists, and counselors abound; yet there are not enough of them to treat the plague that has made the souls of mankind sick. Is this what God designed for man—a future without hope? No, Beloved, no! This is what has happened to man because he has chosen to believe Satan, the father of lies. God knows the thoughts that He has for those who are His, "plans for welfare and not for calamity to give you a future and a hope" (Jeremiah 29:11). Christians must never look to the future or even at today except from the perspective of His sovereignty. For if God is not sovereign then you cannot give thanks in all things (1 Thessalonians 5:18), for God cannot cause all things to work together for good to them who love Him and are the called according to His purpose, and the events of your life can never be used to make you into His image (Romans 8:28, 29). Rather you are the victim of man, Satan, nature, or fate.

Oh, no, Beloved, God is sovereign. And He assures you: "Surely, just as I have intended so it has happened, and just as I have planned so it will stand. . . . For the Lord of hosts has planned, and who can frustrate it? And as for His stretched-out hand, who can turn it back?" (Isaiah 14:24, 27).

January 8

"Does God permit cancer, death, famine, nakedness, danger . . . in a Christian's life? Do you mean to tell me that a God of love permits such things? No, thanks! If that's your God, then I want no part of Him!"

Have you ever heard statements to this effect? If you have ever discussed the sovereignty of God, you have. Possibly you have even had these thoughts yourself. I understand. They are natural and normal reasonings of the human mind. Yet, Beloved, the human mind cannot reason them out apart from the veracity of His Word. " 'For My thoughts are not your thoughts, neither are your ways My ways,' declares the Lord. 'For as the heavens are higher than the earth, so are My ways higher than your ways, and My thoughts than your thoughts' " (Isaiah 55:8, 9). "And do not be conformed to this world, but be transformed by the renewing of your mind, that you may prove what the will of God is, that which is good and acceptable and perfect" (Romans 12:2).

Let us answer these questions about adversity and sickness from God's Word, and humbly submit to what He speaks whether we can rationalize it or not. We must take one precept at a time, day by day. So be patient, listen, and wait for His revelation; just beware that you lean not to your own understanding.

First we want to look at adversity and how it fits into God's sovereignty. This will take several days. Listen to what God says of Himself through the prophet Isaiah, then meditate upon it and we'll talk about it tomorrow.

> "I am the Lord, and there is no other; besides Me there is no God. I will gird you, though you have not known Me; that men may know from the rising to the setting of the sun that there is no one besides Me. I am the Lord, and there is no other, the One forming light and creating darkness, causing well-being and creating calamity; I am the Lord who does all these" (Isaiah 45:5–7).

January 9

In Isaiah 45:7, God tells us that He is the One who causes well-being or peace and who creates calamity. The word calamity is *ra* in the Hebrew, and in the King James Version it is translated *evil*. It refers to distress, affliction, sorrow, or trouble.

The word for create is *bara*, which means *to create, to cut down, to select, feed, choose, dispatch*. It is used in this passage to show the unfolding of God's purposes in history. It does not make God the author or instigator of evil, for "Let no one say when he is tempted, 'I am being tempted by God'; for God cannot be tempted by evil, and He Himself does not tempt any one" (James 1:13). Rather, what God is saying is that if evil occurs, He permits it, and He will use it to achieve His ultimate goal and glory. For He makes even the wrath of man to praise His name (Psalms 76:10; Exodus 9:16).

Thus when adversity comes into your life, Precious One, you can rest in the fact that first it had to be filtered through His sovereign fingers. And those are fingers of love, for God is love! If you are familiar with the Old Testament and the history of God's chosen people, Israel, you know that many times God used the adversity brought by other nations to chasten Israel. Yet that chastening (discipline) came because He loved them (Hebrews 12:5, 6; Proverbs 3:11, 12). However, God then held the nations accountable to Him for their evil behavior toward Israel.

"I can't understand it. It doesn't seem fair!" Is that what you are thinking? Remember, God's ways are not your ways, His thoughts are not your thoughts. Faith submits, taking God at His word and resting in His character. In the days to come you will see that this Sovereign One who sits upon the throne of the universe is just, merciful, holy, righteous—a God of love. Rest and listen. Remember Job? Why not read the first chapter of Job? When you do, write out who permitted Job's adversity or calamity. Then we will discuss it tomorrow.

January 10

Our question goes back to the eighth day of this month—"And what about adversity in a Christian's life? Does God permit that? Cancer, death, famine, nakedness, danger. Do you mean to tell me that a God of love could permit such things?"

Did God permit it in Job's life? Yes, He did. When Satan challenged the reason for Job's fear (or reverence) of God, did God not say to Satan, "Behold, all that he has is in your power, only do not put forth your hand on him" (Job 1:12)? And what did Satan do? Why, he brought calamity upon calamity, wave upon wave as he literally wiped out all that Job had. And what did Job do at the end of that tragic day, after learning of the destruction of his livestock and the death of his servants and his sons and daughters?

> Then Job arose and tore his robe and shaved his head, and he fell to the ground and worshiped. And he said, "Naked I came from my mother's womb, and naked I shall return there. The Lord gave and the Lord has taken away. Blessed be the name of the Lord" (Job 1:20, 21).

Tell me, Job, from where did this calamity come? "The Lord gave and the Lord has taken away." Job looked beyond secondary causes to the sovereignty of God, and he bowed his knee without bitterness. "Through all this Job did not sin nor did he blame God" (1:22). Yet the adversity was not over. Satan would again be permitted to touch Job, this time with boils. Yet he could not take Job's life for God would not give him permission. "So the Lord said to Satan, 'Behold, he is in your power, only spare his life'" (Job 2:6).

O Precious Child of God, are you in great travail of soul because of some adversity? Fear not, your Father is filtering it through fingers of love. As it was with Job, so it will be with you. It will result in good.

January 11

"But how?" you say. "How could it ever result in good? There's no way!"

No, there doesn't seem to be any way, does there? It all seems so senseless, so painful, so cruel, so unjust. I understand, yet we have such limited perspectives. We are so bound by our humanity, our concepts, our evaluations. Our vision is so shortsighted, our perspective so temporal. "Eye hath not seen, nor ear heard, neither have entered into the heart of man, the things which God hath prepared for them that love him" (1 Corinthians 2:9 KJV). No, Beloved, things like this cannot be understood with the senses; they must be revealed by His Spirit (1 Corinthians 2:10). May God grant you that revelation, wherever you are, according to your deepest need. And may you give Him time to speak to you. May you be still and know that He is God. And in knowing that, may you bow your knee before Him in total meekness.

Job was to suffer much. He endured boils. When his wife suggested that he "curse God and die," he responded, " 'You speak as one of the foolish women speaks. Shall we indeed accept good from God and not accept adversity (*evil*)?' In all this Job did not sin with his lips" (Job 2:9, 10). No, Job did not sin with his lips. Even so, his days were only to increase in the bitterness of adversity as pious friends came to point out his seeming transgressions.

O Job, I know it must have seemed unbearable at times, but I thank you for going before me. I know, my Dear Brother, it must have caused you anguish of soul that I have never known; yet I thank you, for your tragedy has left me a legacy of untold wealth. And not me alone, but millions besides me. Without your story, there would be areas of darkness in my understanding. Job, among other things I understand that now, "Whether for correction, or for His world, or for lovingkindness, He causes it to happen" (Job 37:13). I now look at the wars of man and can see how my God, through the weather, turned the course of history as in the Normandy Invasion and the Battle of Midway.

O Job, I bow with you before our God and I say as you did during the days of your great affliction, "I know that Thou canst do all things, and that no purpose of Thine can be thwarted" (Job 42:2). And there on my knees beside you, I find peace, and in this meekness, I inherit the earth (Matthew 5:5).

January 12

Adversity. Why does God permit it? O Beloved, can you not see its purpose by now? It is to refine us, to consume the dross so that we can come forth as pure gold tried in a furnace of fire seven times. Remember, the thoughts He has of us are thoughts of good, not evil, to give us a future and a hope (Jeremiah 29:11). And what is that future but to share in His glory? "For I consider that the sufferings of this present time are not worthy to be compared with the glory that is to be revealed to us" (Romans 8:18). Therefore "in this you greatly rejoice, even though now for a little while, if necessary, you have been distressed by various trials, that the proof of your faith, being more precious than gold which is perishable, even though tested by fire, may be found to result in praise and glory and honor at the revelation of Jesus Christ" (1 Peter 1:6, 7).

When Job's trial was over, and Satan saw that Job truly feared his God and did not have merely a fair weather faith of bless-me-God-and-answer-my-prayers-but-don't-make-it-rough-and-I-will-worship-You, then God restored the fortunes of Job and increased all that he had twofold. But was that all? Was it simply a matter of material gain for Job once the trial was over and his faith was proved? Oh, no! It was far more than that. Job himself said, "I have heard of Thee by the hearing of the ear; but now my eyes see Thee; therefore I retract, and I repent in dust and ashes" (Job 42:5, 6). Now Job knew his God as he had never known Him. This, Beloved, is the purpose of adversity in your life. It is filtered through His fingers of love so that you might say with the Psalmist, "It is good for me that I was afflicted, that I may learn Thy statutes" (Psalms 119:71). "But the people that do know their God shall be strong, and do exploits" (Daniel 11:32b).

Through adversity Job came to know His God even better, and it will be the same for you and for me.

January 13

Today I feel that God would simply have me share with you this precious poem that was given to me by a dear saint of God. I do not know who wrote it for it bears no author's signature.

The Refiner's Fire

He sat by a furnace of sevenfold heat,
  As He watched by the precious ore,
And closer He bent with a searching gaze
  As He heated it more and more.
He knew He had ore that could stand the test

And He wanted the finest gold,
To mold as a crown, for the King to wear,
Set with gems of price untold.
So He laid our gold in the burning fire,
Tho' we fain would say Him, "Nay";
And watched the dross that we had not seen,
As it melted and passed away.
And the gold grew brighter and yet more bright,
But our eyes were dim with tears,
We saw but the fire—not the Master's hand,
And questioned with anxious fears.
Yet our gold shone out with a richer glow
As it mirrored a Form above,
That bent o'er the fire, tho' unseen by us,
With a look of ineffable love.
Can we think it pleases His loving heart
To cause us a moment's pain?
Ah, no! but He sees through the present cross
The bliss of eternal gain.
So He waited there with a watchful eye,
With a love that is strong and sure,
And His gold did not suffer a bit more heat
Than was needed to make it pure.

January 14

Have you ever wondered what purpose prayer has if God is sovereign? After all, if it's going to happen, then it's going to happen. So why should I pray?

These thoughts have occurred to me, although I must admit they have come as a result of preparing myself as a teacher of God's Word rather than as personal questions of my own heart.

To me, accepting God's sovereignty doesn't mean that I must make every other truth in God's Word submit to the logic of His sovereignty. Maybe it is my naiveté or my lack of formal education, but I just don't have problems trying to make all my doctrines fit into a logical sequence with one doctrine totally supporting, explaining, or amplifying the other according to my human reasoning. To illustrate my point, let me ask you how you explain the doctrine of election, predestination, and the free will of man. If you are like many, you will buy one and discard the others because you cannot make them "fit"! Others of us accept all three doctrines because we feel that if Scripture says it, we are to accept it and believe it even if we cannot make it totally jibe! When I cannot make it all fit together, I simply say:

> Oh, the depth of the riches both of the wisdom and knowledge of God! How unsearchable are His judgments and unfathomable His ways! For who has known the mind of the Lord, or who became His counselor? Or who has first given to Him that it might be paid back to Him again? For from Him and through Him and to Him are all things. To Him be the glory forever. Amen (Romans 11:33–36).

To me this is far better than taking doctrines to extremes.

Why don't you stop and ask God how balanced you are? Are you a real student of His Word, or are you an opinionated follower of men? If you are the latter, you are still precious, but you are carnal. I say that in love. That was the problem in Corinth (1 Corinthians 1:10–17, 3:1–5).

January 15

Deuteronomy 32:39 says, "See now that I, I am He, and there is no god besides Me; it is I who put to death and give life. I have wounded, and it is I who heal; and there is no one who can deliver from My hand." If God wounds and heals, kills and makes alive, then why pray when we or one of our loved ones becomes sick? Why not just accept it with a certain fatalistic attitude? Because, Beloved, God bids us pray. "Is anyone among you sick? Let him call for the elders of the church, and let them pray over him, anointing him with oil in the name of the Lord; and the prayer offered in faith will restore the one who is sick, and the Lord will raise him up, and if he has committed sins, they will be forgiven him. Therefore, confess your sins to one another, and pray for one another, so that you may be healed. The effective prayer of a righteous man can accomplish much" (James 5:14–16).

How God's sovereignty and prayer fit together I do not completely understand, but I do know that laced throughout the tapestry of God's Word is the golden thread of His sovereignty. Yet side by side, looping over and under in a beautiful and intricate pattern, is the silver thread of the redemptive power of prayer. Neither distracts from the other nor mars God's perfect pattern.

God takes pains to let us see Asa's failure to turn to God when "in the thirty-ninth year of his reign Asa became diseased in his feet. His disease was severe, yet even in his disease he did not seek the Lord but the physicians" (2 Chronicles 16:12).

Yet God gives us an account of king Hezekiah, who in his illness cried out to God and was healed. God sent the prophet Isaiah to tell him to set his house in order because of his impending death. "Then he turned his face to the wall, and prayed to the Lord, saying, 'Remember now, O Lord, I beseech Thee, how I have walked before Thee in truth and with a whole heart, and have done what is good in Thy sight.' And Hezekiah wept bitterly" (2 Kings 20:2, 3).

God stayed his death saying, "I have heard your prayer, I have seen your tears; behold, I will heal you" (20:5).

Oh yes, Beloved, our times are in His hands; He holds the keys to hell and death; yet He bids us pray (Psalms 31:15; Revelation 1:18). Don't try to figure it all out! Just believe Him, do what He says, and rest.

January 16

I receive so many letters from people who are hurting and confused. They are usually hurting in the area of interpersonal relationships, often involving divorce, or in the area of physical illness. Their confusion comes because they have believed God to alter their situation and He hasn't. Either the loved one has not come back, the marriage has not been healed, or God has not given them another husband or wife.

For example, I read a letter last night from a woman who had been married and divorced five times. Then she was saved. And what is her heart's cry now? "I'm very alone. However, I don't just want someone, anyone, and I **definitely** don't want an affair! My greatest desire is (only if it's possible without going to hell) to meet and marry a good Christian man! To fulfill what God intended for my life!" Her confusion is over whether or not she can have a good marriage and if not, why not? After all, a good marriage, to her, is fulfillment. Her letter is not unique. Oh, granted, the majority have not been divorced as many as five times, but many have been divorced at least once. And if they are not divorced, then it is a matter of infidelity, and they want the infidelity stopped or they want to be set free from the marriage so they can find someone else and live happily ever after. Their confusion is, in essence, "If I am praying and believing God, why doesn't He in some way alter my situation?"

It is the same with those who are physically ill. Someone wrote: "I was left with an injured nerve in my leg (I'm 65). I'm not able to do much. I believe God has saved me, and I have prayed so much for my healing. Sometimes I feel like He doesn't hear my prayers because the nerve hasn't healed back. God made that leg, and I believe He can make it back as He did the first time. Am I deceived, or is it not God's will to heal me? Write me your thoughts and pray for my healing." Physical healing is foremost in their minds; and I can understand this because of all that they see from religious programs on television. Their confusion is, "Why, if I believe, am I not being healed like others?"

Their confusion, to put it another way, is, "Doesn't God want me to be happy? Surely if I am a child of God, I'm not to suffer such disappointments, am I???"

Are we? If God is God, if He is sovereign, if He honors faith and answers prayer, why doesn't He always intervene and alter our situation? Good question, isn't it? What's the answer? Ask God and then we'll talk about it tomorrow.

January 17

When we walk through God's magnificent museum of truth, surveying the various portraits of the Sovereign Ruler of the universe, do we catch grotesque or fearful images of different aspects of God's character that show Him to be a cruel or malicious despot? No, of course not! The One who sits upon the throne of the universe is a God of love. The Scriptures state it very plainly, "God is love" (1 John 4:8). God's actions demonstrate it very clearly, "For God so loved the world that He gave His only begotten Son . . ." (John 3:16). The very essence of God's being is love.

Love is not merely an attitude with which God clothes Himself at times; rather it is an attribute that so permeates His being that He could never divest Himself of it. To do so would make Him less than God. Therefore, whatever actions or commandments issue forth from His throne must come forth from love. Even His judgments! Why? Because God is love.

How well do you understand love? How deep is your comprehension of love? How pure? How broad? Can we, as redeemed sinners not yet made perfect, begin to comprehend "the breadth and length and height and depth and to know the love of Christ which surpasses knowledge" (Ephesians 3:18, 19)?

Can we, with our finite reasoning power, begin to judge whether or not God is acting in love? After all, is He not the source and therefore the author of love? Could we even begin to know love or to act in love if it were not for Him? Would we have a clear, untainted demonstration of the purity of love if we had not seen or heard of it from Him? How then can we sit in judgment of God and accuse Him of not being loving if He does not conform to our evaluation of love's behavior? What folly!

Yet, is this not what we do when God's actions do not concur with or live up to our expectations? Doesn't a loving God want us to be happy? Surely he will not leave us in disappointment with our prayers not answered when we have prayed in faith believing, will He?

O Precious One, if you are hurting, if you are confused, if you are disappointed in God, don't be. Believe Him when He says, "I have loved you with an everlasting love; therefore I have drawn you with lovingkindness" (Jeremiah 31:3).

January 18

Oh, what peace, what rest would be ours now if only we would live in the full knowledge of His sovereign love. Granted, we would still suffer pain and tribulation, for these are to be our lot in one way or another simply because we belong to His Kingdom. When Christ returns as King of kings and rules this earth with His rod of iron, then the hurt, the pain, the suffering, and tribulation will end (Daniel 7:13, 14, 22, 27; Revelation 2:25–27). But until then God would have us look beyond our circumstances and our evaluation of our lot in life to His sovereign throne and know that "from Him and through Him and to Him are all things" (Romans 11:36). He would have us know that our disappointments are His appointments, working a far more eternal weight of glory.

> "Disappointment—His *appointment*,"
>> Change one letter, then I see
> That the thwarting of my purpose
>> Is God's better choice for me.
> His appointment must be blessing,
>> Tho' it may come in disguise,
> For the end from the beginning
>> Open to His wisdom lies.
> "Disappointment—His *appointment*,"
>> Whose? The Lord, who loves me best,
> Understands and knows me fully,
>> Who my faith and love would test;
> For, like loving earthly parent,
>> He rejoices when He knows
> That His child accepts UNQUESTIONED
>> All that from His wisdom flows.
> "Disappointment—His *appointment*,"
>> "No good thing will He withhold,"
> From denials oft we gather

Treasures of His love untold.
Well He knows each broken purpose
   Leads to fuller, deeper trust,
And the end of all His dealings
   Proves our God is wise and just.
"Disappointment—His *appointment*,"
   Lord, I take it, then, as such.
Like the clay in hands of potter,
   Yielding wholly to Thy touch.
All my life's plan is Thy moulding,
   Not one single choice be mine;
Let me answer, unrepining—
   Father, "Not my will, but Thine."
                              —Edith Lillian Young

January 19

Have you ever wanted something so badly that you wondered how you could survive without it? What you wanted just had to be right; it had to be the best thing for you. Nothing you could think of could have been better. Yet it never came to pass! You begged, you pleaded, but it didn't happen. God did not answer your prayers. And when all your hopes, dreams, and expectations were dashed against the hard, cold wall of reality, you finally saw that it would never be. How did you handle it then? Did you thank God, accept it, and walk away from the rubble? Could you trust in His sovereign love and say with the poet,

From denials oft we gather
   Treasures of His love untold.
Well He knows each broken purpose
   Leads to fuller, deeper trust;
And the end of all His dealings
   Proves our God is wise and just?

Or did you stoop down to examine the broken bits of what might have been and shed quiet tears of pity? Maybe you gathered all the pieces in a box carefully marked "Shattered Hopes, Dreams, and Expectations" and then stored them in the attic of your memories. Many times, in my early years as God's child, that is what I did. Then on rainy days of disappointment, I would get them out of the attic and work on restoring them. Carefully I would examine each piece, dreaming of what-could-have-been-if-only-I-had-done-things-differently. When I did this, I would catch myself in a season of depression. In turn the depression would make me angry with the reality of my present relationships or situations, for they seemed usurpers of what-could-have-been if only I had had my way or if only God had answered my prayers.

The gloom of depression would last as long as I let it. I learned that all I had to do to end it was to put the broken pieces back in the box, tie a string about it, and remove them from my thoughts. Once again I could store them in the attic, safely tucked away for another rainy day of disappointment, to be followed by a season of depression.

Then one day, when I fully accepted His word that "as for God His way is perfect," and when I quit struggling and snuggled into the arms of His sovereign, infinite wisdom and love, there to rest, I threw the box away. "Forgetting what lies behind," I determined I would always reach "forward to what lies ahead" and "press on toward the goal for the prize of the upward call of God in Christ Jesus" (Philippians 3:13, 14).

What about you, Beloved? Have you decided to fully trust or are you going to indulge yourself on rainy days of disappointment?

January 20

Do you sometimes even wonder if there is a God who cares, who loves, who sees, who knows what is going on in your life? At times does it all seem so frustrating, so futile that you just want to run away? Or maybe just escape into the oblivion of alcohol, or the temporary, quiet, anesthetic bliss of drugs, or the warmth and seeming security of illegitimate arms? I understand. I was there once. Caught in a marriage that was a nightmare compared to my idealistic dreams, I felt enslaved for the rest of my life, held prisoner in a dungeon of misery and wretchedness from which I might never escape. I had been taught that marriage is permanent. Only death could sever my chains and yet, I reasoned, if Tom died before me it probably wouldn't happen until I was an old woman. And who wanted old women? Oh, would I never know the one thing I had ever really wanted, a marriage where two people were head over heels in love with each other—totally content, totally fulfilled because they belonged to one another forever?

I tore the platinum wedding band from my hand and threw it across the room. My finger was naked for the first time in six years. Round and round it rolled making a mockery of the words engraved inside, "Our Love Is Eternal." Disillusioned, hurt, longing for unconditional love, I gathered my sons in my arms and ran. I ran to a wilderness filled with illegitimate arms offering warm but temporal security, not knowing there was a God who sees, who cares—who, if I had turned to Him, would have sent me back and saved me so much grief.

What about you? Where are you? He knows. He sees. Your God is omniscient, all-knowing. You don't have to run away. Stay. He will meet you where you are.

Take time today to talk with the One who sees and, seeing, cares. Pour out your heart to Him. Ask Him to meet you where you are and to sustain you. There, in faith, thank Him for being a God who can be touched with the feeling of our infirmities (Hebrews 4:15).

January 21

The harsh treatment was too much. She ran. Leaving the security of home, she fled to the wilderness. It wasn't fair. It wasn't her idea that she sleep with her mistress's husband. She could not stand the jealousy. Then He found her. Face to face with the angel of the Lord, Hagar realized that there was a God who sees. He saw. He understood. And because she knew that He knew, she could go back to Sarai and Abram. She could endure. God had revealed Himself to a mere slave! How awesome it was to have seen God and remained alive! "Then she called the name of the Lord who spoke to her, 'Thou art a God who sees'" (Genesis 16:13). Hagar could stop running, because she knew that God lived, that He cared, and that she had His promise.

O Beloved, does it sometimes seem too hard to bear? Does your situation seem unfair, unjust? A situation not of your choosing, not really of your making? You look at others and they don't seem to be experiencing your pain, your hardship, your suffering. And as you look at them, the reality of your circumstances becomes even more grim. Why couldn't you have what they have? Why are you having it so bad when others aren't? You feel cheated.

Are you? Has God cheated you? Did He cause it all to happen? Or are your circumstances the awful wages of sin, the sin of mankind or your own personal sin?

Obviously, all suffering, all distress has come because man chose to believe the serpent's lie. Sin entered the world and with it came its awful wages—death (Romans 5:12; 6:23).

Yet, there is a God who sees. A God who loves. A God who reigns. A God who redeems.

O Precious One, quit looking at your circumstances. Quit feeling cheated. Quit running away and run to the One who can take it all and make it result in good. Turn to the Redeemer.

"For if He causes grief, then He will have compassion according to His abundant lovingkindness. For He does not afflict willingly, or grieve the sons of men. . . . Why should any living mortal, or any man, offer complaint in view of his sins?" (Lamentations 3:32, 33, 39).

January 22

Much of my past has faded into the insignificance of years gone by, but I can still recall one scene as vividly as if it happened yesterday.

I was not even a year old in Christ. The boys and I had just come home from church, and Tommy and Mark were downstairs playing when the phone rang. It was the admissions desk at Johns Hopkins Hospital where I was to go for surgery; I was scheduled to enter the hospital that afternoon. They gave me a message to call a number in Cleveland, Ohio, and I recognized it immediately as my in-laws' phone number. Little did I realize what they would say to me.

My husband Tom and I had been divorced for several years. Yet my Heavenly Father had finally brought me to the place where I was willing to go back to Tom if that were His will. Tom had been on my heart recently; I had even thought of writing him. He had been concerned about my forthcoming surgery and since this was the day I was to enter the hospital I assumed that Tom was trying to reach me and wish me well. I did not know that an entirely different message awaited me, and that I would never hear Tom's voice again.

When I reached my father-in-law, his first words were: "Tom is dead. He hung himself." I was sitting on the edge of the bed, but that wasn't solid enough. Hearing that news, I slid to the floor and sought refuge on my knees where I could get my bearings. Our conversation was brief; talking was too difficult. I assured Dad Goetz I would be home as soon as I could get there.

The receiver never left my hand as I hit the buttons, waited for the dial tone, and frantically called my pastor. The phone rang and rang and rang. I just *knew* the pastor was home; he had to answer. So I let it ring and ring until finally, in numbness, I accepted the fact that, need him or not, he was not there. If it were not for God, I would almost feel betrayed. *Where were you when I needed you?*

"Where were you?" It may be a question you can ask of men, but you can never ask it of God. He would say, "I'm omnipresent, my child. I was there all the time."

O Beloved, He is there. You can find Him, on your knees. Call on Him.

January 23

"Behold, I am the Lord, the God of all flesh; is there anything too hard for me? . . . Call unto me, and I will answer thee, and show thee great and mighty things, which thou knowest not" (Jeremiah 32:27; 33:3 KJV).

I will be eternally grateful to my God for not allowing my pastor to be home. For if he had been, I might have missed what God said to me that day. And over the years, when the past has come back like a flash flood to drown me in morose memories, my Heavenly Father's words have kept my head above the waters.

When I hung up the phone, I cried out, "Oh, God. . . ." As I said, He had been there all the time waiting for me to call. "Oh, God" was all I had to say. He knew it all. He had known it before the foundation of the world, and He had the answer, the way of escape. I could bear it, or He would not have allowed it to happen.

When I said, "Oh, God," He said three things to me that I will never forget. They were spoken in that intimate, still, small voice to my heart. Now, mind you, I was but months old in the Lord. No one had taught me to memorize Scripture, yet I had read and read God's Word, literally devouring the pages of the New Testament in wonder and in awe. The first thing God said to me was, "All things work together for good." It was Romans 8:28, a verse that I had read and thought upon, though I didn't know just then where to find it.

Here was a word from my God and Father, a sure promise in which, believing, I could find solace. God is in control and, because He is sovereign, He can take each and every situation in a believer's life and cause "all things to work together for good" (Romans 8:28). The good, the end result of all, will be to conform His children to the image of His Son. If that is God's goal and everything in a believer's life has that end, then I could believe the next thing God said to me. What was it? We will look at it tomorrow (unless you can't wait!).

For today, let me ask you a question: Precious One, where do you run to in the day of trouble? To the arms of flesh or to the God of all flesh who said, "Call upon Me in the day of trouble . . ." (Psalms 50:15)?

January 24

The second thing God said to me was, "In everything give thanks." Apparently at the time, that was enough for His new babe in Christ. And so I said, in childlike trust, "Thank You, Father." I couldn't have told you where that verse was then, but I can tell you now (1 Thessalonians 5:18). And I can tell you, looking back on it in its fullness and its context and from the perspective of God's sovereignty, that all untoward circumstances of life, all ploys of men or of Satan, and even all mistakes are so watched and so supremely governed and overridden by God that ultimately they will be used to achieve God's will for each one who belongs to Christ Jesus. This, Beloved, is our heritage as children of the Sovereign God.

And does this promise only cover the days of my life after I came to know Jesus Christ as my Lord and Savior? No, I do not believe so. When God says, "All things work together for good," I believe He means all the things that have happened in your life since you were first conceived in your mother's womb. Thus even the way you were formed, even the parents that conceived you are part of God's plan to conform you into His image, "just as He chose us in Him **before the foundation of the world**" (Ephesians 1:4).

Nothing in your life is an accident of fate; nor are you a victim of the selfish folly of man or the destructive caprice of Satan. Rather your sovereign Father God who sits in the heavens and makes the earth His footstool has only permitted those things in your life which He could cause to work together for your good and your Christlikeness and thus for His glory. Because of this, **you can give thanks in everything,** "for this is the will of God in Christ Jesus concerning you."

O Precious One, do you realize what peace would be yours if you would only believe what God has said and bow your knee in humble, trusting thanksgiving? Then, you would cease to belch the gall of bitter memories of horrible days gone by, days either of your making or of another's, that have been overruled by His promises and His sovereign rule. With a touch from His sceptre they have been turned into good—your eternal good.

May God grant you, as you go back and reread today's devotional, to see it all through the prism of His infallible Word.

January 25

The third thing that God said to me when I learned of Tom's suicide was, "I will not give you anything that you cannot bear." Oh, what a promise that was to me! I could bear it! I could endure it! It would not overwhelm me! My Father, my omniscient, omnipresent, omnipotent Father would never allow anything to come into my life without first filtering it through His fingers of love so that I might bear it. His grace was sufficient (2 Corinthians 12:9).

A year or two after Tom's death I would memorize four assurance verses, one of them being 1 Corinthians 10:13. In studying the meaning of temptation in that verse, I would understand that it could also be translated *trial* or *testing*. "There hath no temptation (*trial* or *testing*) taken you but such as is common to man; but God is faithful, who will not suffer you to be tempted (*tried* or *tested*) above that ye are able, but will, with the temptation, also make a way to escape, that ye may be able to bear it." It was true, and it was mine for the obedience of faith; no matter what came my way, my God would provide His way of escape that I might bear it. I need not surrender, retreat, or give in; through Him I could conquer in all things (Romans 8:37). I could do all things through Him Who would continuously infuse His strength into me (Philippians 4:13).

Those three things which God had spoken to my heart, plus the hours that I had spent reading God's Word, enabled me to sit in the pew, looking at Tom's casket, which rested on the very spot where we once stood and took our vows. "In sickness and in health. . . ." Tom had been sick, mentally sick, manic depressive. "For richer or for poorer . . . until death do us part." But death had not parted us. I had. When the marriage got so bad I thought I couldn't take it any longer, I had walked out. But not before lacerating him irreparably with a tongue "set on fire of hell" (James 3:6).

I might as well have put the rope around his neck myself. I knew it. I was guilty, and I could live my life over and over again chasing "what ifs" or "if onlys" down the corridors of my imagination. But to do so would be to deny what I knew about God and what He had said to me. No, I had acknowledged my sin; I had sought His forgiveness; I had heard His cry from Calvary's tree as He hung there cursed for me, "Father, forgive Kay for she knows not what she does." And I really had not known, at least not from the true perspective of life, for I was blind. If I had seen then as I do now, I never would have left Tom. However, it was done. Tom was dead. I had to live. And how would I live? I would live by every word that proceeded out of the mouth of my God (Matthew 4:4). "All things work together for good. In everything give thanks. I will not give you anything you cannot bear." It is true, Beloved!

January 26

One of the names for God is Jehovah-jireh. It means *the Lord will provide*. Abraham was the first to use this name for God when God tested him at Mount Moriah. Until this time, Abraham had received all of the benefits of God's covenant. Now it was time to test Abraham's covenant commitment to God. Would Abraham love God enough to give up his only son if God asked him? You probably know the story well; it's recorded in Genesis 22. As Abraham took the knife to slay his son at God's command, "the angel of the Lord called to him from heaven, and said, 'Abraham, Abraham!' And he said, 'Here I am.' And he said, 'Do not stretch out your hand against the lad, and do nothing to him; for now I know that you fear God, since you have not withheld your son, your only son, from Me' " (Genesis 22:11, 12).

It was then that Abraham knew that when God tested, He also provided. There is always His provision for every situation of life, every trial, every testing, every temptation. Remember 1 Corinthians 10:13. Genesis 22:14 says, "And Abraham called the name of that place The Lord Will Provide, as it is said to this day, 'In the mount of the Lord it will be provided.' " And where is the mount of the Lord? Mount Moriah, the "mount of the Lord," is where the temple would be built. There men would meet with God and in time learn of the Savior through whom God would provide all of man's needs. "But my God shall supply all your need according to his riches in glory by Christ Jesus" (Philippians 4:19 KJV).

The Father knows how to give good gifts to his children, for "every good thing bestowed and every perfect gift is from above, coming down from the Father of lights, with **whom there is no variation, or shifting shadow**" (James 1:17). He is the immutable God. He changes not, for He is the same yesterday, today, and forever (Hebrews 13:8). The Jehovah-jireh of Abraham is your Jehovah-jireh, the God who provides. And yet to whom do you run in time of trouble?

O Precious One, whatever your need, learn to run first to the outstretched arms of Calvary where you will find His all-sufficient grace, grace to help in time of need (Hebrews 4:16). Then wait . . . wait on the Lord, that He might provide in His perfect way and His perfect time all your need. Not to do so is to end up in the horrible distress that comes when we will not walk in obedience of faith.

January 27

I have known God as my Father for eighteen years now, and I could tell you one story after another of how He has so faithfully provided all that I have needed. There is no way you can "out-believe" God, for every act of faith is met with His just recompense of reward.

After Tom's death, I began to feel that God wanted me to attend

Bible school. Having had surgery on my neck and being locked into an immobilizing neck brace, I was on leave of absence from Johns Hopkins where I worked on a research team as a registered nurse. After much prayer and a period of recovery serving as a nurse at Child Evangelism's summer camp, I met a couple who were leaving soon to go to Tennessee Temple Bible School in Chattanooga, Tennessee. Having sought out positions as a school nurse, only to have these doors close, I felt God wanted me to go to Tennessee Temple. I made application, but there was no time to wait for a response; by faith I rented the other half of a U-Haul truck from my new friends and set out for a state, a city, and a school I had never seen. With a small amount of cash in my pocket, $350 in the bank, a station wagon loaded down with two sons, a dog, and a potted tree, I set off with His promise, "Faithful is He who calls you, and He also will bring it to pass" (1 Thessalonians 5:24).

I had read the biographies of George Mueller, Dwight L. Moody, Charles Haddon Spurgeon, Robert Murray McCheyne, and Madame Guyon. Their God was my God, the God who provided all their needs. I was a little like Abraham as he went out not knowing exactly where he was going. I knew I was headed for Chattanooga, Tennessee, but that was all. The only people I knew there were the two new friends I was traveling with. I had no job, no home, and, as of yet, no school! We drove through the long dark night arriving in Chattanooga with the morning sun.

Now that I was there, what was I going to do? As I walked through the carport into my friends' empty house, I was thinking of our needs, the boys and me. We had to live somewhere, but where? All I owned was in half of that truck. Where would I put it? If I stored it in some warehouse, the rent would probably eat up most, if not all, of my meager savings. As I walked into their house, I did, I guess, what every woman does when she walks into a new house. I went to the window over the kitchen sink to survey the rest of the neighborhood. And there, across the backyard, was a little brick house. I couldn't believe my eyes! Was it really empty? I had to find out; I couldn't wait. Jehovah-jireh—THE LORD WILL PROVIDE. Do you know His name?

January 28

I dashed across their backyard crying out, "Maybe this is what God has for us." Nose pressed against the glass, hands cupped over my eyes to shut out the glare, I twisted and turned to see all that I could through those glass patio doors. Then I ran to the front of this little three bedroom brick house. There it was—For Sale.

I flew back to my friends' home saying the telephone number over and over again so that I wouldn't forget it. The salesman didn't waste any time getting out there. He could spot a prospective buyer when he heard one! Why, he couldn't have missed! Or at least he thought so until he met me and found out that all I had to my name was $350, no husband, and no job—just two boys and a dog! He stood there shaking his head. Not only did I want to buy his house. I also wanted him to let me store my furniture in its garage until the loan was approved. What he was thinking was, *Who would approve her loan*??? Yet God overruled his better judgment, and, thinking he was humoring me, he said he would apply for the loan on Monday.

O Beloved, if only we could see that man's extremities are God's opportunities! When do we need God? At all times. But when do we realize we need Him? When do we usually turn to Him? Right! When there is no other way of escape. When we can't swing it ourselves. It's sad, but it's true, isn't it? When we find that we cannot handle it ourselves and we run to Him, what do we find? We find a God of mercy, a God of compassion, a God who does not give us what we deserve, but a God who rules from a throne of grace—unmerited favor.

> The Lord's lovingkindnesses indeed never cease, for His compassions never fail. They are new every morning; great is Thy faithfulness. "The Lord is my portion," says my soul, "Therefore I have hope in Him." The Lord is good to those who wait for Him, to the person who seeks Him (Lamentations 3:22–25).

Think upon these things and tomorrow I will continue our story, His and mine.

January 29

The down payment on the house was to be $600, but since they had not installed an air conditioning unit, they would let me have it for $350 down. I was so excited! Yes, I could store my furniture in the garage although he really shouldn't permit it. At this point, I could hardly contain myself. But I did have to get a job before I went to apply for that loan. Monday morning, I arrived bright and early at the hospital closest to our new home-to-be and walked out with a job. Then I went back to look at the house again. I remember walking across its backyard to the place where I stopped and prayed. I could probably take you to that spot today. "Father, I want this house only if it's Your will. So Lord, if it's Your will make them approve the loan. But if it's not, then don't let them approve it; for You will have to make the payments on this house."

That afternoon as I sat in the FHA office, answering all the questions, I timidly said, "If the Lord wants me to have this house, He'll have this loan approved." A muffled "What?" came from the head bent over my forms as the girl continued her writing. Although she never looked up, I repeated what I had said, this time a little louder. Having gotten it out once, I now had more boldness, "If the Lord wants me to have this house He will have this loan approved." With that she dropped her pencil and asked incredulously, "Who?" "The Lord God. He will have this loan approved. I've prayed about it." Her head went back down, still shaking.

The loan was approved. And was the real estate agent surprised! "Do you know how many couples have tried to buy this house and could not get their loans approved?" No, I didn't know, but it didn't matter; God had set aside that house for me. It was His provision and I would live there for only $90 a month (including utilities), until His next provision came along. There was one other thing that I felt we needed and that I had asked God to provide—a husband!

"Behold, I am the Lord, the God of all flesh: is there anything too hard for me? . . . Call unto me, and I will answer thee, and show thee great and mighty things, which thou knowest not" (Jeremiah 32:27; 33:3 KJV).

January 30

It's true, Beloved. The people who know their God can not only stand firm but they can do exploits for Him, even in the midst of adversity. Within the year I was to learn another aspect of His sovereignty as God allowed someone to reach between His omnipotent fingers and touch me in a hurtful way. "For promotion cometh neither from the east, nor from the west, nor from the south. But God is the judge; he putteth down one, and setteth up another" (Psalms 75:6, 7 KJV). God, in His sovereignty, would put me down. When he knew my faith was mature enough to bear it, He would allow me, in a small way, to be persecuted for my faith. I would lose my job and run out of money. Yet even that would be filtered through fingers of love; and it would only be for a season, for learning more about the character and ways of my Sovereign Father.

I will share all this with you next month, Beloved, even how God brought Jack and me together. As we walk through the Museum of the Character and Sovereignty of Our God, I want you to see the practicality of it all, and to apply it to your life so that no matter what, you may stand firm. It is hard for me to convey the sense of urgency I feel, and the burden. I am so concerned because I feel the time is coming even closer when our faith here in the United States of America and in Canada will be tested to the core. And what will we do then? How will we stand? We are so ill-prepared because we do not know our God. We know **of** Him, but we really do not know **Him.** And why? Because we are too busy, too involved, too entangled with the affairs of this life. Thus we know barely anything of His life.

The setting of Daniel 11:32b—"But the people that do know their God shall be strong, and do exploits"—is the end times, "a time of distress such as never occurred" (Daniel 12:1). As you read from Daniel 11:32 on through the end of Daniel, you will see several references to "those who have insight." Many of these will endure great difficulties, and yet they are the ones who "will give understanding" to others (11:33) and who "will shine brightly like the brightness of the expanse of heaven" (12:3).

Beloved, I am preparing for that time. I have determined that I will stand for my God no matter the cost. To stand, I must know Him. To know Him, I must have time with Him, time alone and time in His Word. Then not only will I have insight and be able to stand, but I will also be able to do exploits for Him.

What about you? Will you get to know your God?

January 31

Her letter was very brief. I ached as I read it. She was desperate, confused. She had seen my television program and wanted the free booklet I had written on death. "Our two sons, ages nineteen and thirty-one, were found murdered in their older brother's car. Where was God? How could He allow such a thing?"

Have you ever heard of some horrible tragedy and wondered the same thing? Where was God?

Several days ago, while speaking at Mount Hermon conference grounds on the West Coast, I was asked to report to the administration building late one evening. I knew something was wrong; I just didn't know what. When I told the girl at the desk my name, she said, "I'm afraid I have bad news for you. Your husband just called. Dan De-Haan was killed in a plane crash." My response to her was a simple,

"Thank you," but to God I said, "Father, this is so hard to understand."

Dan was only thirty-three. He loved his God and served Him fully. He and Penny had only been married about eight years. When Dan was still single, we taught teens side by side. Then God brought Penny, a widow with two sons and a daughter, into his life. Her first husband had been killed in a plane crash also.

Again I repeated the words, "Father, this is so hard to understand." I couldn't understand why God would let it happen, just as that dear mother couldn't understand why God would allow her two sons to be murdered. I still do not understand.

"Maybe it was an accident." That is what some would say. But if that were the case, then God had nothing to do with it! And if God had nothing to do with it, then where was God? Dan was God's son, a faithful son, a man greatly used of Him. Did God not know that Dan was in trouble as he piloted that little, single-engine plane through the fog at night?

And what about the two sons who were murdered? Did God not know they were in danger? How could God allow Dan to die? How could God allow this woman's two sons to be murdered?

I do not know how God could allow either; I only know that He did. And although I cannot understand it or explain it, it is all right, for I know my God. "See now that I, I am He, and there is no god besides Me; it is I who put to death and give life. I have wounded, and it is I who heal; and there is no one who can deliver from My hand" (Deuteronomy 32:39).

"But," you say, "what kind of a God is that?" We will see as we continue to look at God's character and His sovereignty.

So That You May Know Him . . .

These are only some of the facets of God's character—commonly referred to as the attributes of God. I challenge you to study and meditate on these and to ask God to reveal Himself to you in new and deeper ways.

Omniscient—God knows all. He has a perfect knowledge of everything that is past, present, or future. Job 37:16 and Psalms 139:1-6.

Omnipotent—God possesses all power. He is able to bring into being anything that He has decided to do, with or without the use of any means. Genesis 18:14; Job 42:2; Jeremiah 32:27.

Omnipresent—God is present everywhere, in all the universe, at all times, in the totality of His character. Proverbs 15:3 and Jeremiah 23:23, 24.

Eternal—God has no beginning, and He has no end. He is not confined to the finiteness of time or of man's reckoning of time. He is, in fact, the cause of time. Deuteronomy 32:40 and Isaiah 57:15.

Immutable—God is always the same in His nature, His character, and His will. He never changes, and He can never be made to change. Psalms 102:25-27; Malachi 3:6; and Hebrews 13:8.

Incomprehensible—Because God is God, He is beyond the understanding of man. His ways, character, and acts are higher than ours. We only understand as He chooses to reveal. Job 11:7; Isaiah 55:8-9; Romans 11:33.

Self-Existent—There is nothing upon which God depends for His existence except Himself. The whole basis of His existence is within Himself. There was a time when there was nothing but God Himself. He added nothing to Himself by creation. Exodus 3:14 and John 5:26.

Self-Sufficient—Within Himself, God is able to act—to bring about His will without any assistance. Although He may choose to use assistance, it is His choice not His need. Psalms 50:7-12 and Acts 17:24, 25.

Infinite—The realm of God has no limits or bounds whatsoever. I Kings 8:27 and Psalms 145:3.

Transcendent—God is above His creation, and He would exist if there were no creation. His existence is totally apart from His creatures or creation. Isaiah 43:10 and 55:8, 9.

Sovereign—God is totally, supremely, and preeminently over all His creation. There is not a person or thing that is not under His control and foreknown plan! Daniel 4:35.

Holy—God is a morally excellent, perfect being. His is purity of being in every aspect. Leviticus 19:2; Job 34:10; Isaiah 47:4; Isaiah 57:15.

Righteous—God is always good. It is essential to His character. He always does the right thing. Ultimately, since He is God, whatever He does is right. He is the absolute. His actions are always consistent with His character, which is love. Deuteronomy 32:4 and Psalms 119:142.

Just—In all of His actions, God acts with fairness. Whether He deals with man, angels, or demons, He acts in total equity by rewarding righteousness and punishing sin. Since He knows all, every decree is absolutely just. Numbers 14:18; 23:19; Psalms 89:14.

Merciful—God is an actively compassionate being. In His actions, He responds in a compassionate way toward those who have opposed His will in their pursuit of their own way. Psalms 62:12; 89:14; 116:5; Romans 9:14–16.

Longsuffering—God's righteous anger is slow to be kindled against those who fail to listen to His warnings or to obey His instructions. The eternal longing for the highest good for His creatures holds back His holy justice. Numbers 14:18 and 2 Peter 3:9.

Wise—God's actions are based on His character which allows Him to choose righteous ends and to make fitting plans to achieve those ends. Isaiah 40:28 and Daniel 2:20.

Loving—The attribute of God which causes Him to give Himself for another, even to the laying down of His own life. This attribute causes Him to desire the other's highest good without any thought for Himself. This love is not based upon the worth, response, or merit of the object being loved. Jeremiah 31:3; Romans 5:8; 1 John 4:8.

Good—This attribute of God causes Him to give to others in a way which has no motive and is not limited by what the recipients deserve. 2 Chronicles 5:13 and Psalms 106:1.

Wrathful—There is within God a hatred for all that is unrighteous and an unquenchable desire to punish all unrighteousness. Whatever is inconsistent with Him must ultimately be consumed. Exodus 34:6, 7; 2 Chronicles 19:2; Romans 1:18.

Truthful—All that God says is reality. Whether believed by man or not, whether seen as reality or not, if it is spoken by God, it is reality. Whatever He speaks becomes truth as we know it. Psalms 31:5 and Titus 1:2.

Faithful—God is always true to His promises. He can never draw back from His promises of blessing or of judgment. Since He cannot lie, He is totally steadfast to what He has spoken. Deuteronomy 7:9 and 2 Timothy 2:13.

Jealous—God is unwilling to share His glory with any other creature or give up His redeemed people. Exodus 20:5; 34:14.

"This is what the Lord says: 'Let not the wise man boast of his wisdom or the strong man boast of his strength or the rich man boast of his riches, but let him who boasts boast about this: that he understands and knows me, that I am the Lord, who exercises kindness, justice and righteousness on earth, for in these I delight,' declares the Lord" (Jeremiah 9:23, 24 NIV).

FEBRUARY

When We Ask "Why?"

February 1

There is one truth that I know and understand. It is the sovereignty of God. This truth holds everything else together. It's the truth I run to crying, "Abba, Father." There, in childlike trust, I can bury myself in the folds of His garment. There I can shut out all the whys, wherefores, and hows as God picks me up, holds me, and then lifts me up in outstretched arms and looks straight into my eyes. There my questions disappear, for I have seen His face, a face that reveals His character. And that is all I need to see! Just Him ... "for He cannot deny Himself" (2 Timothy 2:13). Whatever has happened, whether I can understand it or not, is all right; for I know that, as my God rules from His sovereign throne, He cannot deny who He is!

The God who does according to His will in the army of heaven and among the inhabitants of the earth (Daniel 4:34, 35) is first and primarily a loving, holy God. There is not a person or thing that is not under His control and foreknown plan. He is a wise and just God, righteous in all His ways. Merciful and longsuffering, He is a good God who is immutable, never changing, and never, never failing. Oh, true, His righteousness does require that His wrath punish all unrighteousness, yet this is only right; for to let unrighteousness go unjudged would be wrong. God cannot do what is wrong.

And from where did such a God come? He has always been. He is the eternal, self-existent, self-sufficient God who is infinite in His realm and truthful in all His words. Omniscient, omnipotent, omnipresent, He is incomprehensible. He is a jealous God who will share His glory with none. He is transcendent above all creation.

This is my God. This is the One to whom I run when I cannot understand or when everything seems wrong. In His presence I find answers that enable me to cope with life. There I can live in the absolute certainty "that all things work together for good to them that love God, to them who are the called according to his purpose" (Romans 8:28 KJV).

And you, Precious One, what is your God like? How far can you trust Him? You will be able to trust Him only to the extent that you know Him!

February 2

If I could share only one truth with you, Beloved, it would be the character and the sovereignty of God. Knowing your God and understanding His sovereignty will hold you when nothing else will. If a child of God can understand early in his Christian walk who God is and that He is in control of everything, it will save him much heartache. It is a truth that will give you inexplicable peace—peace that will shelter you in the worst of storms, peace that will calm the overwhelming waves of depression that would seek to slap you down and catch you in an undertow of despair, peace that will enable you to see far beyond today and tomorrow, to the shores of eternity, peace that will cause you to endure as seeing Him who is invisible (Hebrews 11:27).

When we say to Him, "God, I cannot understand why," we still need to know that we can trust Him—understand or not!

Isaiah 26:3 says, "Thou wilt keep him in perfect peace, whose mind is stayed on thee, because he trusteth in thee." A mind stayed upon God is a mind at peace. But what does it mean to stay your mind upon God? Is it simply saying over and over again, "I believe in God"? No, I do not believe so. Rather, it is concentrating on the aspects of the character of God that would appropriately deal with or apply to the situation in which you find yourself.

For instance, where was God when Dan got into trouble as he, an inexperienced pilot, flew into the fog? Or where was God when those two sons were being shot to death in their brother's car? God was there. He is present everywhere. And although He did not deliver them from death, He sustained them. God cannot lie; He is righteous. His promises, which are yea and amen (true and so be it), were theirs in their moment of distress. "For He Himself has said, 'I will never desert you, nor will I ever forsake you'" (Hebrews 13:5). Even in that time of human tragedy, God was there operating in His mercy. He could have stopped it all, changed the circumstances, and come to their rescue. Yet He did not. Why? I do not know. I do not understand. I only know that, understand it or not, it is all right. I can say this because of His character.

O Precious One, this month may God grant us insight into His character and the marvelous peace that results from such knowledge.

February 3

It was August 17, 1978. Elaine Mason and Rondelle Stevenson had taken several days off to bask in the Florida sun and listen to tapes. In not too many days they would travel with Jack and me to the Holy Land, or at least that is what they had planned. At seven o'clock in the evening, they were settled in their room, listening to tapes on prophecy from Moody Bible Institute. The porter had just delivered the cheeseburgers they had ordered from the motel restaurant and he was returning to get their Cokes. He left the door to their room ajar . . . it would be just a minute or two. Little did he realize that he had only those few minutes to live.

Suddenly the door flew open. In burst two men with black stockings covering their faces. Each had a gun. "One held a gun on us while the other went through our luggage," says Rondelle. "Then they asked us several questions—were Elaine and I married, were we by ourselves. One said, 'If anyone comes through that door, they're dead.' "

"Because of having been at Reach Out and having studied the Word, we were able, I think, to stand in the midst of all of this," says Rondelle. "Afraid, but knowing where to turn, I kept saying the Father's name over and over while Elaine said, 'Father, I am Your child. I am Your child.' We had learned that God is sovereign and that everything that happens is filtered through His fingers of love. We knew we were in His hands. We don't know why, but we never felt led of God to command them to leave us alone. We just knew we were in God's hands and that He was sovereign."

When this happened, Rondelle was only two years old in Jesus Christ. She had wanted to be saved for years, but not until she found herself in the middle of a heart-breaking crisis had she finally said to God, "I give up." That was all He had been waiting for! At that time she and Elaine had been driving to Reach Out from Cleveland, Tennessee, each week to attend the *Precept* course on Romans. She was saved while we were studying Romans 3. Now, two years later, they were teaching Sunday School. "I had just taught Romans 8:28 before we left for Florida," she says. "As I sat in that motel room, it kept going through my head, 'And we know that all things work together for good to them that love God, to them who are the called according to his purpose.' " They had learned about God's sovereignty in the Word, but they experienced it in that motel room.

I will continue their story tomorrow. But before you read on, let me ask you, "What if that had been you? Would you have been ready to die? Would you have realized you were in God's hands rather than the gunmen's?"

February 4

Rondelle continued: "They continued to hold us for about twenty minutes. I kept wondering where the porter was. They searched all over our room. One took his shirt and began wiping off fingerprints. At one time, one was on each side of my bed trying to take my watch off until finally, unable to do so, they made me take it off myself.

"When the porter knocked, the men opened the door and got behind it so that he couldn't see them. As the porter walked through the door, he must have seen the fear on our faces, and he turned toward them. One of them shot him right below the eye causing him to fall across the foot of the bed onto the floor. He was killed instantly. The man that shot him ran out the door. The other one stepped across the porter's body, reached out with his gun and shot Elaine under her right eye. The bullet came out just beneath her left ear. Elaine fell backwards onto the bed and lay there drowning in her own blood. Then he turned and shot me. The bullet went in my left cheek and exited under my left ear. I knew that was my last breath. I just knew that anyone who was shot in the head would die!

"Before he shot us, I thought my heart would beat out of my body from sheer fright. But just as soon as I thought I would die any minute, all I could think about was seeing Jesus. I didn't think about my children; I didn't think about my husband. There was just a kind of anticipation. I thought, 'I'm going to see Jesus, I'm going to see Jesus at any time.' I wasn't sad. It was really a happy time, and I was very calm. I just knew that at any minute I would be with Him. When the man shot me, I was leaning back against the back of the bed. When he ran out of our room, I remember saying, 'Father, forgive him.'

"I called the desk and told them that we had been robbed and shot. Elaine was trying to say something to me but I couldn't understand her. I kept saying, 'Elaine, turn over, turn over.' You might think that the things that happen to us are coincidence, but they're not. At the very time that the motel called the police and the ambulance, there was a paramedic passing by on his way home from work. When he heard the call going out to the police over his radio, he turned into the motel, came straight to our room, and saved Elaine's life.

"The king is not saved by a mighty army; a warrior is not delivered by great strength. A horse is a false hope for victory; nor does it deliver anyone by its great strength. Behold, the eye of the Lord is on those who fear Him, on those who hope for His lovingkindness, to deliver their soul from death, and to keep them alive in famine. Our soul waits for the Lord; He is our help and our shield" (Psalms 33:16–20). We will finish the story tomorrow. Why don't you meditate for a few minutes on this Scripture. It is God's Word.

February 5

Not only had Elaine been wounded worse than Rondelle. She had also lost a lot of blood. As she lay in the hospital the first three days, all she said over and over was, "No man can take my life. God is sovereign, and He holds the keys to life and death."

"When I was shot I had an anticipation," recalls Elaine. "I don't know how else to explain it except I had an anticipation, and I saw a light. My next thought was that I would see Jesus. When I came to myself, I thought, 'That's no light; that's the ceiling.' Then I remembered telling Rondelle to telephone for help. And I remembered her saying to me, 'Turn over! Turn over!' but I couldn't. I felt just like my head was pinned to the bed. Then the paramedic came in the door. Immediately Rondelle told him to turn me over.... At the hospital all that night when I kept saying over and over, 'No man can take my life. God is sovereign, and He holds the keys to life and death' (Revelation 1:18), a lot of those doctors couldn't get over what I was saying. One of the doctors said, 'I would sure like to know your God!'

"You know, when those men were in our room we never begged or pleaded. Even when we were shot, we never moved or flinched. The gunman put the gun right up to our heads and shot and we never lifted a finger. I have thought of it so many times. The doctor said if I had moved even a fraction either way, the bullet would have hit my jugular vein. It was so close that it clipped a nerve. Being shot at such a close range blew my eyeball out, but it also saved my eye. Isn't that something! If my eye had not been blown out, it would have been destroyed. Also, because I was sitting on the edge of the bed with my feet on the floor (I had my hamburger on my lap), and because the gunman was above me, the bullet went in at such an angle it just missed everything. God had it all under control."

That is it, Beloved. No matter what happens, whether good or bad, God is in control. If that were not true, we would be in the hands of mere men or victims of the whims of fate!

Listen to what God says, "I am God, and there is no other; I am God, and there is no one like Me, declaring the end from the beginning and from ancient times things which have not been done, saying, 'My purpose will be established and I will accomplish all My good pleasure' " (Isaiah 46:9, 10).

February 6

How do you handle tragedies? Our minds are memory banks, able not only to call up the statistics of each event but also to flash on the screen such vivid pictures that you feel the emotions all over again. Will you never be free of the pain, the loneliness, the anger, the anguish, the morbidity of it all? Even the slightest touch and the scanner is at work searching out the past. A word, a look, a sight, a sound, a fragrance, a certain time of year, a certain type of day—and the whole event is recalled. How do you handle it? Never talk about it? Become bitter? Blame God? Take pills? Drink? Become a recluse? Never get over it? Or live with "what ifs" or "if onlys"?

Elaine said, "I relived that porter's death so many times. Every time I saw a black person, it was like triggering a tape recorder. I kept wishing I had cried, 'Don't come in here!' so that maybe I could have saved his life. Finally, after reliving this so many times, I realized that I had to set my mind on things that were pure and lovely and worthy of praise . . . I had to 'Philippians 4:8' it! When I obeyed God, I had peace. I quit reliving it, and the peace of God mounted guard around my heart and mind."

And you, Beloved, how do you handle your tragedies? Have they maimed, crippled, or destroyed you? Or do you 'Philippians 4:8' them?

> Finally, brethren, whatever is true, whatever is honorable, whatever is right, whatever is pure, whatever is lovely, whatever is of good repute, if there is any excellence and if anything worthy of praise, let your mind dwell on these things (Philippians 4:8).

If you will bring every thought under the inspection of Philippians 4:8 and reject each thought, each memory which does not meet its qualifications, then, Beloved, "the God of peace shall be with you. . . . And the peace of God, which surpasses all comprehension, shall guard your hearts and your minds in Christ Jesus" (Philippians 4:7, 9). This is God's promise to you. It is yours for obedience!

February 7

But how can such tragedy, such pain, ever work together for good? What's the good in Dan's plane crash, in sons being murdered, in being shot through the head, or in anything that brings distress of any kind? How can a God of love and mercy, if He is sovereign, allow such things?

I feel that it is needful to speak of this again, and look at it from a slightly different perspective. First of all, we must remember that we are eternal beings. All of life, whatever it brings, is God's means of preparing us for eternity. Every human being will live forever either in heaven or in the lake of fire. When we pass from physical life into physical death that is not the end. To believe so is to be deceived and thus damned forever. No, physical death is merely a temporal tunnel that brings you out of the physical world into the presence of God or into the abode of the damned. Those who are damned will be condemned for all time to the eternal fire (Matthew 25:41–46) where their worm dies not (Mark 9:44). Those, however, who believe on the Lord Jesus Christ and do His will (Matthew 7:21) will enter into the kingdom of heaven and will live in the presence of God forever and ever, and God "shall wipe away every tear from their eyes; and there shall no longer be any death; there shall no longer be any mourning, or crying, or pain" (Revelation 21:4). God will make all things new (Revelation 21:5).

Therefore, the death of a Christian brings distress **only** to the ones who are left behind. For the true child of God, to be absent from the body is to be present with the Lord (2 Corinthians 5:8); therefore, to die is gain (Philippians 1:21). I promise you that anyone who has ever entered into heaven would never choose to come back to earth.

But what if the one who died was not a Christian? How can a tragedy like that work together for good? For the one who died without Christ, it did not work together for good; God did not promise that it would. His promise is only to those "who love God, to those who are called according to His purpose" (Romans 8:28). Yet, Beloved, that person never would have been saved, even if he or she had lived hundreds of years. God knew that (John 6:37, 39; 10:26–29). He knew that person would refuse to come to Him so that he might have life and, therefore, another very valid aspect of God's character, His wrath, is shown. "For the wrath of God is revealed from heaven against all ungodliness and unrighteousness of men, who suppress the truth in unrighteousness, because that which is known about God is evident within them; for God made it evident to them" (Romans 1:18, 19).

He knew God was God, but he rejected this knowledge. Therefore, because he refused His righteousness, he experienced His wrath. "But how can his death have any merit?" We will look at it tomorrow. In the meantime, let me ask you, "If you were to die, how would it be for you?"

February 8

Death serves as a constant reminder that this life, as we know it, is temporal. The wail of sirens, the ink on newspapers, the coverage of television, the tears of the bereaved ever herald the truth, "It is appointed unto men once to die" (Hebrews 9:27 KJV). All mankind knows that even if they do not believe the remainder of that statement: "but after this the judgment."

And so God, in His sovereignty, uses death to bring life. At Dan DeHaan's funeral, the pastor gave an invitation from God. When Elaine and Rondelle share their testimony, they give an invitation from God. And what is God's invitation? "Will you believe on the Lord Jesus Christ so that you might have life? Will you bow before Me and say, 'My Lord and my God'? Will you freely receive and walk in My righteousness? Will you give up and surrender your all to Me, deny yourself, take up your cross, and begin following Me for the rest of your life?"

Thus death and tragedy work together for good, for they become a platform for the gospel of Jesus Christ. From that platform, the dead can yet speak (Hebrews 11:4), testifying by their lives as to where they will spend eternity, for true faith has works which others can see (James 2:14–26). Or if there has been a near-death conversion, there is that testimony of a life that came so close that it cried out, "For what does it profit a man to gain the whole world, and forfeit his soul? For what shall a man give in exchange for his soul?" (Mark 8:36, 37).

Both Elaine and Rondelle said, "If we had not yet received Christ, at least we would have had twenty minutes in which to decide; that poor porter had no time. He did not know that when he walked from the restaurant kitchen into our room he would be walking into eternity. The verse God gave us that explained the whole purpose of our seeming tragedy was Genesis 50:20: 'And as for you, you meant evil against me, but God meant it for good in order to bring about this present result, **to preserve many people alive.**' Through our testimony many people have been saved, and that makes it all worthwhile."

And you, Precious One for whom Christ died, if you have not accepted God's invitation, may I ask why not? Why don't you write out your answer in your notebook and then consider whether or not it is worth it? Remember: you are eternal.

February 9

I have said that "all of life, whatever it brings, is God's means of preparing us for eternity." Well, I want to explain this, for understanding it can keep you from bitterness.

The dear woman who wrote me about the murder of her two sons said, "Sometimes I think there is no God. Why did my two sons have to die? Why?" I have hurt also. My sons were not murdered, but their father murdered himself. I hurt with her. I understand her pain. I am sure multitudes have felt the same way—the Jews in the midst of the holocaust, the woman who is repeatedly raped by her captors, the Chinese who watched Chairman Mao and his men kill hundreds of thousands, the Africans who watched Idi Amin's men dismember their loved ones part by part. Does a God who is in control sit on His heavenly throne and idly watch such things and not have a purpose for them? Does He waste pain, tragedy, suffering, tears, broken hearts? Or does He redeem them from the waste bins of life's marketplace and recycle them, using them for His glory and our ultimate good? He recycles them. And, although that process may be very painful, someday we will see "that the sufferings of this present time are not worthy to be compared with the glory that is to be revealed to us" (Romans 8:18). His grace is there, available to all, sufficient for any and every circumstance of life (2 Corinthians 12:9). It is ours for the appropriation of faith. We must simply take God at His Word: "See to it that no one comes short of the grace of God; that no root of bitterness springing up causes trouble, and by it many be defiled" (Hebrews 12:15).

Not to receive His grace, to fall short of it by not believing God, will result in a tragedy far greater than the one that has caused your bitterness. And not only that; your bitterness will defile others. Our tragedies are permitted for two reasons: that we might become more like Jesus and that others might see the reality of our God and long to know Him as we know Him. "For we who live are constantly being delivered over to death (death to my will, my way, my life) for Jesus' sake, **that** the life of Jesus also may be manifested in our mortal flesh" (2 Corinthians 4:11). The more trials we experience, the more we become like Jesus, if we appropriate His grace. Therefore, all of life, whatever it brings, prepares us for eternity. It makes us realize that life is temporal, thus preparing us for eternity. It shows others the reality of our God and the surety of His Word. "Your momentary, light affliction is producing for [you] an eternal weight of glory far beyond all comparison" (2 Corinthians 4:17).

February 10

"Can you discover the depths of God? Can you discover the limits of the Almighty? It is high as the heavens, what can you do? Deeper than Sheol, what can you know? Its measure is longer than the earth, and broader than the sea. If He passes by or shuts up, or calls an assembly, who can restrain Him?" (Job 11:7–10).

Incomprehensible! That is what God is. Because God is God, He is beyond our understanding. You cannot always figure God out. Try though you may to make Him logical, to confine Him to your box of human reasoning and comprehension, you cannot. He will not, He cannot be put into a box. He is God. His ways, His acts, His character are higher than ours.

Oh, the depth of the riches both of the wisdom and knowledge of God! How unsearchable are His judgments and unfathomable His ways! For who has known the mind of the Lord, or who became His counselor? Or who has first given to Him that it might be paid back to Him again? For from Him and through Him and to Him are all things. To Him be the glory forever. Amen (Romans 11:33–36).

Have you realized that you can only understand that which God chooses to reveal to you? Have you accepted the fact that He is God and that you are mere man, that because He is incomprehensible, there will have to be times when you will need, by faith, to cease trying to figure Him out and rest simply in His character and the fact of His sovereignty?

Oh, how good it is to become a child, to *snuggle* and not to *struggle,* to see that it is enough just to accept the fact that He is the Father and you are the child. Young children do not try to figure their father out; they simply take him at his word.

Have you been struggling? Are you confused because you cannot figure Him out? Do you wrestle with "whys"—with "hows"? Snuggle—just snuggle like a child. It matters not; you are in His arms. Oh, what rest you will find for your tormented soul!

February 11

"That I may know Him" (Philippians 3:10). This was the passion of the Apostle Paul's life. And it is the passion of my life. Is it the passion of your life?

And how do we come to know Him? I believe it happens primarily in three basic ways: First, we come to know Him through His Word as the Holy Spirit guides us into all truth and takes the things of God and reveals them to us (1 Corinthians 2:9–16). Secondly, the various experiences of life teach us more about Him. For instance, how will you realize that God is faithful if He never permits you to be in a situation where you can see His faithfulness? Thirdly, I believe we come to know Him through the experiences and testimonies of others.

Which of the latter two ways do you feel would be the more effective? And if you were to know God through His Word and yet were never able to experience its reality in the test tube of life, how well do you think you would know Him? Right—not very well! No, it takes experience. And this is the meaning of the word *know* in Philippians 3:10. It means *to know experientially.*

Tomorrow, I am going to begin to share with you some of the experiences that have given me a deeper, personal knowledge of God. To be honest, at times, they were challenging and painful, yet I tell you before God that I would not have missed one of them. Along with His Word and the testimonies of others, they are what have made me what I am in Him. And they have given me a confidence in my God that I would not exchange for anything on this earth. Because of where I have been with Him, I can face tomorrow.

Now, you may say, "But if it brings pain, then I'd rather not know Him." To that, Beloved, I would say, "But can you bear to live without really knowing Him, for that truly is unbearable pain?"

Take a few minutes and talk to God about Paul's words in Philippians 3:8, "More than that, I count all things to be loss in view of the surpassing value of knowing Christ Jesus my Lord, for whom I have suffered the loss of all things, and count them but rubbish in order that I may gain Christ."

What does the Spirit bring to your mind as you meditate on this verse? Write it out.

February 12

You have, in all probability, sung the chorus, "God is so good, God is so good, God is so good, He's so good to me." It's sweet, simple, and as far as the words go, easy to remember. But the question is, "Is it a song for every day? Any day? Sure, the words are easy to remember, but is it true?"

Yes, Beloved, it is true. The Psalmist wrote, "Praise the Lord! Oh give thanks to the Lord, **for He is good;** for His lovingkindness is ever-lasting" (Psalms 106:1). If God is good then He can never act apart from His goodness, and I can sing the chorus anytime and at all times, even when things do not seem to be going my way! If God is sovereign, and He is, then all that He does as Supreme Ruler of the universe is good, because God is good.

I was on duty at the hospital and another nurse reported me. Normally I worked in obstetrics, in the delivery room, but that night, my regular night off, I was needed to help cover on another floor. Things were rather slow. As I made my rounds, I came upon one dear old man who was absolutely terrified. From what I had heard at report he was a patient to be avoided; yet my heart went out to him. He needed peace. So after asking him if he would let me read God's Word to him, I took the Gideon Bible from his bedside drawer and read him passage after passage. Peace came for him, and it was precious.

A trial came for me, and it was precious. Through that trial I would come to know God as my Jehovah-jireh (the Lord will provide) in an even deeper way. And through that trial the reality of my faith would once again be confirmed to me.

The next day I was asked to report to the Director of Nursing. "Kay," she said, "your nursing is beautiful, but you will have to stop telling your patients about Jesus." Had my patients complained? "No, but you can't talk about Jesus. God Almighty doesn't need people like you to go around telling them of His existence."

"I'm sorry, Mrs. _____, I cannot stop. I will just have to quit my job."

"No, we don't want you to do that. Your nursing is beautiful. You just need to be quiet about God and the Bible."

The conversation went back and forth. I couldn't quit telling people about Jesus. They needed Him. Without Him there was no peace.

I quit. I had no savings; I lived from hand to mouth. My two boys and myself—and our God, who is so good.

February 13

The next day I was out looking for a job. I had a school bill to pay, children to feed, and a house to make payments on. That afternoon I had a job if I wanted it. The only problem was that I knew it was not the job for me. Nothing was right about it, and I knew that it wasn't where God wanted me.

It would be two weeks before I would work again, and then two more weeks before my first paycheck. It wasn't long before my money ran out. I began every day singing to my Jehovah-jireh, my God who promised that He would supply all my needs according to His riches in glory through Christ Jesus my Lord (Philippians 4:19)! The gas gauge on Bluie, my faithful station wagon, acted like it had Parkinson's disease. Then one day it quit shaking and had a stroke. It wouldn't move. So every morning when the boys and I piled into the car to go to school, we sang, "Give me gas in my car, keep me going, going, going. Give me gas in my car, I pray." It was a chorus that we loved, so we just adapted the words to fit our need. Wish I could sing it for you! You would understand why the Lord kept us waiting only weeks instead of months. *You should hear my singing!!!*

I couldn't tell how much gas I had; I only knew that if it were empty I had no money to fill it. The day I ran out I was on the school campus so there were plenty of friends to come to my rescue. Someone that day had given me two dollars. Then a bag of groceries appeared in our kitchen. God is good, so good, but would I have ever realized just how good if I had never found myself between a rock and a hard place? When those times come, He is still good. He never changes. His lovingkindnesses are new every morning.

The job He provided was at The Diagnostic Hospital. When they hired me, they weren't even looking for a nurse. They just hired me—at fifty cents an hour more than I had been earning, plus all of my uniforms were done free! There, in the year to come, I would freely share Jesus Christ with my precious patients. But even more exciting, I would witness to one of the doctors who hired me, Dr. Maurice Rawlings. Years later, Maurice would be saved and would author three best-selling Christian books. And who would help him with the scriptural part of *Beyond Death's Door* and *Before Death Comes?* I would!

I will never forget the first night when we went over the manuscript of *Beyond Death's Door.* We were sitting on the couch, holding hands, praying. Suddenly I felt Maurice looking at me. When I looked up, he was shaking his head. "Kay," he said, "who would ever have thought we'd be holding hands praying?!"

"He indeed is good for His lovingkindness is everlasting" (2 Chronicles 5:13b). "The Lord's lovingkindnesses indeed never cease, for His compassions never fail. They are new every morning" (Lamentations 3:22, 23a).

February 14

"Father, do you want me to have a husband?" I needed to know. I had looked all over our Bible school and college campus and hadn't seen any likely candidate. There were none at church that I knew of, so the prospects of finding a husband really seemed pretty dismal! Yet if God wanted me to have a husband, He certainly wasn't limited by our campus or the membership of our church. There was a whole big world out there and my omniscient Father knew everyone, so I decided I needed to discuss the matter with Him in prayer. When I ascertained that He wanted me to have a husband, then I fully committed the entire situation to Him.

"Father, You are omnipresent and there is nothing too hard for You; You are omnipotent. Therefore, will You please search the world over and bring me the husband of Your choice. You know I have trouble picking out men, so You pick one for me and bring him to me." I must have said more, but I don't remember it. I do know that I said that. I had prayed according to the attributes of my God. Now I would wait and see what He would do.

I prayed that prayer in November or early December, 1964. What inspired it was a paper I was writing on Genesis. Before we left on Christmas break, we had to hand in a paper that dealt with some aspect of the first twenty-five chapters of Genesis. I slipped in right under the wire! I chose Genesis 24. The theme of that chapter had become dear to this young widow with two sons! In Genesis 24, Abraham sent out his servant (probably Eliezer, Genesis 15:2) to find a bride for his son, Isaac. I titled my paper: "On Hunting Husbands and Winning Wives." In that paper I showed, first of all, how God sends His Holy Spirit out to obtain a bride for His Son, the Lord Jesus Christ. Then— and I spent far more time writing on this point—I explained how God, because He was omnipresent, could search the whole world over and find the perfect mate for each of us. After all, was He not omniscient, the all-knowing, all-wise God! If he were sovereign and omnipotent, then, in His own way and in His own time, He could bring a man and a woman together to become one with Him. "Is anything too difficult for the Lord?" (Genesis 18:14).

I think I got an A on my paper. I know I got an A+ on my prayer. I will tell you about it tomorrow.

For today, why don't you think about Genesis 18:14? "Is anything too difficult for the Lord?"

February 15

On Christmas break, the boys and I drove to Michigan to be with my family. In my zeal as a one-and-a-half-year-old child of God, I had written to every member of my family, explaining how to be born again. Well, that went over like a porcupine in a balloon factory. No one wanted to discuss the subject; my porcupine needles had already done their damage. Anyway, in my zeal I blew it. The whole family became upset, and we went to our separate rooms to cry. We're lovers, not scrappers! I never felt so all alone. As I talked with Him there on my knees beside the bed, I felt like Elijah, so alone. I was just kneeling, saying nothing, just hurting and needing comfort. I loved my family. I loved my God. I didn't want to hurt either. Then He spoke, in a still, small voice in my mind. What He said caught me off guard!

"You are going to marry Jack Arthur." That was all. That was enough! It certainly took my mind off my hurt. I wouldn't be alone any more; I'd have a husband, a husband who understood me.

Someone had told me about Jack. "He's a bachelor who really loves the Lord." Jack was a missionary with the Pocket Testament League serving in South America. Our church had prayed for him because he had been stoned for preaching the gospel.

When I returned to school, I told two of my friends separately. I thought I'd better because, otherwise, if it happened, they would never believe that God had already told me.

I had heard about Jack, but I didn't know what he looked like. So the first thing I did was get his missionary prayer card with his picture so I would recognize him when he came along! God had searched the world; there Jack was in Argentina and Kay in Chattanooga, Tennessee. Now, He would have to bring Jack to me.

I would wait almost six months before I would see Jack face to face. We would meet for the first time in the Happy Corner at Tennessee Temple. At one time, as an older student, Jack had managed the Happy Corner, never realizing that it would be the "field" where he would meet his Rebekah—and her two sons!

"For all this I considered in my heart even to declare all this, that the righteous, and the wise, and their works, are in the hand of God" (Ecclesiastes 9:1 KJV).

February 16

It was June, beautiful June when the evenings are long and warm and you just want to be out enjoying it all—going somewhere, doing something, anything, just to be outside.

Late that Friday the call came from The Diagnostic Hospital. "Kay, we won't need you tonight. We have no patients." They may not have needed me, but I needed them. I needed that twelve hours of pay. I had a school bill due. Why had they closed the hospital? We only had twelve beds at the time, but they had never closed it before. Even though we had no patients, someone might have come to the clinic at night. Immediately I was praying, "Father, why did You let them close the hospital? You know I have a school bill to pay. I need that money." His answer came quickly, "In everything give thanks." "All right, Father. I don't know why, but thank You anyway."

An unexpected night off . . . a warm, June evening. The boys and I would go to a recital at school. Someone else had the same idea. Jack was passing through Chattanooga on his way home to visit Pop. Mom and Pop, his grandparents, had raised him, and Pop's life seemed to be ebbing away. However, on the way to Indiana there was another father to be visited, Jack's spiritual father, Dr. Charles Weigel. On that lovely, warm June evening, Jack and Dr. Weigel walked over to Philips Memorial Chapel to hear the recital. Oh, how Dr. Weigel loved to sing! Our hearts thrilled when he stood in chapel, threw up his hands, pulled out all the stops and sang his famous hymn, "No One Ever Cared For Me Like Jesus." Little did I realize that Jack was his beloved son in the gospel. If I had, I probably would have become friends with Dr. Weigel! I had thought seriously, at first, about helping God bring Jack and me together. I thought about writing Jack in South America and telling him that this sweet, young widow with two sons was praying for him as she attended his alma mater! But then I came to my senses, "No, Father, if this is of You then You can bring it to pass without my help."

"Unto God would I commit my cause, who doeth great things and unsearchable, marvelous things without number" (Job 5:8, 9).

February 17

After the recital the boys wanted an ice cream cone from the Happy Corner, and I wasn't in any hurry to get home. It was our night out.

The young man at the soda fountain had just placed two chocolate ice cream cones into my hands when I heard the words, "Mr. Arthur, would you please sign my Bible." I had the boys praying for Jack, so they had recognized him from his picture. Of course, I hadn't told them what God had told me. If I had they would have blown it for sure!

I gladly delivered the ice cream cones to my sons, and immediately introduced myself. How I did it I don't know, but I made sure Jack knew he was talking to a widow. I really don't remember too much of our conversation that night. I was too nervous and excited. I remember fretting inside about my hair. I had just had it cut and it was soooo short! What if he didn't like short hair? There was one thing, however, that Jack said that night that I did remember! He said, "In December, I'm going back to South America." And in my mind I said, *Well you don't know it, but I'm going with you!*

Jack left Chattanooga the next day, and I went to see the school registrar. If I was going to South America as Jack's wife, I had better go to summer school and graduate so I'd be ready when he got back.

Well, I graduated. But still no Jack! "Father, did I get my signals crossed?" As I searched my Bible frantically for answers, several verses seemed to assure me that I had heard God correctly. Still, that didn't produce Jack, so I enrolled in college. And just when I had gotten into my Greek alphabet, he appeared on the scene. We bumped into one another on the corner of Orchard Knob and Union right there on Temple's campus. That night we went out to dinner. In November, Jack asked me to marry him. To which I replied, calmly, "Jack, I have something to tell you. God told me I was going to marry you eleven months ago!" When we told the boys, Mark said, "Well, God says, 'Ask and you shall receive.' " We had been praying for a daddy . . . I just hadn't mentioned any names!

Jack said laughingly, "I never had a chance!" He didn't. Our Father knew we needed to be together. He had a work for us to do!

"Truly I have spoken; truly I will bring it to pass. I have planned it, surely I will do it" (Isaiah 46:11b). What, Precious One, has God spoken to you? If He has spoken, then rest assured; If He has planned, none shall frustrate Him.

February 18

When you read or hear about how God blesses and deals with others, do you feel a twinge of jealousy? Or, do you feel that God has favorites and that you are not one of them? Have you ever asked God for things that others have asked for? Have they been granted their requests while you have been left out? Or do you feel unloved because God does not always give you what you want or what you ask for? Sometimes it's hard to take, isn't it? Others seem to have so much, more than they really need, while you can hardly make ends meet!

And where is the just God that you have heard or read about? Where is the God that is no respecter of persons? He is there, Beloved—holy, righteous, just in all His ways. Do not walk by the sight of your eyes, nor the passions of your heart. Do not listen to that subtle voice of accusation. You cannot see or know all that God is doing. Remember: God is incomprehensible. Do not try to figure Him out; rather learn of Him. You cannot trust someone that you do not really know.

For the next several days I want to share with you God's holiness, righteousness, and justice, the three aspects of His character that will help you when the liar seeks to defame your God and Father. You need to be prepared to stand when he whispers, "If God really loved you then . . ." or "See, you're not special to God like that one, for if you were, God would. . . ." Let me arm you with several Scriptures that describe your God. As you read them, underline any significant words or phrases that describe His character. Then meditate on the implications of calling such a God, "Father."

> "Speak to all the congregation of the sons of Israel and say to them, 'You shall be holy, for I the Lord your God am holy' " (Leviticus 19:2). (To be holy means to be morally excellent. It is purity of being in every aspect, that which is set apart and, therefore, untainted with ungodliness.)
> "The Rock! His work is perfect, for all His ways are just; a God of faithfulness and without injustice, righteous and upright is He" (Deuteronomy 32:4).
> " 'The Lord is slow to anger and abundant in lovingkindness, forgiving iniquity and transgression; but He will by no means clear the guilty, visiting the iniquity of the fathers on the children to the third and the fourth generations' " (Numbers 14:18).

February 19

He was one hundred and twenty years old, and he blew it! For the last eighty years of his life he had been waiting for this event. The whole thrust of his existence had been to bring the children of Israel out of the land of Egypt, the house of bondage, so that he might take them into Canaan, the land of promise. Now, Moses would never set foot in the land flowing with milk and honey, for he had disobeyed God by failing to treat God as holy in the sight of the sons of Israel. Oh, how my heart ached for Moses. Here was something else that was hard for me to understand.

It all occurred at Kadesh, at the waters of Meribah (Numbers 20:1–13). There, Israel again contended with God. They had come, by

God's leading, to the wilderness of Zin and once again had found themselves in a no-water situation. As was their custom when things became difficult, they complained bitterly and cried, "If only we had perished when our brothers perished ... Why then have you brought the Lord's assembly into this wilderness, for us and our beasts to die here?" (Numbers 20:3, 4). For forty years Moses had put up with this! Whenever anything went wrong the people always murmured—not against God, their Divine Leader—but rather against Moses. Now it was happening again. Once again Moses fell on his face before the Lord and God met him there. "Take the rod; and you and your brother Aaron assemble the congregation and **speak** to the rock before their eyes, that it may yield its water" (Numbers 20:8).

This was the second time in their forty years of wilderness living that they had come to a no-water situation. The first time occurred at Rephidim on their way to Mount Sinai where they would receive the Ten Commandments and the pattern for the tabernacle. That time God brought water from the rock after Moses struck it. "You shall strike the rock, and water will come out of it" (Exodus 17:6).

In both situations, God brought forth water from the rock; yet this second time He would not ask Moses to strike the rock but simply to speak to it. And this is where Moses failed. To put it in everyday language, he blew it. He blew it because he did not treat God as holy. He did not do God's work God's way. He struck the rock anyway. And because God is immutable, because He cannot change, God had to deal with Moses. Moses would be punished. And what a hard punishment it was! Hard, but just. God is always just. You can rely on it.

Oh, you may shake your fist; you may cry bitterly; you may pout; **but it is right.** So bow with Moses before your God and say, "All His ways are just ... righteous and upright is He" (Deuteronomy 32:4). Think upon it. Rest in it.

February 20

What was so bad about Moses striking the rock? It worked the first time, didn't it? Water came out both times, didn't it? Both times the people and their cattle drank and were satisfied, weren't they? Of course it worked; **but it was still wrong!** Because Moses disobeyed. Because Moses got provoked.

And the Lord spoke to Moses, saying, "Take the rod; and you and your brother Aaron assemble the congregation and speak to the rock before their eyes, that it may yield its water. You shall thus bring forth water for them out of the rock and let the congregation and their beasts drink." So Moses took the rod from before the Lord, just as He had commanded him; and Moses and Aaron gathered the assembly before the rock. And he said to them, "Listen now, you rebels; shall we bring forth water for you out of this rock?" Then Moses lifted up his hand and struck the rock twice with his rod; and water came forth abundantly, and the congregation and their beasts drank (Numbers 20:7-11).

The rock, according to 1 Corinthians 10:4, was a symbol or picture of the Lord Jesus Christ. "And all drank the same spiritual drink, for they were drinking from a spiritual rock which followed them; and the rock was Christ." Thus, the water from the rock became symbolic of the Holy Spirit given to each one who believes in the Lord Jesus Christ.

Jesus stood and cried out, saying, "If any man is thirsty, let him come to Me and drink. He who believes in Me, as the Scripture said, 'From his innermost being shall flow rivers of living water.' " But this He spoke of the Spirit, whom those who believed in Him were to receive; for the Spirit was not yet given, because Jesus was not yet glorified (John 7:37-39).

The Holy Spirit could be given only through Jesus Christ's death, burial, resurrection, and glorification. Once the Holy Spirit comes to indwell us, we are complete in Jesus (Colossians 2:9, 10). Anything we need will be ours by virtue of Christ's sacrificial death which sanctified and perfected us once for all time (Hebrews 10:10, 14). This means that, when Moses struck the rock a second time, it was a picture of crucifying Jesus a **second** time, which was not necessary. All you ever needed was given to you through His death at the time of your salvation. The water is there, yours for the believing, the asking—all you will ever need. Speak to the Rock who supplies **all of your needs** (Philippians 4:19). You cannot crucify Him over and over; His one death was sufficient for all time (Hebrews 10:10-18).

Think on it. To understand it is to have your thirst satisfied. We'll continue tomorrow. You are dear to be so patient. How thankful I am that you want to learn. Oh, I love sharing with you and I thank our Father for this privilege.

February 21

Remember now, we are looking at the character of our God. We want to know, we need to know the attributes of this One who is the

Sovereign Ruler of the universe. "But the people that do know their God shall be strong, and do exploits" (Daniel 11:32b). God wants you to be strong in Him. To do this, you must know Him. That is why He has laid this devotional on my heart for His precious church. So hangeth Thou in there, Precious One. Learn, apply, and grow.

Moses wrote, " 'The Rock! His work is perfect, for all His ways are just; a God of faithfulness and without injustice, righteous and upright is He' " (Deuteronomy 32:4). This verse is part of a song Moses wrote, and do you know when he wrote it? After God had told him that he could not go into the land of Canaan with the children of Israel. Listen to God's words again in Numbers 20:12:

> But the Lord said to Moses and Aaron, "Because you have not believed Me, to treat Me as holy in the sight of the sons of Israel, therefore you shall not bring this assembly into the land which I have given them."

God's judgment was not easy for Moses to accept. As a matter of fact, Moses pleaded with God to rescind his punishment:

> " 'O Lord God, Thou hast begun to show Thy servant Thy greatness and Thy strong hand; for what god is there in heaven or on earth who can do such works and mighty acts as Thine? Let me, I pray, cross over and see the fair land that is beyond the Jordan, that good hill country and Lebanon.' But the Lord was angry with me on your account, and would not listen to me; and the Lord said to me, 'Enough! Speak to Me no more of this matter' " (Deuteronomy 3:23–26).

And why didn't God give in to Moses? God said it was, "Because you broke faith with Me in the midst of the sons of Israel . . . because you did not treat Me as holy in the midst of the sons of Israel" (Deuteronomy 32:51).

But how could a God of love be so hard on Moses? He had to be, Beloved, because He is also a just God, righteous in all His ways. Whether He deals with man, angels, or demons, He acts in total equity by rewarding righteousness and punishing sin. Since He is omniscient, knowing all; every one of His decrees is absolutely just. Moses knew this, for, just before he went up to Mount Nebo to die at 120 years of age, he spoke this song, " 'The Rock! His work is perfect, for all His ways are just; a God of faithfulness and without injustice, righteous and upright is He.' " O Beloved, will you not sing Moses' song?

February 22

Please do not think I am saying that if others have something, and you do not, it is because you must have done something wrong. Oh, no! I am **not** saying that. I simply used Moses' situation to show you that Moses knew God's character. Remember, the murmuring, complaining children of Israel were permitted to go into Canaan, but Moses wasn't. Yet Moses never said, "God, that is not fair! I never complained in all the forty years we spent in the wilderness. I never refused to go into the land that You had the twelve men spy out from Kadesh-barnea. Why aren't You treating me the same as everyone else?" No, Moses never said any of this, because Moses knew God's character. He knew that God deals with each of us in a fair and righteous way. His actions are always consistent with His character, which is love. Love always seeks another's highest good (1 Corinthians 13:4–8). Nothing can ever separate you from His love. "Who shall separate us from the love of Christ? Shall tribulation, or distress, or persecution, or famine, or nakedness, or peril, or sword?" (Romans 8:35).

No, if there are difficulties in your life but not in the lives of others, it is not a sign that God does not love you. Rather, in His love He has permitted these things. "Why?" you ask. I do not know; but it will serve some purpose, for God is loving, righteous, and just.

When Jesus told Peter the way in which Peter was going to die (apparently also by crucifixion), Peter wanted to know how John would die. Would God treat John the same as Peter? To which Jesus (in His love, justice, and righteousness) replied, "If I want him to remain until I come, what is that to you? **You follow Me!**" (John 21:22).

O Precious Child of God, do not miss what God has for you by looking at the lives of others and thinking God has favorites or that He is a respecter of persons. Remember He is a holy, righteous, just, and loving God. Follow Him.

February 23

Fear. It can do awful things to a person. Its purpose is to immobilize you, paralyze you, make you impotent. Its source is never God. Note that I said fear *never, never* comes from God. How could fear come from the One whose name is Jehovah-shalom, the Lord is Peace (Judges 6:24)? Have you not heard the words of Jesus: "Peace I leave with you; My peace I give to you; not as the world gives, do I give to you. Let not your heart be troubled, nor let it be fearful" (John 14:27)?

Yet hearts are troubled; Christians are fearful. I believe behind all fear is the father of lies, the devil. Fear comes when we believe him rather than God.

For the next three days we will look once again at our Sovereign God, the God who is love, and therefore, can never act independently from His love. Insecurity breeds fear. People who know without a shadow of a doubt that they are loved are rarely insecure. Therefore, if you are ever going to know rest from fear you must first understand and accept the fact that God loves you unconditionally. That will be harder for some of you because you have not known much love here on earth. It will require a real exercise of faith on your part; yet, if you will believe God, your faith will remove mountains—of rejection, bitterness, fear, anger, and rebellion—by a grain of mustard-seed-sized faith (Matthew 17:20)!

God loves you, unconditionally and sacrificially. He loved you before you ever loved Him. "In this is love, not that we loved God, but that He loved us and sent His Son to be the propitiation (satisfaction) for our sins" (1 John 4:10). "But God **demonstrates His own love** toward us, in that while we were yet sinners, Christ died for us" (Romans 5:8). Read it again, Beloved. It is not just so many words that you nod your head to and say uh-huh . . . sure, sure. It's *truth, life, fulfillment, peace, security.* God so loved you that He sacrificed His only Son for you. What more could He do to prove His love? And so that you will never ever be alone, He has sent His blessed Holy Spirit to live within your very own body. God wants to be with you, God longs to be with you. Thus "the love of God has been poured out within our hearts through the Holy Spirit who was given to us" (Romans 5:5).

Believing that God loves you, and receiving His love, will cast out fear for "perfect love casts out fear" (1 John 4:18). Today, if you in any way doubt God's love for you, why don't you tell Him? "Father . . . oh, how I need a loving Father. Father, I will choose to believe that You love me . . . help, Thou, my unbelief."

February 24

"Fear hath torment" (1 John 4:18 KJV). No argument there! If you have ever been fearful, you know the torment that fear brings.

If you are ever going to learn how to deal with fear, there are a number of facts that you need to know. Some I have already mentioned; however, they are worth repeating, so bear with me.

First, recognize that fear is never from God: "God hath **not** given us the spirit of fear; but of power, and of love, and of a sound mind" (2 Timothy 1:7 KJV).

Secondly, believe that God loves you with a perfect love. You could not be loved any more or any better.

Thirdly, true acknowledgment of this love will cast out fear. "There is no fear in love, but perfect love casteth out fear because fear hath torment. He that feareth is not made perfect in love" (1 John 4:18). Let me repeat the last part of that verse from the NASB: "the one who fears is not perfected in love." This means that when I am fearful it is because I am failing in some way to comprehend God's love for me. Let's take a deeper look at what it means to be loved by God.

Because God loves us and because we have received the gift of His love, the Lord Jesus Christ, "there is therefore now no condemnation" (Romans 8:1). You never need to fear that God will ever pass sentence or judgment against you.

Because God loves you, "He Himself has said, 'I will never desert you, nor will I ever forsake you,' so that we confidently say, 'The Lord is my helper, **I will not be afraid.** What shall man do to me?' " (Hebrews 13:5b, 6). The Sovereign God of love will never abandon you nor leave you in the lurch. He is always there. Therefore, since you are never abandoned to the hands of man, you need not fear, because whatever comes must be filtered through His fingers of love.

Because God loves you, and because His Son prays for you according to His will, He will keep you from (out of the power of) the evil one (or evil). " 'I do not ask Thee to take them out of the world, but to keep them from the evil one' " (John 17:15). Satan cannot do a thing to you without God's permission. And if God grants Satan permission to touch you as He did Job, you need not fear, for it will work together for good (Romans 8:28), be used to make you more like Jesus (Romans 8:29), and will never be more than you can bear (1 Corinthians 10:13).

I have another "because" for you, but I will share it with you tomorrow. You have enough to think upon today.

February 25

Fear is a natural response to something that we feel is going to hurt us, something that threatens our well-being. And although it is a natural response, still its root cause lies in unbelief. When we fear, we are afraid that we will find ourselves in a situation that will hurt us or that we cannot handle. Yet God is there, never leaving us nor forsaking us (Hebrews 13:5), constantly infusing His strength into us (Philippians 4:13).

When we fear, we feel as if things have gotten out of control. Yet

God said that "He does according to His will in the host of heaven and among the inhabitants of earth; and no one can ward off His hand or say to Him, 'What hast Thou done?' " (Daniel 4:35), "For the Lord of hosts has planned, and who can frustrate it?" (Isaiah 14:27a).

When we entertain fear, we are allowing something that God does not send into our lives, for "God hath not given us the spirit of fear" (2 Timothy 1:7). We are failing to appropriate the power that is ours through His resurrection, the love which guarantees our highest good, the sound mind which we can have by bringing every thought captive to the obedience of Jesus Christ (2 Corinthians 10:5).

At the root of it all is a fear for our life. Remember, yesterday I told you that I had one more "because" for you? Well, this is it. Since fear in some way involves a threat against life, you need to know that God says that no man has the power of death, nor does Satan. Jesus Christ through His own death rendered "powerless him who had the power of death, that is, the devil" so that He "might deliver those who through fear of death were subject to slavery all their lives" (Hebrews 2:14, 15). Therefore, you are to be **"in nothing** terrified by your adversaries, which is to them an evident token of perdition, but to you of salvation, and that of God" (Philippians 1:28 KJV). Jesus says, "I have the keys of death and of Hades" (Revelation 1:18); therefore, "do not fear those who kill the body, but are unable to kill the soul; but rather fear Him who is able to destroy both soul and body in hell" (Matthew 10:28). To fear for my life or for the lives of my loved ones is to deny God's control over death. Can't you see how liberating this is, for fear locks us up in a prison of impotence? And that is just what Satan wants! You must say, with the Psalmist, "When I am afraid, I will put my trust in Thee" (Psalms 56:3). The cure for fear is to know the character and sovereignty of your God and to live accordingly. Be cured.

February 26

How does one, in a practical way, live out the character and sovereignty of God? How do you work it into your day-by-day existence? Let me share with you one incident from my own life when I had to put practically everything I knew into faith's action.

A horrible storm was brewing, the kind that makes you pray for protection. It was only dinner time, but the heavens seemed angry. Wearing the gloom of charcoal gray and an ominous scowl of clouds, they thundered at the earth. The wind was violent, at times screaming and beating the trees. The youngest saplings bowed their heads, cowering almost to the ground. Heaven and earth were going to have it out. And we knew that, except for God's merciful protection, we would not fare well.

The dinner bell had rung, and Jack and I scurried to the shelter of our dining hall. Oh, but it was good to be inside. Shivering and rubbing my hands together, I scanned the barn for our nine-year-old son, David. Not finding him, I went out and bellowed over the storm. Then I returned, picked up my plate and sat down. Being a typical mother of a typical nine-year-old, I was telling Jack how David needed to learn to be on time for meals. Exploring Reach Out's thirty-two acres, hunting snakes, fishing in the creek, or climbing in the cave were allurements that made David oblivious to time. Still he didn't come.

When rain began pelting the barn's tin roof, concern took hold. "Honey, we've got to find out where David is," I said. Translated that meant, "You go out in the rain and find him." Jack left and in a few minutes returned to the table to resume his meal.

"Where is he?"

"Don't worry," Jack replied in the casual manner of a father, "I'm sure he will be here in a minute." Jack was raised on a farm and understood the preoccupations of a nine-year-old, but after two more bites my "mother alarm" was making an awful noise in my breast. I had to find our son. By now the heavens were crying with hysterical torrents of wrath.

Jack and I were drenched when we got to the car. Surmising that David was not on the ranch, we drove down Noah Reid Road—honking, trying to out-yell the wind while frantically looking for him.

Then the Holy Spirit brought to my remembrance Philippians 4:5–7, "The Lord is near. Be anxious for nothing, but in everything by prayer and supplication with thanksgiving let your requests be made known to God. And the peace of God, which surpasses all comprehension, shall guard your hearts and your minds in Christ Jesus." Meditate on those verses in light of what we have learned this week. How do they fit?

February 27

Be anxious for nothing when your child is missing in a horrible storm? Suddenly I found myself thinking of an acquaintance in our city whose son had just been murdered. They found his body in a ravine at the back of their home. Now our son was missing. What if . . . ? "What ifs" always come; the enemy will see to it! That is his business, to do anything to keep our minds off of the truth of God.

Not finding David, we returned to the barn to see if he had come home by now. I anxiously waited in the car. Jack returned, shaking his head. As he reached for the ignition key, he told me, "Some of the boys are going to help us look. You and I'll go down and try the bridge and then the railroad tracks." I looked over at the creek. It had already covered its banks.

As we left the property, I wanted to blame Jack. Surely he should have checked on David that afternoon! You know what you want to do in a trial—to find a scapegoat. But there was God's word again, "Let your forbearing spirit (or sweet reasonableness) be known to all men. The Lord is near (at hand)." I didn't have to have a scapegoat, for the Lord was there for me to lean on. I was to stop being anxious; I was to pray. I had taught Philippians 4:5–7 a number of times. I knew that the word for prayer in Philippians 4:6 meant general prayer—prayer that looked at the character of God and the promises of God that fit the particular situation. So I prayed accordingly.

"Father, You are our Sovereign God who has everything under control. You are omniscient and although we don't know where David is, You do. And, Father, You are omnipresent, so if he is frightened, alone, or if someone is hurting him, let him be aware of Your presence." Now supplication (specific requests) merged with general prayer. "Father, bring to his remembrance the Scriptures and truths we have taught him. I know, Lord, that nothing can happen without Your permission, and I submit to You." Peace and calm came. I no longer wanted to blame Jack. I still wanted David very much, but I realized that there was nothing more that I could do, so I rested in His sovereignty and His love. By faith I thanked Him for the whole situation. Every time an anxious thought came to my mind I rejected it and turned instead to all that I knew about my God.

We hunted, searched, called, and came home without him. And David was there! He had been playing with a friend and had temporarily lost his way. One of the boys found him down on the road.

O Beloved, this is the practicality of knowing God—clinging to what you know and living according to every word that proceeds out of the mouth of God.

February 28

They stood weeping. Ezra read and explained the book of the Law, and they saw the truth of God's Word (Nehemiah 8:4–9). Grief overwhelmed their hearts as a tidal wave of bitter memories flooded their minds and washed away the joy of the occasion. They saw their failure. They had failed to believe God's Word and had faithlessly assumed that God would respond likewise. They did not comprehend the fact that "if we are faithless, He remains faithful; for He cannot deny Himself" (2 Timothy 2:13).

Israel had either forgotten or had not believed God when He said, "Know therefore that the Lord your God, He is God, **the faithful God,** who keeps His covenant and His lovingkindness to a thousandth generation with those who love Him and keep His commandments; but repays those who hate Him to their faces, to destroy them; He will not delay with him who hates Him, He will repay him to his face" (Deuteronomy 7:9–10). They thought they could walk their own way. They assumed that being a chosen nation gave them special privileges, and it did; but they forgot that with those privileges also went grave and awesome responsibility. And aren't we much the same? Before they entered Canaan, the land of covenant, God had gone over the precepts of life a second time. Moses recorded it all in the book of Deuteronomy as a permanent testimony. They had it in their hands; they had it read and proclaimed by prophets, priests, and kings; yet for the most part, they ignored it. Like so many today, they wanted God's blessings without obedience.

God had set before Israel "life and death, the blessing and the curse." He had told them to "choose life in order that you may live, you and your descendants, by loving the Lord your God, by obeying His voice, and by holding fast to Him" (Deuteronomy 30:19, 20).

Just as God said, Israel had known destruction and captivity. Seventy years of captivity! Now, compared to former days, only a handful of Israelites lived in the land. Gone were the days of blessing under David and Solomon. Gone was the glory of the temple. Things were not the same, nor would they ever be, and as they heard Ezra read God's Word, they knew why. They had failed to count on God's faithfulness, not only to bless, but to chasten!

Oh, Beloved, do not do as they did. Heed His Word; believe it; live by it. Because God is faithful, every word shall come to pass ... the blessings **and** the cursings!

February 29

How bitter are the tears of what-might-have-been! They seem as if they will surely strangle us. Your eyes swell until you can hardly see; your nose becomes so stuffy you can hardly breathe; your strength ebbs until you can hardly function. You wonder if life is really worth living, if you can ever know joy again.

Now you see where you failed. Now you realize how wrong you were—foolishly wrong. "The Lord is righteous; for I have rebelled against His command; hear now, all peoples, and behold my pain" (Lamentations 1:18). God has chastened you, and you know it is right for He is holy, righteous, just. He cannot deny Himself; He must stand by His word. "The Lord has done what He purposed; He has accomplished His word which He commanded from days of old. He has thrown down without sparing" (Lamentations 2:17).

So what do you do? Give up? Weep bitter tears of regret for the remainder of your days? No, Beloved, no. Read Lamentations and look for your God. Lamentations was written by Jeremiah during the Babylonian captivity. Chronologically it comes before the books of Ezra and Nehemiah which give us an account of the return of the remnant of Israel to their land. Lamentations is a record of the sorrows of Israel due to God's just judgment. Yet Lamentations is more than just a record of their sorrows. It is another glimpse into the character of their God. And that is what I want you to see. Our just, holy, righteous, faithful, sovereign God is also longsuffering and merciful. By longsuffering I mean that His righteous anger is slow to be kindled against those who fail to listen to His warnings or obey His instructions. His eternal longing for the **highest** good for His creation holds back His holy justice. Thus, for century after century, God had sent Israel prophet after prophet, waiting for repentance; but Israel would not repent. They did not consider that God's longsuffering and goodness were intended to lead them to repentance (Romans 2:4). So He took them into captivity, but He did not abandon them. God is merciful. He responds in compassion toward those who have opposed His will in pursuit of their own way.

> The Lord's lovingkindnesses indeed never cease, for His compassions never fail. They are new every morning; great is Thy faithfulness. "The Lord is my portion," says my soul, "therefore I have hope in Him." The Lord is good to those who wait for Him, to the person who seeks Him. It is good that he waits silently for the salvation of the Lord. . . . For if He causes grief, then He will have compassion according to His abundant lovingkindness. For He does not afflict willingly, or grieve the sons of men (Lamentations 3:22–26, 32, 33).

So dry your tears; put away your weeping. If you have repented, acknowledging your wrong and turning from disobedient ways, He stands there in His mercy, reaching out with open arms, bidding you to come, saying, "Do not be grieved, for the joy of the Lord is your strength" (Nehemiah 8:10b).

Now, Beloved, behold your God and live—live according to His character and His sovereignty.

MARCH

Listen to Me!

March 1

"Listen to me. Listen, please listen." The words seem to have been wrung from a heart filled with agony, "I love you."

"Love me? How . . . how have you loved me?" Her high-pitched retort was haughty, indignant. It came from pouting lips. Her scowling words caused thunder claps in the atmosphere. The warm front of His unending love had suddenly collided with the chilling winds of her insolence. It was inevitable. A storm was certain, a storm that would last four hundred years. These were to be His last words if she would not listen, if she would not return and be the wife she was supposed to be. And she did not listen. Thus silence reigned for four hundred years, and Israel did her own thing—living her own life, yet bearing His name.

Then, in the fullness of time God broke the silence. Again He said, "I love you," and to prove it He offered up His only Son. Still she would not listen. She continued on her haughty way. Who needed Him on His terms? She was fine. There was nothing wrong with her! "If He loved me, I mean really loved me, would He not give me my way? Would He not do what I want Him to do? Would He not reward me for the things that I do for Him? What good has it done me to be His wife anyway? Besides, He doesn't even honor what I do for Him. It's vain to belong to Him."

She could not see where she was wrong and would not believe that He really loved her. She was so determined that she was right that it was impossible to reason with her. She would not listen to Him, or to His prophets. And even when His Son came she would not listen to Him.

O Jerusalem, Jerusalem, who kills the prophets and stones those who are sent to her! How often I wanted to gather your children together, the way a hen gathers her chicks under her wings, and you were unwilling.

75

Behold, your house is being left to you desolate! For I say to you, from now on you shall not see Me until you say, 'Blessed is He who comes in the name of the Lord!' " (Matthew 23:37–39).

Have you ever sat where God sat and loved anyone like Israel? Have you ever loved anyone who would only love you—and believe that you loved her—on her terms? Have you ever loved someone who insisted on making her own rules and was only happy as long as you played the game her way? Yet because you knew that the way was wrong, you could not go on accepting it. So you talked, or rather, you tried to talk. But really there was no reasoning! She just could not see, would not see, would not admit that she was wrong. Every time you showed her her failure, she retorted, "Where have I . . . ?"

O Beloved, this month God wants to talk to His church, Christ's espoused wife. There is something wrong, drastically wrong. He loves us, but we have wandered. He wants us to return. Will we listen?

March 2

O Precious Ones, the word that God has given me for you this month is not an easy word; yet it is a word of love. How I pray that you will receive it as such. So many times we think that love is expressed only with words of praise, kindness, comfort, appreciation. Yet we forget what God said through the writer of Hebrews: "My son, do not regard lightly the discipline of the Lord, nor faint when you are reproved by Him; **for those whom the Lord loves He disciplines,** and He scourges every son whom He receives" (Hebrews 12:5, 6).

Genuine love is not gullible. It does not accept what is false. Rather, love hates falseness because it deludes us and keeps us from the truth. And it is the truth that sanctifies us (John 17:17), that sets us free to be all that we are meant to be (John 8:32). Love and discipline go together, for love desires another's highest good, even if it costs the love of the beloved. Love never seeks its own (1 Corinthians 13:5).

I know that God's word of love to the church in general is, "I am not pleased with you. . . . Return to Me, and I will return to you" (Malachi 1:10; 3:7). Now, Beloved, you may disagree with me, but I plead with you to hear me out, for, like Jeremiah I must be obedient to what God has said (Jeremiah 1:7, 8, 17).

The message that God has laid upon my heart for those who profess Christ is the message of the last of the Old Testament prophets, Malachi. Now granted, I know that many of you have not strayed from God like Israel did in the days of Malachi. Your Christianity does not weary Him; rather, it brings Him great joy. Yet, Precious Ones, we are members of a church. We have joined hands with others who profess to know Him and who are caught up in the formality of worship; who think they are doctrinally sound and yet who do not esteem His words more precious than their necessary food; who claim Him with their lips yet deny Him with their lives; who have a form of godliness yet know nothing of His power; who bring their gifts to the altar but who will not lay down their lives for the sake of the gospel; who despise other Christians because they are too zealous, too extreme, too holy, too consecrated. To those, God would speak this month in loving rebuke and warning.

And yet, just as there was a faithful remnant in the days of Malachi of "those who fear the Lord and who esteem His name" (3:16), so there is today, and God has a word for them also. Thus we must all listen carefully.

May we hear the words that He would speak to us, and then arise and speak His truth from the housetops that some might listen and return to Him.

March 3

Today I believe God would have us stop and assess where we are with Him. If you are using this book for family devotions, it would be good for you to do this honestly and openly before one another. Confession is good for the soul. However, as one bares his soul honestly before you, you must be careful not to criticize or to condemn, but rather to intercede on one another's behalf.

Now then, what are you going to assess? You are going to honestly assess your walk with the Lord. Why? Because if your walk with the Lord is not what it ought to be, then you are on the road of indifference and thus disobedience. To continue walking that way will only lead you farther away and if you do not return to Him, you will experience the just judgment of God. Remember, whom the Lord loves, He disciplines. If there is no discipline, then it's because you are not His (Hebrews 12:6, 7)! One more "because"—because God keeps books. He has a book of remembrance "written before Him for those who fear the Lord and who esteem His name" (Malachi 3:16). These are the ones whom God will spare "as a man spares his own son who serves him" (v.17). God keeps an account of each life and there is a day of reward when each of us is judged "for his deeds in the body, according to what he has done, whether good or bad" (2 Corinthians 5:10). Let's judge ourselves rightly so that we need not be "disciplined by the Lord" (1 Corinthians 11:31, 32).

Tomorrow we will finish our self-examination. Now notice, Precious One, it is *self-examination.* You can never see to take a mote out of your brother's eye until you have taken the beam from your own (Matthew 7:5).

Today, we are going to look at two questions. First, do you honor God as a child is to honor his parents and as a servant is to honor his master? Now, before you answer that, stop and think about what it would mean to honor God in this way. Wouldn't it mean to give Him first place in your life and to obey all that He says, to love Him supremely before all others and all else—sports, television, job, everything? Now answer that first question noting exactly where and how you fail.

Secondly, are you giving God the very best of your life? I mean, do you spend quality time with Him, or do you just give Him your last few tired minutes of the day? And what do you give Him of yourself, your possessions?

March 4

One more day of self-examination and then we will be prepared to receive God's Word to us from Malachi.

Is it tiresome for you to serve God, to walk the Christian walk? By that I mean is it difficult and boring for you to study your Bible consistently in order to learn His Word? Is it a drag for you to have a daily time of worship and prayer and to be in His Word? Do you even do it? Does going to church or serving God seem a burden to you?

Do you say that you do not have time to study God's Word, pray daily, or worship Him as you should, and yet you find that you do have time for what you want to do—watching television, reading the paper, working on your hobbies, or pursuing your career beyond what is necessary?

When you give others advice or instruct your children, do you speak the truths of God's Word uncompromisingly, without wavering regardless of whom you are speaking with or regardless of the particulars of the situation? In other words, do you advise and instruct people the way God would have you to do so?

If you are married, what is your marriage like? Men, are you fulfilling your role as a husband should? Are you assuming the responsibilities of headship and ruling in the attitude of Christ as the sacrificial lover of your wife (Ephesians 5:25–33)? Are you providing for your household? Are you bringing your children up in the discipline and instruction of the Lord (Ephesians 6:4)? Women, are you submitting to your husband as to the Lord (Ephesians 5:22) even if he is in rebellion against God's Word (1 Peter 3:1–6)? And are you a sensible and pure woman who is a faithful keeper of her home (Titus 2:5)? Do you seek to be strong in all moral qualities, doing your husband good and not evil so that he can safely trust you (Proverbs 31:10–12)? To do all these things as a husband or wife means that you are faithful to the covenant of marriage and are not seeking to deal treacherously with one another.

Are you robbing God? Do you hoard your money and possessions or do you generously give to the Lord's work?

And last but, as the saying goes, not least, do you speak against God? Do you murmur and complain saying that it does not pay to serve Him? Do you profess to be doing what He says and yet say you are not honored by God, that there's no profit in serving Him? If your answer is *yes,* are you serving God His way? Are you hearing Him?

March 5

Before we begin to hear the Word of the Lord through the prophet Malachi, I would like to put the book of Malachi into its historical context.

To know the setting of an Old Testament book, I always go to Irving Jensen's work, *Jensen's Survey of the Old Testament,* by Moody Press. Irving Jensen, G. Campbell Morgan, Charles L. Feinberg, and J. Sidlow Baxter all concur that the books of Nehemiah and Malachi are closely associated as they both deal with parallel problems existing in Israel after the Babylonian captivity. Some believe that Nehemiah and Malachi were contemporaries. Others say that Malachi followed Nehemiah. In Nehemiah, there is no direct reference to Malachi, and in Malachi there is no reference to Nehemiah as governor (Malachi 1:8). Baxter, in *Explore the Book,* puts "the ministry of Malachi somewhere between 420 and 397 B.C.,"[1] while Jensen says that "Malachi probably wrote his book around the time of Nehemiah's visit to Babylon, in 433 B.C."[2]

For years God had warned His people through His prophets that He would judge them with the sword and with captivity if they did not repent. For some reason, that warning seemed hard to believe. After all, they were God's elect nation. Prophets came and went, all burdened with the oracle of the Lord. But God's people would not listen. In 722 B.C. the Northern Kingdom of Israel was taken captive by the Assyrians; then in 586 B.C. the last of the Southern Kingdom went into Babylonian captivity. But, oh, the grace of God! In the midst of all the turmoil came the word of the Lord through Jeremiah: the Babylonian captivity would only last for seventy years (Jeremiah 29:10). Under Cyrus, the king of Persia, they would be allowed to return to their beloved land and the holy city of Jerusalem.

When they returned seventy years later, it seemed at first that the captivity had taught them their lesson! The temple was restored, the sacrifices were reinstituted, and the walls were rebuilt under Ezra and Nehemiah. With the restoration came tears of repentance, words of confession, and a determination to be obedient to God's Word (Nehemiah 8-10). However, the sins that Nehemiah had addressed and seemingly dealt with in his days are the same sins that Malachi cried out against in his prophecy. The corruption of the fathers, rather than being thoroughly dealt with and removed, had spread like a malignant cancer to almost the entire body. "When Malachi wrote his book, the Jews as a nation had been back in the land of Canaan for about one hundred years. Prophets like Haggai and Zechariah had predicted that God's blessings would be given to the people in the days to come, especially in 'the day of the Lord.' However, several decades passed and these prophecies of hope were still unfulfilled. The days had become increasingly drab and dreary. It was a period of disappointment, disillusionment, and discouragement . . . of blasted hopes and broken hearts. The Jews' faith and worship were eroding, and their daily lives showed it. In this backslidden condition they were hypercritical of God's ways."[3]

Does it sound familiar, Beloved? Is it not also sin to cause Christ's church to waste away? Have not many grown weary in waiting for the Lord's coming? Do not multitudes in the church find their lives filled with disappointment, disillusionment, and discouragement? Are they not a people with blasted hopes and broken hearts? Are they not so caught up in the formality of their Christianity that they are missing the beat of His heart? And what is God's Word to them . . . to you?

March 6

Has there ever been a time when you, as a Christian, felt that God did not love you? Why did you feel that way? What happened that caused you to doubt His love?

The opening words of Malachi are God's words: "I have loved you." No sooner are they said, than the retort comes back, "Wherein . . . how hast thou loved us?" *Wherein* (KJV) or *how* (NASB) is stated seven different times, each one a rebuttal to God's exposure of their shortcomings. Obviously God and His people are at odds. God is not pleased with them and they are not pleased with God. The atmosphere is electric and Israel is murmuring: *Why is He complaining? What's wrong? Certainly there is nothing wrong with us. I tell you, it certainly is vain to serve the Lord. Where has it gotten us?* "What profit is it that we have kept His charge, and that we have walked in mourning before the Lord of hosts?" (3:14). *He says He loves us. How has He loved us?*

Because things were not going their way, Israel (not all, but as a whole) doubted God's love. They apparently never once stopped to consider that maybe there was something wrong in their lives, or it never occurred to them that God might be permitting difficulties or disappointments in order to refine them as silver so that they might "present to the Lord offerings in righteousness" (3:3). Apparently they had failed to recognize a loving Father's responsibility to discipline His children. At any rate, they refused to believe that God loved them because, according to their estimation of love, He certainly wasn't showing it. In no way would they consider themselves the cause of their own distress, disappointment, or disillusionment.

They were wrong. Wrong and blind. The formality in their worship kept them from examining their hearts and their motives. They were in a state of spiritual decline, but they could not see it because they were still going through the motions of worship! And so it is with the church at large today. We are only happy with God when things are going **our** way. As long as we seem to have His blessing, as long as things are running smoothly and we have no lack of good things, as long as we do not feel we have to toe God's line, then we are willing to believe God loves us. But let God make righteous demands on us, or withhold what we want, and then we pout and with insolent lips say, "How have You loved me?"

God loves you unconditionally, Beloved. The question is: do you love Him unconditionally? Have you ever thought that maybe the reason you, at times, doubt His love for you is because you are not really loving Him as you should?

March 7

I remember many times standing before my father with a tear-stained face, disappointed, angry, or pouting and hearing him say to me, "Kay, I love you so much that even if you hate me, I am going to do what is right and best for you." His love transcended mine. Yet many times, even after hearing those words, I would run to my room, throw myself down on my bed and murmur out loud, "You'll be sorry. I'll never love you, kiss you, or hug you again. You'll see." But it was I who would later see. It was I who would later be sorry. Oh, how I wounded my precious mother and father down through the years. I guess they are the wounds of parenthood that we all must be willing to bear. They are the product of a child's immaturity, and Jack and I as parents have borne our share as well. Even now they are not over for our children oft times sit in judgment when they do not have all the facts straight, just as I did as a young adult. And, as I watch our oldest enter into fatherhood, I know that someday he, too, will sit where we have sat and will look back and shake his head at some of the things he said or did in ignorance and blindness. Yet, try as they may, parents at the time cannot convince their children of their love. There simply will be times when children feel their parents have failed.

Yet, desiring the other's highest good, love bears, believes, hopes, and endures all things. And so it was with God and Israel in the book of Malachi. It was God's cry of wounded love for His people, a love that was willing to risk being loved for His children's good just as Daddy was willing to risk my love for my own good. It was a love that could not rejoice in unrighteousness (1 Corinthians 13:6) and therefore had to rebuke, speaking the truth (Ephesians 4:15), and, if necessary, wound in order to heal. Yet, even if they would not listen or acknowledge their wrong and although He would be forced to chasten them, nevertheless God would not abandon them. Nor would God ever take "into account a wrong suffered" (1 Corinthians 13:5). We see this in Malachi. Oh, God shut up the heavens . . . for four hundred years He retreated in silence because they would not listen. Yet He did not retreat into silence without leaving them hope . . . a promise to cling to! "Behold, I am going to send My messenger, and he will clear the way before Me. And the Lord, whom you seek, will suddenly come to His temple" (Malachi 3:1). Jesus, the Messenger of God's unfailing covenant, the ultimate expression of God's love, would come. Whether they believed it or not, whether they recognized it or not, God loved them. And, Beloved, He loves you too. Maybe He has been silent for a while, but He is still there. Cling to His promise: "I will never leave thee, nor forsake thee" (Hebrews 13:5 KJV).

March 8

The problem with God's people in Malachi's day is the same as the problem with the church today. Irving Jensen expressed it this way: "The Jews' faith and worship were eroding, and their daily lives showed it." The question is: Why does faith erode? Erosion is a gradual eating or wearing away. What causes it?

Let me ask you, Beloved. Was there a time when you were more zealous for the things of God—a time of first love with all its newness, joy, discovery, anticipation, a time when you would have gone anywhere, done anything God would have asked of you? Was there a time when you longed to serve Him without distraction? Notice, I said *was there*. What happened? You still worship Him, go to church, give of your monies, and are active in some work for Him; but things are different, aren't they? And it's not that you have settled down into maturity but rather that you have lost something.

Malachi's message shows us where God's people had failed. They still went through the motions of worship, bringing their sacrifices to the temple (Malachi 1:7, 8, 11) as we do our offerings. The priests still performed their duties as we do our ministries. They wept in prayer before God's altar (2:13) as we do in times of need and crisis. Yet it was all done by rote; the passion was gone, as, for the most part, is ours. Our problems are the same as Israel's. Time passes, cultures come and go, men are born and die, and yet the nature of man remains the same. So history repeats itself, for man makes history. And it is what is in man's heart that makes the difference. If you have strayed from God, if your Christianity is mere formality, if the zeal, the passion is gone, something is wrong in your heart. The love of God is not there! Only love can maintain true fellowship with God. Israel, like the church today, suffered from heart failure.

If you serve Him from a fear of what He will do if you do not serve Him, you will soon lose your fear and your service. If you serve God on the basis of policy, you will surely fail sooner or later. There never was a more dishonest principle of action than this, "Honesty is the best policy." The man who is only honest because it is a good policy will be dishonest the moment he thinks there is an opportunity to gain by it. The man who is only loyal to God because he wants God to save him from hell, is not mean merely, but will utterly fail to be loyal to God for long. There is only one motive strong enough to maintain relationship to God: *Love.*

Now see what the death of love issues in. Callousness. "Wherein hast thou loved us?" the people asked. The prophet said: "You have lost your love for God; and now you are questioning God's love for you." That is always so; callousness results from the death of love.[4]

Oh, Beloved, have you lost your first love? Or do you feel its very life ebbing away? Do not let it go. Rather put to death that which has caused your love to die! Nothing, Beloved, is of more value than a heart aflame with love for God. Nothing.

March 9

Beloved, before we go any further, you need to carefully read Malachi 1:6–14, written below. In verse ten, you will notice the phrase, "I am not pleased with you." As you read, note why God is not pleased with them, marking each reason with a pen in some distinctive way so it will stand out on the page. Then meditate on what you observed, asking God to show you how your life compares with what God is saying in this passage. Give yourself time, Beloved. I promise it will be worth it.

"A son honors his father, and a servant his master. Then if I am a father, where is My honor? And if I am a master, where is My respect? says the Lord of hosts to you, O priests who despise My name. But you say, 'How have we despised Thy name?' You are presenting defiled food upon My altar. But you say, 'How have we defiled Thee?' In that you say, 'The table of the Lord is to be despised.' But when you present the blind for sacrifice, is it not evil? And when you present the lame and sick, is it not evil? Why not offer it to your governor? Would he be pleased with you? Or would he receive you kindly?" says the Lord of Hosts. "But now will you not entreat God's favor, that He may be gracious to us? With such an offering on your part, will He receive any of you kindly?" says the Lord of hosts. "Oh that there were one among you who would shut the gates, that you might not uselessly kindle fire on My altar! I am not pleased with you," says the Lord of hosts, "nor will I accept an offering from you. For from the rising of the sun, even to its setting, My name will be great among the nations, and in every place incense is going to be offered to My name, and a grain offering that is pure; for My name will be great among the nations," says the Lord of hosts. "But you are profaning it, in that you say, 'The table of the Lord is defiled, and as for its fruit, its food is to be despised.' You also say, 'My, how tiresome it is!' And you disdainfully sniff at it," says the Lord of hosts, "and you bring what was taken by robbery, and what is lame or sick; so you bring the offering! Should I receive that from your hand?" says the Lord. "But cursed be the swindler who has a male in his flock, and vows it, but sacrifices a blemished animal to the Lord, for I am a great King," says the Lord of hosts, "and My name is feared among the nations."

March 10

Yesterday, as you meditated upon Malachi 1:6–14, I'm sure you noticed that one of God's complaints with His people was their improper attitude toward Him. They were treating Him with contempt! They called Him "Father," but did not give Him the honor due a father. They called Him "Master," but did not respect Him as a servant should. Rather they were despising His name. They were filled with disdain, for they looked down upon His altar. What they were offering to God was less than the best! And they could not see or would not admit that they were wrong.

It was more or less a case of, "I'll give God what I want to give Him and if He doesn't like it, then that's His tough luck." They were calling the shots, so to speak. They wanted all the privileges that went with being children of God, but not all of the responsibilities. They didn't mind calling Him "Master" as long as they could do what they wanted. Does it sound familiar? Look around you at the church. Take a good look at the people with whom you worship every Sunday. And while you look at them, look also at yourself. Don't most of them claim to know God as Father? Do they not profess Jesus Christ as Lord (Master) and Savior? And if you asked them where they will spend eternity, would not most of them say, "In heaven"? Yet, do they, do you, give God **all** the honor that is due Him as Father? To honor Him is to treat Him with great respect, high regard. It is to realize that because of Who He is, He is to be reverenced. Yet, in our society today we know little of reverence.

I was sickened several days ago and angry with a righteous anger as I saw the news coverage of a disc jockey in town who called for contributions to be sent to our President's wife because she could not find proper tablecloths for the White House. The attitude of the disc jockey and the contributions of the people showed great disdain for the presidency of the United States. On display were paper plates, ketchup bottles, paper tablecloths, and other shams that were a very sad commentary on our times. Agree or not with Mrs. Reagan's desire for lovely table linens, there is an honor, a respect, due her name because of the position she holds. We are spoiled, overindulged, ungrateful children. If we lived behind the iron curtain for a short time we would fall down on our knees in humble gratitude for what we have here. Yet to achieve such gratitude would probably require our overthrow; if we do not straighten up, that may be exactly what God will have to do!

Israel would not give God the honor due His Fatherhood, nor would they give Him respect as a Master; they would not listen or obey. They only wanted God with all His benefits and blessings on their terms.

What about you, Beloved? You are loved by God, but do you embrace His love with a loving heart that longs to honor Him as Father and respect Him as Master? Honestly, who calls the shots in your life?

March 11

The wonder of wonders is that the eternal God gives man a free will! Man can choose his own way. God sets before him blessing or cursing, life or death, and then leaves the choice to him. The words that were spoken to Israel are for the church also, "for whatever was written in earlier times was written for our instruction" (Romans 15:4). Listen carefully: "I call heaven and earth to witness against you today, that I have set before you life and death, the blessing and the curse. So choose life in order that you may live, you and your descendants, by loving the Lord your God, by obeying His voice, and by holding fast to Him; for this is your life and the length of your days" (Deuteronomy 30:19, 20).

There it is again: the way to succeed, the motive of all behavior and all service, the way to maintain a true and vital relationship with God: "Choose life . . . by loving the Lord your God." This is where Israel failed. And if you and I fail, Beloved, it will be in love. Love is that dynamic that is willing to do whatever is necessary to demonstrate its reality . . . like crucifying your only son!

Israel loved only in word, not in deed. They did not honor and respect God. You would think they would have learned their lesson. If God is God, He must be obeyed. His people cannot alter His just requirements and laws according to their own desires and then expect God to compromise and meet them on their level! Yet this is exactly what they did and, although God sent prophet after prophet to warn them, still they did not listen. Hear the words of Isaiah. They parallel the problem in Malachi's day, and yet they are separated by approximately three hundred years.

> Listen, O heavens, and hear, O earth; for the Lord speaks, "Sons I have reared and brought up, but they have revolted against Me. An ox knows its owner, and a donkey its master's manger, but Israel does not know, My people do not understand." Alas, sinful nation, people weighed down with iniquity, offspring of evildoers, sons who act corruptly! They have abandoned the Lord, they have despised the Holy One of Israel, they have turned away from Him. Where will you be stricken again, as you continue in your rebellion? (Isaiah 1:2–5a).

Israel did not listen, but rather trampled under foot the love of God. So God sent them into captivity, the curse of disobedience. Then Malachi, bearing God's burden, came to them after their restoration and spoke the same message again. And again they did not listen. Thus another captivity awaited them: the iron vise of the Roman Empire.

O Beloved, there it is, set before you. Life or death, blessing or cursing. You can choose your way, but you cannot choose the consequences. Choose life ... by loving your God, by obeying His voice.

March 12

Have you ever helped pack a missionary barrel? What *is* a missionary barrel, you say? It is usually (not always) a collection of things that people do not need or want anymore. Leftovers! It is less than better or best, because better and best are kept in the closet at home. Now to the naked or poor, the things in a missionary barrel are better than nothing. Yet even much of what comes is given up on the rubbish heap because it is unusable even in a jungle or a foreign country.

Now suppose we had the opportunity to appear at the White House to present our President with a gift. What would we take him? Something from the missionary barrel? Absolutely not! We would take him something we treasured, something we hoped he would prize. The gift for the mission field is in essence supposed to be a gift to the Lord, a gift for the furtherance of His Kingdom. And the gift for our President? Well, it's a gift for the President! The latter gift gets the praise and recognition of men; the former, the praise and recognition of God. And there are so many that love the praise of men more than the praise of God!

> "But when you present the blind for sacrifice, is it not evil? And when you present the lame and sick, is it not evil? Why not offer it to your governor? Would he be pleased with you? Or would he receive you kindly?" says the Lord of hosts (Malachi 1:8).

And what do you, Beloved, give to God—**of your time?** Does He get the first hour or hours of the day or the last few sleepy moments? **Of your talents, gifts, abilities?** Are they all spent in your pursuit of the pride of life or on things that have no eternal value whatsoever? **Of your possessions?** Does your gift come off the top or do you give whatever is left over after your desires are met? **Of your service?** Do you work as unto Him or for personal praise and recognition? Are you willing to do things His way, or must it be exactly the way you want it or not at all?

What are you packing in God's missionary barrel, Beloved? What are you giving to Him? The blind, the lame, the sick, or your best?

March 13

Not too long ago I asked my Sunday School class why they came to Sunday School. Was it out of a sense of duty or moral obligation or were they coming to really learn God's Word? And, if they were coming to learn, were they willing to pay the price of disciplined study? Or did they simply want to be fed predigested food? Now don't get me wrong; there are many dedicated people in my Sunday School class. Yet I cannot help but wonder as I see our lack of zeal, our lack of discipline, how many go to Sunday School and church because of a burning desire to worship God and to grow in the knowledge of Him that they might be equipped for the work of the ministry (Ephesians 4:11–13).

What difference would it make in the lives of churchgoers if the doors of our Sunday Schools and churches were barred shut? Would it simply give us two more hours a week to do our own thing without a guilty conscience, or would we beg and plead for the doors to be opened again that we might worship our God and learn more of Him? The Jews in Malachi's day, for the most part, wouldn't have minded at all if the doors to the temple had been shut and barred. To them it was "tiresome" to serve the Lord. They looked on the whole system of worship as a mere formality, and they sniffed at it with contempt! How soon they had forgotten the pain of their deserved captivity. Now that the fetters of captivity were gone and all was at ease in Zion, who needed God?

Prayerfully read Isaiah 1:10–14 in your Bible.

It is hypocrisy, Beloved, to go through the motions of worship and sacrifice when you are not motivated by love. It is vain to give God the blind, the lame, the sick of your life when you keep the best for yourself or when you expend yourself for the things of this life! And so God cries, " 'Oh that there were one among you who would shut the gates, that you might not uselessly kindle fire on My altar! I am not pleased with you,' says the Lord of hosts, 'nor will I accept an offering from you' " (Malachi 1:10).

March 14

" 'I am a great King,' says the Lord of hosts, 'and My name is feared among the nations' " (Malachi 1:14). Yet Israel was swindling Him! Can you imagine cheating God? Yet that is what they were doing. " 'But cursed be the swindler who has a male in his flock and vows it, but sacrifices a blemished animal to the Lord, for I am a great King. . . .' " The nations would fear His name, yet His people would not! Amazing, isn't it?!

Several months ago I was introduced to a very remarkable black woman who had just finished hearing me teach. She was a Muslim, a very curious one. She could not get over what I said or my strong stand. Our rapport was instant. Here was a precious woman who was honestly searching for truth. The friend who brought her had been witnessing to her and praying diligently for her. As we talked, my black friend kept shaking her head. "You know, if you really believe what you are saying, Kay, you couldn't do anything else but live the way you're teaching."

How right she is! She does not know our God or His Son. She does not believe that the Bible is God's infallible Word and yet she, a Muslim, realizes that if I believe what I say I believe, I must live a life that is in total accord with what I profess. I cannot swindle God by professing my total allegiance to Him and then live a life that is a sham.

Beloved, to truly believe on Jesus, as I have said, is to acknowledge His name, the Lord Jesus Christ, and live according to that confession. The word *lord* is *kurios* in the Greek, which means master, signifying power or authority.[5] *Kurios* in the Septuagint (the koine Greek translation of the Old Testament) and in the New Testament is representative of the Hebrew *Jehovah,* the word used for God.[6] God tells us in Romans 10:9, "that if you confess with your mouth Jesus as Lord, and believe in your heart that God raised Him from the dead, you shall be saved." *Jesus* means "God my Savior." *Christ* is the koine Greek rendering of the word "Messiah" or "Promised One." Therefore, to believe on His name is to acknowledge that Jesus is God, my Savior, my Master, the Promised One, and to live in obedience to what I profess. To despise His name, as God said they were doing in Malachi's day, is to claim one thing and do another! They were swindlers because they were cheating God in their sacrifices and worship, giving God less than best. And you, Beloved, where do you stand? How do you measure up? Does your life, your sacrifice for Him give the reverence due to His name? God wants a pure offering that is totally committed!

I urge you therefore, brethren, by the mercies of God, to present your bodies a living and holy sacrifice, acceptable to God, which is your spiritual service of worship (Romans 12:1).

March 15

It's a heavy month, isn't it? The messages are not easy. I'm sorry, Precious One. I cannot help it. It must be said. Someone must love the church enough to wear the shoes of Isaiah, Jeremiah, Ezekiel, Malachi. Before God, I have covenanted to be among the ranks of those who will speak the truth in love. How I pray that you will be among those who will listen. Our time is short, Beloved; I do not set days or hours because that is not scriptural, yet I do believe from my understanding of prophecy that we do not have any longer than the year 2000. And then because I believe in a pretribulation rapture, I would shorten that by seven years at least. Our time is short! According to Jewish reckoning, it is later than we think! The day is far spent; the night is coming. And what about the church? We who profess to be sons of light and of the day consort with those of the night. It is hard to tell one from the other. Percentagewise, few are alert and sober, and are donned in battle array, wearing the breastplate of faith and love, and the helmet of the hope of salvation (1 Thessalonians 5:5–8).

As I write this, it is December 1981. Our world is in chaos. Poland has ousted the Solidarity Union, instituting martial law, and has shut the Polish borders. Israel has annexed the Golan Heights, upsetting Syria, and Israel-American relations are greatly strained. Brezhnev, just before his seventy-fifth birthday, said he thought war between the East and West was a very real possibility. He said, however, that he hoped something could be worked out in arms limitations. Others, the news reported tonight, are talking about a war within three or four years.

Many students of God's Word believe, based on their study of Ezekiel 38, that the future does hold a confrontation between Israel and Russia with Russia being the aggressor. That this is Russia's ultimate intention is obvious. In the 1973 Yom Kippur War, Russia supplied Syria with arms and tanks. During that war, Brezhnev sent a cable to President Nixon saying that Russia had decided to take unilateral action and thus resolve the Israeli problem. American reconnaissance flights reported that the large Soviet warship docked at Alexandria, Egypt was loaded with ballistic missiles with nuclear warheads. "At the same time the Soviet airlift (with Syria) dramatically stopped and all those huge transports were at the ready while crack Soviet parachute regiments moved towards the airfields." It was at this point that President Nixon called a worldwide United States military alert in the five-stage American defense condition.[7] Russia never took unilateral action.

O Beloved, when Russia does make its move toward Israel then events will move with the suddenness of an avalanche. If you are not ready, you'll be buried under it all. And the church is not ready. We must awaken others. We must pray. Our time is so short. If only we knew!

March 16

And where were the shepherds of God's flock in Malachi's time? Why hadn't the priests spoken to the people or barred the doors to the temple until the people saw the error of their ways? Why didn't they put a stop to their contemptible sacrifices? The priests knew God's Word, "But if it has any defect, such as lameness or blindness or any serious defect, you shall not sacrifice it to the Lord your God" (Deuteronomy 15:21).

The shepherds were as guilty as the people. As a matter of fact, in Malachi, it was the priests that God kept taking to task. Why? Because like priests, like people. With leadership go responsibility and accountability.

The Great Shepherd knows the needs of His sheep. However, in our case it is one priest speaking to another, for if you are a believer then you are part of a kingdom of priests unto God. Listen carefully to God's Word:

> And they sang a new song, saying "Worthy art Thou to take the book, and to break its seals; for Thou wast slain, and didst purchase for God with Thy blood men from every tribe and tongue and people and nation. And Thou hast made them to be a kingdom and *priests* to our God; and they will reign upon the earth" (Revelation 5:9, 10).

Therefore, I speak to you, priest to priest. And in doing so, I ask you to listen carefully to the responsibility of priests: "For the lips of a priest should preserve knowledge, and men should seek instruction from his mouth; for he is the messenger of the Lord of hosts" (Malachi 2:7). But Beloved, how can we give instruction if we are too busy with the affairs of this life to gain knowledge? And how can we call others to consecration when we will not consecrate ourselves?

" 'And now, this commandment is for you, O priests. If you do not listen, and if you do not take it to heart to give honor to My name,' says the Lord of hosts, 'then I will send the curse upon you, and I will curse your blessings; and indeed, I have cursed them already, because you are not taking it to heart. Behold, I am going to rebuke your offspring, and I will spread refuse on your faces, the refuse of your feasts; and you will be taken away with it' " (Malachi 2:1-3).

Do you sometimes feel as if your blessings are a curse, that things were better when you were struggling? You were closer to God then. And are your offspring rebuked by God because they are a product of your hypocritical life-style? O, Precious One, this is not the inheritance of those who love their God and of those who pursue holiness. God's plan for us is life and peace (Malachi 2:5), but it cannot be ours unless our hearts are fully His.

March 17

This morning as I was having my quiet time, the Lord impressed upon my heart the peace that was mine for the believing, the obeying. Yesterday, the hot water lines in one of our motel units burst, flooding five rooms with two or more inches of water. Since all the trainees and most of the staff were gone, the mess was not discovered until late last night. What could we do? We could become upset and cry, "Why this, Lord?" or we could believe God, give thanks (Ephesians 5:20), and walk in perfect peace by keeping our minds and hearts stayed upon Him (Isaiah 26:3). We chose to give thanks. Then this morning, as I was meditating on all of this; as I tried to put myself in the shoes of Polish Christians, and as I thought of what the future could hold for us, I thought again of His promises of peace.

God's covenant to Levi (the priests) "was one of life and peace, and I gave them to him as an object of reverence" (Malachi 2:5), and God's covenant to His church is the same. Did not the angels proclaim it when they proclaimed the Messiah's birth saying, "Glory to God in the highest, and on earth peace among men with whom He is pleased" (Luke 2:14)? If you read that verse carefully you will notice it is different than the King James Version which we so often quote, "And on earth peace, good will toward men." The New American Standard's translation is truer to the Greek. It is not peace on earth, but rather peace among men with whom God is pleased! Peace comes through knowledge, and through obedience to that knowledge! "Grace and peace be multiplied to you in the knowledge of God and of Jesus our

Lord" (2 Peter 1:2). "These things I have spoken to you, that **in Me** you may have peace. In the world you have tribulation, but take courage; I have overcome the world" (John 16:33).

Our peace is wrapped up in Him, and if we are not wrapped up in Him, we will not know peace. We can't. He is the Prince of Peace. Outside of His will, separated from a knowledge of Him, or living in hypocrisy, there can be no peace. Rather there must be chastening and "no chastening for the present seemeth to be joyous, but grievous: nevertheless, afterward it yieldeth the **peaceable** fruit of righteousness unto them which are exercised thereby" (Hebrews 12:11 KJV).

O, Beloved, if we will only listen and reverence God, fear Him and His Word, then we will know His life and His peace. It's His covenant to us!

March 18

Oh, how desperately we need people who have determined in their hearts that they will stand for what is right, people who will live for absolutes that transcend their own personal desires, people who are willing to die for something rather than live for just anything. We need men, women, teens, and children of character, of principle, of conviction.

But where are they, and why are there so few? You may even look at yourself and wonder why you are not a person of great conviction. Does resolve of character and conviction belong only to a certain personality type? No, I do not believe so. True, some personalities tend to be more verbal than others. My husband and I are as different as night and day in our personalities. If you were to analyze us according to the popular theory of the four personality types, Jack would be labeled a phlegmatic and I a sanguine. Yet my husband is a man of great conviction who will do what is right because it is right. It does not matter the cost or the discipline. I have seen people, women especially, try to push him into something and I have thought, "Now you have had it, Honey. He is not going to do it. You can't push him when he is convinced he is right." Jack is not bullheaded; he is reasonable and a peacemaker. Yet he is a man with absolutes, a man who would not hesitate to lay down his life rather than compromise His God. If we ever go to prison, I pray that we will go together, for I know he would be a great source of strength to me.

Now, I know all this about Jack because I live with him. But because he is not as verbal as I am, others might not know it until they saw him in a confrontation where truth or principle was involved. And, Beloved, it may be the same with you. Although you may be a quiet, reserved, even-keeled type, under that personality is a hero or a heroine, a brave and noble person who lives intrepidly according to your convictions and the need of the hour. I love Deborah's song in Judges 5 where she says, "The peasantry ceased, they ceased in Israel, until I, Deborah, arose, until I arose, a mother in Israel" (Judges 5:7). Godless Jabin and his army with their mighty iron chariots had oppressed them too long. Even the farmers (peasants) could no longer live on their land. The highways were deserted. It wasn't safe to go out. The people were holed behind the city gates without shields or spears to defend themselves. Deborah had had it. That was no way for children of the Almighty God to live. So she arose, "a mother in Israel."

O Beloved, it is time for us, God's kingdom of priests, to awake and arise, even as did Deborah, the sons of Levi, and others in days of old. I will tell you about it tomorrow. I love you, my heroes and heroines.

March 19

Remember the covenant of life and peace in Malachi 2? Well, God made this covenant with Levi because He saw that the Levites were zealous for His glory and His righteousness. Thus, in Malachi 2, God warns the Levites to continue to listen to Him and to give honor to His name rather than despise it. As you read these verses from Malachi below, give special attention to verse four (in bold type). God is saying that life and peace cannot continue in the face of disobedience and dishonor of God!

"And now, this commandment is for you, O priests. If you do not listen, and if you do not take it to heart to give honor to My name," says the Lord of hosts, "then I will send the curse upon you, and I will curse your blessings; and indeed, I have cursed them already, because you are not taking it to heart. Behold, I am going to rebuke your offspring, and I will spread refuse on your faces, the refuse of your feasts; and you will be taken away with it. **Then you will know that I have sent this commandment to you, that My covenant may continue with Levi,**" says the Lord of hosts. "My covenant with him was one of life and peace, and I gave them to him as an object of reverence; so he revered Me, and stood in awe of My name. True instruction was in his mouth, and unrighteousness was not found on his lips; he walked with Me in peace and uprightness, and he turned many back from iniquity. For the lips of a priest should preserve knowledge, and men should seek instruction from his mouth; for he is the messenger of the Lord of hosts" (Malachi 2:1–7).

There are two different places in God's Word that speak of a time when Levi reverenced God and stood in awe of His name. We will look at them on three separate days. Although the primary cross-reference to Malachi 2:4 is Numbers 25, we will look at that after we have looked at Exodus 32:25–29. Read it and note how Levi played the hero; we'll talk about it tomorrow.

March 20

Moses had been on Mount Sinai too long for the children of Israel. Being impatient and fickle, yet knowing they needed a god, they assembled about Aaron. "Come, make us a god who will go before us; as for this Moses, the man who brought us up from the land of Egypt, we do not know what has become of him" (Exodus 32:1).

Oh, how like so many of us! If God isn't going to run by our time table, then we will run without Him; we'll get us another god. And that is exactly what we do! When we want something, rather than pray and wait for God we decide that if God won't give it to us then we will get it ourselves! And if it takes giving ourselves to other gods, idols of money, position, self-gratification, sensuality, whatever, to appease our appetites, we will do it. We can't shake our heads at the Israelites and wonder how they could be so senseless after they had seen God's mighty hand in the plagues on Egypt and the parting of the Red Sea! Look at us! We have seen One far greater than Moses, One who healed the lepers, raised the dead, gave sight to the blind, calmed the stormy sea and then died on Calvary's tree, was buried and resurrected! We have bowed before Him, cried out for His eternal life so that we might not perish in hell, and then, relieved, gotten to our feet and walked after other gods. And in doing so, like the Israelites, we have corrupted ourselves by turning aside from the way which God commanded us.

And that makes God angry (Exodus 32:10)! Can you blame Him? Of course not, yet we do. The people in Malachi's day could not understand how God could be so upset. They didn't think they were wrong at all! They were saying, "Everyone who does evil is good in the sight of the Lord, and He delights in them" (Malachi 2:17). As a matter of fact, they got upset with God because He wasn't blessing as they thought He should! "Where is the God of justice?" (2:17). But, Beloved, because God is God He cannot look on sin, nor can He bless it.

His holiness, righteousness, and justice demand that it be dealt with! And Moses understood because Moses was a man of convictions. There is a right and a wrong, and they cannot be compromised. Moses' heart burned with a righteous holy anger! And he cried out, "Whoever is for the Lord, come to me!" (Exodus 32:26). And all the sons of Levi gathered together to him. And then they judged sin without partiality whether the sinner was a brother, friend, or neighbor.

Dear One, are you for the Lord? Then come to Him and put to death that sin which so easily besets you. O Dear God, give us men and women who are not so apathetic that they cannot be indignant toward sin.

March 21

Show me the God or gods a man worships, and I will tell you the character of that man. You see, Beloved, we become like that which we worship. The gentile gods were sensual and so, too, were their worshippers. Immorality inevitably follows idolatry. When the sons of Israel joined themselves to Baal of Peor, it was no time before they played the harlot with the daughters of Moab.

Today we are going to look at Numbers 25:1-13, the direct cross-reference for Malachi 2:4, 5. Read the account carefully and then we will discuss it tomorrow.

> While Israel remained at Shittim, the people began to play the harlot with the daughters of Moab. For they invited the people to the sacrifices of their gods, and the people ate and bowed down to their gods. So Israel joined themselves to Baal of Peor, and the Lord was angry against Israel. And the Lord said to Moses, "Take all the leaders of the people and execute them in broad daylight before the Lord, so that the fierce anger of the Lord may turn away from Israel." So Moses said to the judges of Israel, "Each of you slay his men who have joined themselves to Baal of Peor." Then behold, one of the sons of Israel came and brought to his relatives a Midianite woman, in the sight of Moses and in the sight of all the congregation of the sons of Israel, while they were weeping at the doorway of the tent of meeting. When Phinehas the son of Eleazar, the son of Aaron the priest, saw it, he arose from the midst of the congregation, and took a spear in his hand; and he went after the man of Israel into the tent, and pierced both of them through, the man of Israel and the woman, through the body. So the plague on the sons of Israel was checked. And those who died by the plague were 24,000. Then the Lord spoke to Moses, saying, "Phinehas the son of Eleazar,

the son of Aaron the priest, has turned away My wrath from the sons of Israel, in that he was jealous with My jealousy among them, so that I did not destroy the sons of Israel in My jealousy. Therefore say, 'Behold, I give him My covenant of peace; and it shall be for him and his descendants after him, a covenant of a perpetual priesthood, because he was jealous for his God, and made atonement for the sons of Israel.' "

Meditate on what you have read. Are there any idols in your life that have changed your character? Look at what you give yourself to, for if these keep you from fully following God, they are idols. Can you see any truths you can apply to your own life?

March 22

How jealous are you for the holiness of God? How ready are you to stand for righteousness? How far would you go to keep others from iniquity?

God is looking for heroes of the faith, intrepid men and women who will live according to their convictions. When He saw the zeal of Phinehas, the Levite, He knew He had His man. Twice the Levites had stood with Him. Twice He had seen a passion for Himself that overruled all other commitments and loyalties. Yesterday you read of Phinehas, the son of Eleazar, the son of Aaron. Jealous with God's jealousy, he put to death the sin within the camp and in doing so checked the plague that had already taken 24,000 lives. And what does God say about Phinehas, as representative of the tribe of Levi? "True instruction was in his mouth, and unrighteousness was not found on his lips; he walked with Me in peace and uprightness, and **he turned many back from iniquity**" (Malachi 2:6).

Beloved, how do we measure up as priests today? We are to be just as jealous with God's jealousy as Phinehas and the Levites were. I hope that you know there is a godly jealousy. Paul talked of it in 2 Corinthians 11:2: "For I am jealous for you with a godly jealousy; for I betrothed you to one husband, that to Christ I might present you as a pure virgin." And what provoked this godly jealousy? It was a concern that the Corinthians might be "led astray from the simplicity and purity of devotion to Christ" (2 Corinthians 11:3). Wasn't this what happened to the children of Israel as they waited for Moses at the foot of Mount Sinai and when they remained at Shittim?

It also happened at Corinth, taking the same manifestation of immorality. A young man was committing incest with his father's wife (1 Corinthians 5)! But was the church jealous with a godly jealousy for God's name? No, they had let the sin go unchecked. When Paul wrote regarding the situation, his admonition to the church was, "Do you not know that a little leaven leavens the whole lump of dough?" (1 Corinthians 5:6). In other words, unchecked sin spreads. So Paul took the same action the Levites did. He stood against the sin. It had to be checked. The offender was to be put out of fellowship and delivered unto "Satan for the destruction of his flesh, that his spirit may be saved in the day of the Lord Jesus" (1 Corinthians 5:5).

And yet, what do so many do when they see sin in the church? Is it dealt with, or merely whispered about and ignored? And how does one check sin in his own life? We'll talk about it tomorrow.

March 23

Sin is an insidious thing. It usually begins in small ways and spreads until finally you are caught in its vise-like grip wondering how you got there and if there is really any way to be set free. Sometimes sin is so insidious that you do not even realize its presence. It can enter your life so subtly that, were it pointed out to you, you would deny its presence. And thus it was in Malachi's time. Israel could not see her iniquity even when God pointed it out!

Currently I am reading through the Bible again in my quiet time, noting especially what I can learn about prayer. Several days ago I was struck anew and afresh with Genesis 4 and God's dealings with Cain after He rejected his offering. Cain wanted to worship God his own way, on his own terms, and God would not have it! And thus we find Cain angry and pouting!

How typical. We are happy as long as everything is going our way, as long as God agrees with what we want to do, but let Him make any demands on us and it is another story! Cain refused to bring a blood sacrifice; if God didn't like the fruit of his labor He could forget it! "So Cain became very angry and his countenance fell. Then the Lord said to Cain, 'Why are you angry? And why has your countenance fallen? If you do well, will not your countenance be lifted up?' " (Genesis 4:5–7). In other words, you do not have to be unhappy. The misery you are experiencing is of your own choosing. Isn't that so typical? We long for love, joy, and peace, yet refuse to do what is necessary to have them. Love, joy, and peace are ours for the believing, the obeying; all we must do is walk by His Spirit rather than after the desires of our flesh (Galatians 5:16–25). Yet we, in stubbornness, choose not to believe, not to obey! And thus God continues, "And if you do not do well, sin is crouching at the door; and its desire is for you, **but you must master it**" (Genesis 4:7).

Don't we often say, "I do not want to sin, but I can't help it," or "The devil made me do it"? Oh no, Beloved! For a Christian, sin is a matter of choice. Recently I heard about a young man who has attended several of our boot camps at Reach Out. He's in sin, running with the wrong crowd. Recently he said to his mother, "If God doesn't stop me, then I'll go on living the way I am." And what has God got to do with it? It is his responsibility, not God's. God has told us what is right and wrong. He has given us His Spirit to be our Comforter, our Guide, our Enabler; however, the choice is still ours. We must master sin. And the minute we choose God's way, then God will meet us. But, oh, let a little sin in and then you have a monster on your hands. Cain got up and killed Abel!

March 24

Sin. We cover it up. We excuse it. We rationalize it. We do everything but confront it and deal with it honestly and openly. And what does God say? Listen to His Word, "He that covereth his sins shall not prosper, but whoso confesseth and forsaketh them shall have mercy" (Proverbs 28:13 KJV).

If only we realized that sin is never a private affair. When we sin, someone else is always affected. Sin causes repercussions that extend far beyond ourselves, sometimes affecting second, third, and fourth generations. How? Why? Let me explain.

When we sin we are living lives that are un-god-like and unrighteous. By unrighteous, I mean a life that is not lived according to what God says is right. When we live like this, we suppress or hold down the truth through our unrighteousness (Romans 1:18). To do so is to eclipse God or keep men from seeing Him. Therefore, when we sin it hurts others because they cannot see real godliness or righteousness. Also, not seeing godliness or righteousness in our lives allows them to excuse their own sin. "After all," they say, "I'm as good as they are, maybe even better." When Jesus Christ came and lived **as a man,** He as man was tempted by the devil (Matthew 4), but He did not yield. When He as man lived in complete obedience and total dependence upon the Father (John 8:28, 29), He as man took away man's excuse for sin (John 15:22)!

When we live in sin, when we cover our transgressions and do not openly acknowledge and confess them as sin, then our sin affects others because they excuse their sin by ours. "After all, nobody's perfect! What can you expect? Don't be so hard on yourself. We're human, aren't we? We're trying, but we just can't be perfect!"

Are we? **Are we really trying not to sin?** Well, if we were trying then we wouldn't sin. With sin, it is not a matter of trying or not trying. If you are a Christian, it is a matter of yielding. Remember, you have the choice. You can master sin if you will! It is simply a choice. Who is going to run your life, the Spirit of God or your fleshly appetites? Since the Garden of Eden man has sought to cover his sin. Instead of running to God and confessing his sin, Adam made fig leaves and covered himself. (He now knew good and evil!) So God sought him out, and when He confronted Adam with his sin, Adam blamed Eve; then Eve blamed the serpent. They looked for an excuse. O Beloved, can't you see that when you sin, you cannot cover it! God knows it. Others see it, and it gives them their excuse!

March 25

The priests in Malachi's day were covering their sins and the repercussions spread to the whole nation. The Jews looked at their religious leaders and followed suit. Among those who claimed to be God's chosen people there was great sin. Listen to His indictment against the people in Malachi 3:5, " 'Then I will draw near to you for judgment; and I will be a swift witness against the sorcerers and against the adulterers and against those who swear falsely, and against those who oppress the wage earner in his wages, the widow and the orphan, and those who turn aside the alien, and do not fear Me,' says the Lord of hosts." The people and the priests were not distinguishing "between the righteous and the wicked, between one who serves God and one who does not serve Him" (3:18).

And so it is today. There is sin in the camp. Grievous sin. Divorce abounds not only in the ranks but among the leadership. I know pastors, authors, and leaders who are guilty of immorality and divorce (without biblical grounds). Yet no disciplinary action has been taken and they have moved from one church to another or continued writing Christian books or holding positions of leadership in Christian organizations. O Beloved, we are to pursue "holiness, without which no man shall see the Lord" (Hebrews 12:14). I cannot call you to holiness if I will not be holy myself. As the priest, so the people!

When we cover our sin, God calls it "dealing treacherously." The Hebrew word is *bagad,* and it means to cover (as with a garment), to act covertly, deal deceitfully, treacherously, to depart, offend, transgress. Sin *does* affect your brother. It affects him in a horrible, insidious, deceitful way. Your sin encourages him to sin as well. And sin is transgression of the law, whereas love is fulfillment of the law. "For this, 'You shall not commit adultery, you shall not murder, you shall not steal, you shall not covet,' and if there is any other commandment it is summed up in this saying, 'You shall love your neighbor as yourself.' Love does no wrong to a neighbor; love therefore is the fulfillment of the law" (Romans 13:9, 10).

God loves you. The question is: Do you love Him? And you say you love others. Do you? If you do—if I do—then we will pursue holiness instead of excusing and covering our sin.

March 26

Divorce. It is one of the things that God literally hates. It destroys the home, the bedrock of any nation. But they say, in whimpering tones of self-indulgence, "Surely God doesn't want people to be unhappy, does He?" My Precious Ones, let me say this: God is not concerned about your happiness; He is concerned about your holiness. Be holy and you will be happy. (I use the term "happy" because it is the language of our culture.) True happiness is experienced through a right relationship with God. Look around you, talk to people, observe their lives and you will discover that a person can have every material possession, fame, beauty and five lovers and still be dissatisfied and unhappy. But talk to a person pursuing holiness who is in a right relationship with God, and you will find that he can live in the meanest of circumstances with the meanest of people and still know the joy of the Lord which is his strength and the source of his right relationship with others.

Yet what are we doing in our nation and in the church? We are putting away our wives, our husbands. Do you realize that today a child that still has his original parents is an oddity to his schoolmates? And what does divorce do to a man or woman? It defiles them. And what does it do to the land? It pollutes the land, for it stops or hinders our having godly offspring.

Oh listen, America! Listen, you people of the world! Listen, church! Listen to the Word of the Lord.

"The Lord has been a witness between you and the wife of your youth, against whom you have dealt treacherously, though she is your companion and your wife by covenant. But not one has done so who has a remnant of the Spirit. And what did that one do while he was seeking a godly offspring? Take heed then, to your spirit, and let no one deal treacherously against the wife of your youth. For I hate divorce," says the Lord, the God of Israel, "and him who covers his garment with wrong," says the Lord of hosts. "So take heed to your spirit, that you do not deal treacherously" (Malachi 2:14–16).

The priests and the people were dealing treacherously. They were divorcing their wives and not calling it sin. They divorced them and never blinked an eye, shed a tear, or missed a beat as they marched to the destroyer's cadence right into God's temple without the slightest shame. They divorced their wives and sought God at the altar. Yet at the altar they wept. "You cover the altar of the Lord with tears, with weeping and with groaning, because He no longer regards the offering or accepts it with favor from your hand" (Malachi 2:13).

He can't. You can weep all you want, but He can't. He is God. And you either march to His cadence, or you don't march at all!

March 27

Isn't it strange how that when we get hurt we cry for justice? "It's not right. They shouldn't be allowed to get away with it. It just isn't fair. That's all there is to it." We insist on justice, because we have been wronged. But what do we want when we are the guilty party, the one who has wronged another? Mercy, of course!

Iniquity abounded in Israel. Men did not honor or respect God; they profaned His altar with unsuitable sacrifices; ungodly and partial instruction was given by so-called men of God; brother dealt treacherously against brother; divorce was rampant among those who professed to be God's servants; tithes and offerings had been withheld from God and yet they cried, "Where is the God of justice?" (Malachi 2:17). They wanted justice from God because they had been hurt, yet they did not want the God of justice. In other words, give me God to meet my demands and plead my case, but don't put the demands of the holy God on *me*. I want the gifts but not the Giver, the redemption for my sins but not the Redeemer.

And how about you, Beloved? Do you want all the benefits of God without the obligations of godliness?

They had asked the question, "Where is the God of justice?" They would get their answer. He was coming! " 'Behold, I am going to send My messenger, and he will clear the way before Me. And the Lord, whom you seek, will suddenly come to His temple; and the messenger of the covenant, in whom you delight, behold, He is coming,' says the Lord of hosts" (3:1). And yet, when He came, it would not be to bring the unjust justice, to lift them out of the rebellious, willful, self-dug pits, but rather to execute judgment upon the earth.

> " 'But who can endure the day of His coming? And who can stand when He appears? For He is like a refiner's fire and like fuller's soap' " (Malachi 3:2).

He would come as the Lamb of God to take away the sin of the world, but only those who knew they needed a lamb would recognize His coming. And so, for all those who were arrogant doers of wickedness (Malachi 3:13–15) as well as for those who feared the Lord (3:16), there would be a forerunner who would clear the way of the Lord. John the Baptist. And what would be his message? "Repent, for the kingdom of heaven is at hand" (Matthew 3:1, 2).

There it was . . . the offer of a Kingdom in which justice would reign. And the key that would grant entrance into that Kingdom hung on a ring of repentance! Do you really want justice, or would you prefer mercy? Have you ever repented?

March 28

"A voice is calling, 'Clear the way for the Lord in the wilderness; make smooth in the desert a highway for our God. Let every valley be lifted up, and every mountain and hill be made low; and let the rough ground become a plain, and the rugged terrain a broad valley; **then** the glory of the Lord will be revealed, and all flesh will see it together; for the mouth of the Lord has spoken' " (Isaiah 40:3–5).

This was to be the ministry of John the Baptist. It was the custom of eastern kings to send men before them to remove every barrier and obstacle in their path. "In this instance, it meant removal of opposition to the Lord by the preaching of repentance and the conversion of sinners to Him."[8]

So, in spite of the blindness of their eyes and the hardness of their hearts, God did not consume the sons of Jacob, but rather reached out to them again. Because He loved them (Malachi 1:2) and because He is a covenant-keeping God (3:1) and because He, the Lord, does not change (3:6), He would reach out to them once more. This time, it would not be through prophets but through His Son and His Son's messenger. The message of both would be the same: "Repent."

And what does it mean to repent? The Hebrew word *shubh* used for repentance in the Old Testament carries the idea of a radical change in one's attitude toward sin and good. It implies a conscious moral separation and personal decision to forsake sin and to enter into fellowship with God. There is no fellowship with God, Beloved, if you insist on continuing in sin. "If we say we have fellowship with Him and yet walk in the darkness, we lie and do not practice the truth" (1 John 1:6). Therefore, repentance is a turning to God from sin, a change of mind resulting in a change of direction.

Before any man, woman, or child can truly be saved, he or she must see the need of salvation and of a Savior. It is one thing to know you need salvation and another to know you cannot save yourself. When you see your total inability to make yourself right with God, then you recognize your desperate need for a savior; and how many there are who have never seen their need! There are so many sitting in church pews who are typical of the Old Testament Jews sacrificing in the temple—involved in religion, calling upon the one true Jehovah God, going through the rituals of worship, having a zeal for God but not in accordance with knowledge. "For not knowing about God's righteousness, and seeking to establish their own, they did not subject themselves to the righteousness of God" (Romans 10:3). They have not repented; they have seen no need to do so. Thus they are religious, but lost. What about you?

March 29

John the Baptist's message was very clear, very direct. It needed to be. The people were set and comfortable in their ways. Caught up in their sects, convinced they were right, they did not know it was a case of the blind leading the blind. They boasted in a law they broke and thus they dishonored God. Their praise came from men, certainly not from God (Romans 2:17–29). Speaking of the One to come, John said, "His winnowing fork is in His hand, and He will thoroughly clean His threshing floor; and He will gather His wheat into the barn, but He will burn up the chaff with unquenchable fire" (Matthew 3:12). John was letting them know that when the Christ came He would winnow the grain to expose what was wheat and what was chaff.

Do you like preaching that winnows the grain? I believe we need more of it, much more. And I do believe that if we love God and man then we will preach a message that will separate the wheat from the chaff, even as did Malachi. But as you preach, remember it was preached from the foundational truth: "I have loved you." Tell them of God's love, "For God so loved the world, that he gave his only be-

104

gotten Son, that whosoever believeth in him should not perish, but have everlasting life" (John 3:16 KJV). But also tell them that "except ye repent, ye shall all likewise perish" (Luke 13:3 KJV). "Not every one that saith unto me, Lord, Lord, shall enter into the kingdom of heaven, but he that doeth the will of my Father which is in heaven" (Matthew 7:21 KJV). And when you preach, ask them if they are doing the will of God or if they are calling the shots, walking the way they want to walk, yet saying, "Lord, Lord."

"Therefore bring forth fruit in keeping with your repentance . . . the axe is already laid at the root of the trees; every tree therefore that does not bear good fruit is cut down and thrown into the fire" (Matthew 3:8, 10). "So then, you will know them by their fruits" (Matthew 7:20).

Walk through the vineyards of your life, Beloved, and inspect your fruit. Record your findings.

March 30

A good way to inspect your fruit is to look at your walk. I say "walk" because some of us are so introspective and so full of self-condemnation that we cannot trust ourselves to objectively look at our hearts. "Little children, let us not love with word or with tongue, but in deed and truth. We shall know by this (deed and truth) that we are of the truth, and shall assure our heart before Him, **in whatever our heart condemns us;** for God is greater than our heart, and knows all things" (1 John 3:18–20).

We counsel so many dear ones who have a hard time accepting the fact of God's unconditional love and commitment that I feel I must say what I am saying for their benefit. Perhaps this is a problem for you. Messages like this month's devotionals sometimes bring condemnation to sensitive souls who long to please God, yet never feel that they can measure up!

Many of those in this category have never known unconditional love from their parents. They have received condemnation instead. Therefore, it is hard to relate to God as One Who loves unconditionally, and this gives them difficulty with their faith. They heap condemnation upon themselves and thus put themselves into "the pits." However, even though there is a risk that some might have difficulty in this area, messages like Malachi's must be delivered.

To all those who fear the Lord, and especially to those of you who too quickly condemn yourselves, let me give you a blessed word from Malachi. God knows those who fear Him. He knows the hearts of all men, and there is "a book of remembrance . . . written before him for those who fear the Lord and who esteem His name. 'And they will be Mine,' says the Lord of hosts, 'on the day that I prepare My own possession, and I will spare them as a man spares his own son who serves him. . . . For behold, the day is coming, burning like a furnace; and all the arrogant and every evildoer will be chaff; and the day that is coming will set them ablaze,' says the Lord of hosts, 'so that it will leave them neither root or branch. But for you who fear My name the sun of righteousness will rise with healing in its wings; and you will go forth and skip about like calves from the stall. And you will tread down the wicked, for they shall be ashes under the soles of your feet on the day which I am preparing,' says the Lord of hosts" (Malachi 3:16, 17; 4:1–3).

O Beloved, never fear, because the Lord knows His own and will lose none of them (John 10:27–29, 17). Hallelujah!

March 31

The way a person handles money tells you a lot about his relationship with God. When the Lord said, "Return to Me, and I will return to you" (Malachi 3:7), they asked "How shall we return?" God's reply was quite interesting, for He dealt with them in the area of their pocketbook! "Will a man rob God? Yet you are robbing Me! But you say, 'How have we robbed thee?' In tithes and contributions. You are cursed with a curse, for you are robbing Me, the whole nation of you!" (Malachi 3:8, 9).

Can you imagine robbing God, from whom comes every good and perfect gift! God, Who has promised to supply all our needs!

It was God who gave the increase and He only asked them for a tenth—the firstfruits, while there remained a whole harvest left for their very own. And here they were begrudging God a tithe of all He had given them. When the whole tithe was brought to the storehouse (the temple or the place of God's designation), did they not partake of it themselves after it had been offered to God (Deuteronomy 12:1–19)? And if they did not partake of every tithe, did not the rest go to the Levites who labored at the temple and to the widows and the poor (Deuteronomy 26:12–15)? Yet they would not release what belonged to God, the tithes and contributions He had asked for! No, as they held back their own lives, so they held back their possessions. Their token giving matched their token living. Find a man who is totally surrendered to God and you will find that everything he has is held in an open hand. What God had commanded, a tenth, would not even trouble him, for a tenth wouldn't be enough to give back to his God.

Beloved, at times I get distressed at the schemes that Christian organizations go through in order to raise support for their ministries. It seems as if people have to be bought in order to get them to give. Where do the Holy Spirit and the guidance of God come into giving? Several weeks ago we received a letter from an acquaintance telling us of a new organization that has been formed to help Christians raise money. Several television ministries are using it and have been very successful. Our friend wanted us to contact them immediately as he knew it would help us tremendously. The organization takes your donor lists and then telephones each one individually urging them to give even more. As I read the letter I prayed, "O Father, keep us at Reach Out from schemes so that we might trust in You." Then, not too long ago, a salesman caught me in our lobby and wanted us to give away things in exchange for donations to the ministry. I called Jack to ask him to deal with the man, but, how I ached. So many people sin in this way, for they give a donation in order to get a gift and then do not deduct the retail cost of that gift from their donation before they write it off as a tax deduction.

Now don't get me wrong. We cannot go on or reach out further without donations that keep our ministry going. Read 2 Corinthians 8 and you will see God's example in giving. We are first to give ourselves to the Lord and then we will beg God for opportunities to give to others and thus to "abound in this gracious work also" (2 Corinthians 8:7) as our abundance is always a means of supply for the needs of others.

How do you give? What is your motive? Are you robbing God? Maybe that is why the devourer is destroying your "crops" and you cannot seem to manage or get ahead (Malachi 3:10, 11).

APRIL

Do You Like Yourself?

April 1

He had been gone a little over three weeks. When he returned home, he seemed like a new man. Friends and family were utterly astonished. What had happened? No one could figure it out! Here was a man who had always been admired and respected as a fine Christian, yet now he was different. Once reserved, he was now open and full of joy. Once undemonstrative, he now even put his arms around the men and around his children, giving them great big hugs! Once very sparing with compliments, he now spoke tender words of affection, praise, and gratitude with ease. Longing hearts eagerly received his new warmth. It was as if somehow he had been unshackled, as if he couldn't wait to put into practice the truths he had learned while he was away.

This lasted two or three days. Then it was gone. The "new" man pulled back inside and locked up. No one ever talked about it, but many times his wife wondered if she would ever find the key that would unlock the door to the man she knew lived inside her husband. She longed to know *that* man more fully. Somehow deep in her heart she knew this was the man he really was.

It was all her fault, or at least for years she assumed it was. They never talked about it. (Why? I don't know. They just never did.) She only knew that a word of honesty spoken in a moment of hurt had pushed this loving, free, demonstrative man back inside the closet of himself. She thought she had heard the lock turn. It must have. He never came out.

She was a Christian also, and she cried out for forgiveness, asking God to show her how to unlock the door. But the years passed. The door remained bolted. Try as hard as she could, search as she would, she could not find the key.

Have you ever looked at a human being and wondered if there were another person locked inside, different from the one you saw? I have. And it has seemed at times that I have caught them pulling back the sheer curtains and peeping out through the windows of their soul. But the minute I caught their eye, they dropped the curtain and were gone. Or so it seemed.

Why? They looked so lovely, so warm, so personable. Why would they hide? Why would they stay behind locked doors? Who, or what, shut them in? Where is the key? Who has it, them or me? Or is there a key at all? I believe there is.

April 2

Several years passed—exactly how many I'm not sure—before the wife ever brought it up; and then it wasn't planned. It just came out. It was a rare moment . . . dinner for four overlooking the bay. This wife and her husband, and another couple were talking about communication and sharing so openly. It was a night of honesty, a time when souls could be bared without fear of judgment or condemnation. No masks had to be worn. They could trust one another. Completely at ease, she told about the man she had once seen in her husband. Then came the inevitable question, "What happened that changed you so?"

The story came out. He had gone to a place far away where no one knew him, where he was his own man. He wasn't who he was because of his family or his wife or his profession. He was simply himself, totally free. And he knew he was loved, accepted, and appreciated just for that! Not because of anything but himself. "Even though I love my wife and children, it felt so good I could have stayed longer!" the husband said. "When I came home I felt wonderful. I felt like I could do something special, instead of just work. I remember wanting to take the things I'd learned and put them into practice. I couldn't wait. But then I tried . . . twice . . . and I failed."

Then she interrupted and told how she felt responsible for closing the door. She had wounded his ego.

It seemed odd to her that he could have forgotten all about it until that night. Apparently the wonderful freedom of total acceptance that he had known had been so *unusual,* so *different,* that it was easy to return to his usual conception of himself. However, that night, as the four of them talked, he slipped back into being what he had been! He looked inside and remembered how he had felt once when he knew he was totally accepted just for who he was. It had freed him for a while, released him to love others unconditionally because he had loved and accepted himself.

What about you? How freely, how unconditionally do you love (accept) others? How freely, how unconditionally do you love (accept) yourself? The latter determines the former.

April 3

Remember what I shared yesterday, how being totally accepted by others had released this man to love people as freely, as fully, as unconditionally as he loved himself? What drew him back inside? What shut the door? What key turned the lock?

I believe the key that fits the lock is love, but not another human being's love, although that does play a part. Rather, it is, I believe, if I am hearing God's Word right, a love of self, a proper, godly self-esteem. Now wait. At least hear me out. I realize some recoil at the slightest suggestion that we are to love ourselves. And yet doesn't God's Word say, ". . . you shall love your neighbor as yourself" (Mark 12:31)?

Isn't this a simile, a comparison of like things? I am to love others **as** I love myself. In Ephesians 5:25 husbands are admonished to love their wives **just as** Christ loved the church. Is that not a comparison? Look at Ephesians 5:28: "So husbands ought also to love their own wives **as** their own bodies." It means what it says. Husbands are to love their wives **as** they love their own bodies, ". . . for no one ever hated his own flesh" (v. 29).

Last night as I wrote down these thoughts, I told God that I wanted Him to use me to bring others to the point of self-acceptance, of self-love, that would free them to love others the same way they love themselves. As I cried out to God, He reminded me of a prayer I had prayed several years ago when I asked Him to love others through me. I believe that all this is part of His answer. Wouldn't you like to learn with me? Or maybe you already know.

So many people—fantastic, wonderful, beautiful, unique creations of God—are locked within themselves, peeping out longingly through curtained windows.

O Father, O Father God, show me—show us—how to love ourselves properly and then to love others as we love ourselves.

April 4

Of course, the key is love. And God is love. And Jesus is God. So ultimately, Jesus is the key. It all centers around Him, the Alpha and the Omega, the Creator of all things and the One by whom all things hold together, the visible Image of the invisible One. Thus, if I am going to ever know love that is totally unconditional, then I must know Him. I can never really love myself apart from God. I must tap the source. I must drill deeply past all the layers of shell and sham, through misconceptions and lies, past the powers of darkness and blindness, until I break through into that one true Fountainhead of Living Water. And then, even discovery is not enough. I must drink deeply. I must imbibe fully until every thirst of my soul is satisfied. Then, having tasted of that sweet, cool purity, I will know the difference between the self-love which the world teaches and that true love—true acceptance of self which God meant me to have.

I must gaze deeply into that Fountain of Living Water until I catch an image of what I am to Him and what I am in Him. I *must* meditate, evaluate, and appreciate what I see as I reflect on Him. I must push back the wisps of hair as I lean over the clear waters of His truth so that my vision will not be marred. And as I look deeply, I will realize that I am unique, one of a kind, foreknown by him and marked out beforehand to become conformed to His image (Romans 8:29). Then, confident ... secure ... free in His love, and having proper self-esteem, I can reach out to others who are locked inside themselves. I can tell them of the key and help them place it in the lock. I can bid them come out, hopefully to stay!

This I believe, Beloved, is the greatest thing I can do for my fellow-man, and for the God Who created us in His image.

April 5

Before we go any further, I feel we need to take a day to see how a person experiences love.

Psychiatrists are now saying that a child first senses whether or not he is loved by the way he is carried in his mother's womb. When we first come into the world, our primary association with love consists of our being made comfortable. Consequently, we associate love with having our needs met! If you love me, you will meet my needs. Beyond this elementary sense of love, we move into a new awareness of being loved as we realize that we are special to others. I believe this was God's purpose in ordaining the family. In a family we receive special attention, special care. We belong. This also explains sibling rivalry. If a new baby, or a brother or sister, makes a child feel that he is no longer special, then that baby becomes a threat to the child's sense of being loved. How vital it is, then, that we are careful to give special attention to each of our children.

Mixed up in all of this is a sense of being loved because we are given our way. You can see this so readily in the way children respond to their parents. For instance, have you ever heard a pouting child say,

"I'm crying because you don't love me . . . you won't give me what I want . . . you won't let me have my way." In other words, you're not treating me as if I'm special. This is why, Beloved, it is so essential that we explain our actions to our children instead of just telling them to be quiet and stop crying or they really are going to get it!

We also feel loved when others respond to the love we give. That is why it is so important to a child, or an adult, to be recognized and appreciated when he offers his expression of love, no matter how feebly. Scribbled pictures, dirty little hands holding dandelions, jelly kisses, sticky hugs, muddy feet trotting across a freshly mopped floor just to say, "I love you"—all must be appreciated and acknowledged. All of this is our introduction to love, and it sets the stage for receiving God's love for us and our love for ourselves.

Now then, can you see how vital it is that we experience God's love? He is the One who meets these needs we have for love! God loved us first (1 John 4:10); He chose us, and therefore showed us we are special (John 16:15); He has supplied all of our needs (Philippians 4:19); He responds to our love (John 14:23). God, through His love and acceptance, wants to give us a strong sense of self-worth.

April 6

The degree to which you are preoccupied with yourself is the degree to which you cannot be occupied with others. The focus must go either on yourself or on others. Thus, in order for you to be freed up to love others, you must first be secure in yourself.

Let me illustrate. You will find many people in Christian ministries who are there because they need to be ministered to, they need to be needed, or they need to feel important. The ministry, instead of becoming a means of meeting others' needs, has become a means of meeting their own needs!

Have you ever talked to someone who was about to be married and asked how he knew this was the girl for him? What is the usual answer? "She's all I have ever wanted. She's perfect for me. She's good looking. She makes me feel important, good, special! She's a great cook. And she likes the things I like. We get along great. I love talking to her. Besides . . . she turns me on!"

All the things the prospective bride is or does, you will notice, are centered around his needs and desires. The focus is on him. Here is someone who will meet his needs. But what will happen if someday she cannot or does not meet his needs? Then where will their relationship be? Will she mean as much to him then as she does now? Have you ever heard a wife say, "I can't figure it out! This isn't the same person I married. He's different. He's changed!" And he probably has! Something has happened or has failed to happen, and he has changed. He has retreated, has run back inside, and turned the lock! Insecurity, hurt, failure or fear of failure, rejection, inadequacy, low self-esteem, a poor self-image—all these can do it! And he never becomes the person God intended him to become; he is never used the way he could have been used had he not been wrapped up within himself.

Is there an answer? Is there a cure? Or are people to remain victims of their failures, and their low self-image? Let's look to God's Word for the answer. Tell me what you think this verse means: "If any man is in Christ, he is a new creature; the old things passed away; behold, new things have come" (2 Corinthians 5:17).

"Yes," you say, "Christians are new creatures, but I know many Christians loaded down with hang-ups so severe that they are totally preoccupied with themselves." I do, too, Beloved. But I believe there is a cure if they will only take it. We'll talk about it step by step in the days to come.

April 7

Where is your focus? On yourself or on others? What about your needs? What are they? How are they met? Are you secure in love or are you desperately searching for it? When you look at yourself, how do you feel? What would you like to change or alter to some degree? How important are people to you? Why? Do you feel like a failure or a success?

These are questions we need to take time to answer, along with other questions. Putting down answers in black and white as objectively as possible can help you evaluate yourself honestly. To do so, Beloved, will help you recognize why you feel and respond the way you do.

When you finish with these evaluations, you need to take them to the mirror of God's Word and reflect on what you see. As you do this, you have a goal in mind: to love yourself. Your objective is to unconditionally, freely, fully accept yourself *as you are* so that you can love others—so that you can accept them unconditionally, freely and fully as they are and therefore minister to them as God would minister to them.

So, Precious One, as we begin, let's cry out to God as the Psalmist did. "Search me, O God, and know my heart; try me and know my anxious thoughts; and see if there be any hurtful way (literally *way of pain*) in me, and lead me in the everlasting way" (Psalms 139:23, 24).

Let's begin . . .

1. When you are faced with meeting a stranger, what are your first thoughts? Will you be at ease or do you feel uncomfortable? Are you concerned about what they will think of you or how they will respond to you? (Don't answer yes or no; write down your honest feelings in your notebook.)

2. How do you feel about walking into a room of people? Do you feel that they are going to look at you, ignore you, or welcome you? And why do you feel that way?

3. When you go into a room of people, what do you do?

4. Now, from answering these questions, where would you say your focus is? On yourself or on others? Can you identify why?

What is your prayer to our Father?

April 8

Have there ever been times when you have dared to dream, when you have let your mind muse about some way that God might possibly use **you** for His glory? Or have you ever looked at others and thought, "Lord, if only I had *that* (whatever it is), then I could be used for You?" I understand, right or wrong; I have been there. Let's do some more searching.

1. How do you feel about yourself physically? Are there things about your physical appearance that bother you or that you think people notice about you? If so, make a heading in the left-hand column of a page in your notebook: **"Things About My Physical Appearance That Bother Me."** List them below this heading. Then, make a heading for the right-hand column: **"What I Could Do to Change Them."** Next to each item in the left-hand column, write out what you could do. (You can be as radical as plastic surgery. Put all the possibilities down.) If it is unchangeable, put that down.

2. Now, evaluate your physical appearance. How much does each listed thing bother you? Give it a number between one and ten, ten indicating the thing that bothers you the most.

3. Those with numbers of three or more need to be dealt with first, so look at each one carefully. Is it physically feasible? Is it economically feasible? Mark it. If nothing can be done about it, then note that.

4. Now then, what are you going to do about those things you can change? To continue to complain or be depressed by them is wrong *if*

you can do something to change them. Therefore, you need to change them *or* live with them without complaining or letting them be your excuse for failure, inadequacy, withdrawal, or depression. At this point, you are responsible. Maturity faces this responsibility head-on and gets with it!

5. If you cannot change whatever needs changing because it is physically or economically impossible, then, if you are going to grow up in Christ, you must accept it. God has permitted it. And, Dear One, if He has permitted it, He is there to help you through the difficulty of accepting it. So run, throw yourself into His waiting arms, bury your head on His shoulder, sob until it is all out, then listen as He pats you on the head and whispers in your ear telling you how He will help you work through it.

Well, Precious One, meditate on these verses; tomorrow we will look at some of the whys and wherefores of accepting yourself.

> For Thou didst form my inward parts; Thou didst weave me in my mother's womb. I will give thanks to Thee, for I am fearfully and wonderfully made; wonderful are Thy works, and my soul knows it very well. My frame was not hidden from Thee, when I was made in secret, and skillfully wrought in the depths of the earth (Psalms 139:13–15).

April 9

What do you think about the fact that God knew what you were going to be like and even permitted you to be that way? Do you feel that it is some kind of a cruel joke or that God chose favorites and you were not one of them? Do you think, *If only I'd . . .* or *if only I were . . . then I could . . . ?* Honestly, Beloved, to think that way seems contrary to God's Word, doesn't it?

I wish I could tell you this in person. Don't you think it grieves God when people are so caught up in themselves that they are not free to reach out to others? Their own shyness, inadequacies, and fears have tied their hands, binding them to the pole of low self-esteem and leaving them battling insanely over temporal insufficiencies. And thus very few hear the clear, glorious gospel from their lips or see it in their lives!

What is the cure? There is only one, as far as I can see, and that is to know what God says, to hear what God says, and then to purposefully order your life accordingly. Everything that you are physically is according to God's sovereignty. Let me explain from the Scripture, then I will illustrate from my life.

We need to go to a familiar but vital passage of Scripture, Romans 8:28–32. As you carefully read this, you can see that it pertains to those who are God's children, the called of God whom God Himself justified and glorified. *Justified* means to declare righteous and thus to put in right standing with God. *Glorified* means to do honor, to make glorious, and signifies the guaranteed state of the child of God with the Godhead in eternity. In Romans 8:30, the verbs *called, justified,* and *glorified* are all in the aorist tense, the active voice, and the indicative mood. The aorist tense signifies an action that takes place at one point in time; the active voice shows that the subject initiates the action of the verb; and the indicative mood indicates reality or certainty. Therefore, it was God who brought you to Himself. He is the Initiator of your salvation and whom He saves, He glorifies. So it is honor that awaits you. But what has this to do with what you are like physically? We will look at that tomorrow; for today, see if you can find the answer yourself.

April 10

Have you ever met people who fret about themselves? They just do not like the way they look. Yet you look at them and think, *they are better looking than I am, so what's their hang-up?* Their hang-up is the fact that they have never accepted themselves the way they are. And, because they cannot accept themselves the way they are, you will find them unable to fully, freely, unconditionally love and accept others. They will either be so preoccupied with themselves that they cannot fully reach out to others or they will look for imperfection and unacceptable physical traits in others. Do not forget: we love others **as** we love ourselves (Mark 12:31).

But how can we love ourselves when we think that we are not up to par physically? Well, let's go back to our Scripture for yesterday. Stop and reread it, and then we will take it apart and see how it relates to what I am saying.

According to Romans 8:29, God foreknew you. The word *foreknow* in the Greek is *proginosko,* and it means to know beforehand. When did God foreknow you? Well, according to what we read in days past from Psalms 139:13–15, He foreknew you before you were ever formed in your mother's womb. He knew what sperm would meet what egg and what genes would be combined to form a unique **you.** And in His book, before you were ever formed, He wrote the number of days that were ordained for you. Remember what God said to Moses when

Moses protested that he was not eloquent but rather slow of speech and slow of tongue? "Who has made man's mouth? Or who makes him dumb or deaf, or seeing or blind? Is it not I, the Lord?" (Exodus 4:11). "And what do you have that you did not receive? But if you did receive it, why do you boast as if you had not received it?" (1 Corinthians 4:7).

Physically, you are sovereignly ordained by God. And what you are physically, Beloved, has a purpose in God's predetermined goal for you as His child. Remember that Romans 8:29 says that you were predestined to become conformed to the image of Christ. The word *predestine* means to mark out beforehand. Thus God marked out beforehand all that was necessary for you, in your uniqueness, to be made like Jesus Christ. This was God's goal for you, Precious One, before you were ever formed in the womb of your mother. And because God is sovereign, because He is the ultimate and supreme authority over all that exists, visible and invisible, and because He is all-knowing and all-powerful, He causes **all** things in your life to work together for good. The good is the accomplishing of the good pleasure of His will.

Think about all this, carefully, and we will continue tomorrow.

April 11

Many people, even Christians, recoil at the word *predestine*. Somehow the word evokes the idea that God is unfair. "What right," they say, "does God have to do that? To predestine people? Why, it makes men nothing but puppets on a string!" But they are wrong. Their reasoning is off. They do not understand either the character of God or the Word of God. God is God. "From Him and through Him and to Him are all things" (Romans 11:36). God is love. He can never act apart from love. In His sovereignty and His love, "He predestined us to adoption as sons through Jesus Christ to Himself, according to the kind intention of His will" (Ephesians 1:5). And in predestining us to adoption as sons, He also predestined us to become conformed to the image of Jesus Christ. Your physical being, Beloved, plays a big part in your being conformed to His image. It is a chisel which God will use on the granite of your humanity. He will use it to bring forth the image of the eternal One Who dwells within.

I have a friend who is strikingly beautiful of face even at fifty! Her flawless, porcelain-like skin covers magnificently high cheekbones. It's a pleasure to look at her. Especially so since she has come to Christ, for the love of Christ lights up her entire countenance. I have looked at her and thought, "Now, Lord, since people have to look at me on television, don't You think You could have done better?" And then, we reason together. I am the way I am . . . scar on cheek, skin full of pores, wrinkles, and so forth, so that women can relate to me. I am just an ordinary looking woman who, like most women, has had to skillfully decorate her exterior! Physically I'm not anything special. And that is what God wanted in order to accomplish His particular purpose in and through me. I bow to it; I bow to Him. I do the very best I can with what I have, and then I forget it. All the fretting in the world cannot change it. I have accomplished the changes I can afford and can effect, and with that I rest my case.

When you are anxious about yourself, the focus is on you—how **you** look, if **you** are pleasing. If it is on you, then it cannot be on others. O Beloved, if this is your focus, how can you reach out to others who are also preocuppied with themselves?

April 12

Maybe it is not the physical *you* that is your hang-up! Maybe it's the *you* that lives inside your physical house, the *you* peeping out through the curtains. The *you* that is afraid to come out. Afraid because you might fail, or be rejected, or might not be appreciated or approved.

Or maybe it's the *you* that is so angry, so hostile that it will be a cold day in hell before you will ever really show your face. Who cares anyway! You don't! Or you say you don't. But really you are hurt, hostile, and angry, aren't you? You just want to be left alone . . . or at least that's what you say. But honestly, you are miserable, aren't you?

Why do people hide? Why don't they come out and really be themselves—healthy, whole, warm, loving, concerned, generous, giving, confident, relaxed? Why can't they come out without trying to impress anyone and be gracious, genuinely caring more about others than about themselves? Why can't they come out in that total freedom that comes from knowing they are completely accepted and therefore free from needing to make any sort of impression whatsoever?

It's because of their concern with who they are or with how they will be received. Somewhere in their background, if you search through the attics of their lives where the past is packed away in dusty boxes, you will find rejection or anger or discontent. I say rejection, anger, or discontent, yet I believe that the root is simply rejection. Anger and discontent, I believe, stem from rejection.

Why is rejection the root of anger and/or discontent? The opposite of rejection is acceptance. If I refuse something, I do not accept it. Anger, then, comes because something has happened to me that I do not like and, therefore, will not accept. Oh, that something, or someone, may be in my life; yet I have not accepted it. Rather, I have rejected it. Therefore, I am angry at its occurrence or presence. It is the same with discontent. Discontent comes from rejection. It is resistance to acceptance. Were I to freely accept someone or something in my life with gratitude and thanksgiving, these would not cause me to be discontented.

Can you see what I'm saying? Can you receive it? How does this Scripture apply:

"Always giving thanks for **ALL** things in the name of our Lord Jesus Christ to God, even the Father" (Ephesians 5:20)?

April 13

I think God would have us stop today and do a little more honest soul-searching before we proceed any further. I know it will help if you will do it. Jesus once asked a man, "Do you wish to get well?" (John 5:6). It was a good question. Some people really do not want to be made whole, to be healed. It would take away their excuse, make them responsible, require them to stop punishing or getting even with the one who hurt them! Thus, God asks you today, "Will you, Beloved One, be made whole?" Believe me, wholeness is yours for the receiving. It is a matter of faith, of believing God. Do not write me off as simplistic; I'm not. It is rather a matter of believing that God's Word has what is necessary to make His child "perfect, throughly furnished unto all good works" (2 Timothy 3:17 KJV). With that, Precious One, let us begin.

Have you ever felt rejection? Ask God to walk back with you to the earliest times you can remember rejection, and then relive each experience individually. When was it? What happened? How did you handle it? Write out all that God shows you.

Now, go back and look over what you have written. Put a star next to those experiences that still hurt or make you angry or depressed.

April 14

Let's do a thorough job of soul-searching and get everything out into the open where we can confront it.

1. When was the last time you felt depressed? What was it over? How long did it last? How did you handle it? Write out your answers.

2. If depression is a constant battle for you, have you had a medical checkup? Are your hormones in balance? This is vital. Is your body chemistry normal? Depression, body chemistry, and hormones have a cyclic effect on one another, so this must be checked out.

3. Is there any way in which you feel at all sorry for yourself? Be honest now. Write down the things which you feel never should have happened to you.

4. Are you angry, in any way? What has made you angry?

Now, if you are in any way angry at something **about yourself**—how you look, how you feel, or how you handled a situation—then this is the cause of your depression. Depression is anger turned inward. The answer is acceptance. Pause and think on that.

April 15

Before you read today's devotional, stop and review all that you wrote down yesterday. Was there any way in which you felt sorry for yourself? If so, then self-pity in all probability has been the major cause of your depression. Why don't you stop and ask God if this is true. Sit quietly before Him and ask Him to speak to you in your mind. Tell Him that you want His thoughts **only** and that you refuse any thoughts that are not from Him. You can trust Him. If this is your sincere prayer, believe me, He longs to answer it. Write down His thoughts toward you.

Now make three columns on a page in your notebook and at the top of the left-hand column write down **"My Fears."** Write them out one by one. Next, label the middle heading, **"Their Cause"** and the right-hand column, **"God's Solution."** After each fear, seek to identify the cause of each. Then ask God to show you His solution for each one.

April 16

Now, let's look at anger, fear, self-pity, and depression in the light of God's Word, for these are things that can keep you from loving yourself as God loves you and thus, from being free to accept, love, and minister to others. Depression (anger turned inward), self-pity, and fear are rooted in rejection—of God's truth, of God's way of meeting the issues of life, of what we are physically—rejection of life's circumstances.

The opposite of rejection is acceptance. So what we have done, in essence, is to say, "God, You have made a mistake. Your Word cannot be true. All things do not work together for good (Romans 8:28). This will not be used to conform me to the image of Jesus Christ (Romans 8:29). I cannot give thanks always for all things (Ephesians 5:20). I cannot give thanks in everything for this cannot be Your will for me in Christ Jesus (1 Thessalonians 5:18). I cannot count it all joy in this trial (James 1:2), nor can I exult in it for it cannot result in patience and proven character (Romans 5:3-4). God, it is more than I can bear; You have allowed me to be tempted beyond what I am able to endure. You have not provided a way to escape (1 Corinthians 10:13). God, I am not fearfully and wonderfully made; You made a mistake when You let me end up this way physically. Your thoughts toward me are not precious (Psalms 139:13-17)! I must be anxious for these things ... peace is impossible (Philippians 4:6, 7). I cannot do all things through You; You do not strengthen me (Philippians 4:13). You are not supplying all my needs according to Your riches in glory in Christ Jesus (Philippians 4:19). I should not suffer (Philippians 1:29). As a matter of fact, the glory and honor that You have promised in the future are not worth the suffering I am experiencing now (Romans 8:17, 18). I cannot cast this care totally upon You and leave it there because if You really cared for me, You wouldn't let me go through this in the first place (1 Peter 5:7). This could not possibly be for Your sake (Romans 8:36) or for the sake of others (2 Corinthians 4:11-18). Your grace is not sufficient (2 Corinthians 12:9). You have lied. You have deceived me. Your word is not true (Psalms 12:6, John 8:44 vs. John 17:17)."

O Beloved, have you, in essence, said any of these things to God? If so, then You have rejected His Word. And is it no wonder that when we reject God's Word, we reap anger, self-pity, fear, and depression?

April 17

When you reject God's Word, your problem is one of temporal vision rather than eternal vision. You cannot see beyond your nose, beyond your mirror, beyond your circumstances, beyond yourself, beyond this life. Unbelief has kept you from accepting yourself as you are and from accepting the circumstances of life as being permitted by God to conform you to His image.

O Beloved, if you would only accept it all as coming from God's hand. Do you not see or believe that God is love? Love is the very essence of God's being. God can never divest Himself of love, for that is what He is! And "In love He predestined us to adoption as sons through Jesus Christ to Himself, according to the kind intention of His will" (Ephesians 1:4, 5). The Father has drawn you to Christ (John 6:44). You did not choose Him, but He ". . . chose you, and appointed you, that you should go and bear fruit . . ." (John 15:16). Therefore, every situation, every circumstance, everything you are goes into preparing you for fruit bearing. God is for you not against you (Romans 8:31). "He who did not spare His own Son, but delivered Him up for us all, how will He not also with Him freely give us all things?" (Romans 8:32). God has you in His hand. No one can snatch you out (John 10:28). Therefore, since God is love and since God is sovereign and since you are in God's hand, whatever comes or happens to you must be filtered through fingers of love. Why then do you refuse these things? Why are you angry? Why are you full of self-pity? Why are you dejected or depressed? Why are you unhappy with yourself? Why are you locked inside yourself? Why won't you love and accept yourself and your circumstances? Acceptance will bring you release. All you have to do is say, by faith, "God, I accept it all as coming from You, filtered through Your fingers of love. Therefore, Father Dear, I thank You and will by faith continue to thank You. I will trust in You with all of my heart. I will not lean on my own understanding" (Proverbs 3:5).

April 18

I always think of a little bantam rooster when I think of the Apostle Paul. According to tradition, Paul did not have much going for him physically. They say he was small of stature, bowlegged and beset with bad eyes that were probably repulsive at times (Galatians 4:14, 15). He was not impressive in either physical appearance or speech (2 Corinthians 10:10). Nor were the circumstances of his life easy. There were times when life was extremely difficult for him. He was slandered and unappreciated even by those whom he had brought to Christ (2 Corinthians 10, 11). He suffered greatly physically. Listen to his testimony: ". . . beaten times without number, often in danger of death. Five times I received from the Jews thirty-nine lashes. Three times I was beaten with rods, once I was stoned, three times I was shipwrecked, a night and a day I have spent in the deep. I have been on frequent journeys, in dangers from rivers, dangers from robbers, dangers from my countrymen, dangers from the Gentiles, dangers in the city, dangers in the wilderness, dangers on the sea, dangers among false brethren; I have been in labor and hardship, through many sleepless nights, in hunger and thirst, often without food, in cold and exposure. Apart from such external things, there is the daily pressure upon me of concern for all the churches" (2 Corinthians 11:23–28).

But Paul's trials and pressures were not just physical; they weighed on him emotionally. Listen again to his story, "We are afflicted in every way, but not crushed; perplexed, but not despairing; persecuted, but not forsaken; struck down, but not destroyed" (2 Corinthians 4:8, 9). Why? How could he come out on top when it seemed that all this was against him? How did Paul handle it all so that he did not wallow in self-pity; so that he did not live a life of fear, turn his anger inward, and become dejected or depressed? How could he constantly reach out to others and accept and love them freely, fully, unconditionally? For love them he did! To the very church that hurt and grieved him the most, he wrote ". . . that you might know the love which I have especially for you" (2 Corinthians 2:4). How did he handle it all? By accepting it. We will look at it tomorrow. But today, Beloved One, let me ask, "Are you any worse off than Paul?" Does your situation, before God, give you the right of rejection?

April 19

How did Paul handle it all? He accepted everything as coming from God and as having an eternal purpose. Paul was so free, so secure in His calling, in His purpose, in His gifts, so confident in God's love that he was able to live for the sake of others.

> I thank Christ Jesus our Lord, who has strengthened me, because He considered me faithful, putting me into service; even though I was formerly a blasphemer and a persecutor and a violent aggressor. And yet I was shown mercy, because I acted ignorantly in unbelief; and the grace of our Lord was more than abundant, with the faith and love which are found in Christ Jesus. It is a trustworthy statement, deserving full acceptance, that Christ Jesus came into the world to save sinners, among whom I am foremost of all. And yet for this reason I found mercy, in order that in me as the foremost, Jesus Christ might demonstrate His perfect patience, as an example for those who would believe in Him for eternal life (1 Timothy 1:12–16).

123

Paul faced what he had been before he met Christ without hiding it. After all it was God Who separated him from his mother's womb and yet waited until all these things had transpired **before** He revealed His Son to him (Galatians 1:15, 16). God did not choose to save Paul until after he had agreed to Stephen's death and had persecuted and imprisoned many others, both men and women (Acts 8:1–3). But Paul not only faced what he had been; he also believed in and received the mercy and the grace of God! He recognized and accepted God's calling "for which I was appointed a preacher and an apostle and a teacher" (2 Timothy 1:11), and with that calling was willing to suffer without shame (2 Timothy 1:12).

Paul accepted it all because his focus was not on himself, but on others; not on temporal things, but on eternal things. "For all things are for your sakes . . . Therefore we do not lose heart, but though our outer man is decaying, yet our inner man is being renewed day by day. For momentary, light affliction (note what Paul calls *light*) is producing for us an eternal weight of glory far beyond all comparison, while we look not at the things which are seen, but at the things which are not seen; for the things which are seen are temporal, but the things which are not seen are eternal" (2 Corinthians 4:15–18).

Where is your focus, Beloved? You will find out by looking at how you accept or reject yourself and the situations and circumstances of your life.

April 20

Low self-esteem is not an emotional or a physical problem. It is a spiritual problem. The key to good self-esteem is a matter of faith. It is all wrapped up in believing God, in believing His Word. If you are unable to love and accept yourself as you are, or if you are in the depths of depression, and the physical cause—if any—has been or is being dealt with, then you can be assured that your future is a matter of choice. Healing is yours if you will choose it. It is found in the person and work of Jesus Christ. It is found in taking God at His Word. I know this may sound simplistic. I know you may think me out of touch with psychology, psychiatry, or psychosomatic medicine. Yet, Dear Precious Ones, listen to me. The Word of God does not allow for anything but a sound mind, a mind under control, healthy self-esteem, and a guarantee that we can always triumph through Christ Jesus.

Now, I know that some of you may be so in the throes of depression or hurt that you can hardly bear to read this. As a matter of fact, you may want to throw me or this book across the room! I understand. I have had friends that have been there. Friends who could hardly bear to read or even hear God's Word because their depression was so deep! Yet, they made it, the same way you can. So, if you want, get alone and throw the book! (I'm too heavy ... 130 lbs.) But, if you throw it, pick it up, grit your teeth, fuss, fume, talk back to me, write me, and let off steam, but read on. There is healing. There has to be, or God is not God and His Word is not true. "Heal me, O Lord, and I will be healed; save me and I will be saved, for Thou art my praise" (Jeremiah 17:14). "He heals the brokenhearted, and binds up their wounds (literally *sorrows*)" (Psalms 147:3). The Hebrew word for heal in these passages is *rapha*. It means *to mend by stitching, to cure, to cause to heal, physician, repair, thoroughly, make whole*. The name of your God, Beloved, is Jehovah Rapha, the God Who heals.

O Precious One, will you not call to Him today, now "... for you who fear (revere) **My name** the sun of righteousness will rise with healing in its wings; and you will go forth and skip about like calves from the stall" (Malachi 4:2).

April 21

In a way, it seems almost humorous, and yet, I do not think the angel was laughing. Gideon was hiding when it happened! You don't normally thresh wheat in a winepress. You do it out in an open field where the wind can catch the chaff and separate it from the grain. This was what that dear angel of the Lord was about to do for Gideon—thresh him! Notice I said "thresh" not "thrash." The Midianites had thrashed him until the poor man was threshing his wheat in hiding and, at the same time, feeling abandoned by God (Judges 6:1–11)! Now, God is going to separate the wheat from the chaff in Gideon's life.

Can you imagine how Gideon must have felt? There he was, hiding and full of doubt, and the angel addressed him thus, "... The Lord is with you, O valiant warrior" (Judges 6:12). Wow! Talk about meeting you at your point of need. "The Lord is with you." Gideon replied, "The Lord has abandoned us and given us into the hand of Midian" (6:13). "O valiant warrior"! He was hiding in fear! How different was God's perspective from Gideon's! And who was right? God, of course. God is a God of truth. He is the One Who has the true perspective on all things. Now, all Gideon needed was to see himself through God's eyes. God saw the wheat hiding inside the chaff. Gideon's focus was on the chaff! "Valiant warrior"—it was there all the time; Gideon just had to see it and God was going to show him, step by step. Gideon would falter and need assurance, and so he would seek signs and put out fleeces. He would do what God said, yet timidly, but God would stay with him until that image of valiant warrior was perfected in flesh and blood.

O Beloved, God will do the same with you! Do you see yourself the way God sees you? Today, write out some of His thoughts toward you, according to the truth of His Word!

April 22

I had already written these devotions to this point when I picked up a book given to me by a dear friend. It is *The Christian Use of Emotional Power* by H. Norman Wright and is published by Fleming H. Revell to which I am slightly partial since they published *How Can I Live, A Devotional Journey with Kay Arthur*. My friends bought it because they had heard Norman Wright in person and were so blessed and aided in their ministry of counseling others.

The book has an excellent chapter on self-image. As I read it, my heart just filled with joy, for here was confirmation of so much that I had been writing. I had also been asking God for a book to recommend to you. Well, here it is! I've only read one chapter, but if the rest is as good as this, you have a winner. It covers so much—emotions, thoughts, worry, anxiety. . . .

Our thought for the day comes from Norman Wright's book and it goes with Gideon.

"It is important to remember that the image a person has of himself is determined mostly through his interpersonal relationships. A person's self-image or self-estimate is the result of the *interpretation he makes* of his involvements with others. What really matters to this person is not what others actually think *but what he thinks they think of him!* It is this *subjective interpretation* that is important to his self-image."[9] Norman Wright quotes Maxwell Maltz's definition of self-image as "the individual's mental and spiritual concept or 'picture' of himself."

When the angel of the Lord told Gideon what He was going to do through him, Gideon didn't see how God could, in the light of who Gideon knew he was! Listen to the conversation carefully.

"And the Lord looked at him and said, 'Go in this your strength and deliver Israel from the hand of Midian. Have I not sent you?' And he

126

said to Him, 'O Lord, how shall I deliver Israel? Behold, my family is the least in Manasseh, and I am the youngest in my father's house' " (Judges 6:14, 15).

It does seem that Gideon's relationship to his family gave him a lower image of himself than the one God had. What about you? Do you see yourself through your own eyes or through God's eyes?

April 23

How does God see you? If your self-image is ever going to be up to par, you must view yourself in the mirror of God's Word. There you will either accept or reject yourself. And with that acceptance or rejection you determine, I believe, the depth of your effectiveness in ministering to others. I have said it earlier—the depth of your love and acceptance of others will be determined by the love and acceptance you have for yourself. The love and acceptance you have for yourself will be determined by your knowledge of and acceptance of the unconditional love which God gives to you.

When Chuck Snyder read Ephesians 3:14–21 one day in Sunday School, I nearly came unglued! The Holy Spirit lifted the veil and I saw it. Read it carefully and then I will share what God showed me.

> ... that He would grant you, according to the riches of His glory, to be strengthened with power through His Spirit in the inner man; so that Christ may dwell in your hearts through faith; *and* that you, being rooted and grounded in love, may be able to comprehend with all the saints what is the breadth and length and height and depth, and to know the love of Christ which surpasses knowledge, that you may be filled up to all the fulness of God (vv. 16–19).

In this passage, Paul is speaking to Christians about the source of power for the inner man. That power comes when Christ dwells in our hearts through faith, when He is at home in our hearts because we believe Him and take Him at His Word. This roots us in love or, to put it another way, establishes us in His love. Then, and this is the key, having been rooted and grounded in love, two things happen (I say "having been" because both verbs are in the perfect tense which denotes a past completed action with a present or continuing result). First, we can **comprehend** the extent of that love—breadth, length, height, and depth. Second, we can then **apprehend,** lay hold of, that love which surpasses knowledge! I say apprehend because the participle *to know* means to know by experience. Thus, being brought into God's love foundationally, we are enabled to comprehend, to know to a greater extent the scope of that love and to lay hold of it and experience it. We'll talk about it more tomorrow.

April 24

For you to refuse to love yourself is to choose sides against God. It is to reject God. Gideon, at first, certainly did not see himself as God saw him, but Gideon came around. He chose to believe God, to trust Him. You must do the same if you are ever to be free to do all God would have you do in ministering to others. For, Beloved, that is what it is all about. "As Thou didst send Me into the world . . ." (John 17:18). ". . . Whoever wishes to become great among you shall be your servant. . . . For even the Son of Man did not come to be served, but to serve, and to give His life a ransom for many" (Mark 10:43, 45). You will never be an effective servant if the focus is on yourself. It must be on others. And only love of self gives you this freedom. "You shall love your neighbor as yourself" (Matthew 22:39).

How does God see you? If you are His, He sees you as justified, put in right standing with God. Once justified, you are reconciled to God, at peace with Him (Romans 5:1). The enmity is gone, the conflict is gone. You are now "accepted in the beloved" (Ephesians 1:6 KJV). Accepted—because of the grace of God. Never to be deserted or forsaken by Him (Hebrews 13:5), you are now members of Christ's body, bone of His bone and flesh of His flesh (Ephesians 5:29, 30). Christ has made you thus; therefore, your past does not matter. God looks at you and says, "There is therefore now **no condemnation** for those who are in Christ Jesus" (Romans 8:1). The things that are behind are truly behind. You are to keep on forgetting (present tense in the Greek, therefore continuous action) the things that are behind and to keep on reaching forward to what lies ahead. You are to press on toward the goal, the image of Christ (Philippians 3:13, 14). To do any less, Beloved, is to disappoint God. It is to fail to accept the love of God, the grace of God, the calling of God.

Don't forget, a person's self-image is developed through interpersonal relationships. So as you develop your relationship with God, remember also that your self-image comes from your interpretation of what others say or do. Be aware that "the person with a poor self-image searches out Scriptures to reinforce his own feelings of condemnation."[10] O Beloved, do not do that. When you read Scripture, don't miss God's heart; Jesus was not sent to condemn but to save.

April 25

It is time, today, for a little more soul-searching. You need to come face to face with your God. "This alone I have found, that God, when He made man, made him straightforward, but man invents endless subtleties of his own" (Ecclesiastes 7:29, NEB). We need to pull back the curtains and expose ourselves. Let it all come out. Let ourselves be seen for exactly what we are and know that, whatever we are, to Him we are acceptable—not because of who or what we are or because of our performance, but only because He has made us acceptable. We can step out of our closets because God, in His love, has unconditionally accepted us. It is His love that makes you adequate, no matter who you are or what you are. You, as God's child, will never have to be accepted on the basis of your loveliness, your performance, your capabilities—these do not matter. You are accepted and, thus, always acceptable because of the abundance of His immeasurable love and grace.

"We do not achieve our worth by accomplishment, but just the reverse. We are able to accomplish because we are worthwhile."[11]

What is your worth to God? Write it out in your notebook. If you in any way feel unacceptable, write it down. If you think you have to perform in any special way or perform any special service in order to be more acceptable to God, write it out.

Now, note the scriptural basis of what you have written, remembering what you have seen thus far. Love you. . . .

April 26

Your thinking determines your self-image and gives you a sense of worth or worthlessness, a sense of adequacy or inadequacy. What you think about yourself and what you **think** others think about you—these are key factors toward proper self-esteem. A person with good self-esteem can look at himself objectively, evaluate his strengths and weaknesses, his gifts and abilities, his personality, and be at home with himself. One who has a proper image of himself also learns how to handle the way others react to him. He does not read meanings into things that others say or do, but rather receives things as they are presented. When we have a proper sense of self-worth or love, we come off the defensive and quit trying to justify, explain, or excuse ourselves all the time. We are able to relax and to get involved with others. Because people are no longer a threat to our sense of worth, we are able to let them see us as we are. We don't have to wear masks or play games in order to be acceptable. O Dear One, can't you see how important it is that we see ourselves as God sees us and believe what He says? It is crucial that our thoughts dwell on these things rather than on what tears us down!

God wants a man to speak truth in his heart (Psalms 15:2) "for as he thinketh in his heart, so is he" (Proverbs 23:7 KJV). Wrong thinking produces a wrong self-image! And a poor self-image is a lie. Every human being has worth in God's eyes, for he was created in God's image! Oh, that image may be distorted, but its remnant is still there (Genesis 9:5, 6)! If you continuously dwell on the negatives, you will become a person, for the most part, incapable of effectively ministering to others, too subjective, and probably very miserable because you will always be wondering what people are thinking about you. Then, you will find yourself wanting or needing their approval, but being difficult or impossible to be around. A person with a poor self-image is an underachiever. His fear of failure, of inadequacy, of imperfection, keeps him from being all that God ordained for him as an individual.

How do you handle it all? How do you develop a good self-image? We will talk about it more tomorrow, but you can know this: It begins in your thinking. Have you ever applied this verse to your own thoughts about yourself?

> Finally, brethren, whatever is true, whatever is honorable, whatever is right, whatever is pure, whatever is lovely, whatever is of good repute, if there is any excellence and if anything worthy of praise, let your mind dwell on these things (Philippians 4:8).

Meditate on it.

April 27

How does one go about developing good self-esteem? We need to look at it together step by step. We're in this together, Precious One. It will take us several days. Oh, how I pray that God will minister to you in a very special and intimate way and that you will receive what He has.

1. First you must deal with the relationships in your past. The basis of a person's self-image comes from his relationship with his family, particularly his parents. If you were raised by someone other than your parents, then you need to begin by asking God if you are suffering from rejection because your parents did not raise you. If so, give that rejection to God with all its implications. And if you are saved, thank

God that He has chosen you. If you are not already His child, then I know He is standing before you with outstretched arms, saying, "I chose you. Will you come to Me that you might have life?" (John 10:10; 15:16).

What kind of an image did you inherit from your parents? What did they tell you about yourself? How did you feel about yourself as a child? Did you feel loved? Upon what basis? Go over these questions with the Lord, asking Him to uncover anything with which you need to deal. Write down what He shows you.

2. What was your relationship to your brothers or sisters like? Was there any sibling rivalry? Did you feel that you didn't measure up to them and, therefore, in some way, had failed? Write down your thoughts.

3. Now then, since school takes up a major portion of our childhood and adolescence, let's check out our relationships with our teachers and our peers. Do you remember any unpleasant or hurtful experiences with teachers or classmates? If so, record these. Tomorrow we will see how to deal with what we have seen today.

April 28

Today, we want to take one more look at the past and then we will proceed with steps toward a good self-image.

1. When you look back, are there any difficult or painful experiences over which you still grieve or over which you still feel bitter or defeated? If so, list these in your notebook.

2. Do you feel bitter or unforgiving toward anyone? List their names and the reason why you feel toward them as you do.

3. Is there anyone whom you just cannot love with the love of the Lord? If so, write out their names and what makes them unlovable.

Now then, Beloved, everything that we have looked at thus far deals with the past, things that never can be changed, never be erased. You can weep over them, moan and groan, and even dream of what life would have been like if these things had never happened to you. Yet it will never alter the fact of their occurrence. You may even feel that they destroyed or marred *the real you* for life. Yet, no matter how tragic or painful they were, I have to say to you, in faith, that all these things will work together for your good, for your transformation into His image. So, let's see what we are to do with them.

1. Admit to God your feelings about each situation and/or person. Tell God everything on your heart. Do not hold back one thing. If you

are angry, bitter, or disillusioned, share it. That was what Gideon did!

2. Then, by faith, despite your feelings, accept each thing as being permitted by God and having a purpose. Do this verbally—say it aloud to God. It is a matter of faith not feeling. Remember, acceptance brings release. "Giving thanks always for all things . . ." (Ephesians 5:20 KJV) knowing that God has known you before you were formed in your mother's womb.

3. Tell God that you refuse every lie that you believed about yourself and that you accept yourself just as you are, fearfully and wonderfully made in His eyes to serve His purpose. Every lie or hurt that was spoken about you was prompted by the devil, the father of lies who uses people for his own deceptive purposes. Thank God that Jesus Christ came to destroy the works of the devil and to restore all things to Himself (1 John 3:8). Tell God, by faith, that you receive that restoration.

April 29

Before we move on to building a healthy self-image, I need to talk to you about forgiveness. Love and forgiveness go hand in hand. You cannot have one without the other, for they were made inseparably one at Calvary. God so loved that He gave His Son and, in giving His Son, He forgave us all our sins. "For I will forgive their iniquity, and their sin I will remember no more" (Jeremiah 31:34). You must accept this forgiveness, if you are ever going to love yourself, and thereby love others. If you can't receive God's forgiveness for yourself, then you will find yourself unable to forgive others. If you will not forgive others, you will be incapable of loving them. Therefore, in an act of faith, verbally receive God's forgiveness and verbally forgive everyone (Matthew 6:12, 14, 15; 18:21–35).

Having dealt thoroughly with the past, let's take a look at ourselves as we are now. You will notice when you read Paul's epistles that he saw himself—past, present, or future—in the light of God's truth. When he says that he had been the chief of sinners, he mentions the grace of God and how it demonstrated God's perfect patience (1 Timothy 1:12–17). So, as we look at ourselves, we must look at the real us, the one hiding behind the curtains.

Norman Wright quotes Paul Tournier's book, *The Meaning of Persons:* "We conceal our person behind a protective barrier. We let it be seen only through the bars. We display certain of its aspects, others we carefully hide."

Remember the devotional for the first day of this month when I talked about the man who for a time came out of the closet of himself? Well, I truly believe he isn't all that he could be because he hasn't fully accepted himself as he is in Christ Jesus. I think he wants to be different than he really is. Possibly he wants gifts or ministries that were not meant for him. Why? Perhaps because others have tried to squeeze him into their Christian mold. I think this is often done. "You should be teaching Sunday School!" "You should be doing evangelism!" "You should be serving on this committee!" A person insecure in his self-image can easily be swayed by statements like these.

Many men and women have moved out of the realm of their talents, gifts, or abilities and found nothing but failure—all because they tried to measure up to someone else's image of themselves. Beloved, you must gain a proper evaluation of yourself if you are going to have a good self-image. Read Romans 12:3, 6 and ask what are the gifts, talents, and abilities that you are certain you have?

April 30

If you are going to have a good self-image then you must accept yourself as you are, with your abilities and your limitations. You must accept yourself as you are without demanding to be the best or not be at all! You are to settle for *being* less than best but not for *doing* less than your best. What you are, you are because of Him for "what do you have that you did not receive?" (1 Corinthians 4:7). And what you do, you do for Him "heartily, as for the Lord" (Colossians 3:23). At that point, you can rest for you have done your best. If you haven't, confess it, accept His forgiveness, and go forward knowing that God is for you, not against you. You are still accepted in the beloved!

Failure or defeat handled the wrong way can hurt your self-image. We must remember that we are still men and women of flesh liable to error and able to sin. A healthy self-esteem not only requires learning to accept our limitations, but also learning how to handle our failures. When you fail, admit it; do not try to cover it up or to blame it on another. Then, thank God that He has covered that failure with the assurance of Romans 8:28, 29. Tell God that you want to grow and learn from that mistake. He will meet you at your point of honest confession.

Another thing that will help you build healthy self-esteem is to become active in the use of your gifts, talents, or abilities. Get involved in the lives of others, not for what they can do for you, but so that you might minister selflessly on their behalf. O Beloved, there is nothing like it to build your sense of self-worth. I am not a woman of great ability, but, oh, how God is teaching me to love, to minister to others; and because of this, I know my life has worth. No matter what your spiritual gifts, you are called to love others.

> And if I have the gift of prophecy, and know all mysteries and all knowledge; and if I have all faith, so as to remove mountains, but do not have love, I am nothing. And if I give all my possessions to feed the poor, and if I deliver my body to be burned, but do not have love, it profits me nothing. Love is patient, love is kind, and is not jealous; love does not brag and is not arrogant, does not act unbecomingly; it does not seek its own, is not provoked, does not take into account a wrong suffered, does not rejoice in unrighteousness, but rejoices with the truth; bears all things, believes all things, hopes all things, endures all things (1 Corinthians 13:2–7).

If you desire good self-esteem, Beloved, love yourself as God loves you, and then love others the same way. Bring them out from behind the curtains, put the key in the lock, set them free—free to be all that God ordained men and women to be! There is no greater ministry.

MAY

May 1

I couldn't believe my eyes! It literally made me sick. In my mind the court had convened, and I, the righteously indignant judge, wanted to know the name of the guilty party! Who had done it? Who had given the order to have it done? Well, it didn't matter. It had to be changed. It couldn't stay like that.

What was the cause of my great consternation? It lay right there before my eyes marring the rhythm of a once beautiful sweep of lawn—three dirt circles filled with nothing but pitiful petunia plants. You couldn't even tell what color they were as they drooped there in their shamefaced immaturity! It made me furious, and I called the court to order. Did they not know that I was going to plant petunias along the border? How stupid to dig up our beautiful lawn! Well, the petunias would just have to be dug up. The grass would have to be put back. It couldn't stay that way.

Frantically, and I mean frantically, I looked for the person responsible for this mess. Our lawn in front of Reach Out's auditorium would soon be restored to beauty. Just as I had decided all of this, I saw the culprit standing by the road, talking with some businessman or visitor. A sudden wave of nausea hit me because I was certain I had the right person; dry dirt was all over him and dust hovered in the air around him so that he looked for all the world like a six-foot version of Pigpen from a "Peanuts" cartoon. It was my husband.

The minute I saw him I knew that I shouldn't do what I was about to do. The courtroom scene changed to a battleground. The flesh stood there in all its glorious battle array anxiously, eagerly waiting for the command to charge. Opposite stood the knowledge of the Word, sword drawn. My will stood, caught in the middle. The flesh was crying, "Charge!" while the Captain of the Word reasoned quietly with me. "He thinks the petunia patches are lovely. Oh, you don't like them, but he does. Look at him, he's worked so hard. What will it matter in the light of eternity? Which is more important, what he wants or what looks good?"

Which side would I join? I was torn, but not for long. Have you ever

135

been caught in a petunia-type of conflict? What did you do? What would you do? Don't be sorry, or pious. Be honest!

May 2

I made my choice. I knew it was wrong. Even as I walked toward the flesh, I could hear the Word of God calling me to its side, to Christ-likeness. Yet, as I walked away, I reasoned, *Surely, if I just share it with Jack, he will see it my way. He has to! They are too ugly. They can't stay there.* The decision was made. The petunia patches had to go. Then I rationalized: *I'll tell him sweetly, gently. He'll agree. He'll put it all back the way it was. He's got to; it's just too unsightly this way.*

I called over: "Jack, as soon as you finish, I have to talk to you. It's very important."

It *was* important. It had to be changed immediately. I'm that way. If it's wrong, it has to be straightened out ASAP—if not sooner! Oh, Kay, when will you ever learn?

The whole time Jack was walking across the lawn toward me, I knew that I should let it pass. But I didn't. I told him it wasn't in good taste, it maimed the beauty of the lawn, it wasn't what I had in mind. Then I described my plans to Jack and tried to make him see the beauty of my way.

Then the words were spoken, sweetly but very firmly: "I am not going to dig up all those petunias I just planted. Besides I think they look beautiful." Did I catch a plaintive note in his tone of voice? Or was it in another voice that called over to the battlefield, "It's not too late to change sides. Don't you want to be like Me? Are the petunias worth missing an opportunity for oneness with Me? Let this mind be in you that was also in Christ Jesus. . . . in honor preferring one another."

Suddenly I turned around. I wanted to be on the right side. I wanted the sweetness of victory. So I stood on tiptoe and kissed the dusty cheek and said, "Okay, honey." A full apology came later that night after I had counseled more with the Captain of the Word.

More than anything else I want to be like Him. But it is hard at times—yet not as hard as it used to be! There was a day when I would have pushed to have the petunias dug up and the grass resodded (seeding would have taken too long!). But then, in days past I didn't long for oneness with my God as I long for it now.

May 3

God's ultimate goal for His children is oneness with Himself. This was the burden of the Son's heart as He prepared to leave His own in the Father's keeping. Jesus did not ask just once. Several times the words came forth, "that they may be one, even as We are."

O Beloved, this is the Father's heart—the Son's heart—the Spirit's heart, that you and I would be one with Him and thus one with each other, that we would be perfected in unity even as they are one (John 17:11, 21). The burden to share this message with you, with the church, has come from the Father, I'm sure. It is His word to us because it is a message much needed by the body of Jesus Christ. We are so fragmented, aren't we? We lack His love for each other, His love that covers and unites. We lack a love for our God that submits and thus genuinely, tenderly whispers, "I love you, Lord" with every choosing of obedience. Although saved, the body as a whole still carries that unpleasant odor of independence rather than oneness. Oh, it is not a disgustingly repulsive and overpowering body odor, but rather a subtle odoriferous whiff that you catch when you get up real close—not obvious at first but definitely there. A shower will not do. We need to soak in a hot tub of truth. Then we need a vigorous scrubbing with a coarse brush of application. The dead skin needs to be rubbed off. Then the sweetness and the pink glow of newness will be apparent to all and we will exude a fresh fragrance to the world. And as we are perfected in oneness then the word will really know that Christ was sent by the Father (John 17:23). You realize, don't you, that the world will never really believe in the reality of Christ until it sees the reality of Him in our lives. And that reality is seen more and more as we become one with Him.

What will it be for you, Dear One? God has drawn a tub for you to soak in. Will you step in and saturate yourself for a month? Will you pick up that coarse brush of application and scrub away? Would you exchange that body odor with the fragrance and glow of oneness? It's yours, if you want it. Do you? Tell the Father about it. Write it down as a commitment, or a refusal.

May 4

The time had come for them to be alone. He had many things yet to say, but not to the world. These were words for His own, for those who had left all to follow Him. They were important words that needed to be said before He went away. His departure was near; the time was short; so He gathered them together in an upper room.

What an evening it was. He washed their feet when they hadn't even considered washing one another's. When heaviness weighted down their hearts because of their Lord's dire predictions, He mingled their sorrow with a promise like the one made through Ezekiel—the promise of the Holy Spirit dwelling within! Over and over again He mentioned love—love for one another, love for the Father.

Then He called them friends. There it was, that covenant term! Abraham had been called the friend of God. Now they were to be called friends of God also. That friendship would cost them the world's love. It would bring the world's hatred, but that was all right. They had been chosen by God. Jesus was going away. He would no longer be there to guide them, but the Spirit would come and take His place. He would guide them into truth. The words came very plainly to them; there were no figures of speech (John 16:29). They knew Jesus had come from God. He would leave the world; they would stay in the world and have tribulation. But they could take courage. Jesus had overcome the world.

They would be scattered (16:32), but even though scattered they would never forget these hours alone with Him, His words, His prayer. And what a prayer He prayed! They heard every word. First He prayed for Himself, then for them, then for those who were yet to believe. They never forgot His plea to the Father on their behalf: ". . . Holy Father, keep them in Thy name, the name which Thou hast given Me, that they may be one, even as We are" (17:11). And along with that, He reassured their hearts over and over in the fact of the Father's love for them—a love just like the Father's for His only begotten Son. That love would cause the Father to keep them even though they would be left in this world.

One. One with Him. One with each other. This is the Father's desire, the Son's desire, and the Spirit's work—for the child of God!

May 5

What Jesus prayed for His disciples, He also prayed for you and me. How important it is that we realize this, so that we do not fall short of His desire, His prayer, His goal for us.

As I share with you, I feel the Lord would have us spend today meditating upon His prayer for us as recorded in John 17. We'll look only at the last eighteen verses.

I ask on their behalf; I do not ask on behalf of the world, but of those whom Thou hast given Me; for they are Thine; and all things that are

Mine are Thine, and Thine are Mine; and I have been glorified in them. And I am no more in the world; and *yet* they themselves are in the world, and I come to Thee. Holy Father, keep them in Thy name, *the name* which Thou hast given Me, that they may be one, even as We *are*. While I was with them, I was keeping them in Thy name which Thou hast given Me; and I guarded them, and not one of them perished but the son of perdition, that the Scripture might be fulfilled. But now I come to Thee; and these things I speak in the world, that they may have My joy made full in themselves. I have given them Thy word; and the world has hated them, because they are not of the world, even as I am not of the world. I do not ask Thee to take them out of the world, but to keep them from the evil *one*. They are not of the world, even as I am not of the world. Sanctify them in the truth; Thy word is truth. As Thou didst send Me into the world, I also have sent them into the world. And for their sakes I sanctify Myself, that they themselves also may be sanctified in truth. I do not ask in behalf of these alone, but for those also who believe in Me through their word; that they may all be one; even as Thou, Father, *art* in Me, and I in Thee, that they also may be in Us; that the world may believe that Thou didst send Me. And the glory which Thou has given Me I have given to them; that they may be one, just as We are one; I in them, and Thou in Me, that they may be perfected in unity, that the world may know that Thou didst send Me, and didst love them, even as Thou didst love me. Father, I desire that they also, whom Thou hast given Me, be with Me where I am, in order that they may behold My glory, which Thou hast given Me; for Thou didst love Me before the foundation of the world. O righteous Father, although the world has not known Thee, yet I have known Thee; and these have known that Thou didst send Me; and I have made Thy name known to them, and will make it known; that the love wherewith Thou dist love Me may be in them, and I in them (John 17:9–26 NAS).

Now as you reread this passage, may I suggest a few things for you to notice and mark? First, note the verse where Jesus clearly says that His requests to the Father are also for us. Write it out in your notebook.

Around each request for oneness, draw a

Note each use of the word *love* by a

Put a fence like this ▦ around each use of the word *keep* or *keeping*.

Record any other insights the Spirit brings to your mind as you meditate on this passage.

139

May 6

We hear much today about setting goals. Some have told us that if we do not set specific goals we will never achieve anything as Christians.

Maybe it is because I am a woman, but I have never really been too goal conscious. As a matter of fact, in my Christian life I have never really sat down and laid out specific goals for myself or for our ministry. This is not because I am against them, but I just don't operate that way. My Christian life of service has been rather a following of His nudgings, His urgings, His proddings, and at times even His holy "pushings" through doors He has opened! Yet I have always had one goal ever since I became His. Still, even though this goal is the desire of my heart, it too has been of my Lord's doing. That goal is to be like Him—at all times, in all circumstances. Yet, as you have seen, at times I have been an onion in a petunia patch!

Recently that goal has become clearer and clearer, as the lenses of life have been brought to focus on infinity. With the passing of years spent in His Word has come a deeper longing for the life that is yet to be. And with this clearer focus on eternal things has come the realization that I have been given this life as a preparation for the next. Oneness is to be realized in this life, not the next! And it is to come in fulness in this life.

It's hard to lay hold of, isn't it? Why do you think that's so? Is it because we see so little of this oneness in the lives of others? I believe so. At times I think that when we compare ourselves with one another, we feel that we aren't so bad off spiritually, at least not compared with the majority around us who profess the name of Jesus the Christ. Yet, every once in a while, by the grace of God we come into contact with someone who gives us a glimpse of the oneness that could be ours, because it is theirs.

This is what happened to me. I heard, and then I met Darlene Rose, a missionary for forty-two years in New Guinea. She lived with us for one week in our home. We shared; we prayed; we ministered side by side. I watched; I listened, and as I did, I saw how far short I was of the goal. For me, Darlene became God's salt. She caused me to long to drink more deeply of the fountain of living waters. Her example was the Father's prod, to press on toward the prize of the high calling in Christ Jesus. Darlene's life was the lens that made me focus more clearly on infinity. And catching a glimpse of the goal in this life made it more attainable.

May God grant you a clearer vision of the reality of His goal for you.

May 7

When our Lord prayed to the Father that His children might "be one even as We are," what exactly was He asking for us? What does it mean to be one even as the Father and the Son are one? Was Jesus praying only for a unity or oneness among believers? No, I do not believe so, for we have an automatic unity of the Spirit by virtue of our birth into the family of God. In Ephesians 4:3, God tells us to be "diligent **to preserve** the unity of the Spirit in the bond of peace." Note: God says "preserve," not "make" or "become." The oneness Jesus is praying for is not *just* a oneness among believers.

Also, I do not believe that our Lord's prayer is that we will all be one doctrinally. This unity of faith comes only *in time* through a knowledge of Jesus Christ and a maturity attained by walking in His ways. Listen carefully to this truth as stated in Ephesians 4:12, 13: "for the equipping of the saints for the work of service, to the building up of the body of Christ; **until** we all attain to the unity of the faith, and of the knowledge of the Son of God, to a mature man, to the measure of the stature which belongs to the fulness of Christ." If the oneness for which Jesus was praying in John 17 was a oneness of doctrine within the body of believers, then it would only be attainable if all experienced it. And this just will **not** come to pass within the **whole** body because we are at different stages of maturity. Oh, true, those mature through years of studying to show themselves approved unto God usually experience a greater unity of the faith among themselves than do others, but this is because of the temperance, mellowness, and teachableness that comes with taking the time to grow and to understand the complexities of the Word. However, put those who are "babes in Christ" and "teens in Christ" (the know-it-all disdaining period) with the "grandfathers" and "grandmothers" in the Word and what will you have? It won't be unity of the faith!

To be one with Him—what then does it mean? We'll look at it tomorrow, Beloved.

Now, let me urge you: "Hangeth thou in there!" It is all going to get so beautifully and wonderfully practical, but first we must carefully build a solid structure of understanding. This is the key. So meditate today on what has been said.

May 8

The oneness for which Jesus prayed in John 17 is, I believe, a oneness of the individual believer with the members of the Godhead. Oh, true, it will bring us into a greater oneness with other believers; however, this oneness with others can never happen apart from our individual oneness with Him. Our oneness with God gives birth to our oneness with others of his family and thus leads us into being "perfected in unity" (17:23)—literally, perfected "into a unity." As the world sees this unity, it knows that God did send Jesus and that God does love the world (17:23).

We'll talk more about this later. Let's return for now to a more comprehensive definition of the oneness Christ prayed for so that we don't fall short of understanding exactly what is on God's heart. In John 17:21 and 23 Jesus explains oneness by using a phrase of comparison—"even as." "Even as Thou Father, art in Me, and I in Thee, that they also may be in Us . . . I in them, and Thou in Me." So, oneness is a relationship with the Father that is like Christ's relationship with the Father. It is Christ in us and God in Christ, thus God and Christ in me! But you may say, "Didn't this oneness come as a result of my salvation? At my salvation didn't God and His Son make their abode in my body?" Yes, Beloved, He did and yet this was **only** the beginning of the oneness for which Christ was praying.

The oneness with God which was lost through sin in the Garden of Eden was regained in salvation. However, it is only *attained* through life. The oneness for which Christ was praying is yet to be attained. How do I know? By the tense of the verbs used. Jesus is praying for those who are **His,** asking that they "may all be one." "May be" is in the subjunctive mood, the mood of probability. It signifies an action which may or should happen but which is not necessarily true at the present. If Jesus had been praying about an existing quality He would have used the indicative mood, the mood of actuality, of reality, but He didn't.

Therefore, the oneness Christ prayed for is a oneness which should happen, a oneness which probably will happen, but which in fact is not yet certain. *The Parsings Guide to the Greek New Testament* states that the verb *may be* is in the active voice which indicates that the subject is responsible for the action of the verb. Thus we are the ones who in essence determine the degree of oneness we desire with Him.

Do you want to truly be one with Him, even as Christ was one with the Father?

May 9

Jesus' prayer in John 17 was the culmination of His time alone with His disciples. The cross loomed before Him. He knew what fear and distress His death would bring to the hearts of His disciples. The Shepherd was to be smitten, the sheep scattered (Zechariah 13:7, John 16:32). Before the scattering came, He had to be alone with them to prepare them for the hours and the days ahead. They would need hope. It was time for truth to be given plainly so that they might believe without a doubt that Jesus had come from God (John 16:30) and so they might take courage (v. 33). That is why He had gathered them together in the upper room. After they celebrated the Passover meal and Jesus inaugurated the New Covenant, He washed their feet. Then Judas left.

> When therefore he had gone out, Jesus said, "Now is the Son of Man glorified, and God is glorified in Him. . . . Little children, I am with you a little while longer. You shall seek Me; and as I said to the Jews, 'Where I am going, you cannot come,' now I say to you also. A new commandment I give to you, that you love one another, even as I have loved you, that you also love one another. By this all men will know that you are My disciples, if you have love for one another." Simon Peter said to Him, "Lord, where are You going?" Jesus answered, "Where I go, you cannot follow Me now; but you shall follow later." Peter said to Him, "Lord, why can I not follow You right now? I will lay down my life for You." Jesus answered, "Will you lay down your life for Me? Truly, truly, I say to you, a cock shall not crow, until you deny Me three times" (John 13:31–38).

I believe it was almost too much for them to contain. If Peter, the bold one, the leader, denied Jesus, what would the rest do? Consternation was written all over their faces, and so He told them not to let their hearts be troubled. He was going away to prepare a place for them, but He would come back and take them with Him to the Father's house. This prompted Philip to say, "Lord, show us the Father, and it is enough for us" (John 14:8).

Oh, how glad I am that Philip said this, for Jesus' answer shows us what it really means to be one with the Father and thus to be able to be perfected in unity by loving one another *even as* Jesus loves us. Only then will the world see again the reality of Jesus and His love.

Today, meditate on how Jesus could show Philip the Father, whom no man has ever really seen because He is spirit.

May 10

"Show us the Father." Isn't Philip's request the same that many have in the world today? "Show me Jesus, and I'll believe in Him!"

Have you not heard some say, "How do you expect me to believe in someone whom I've never seen?" To be honest, this is a rather legitimate request, isn't it? "Show me God, and I will believe."

Is it an impossible request? No! In fact, it is a rather reasonable request that can and should be fulfilled. "How?" you ask. The same way Jesus fulfilled Philip's request. This, Beloved, is what oneness is all about—"one even as we are . . . that the world might believe that Thou didst send me." In Jesus' response to Philip you and I are able to gain a clearer understanding of oneness.

> Jesus said to him, "Have I been so long with you, and yet you have not come to know Me, Philip? He who has seen Me has seen the Father; how do you say, 'Show us the Father'? Do you not believe that I am in the Father, and the Father is in Me? The words that I say to you I do not speak on My own initiative, but the Father abiding in Me does His works. Believe Me that I am in the Father, and the Father in Me; otherwise believe on account of the works themselves" (John 14:9–11).

Jesus was so *one* with the Father that He could tell Philip that because Philip had seen Him, he had seen the Father. Why, the very words Jesus spoke to them were not His, but the Father's. And even the works that Jesus did were the Father's works (John 5:19). Jesus was so *one* with the Father that He never acted independently of the Father. "I can do nothing on My own initiative. As I hear, I judge; and My judgment is just, **because I do not seek My own will,** but the will of Him who sent Me" (John 5:30). Thus Jesus could say to Philip, "He who has seen Me has seen the Father."

This, Beloved, is oneness. Oneness is not a technical state but a vital and essential relationship in all areas of life—oneness in character, in understanding, in purpose, in love. It is a vital fellowship, a sharing in common.

And it is this oneness with God that the world needs to see in our lives. Then when the world says, "Show us Jesus and we'll believe," we can say, "If you have seen me you have seen Him." Does it sound sacrilegious? Please do not assume so, until we share more tomorrow.

May 11

Should a child of God be able to say, "If you want to know what God is like, you can look at my life or listen to my words and you will see the Father"?

The answer to that question must come from the Scriptures, otherwise you would never believe me. And even then, some of you may have a hard time agreeing with it.

Let's begin searching out our answer together in John 14:12, 13 where our Lord Himself makes this astounding statement: "Truly, truly, I say to you, he who believes in Me, the works that I do shall he do also; and greater works than these shall he do; because I go to the Father. And whatever you ask in My name, that will I do, that the Father may be glorified in the Son."

When Jesus says "truly, truly," you can know that it is *truly!* You and I, as believers, are to do the works He did. "But how can this be possible?" you may ask. It is only possible, Precious One, because we have the same Spirit within us as Jesus had—God's Spirit, the Holy Spirit! It will not be by our might or by our power, but *by His Spirit* (Zechariah 4:6). Oneness is ours through abiding in His Spirit. And when we abide in Him—we in Him, and He in us—then we are able to do His works. We speak His words because we do not do anything on our own initiative. The Father does the work through us by His Spirit even as He did through His Son. But even if this is so, are others supposed to be able to see the Father by looking at us? Yes, Beloved, they are.

In 1 Corinthians 11:1, Paul wrote "Be imitators of me, just as I also am of Christ." In Philippians 3:17, Paul said, "Brethren, join in following my example, and observe those who walk according to the pattern you have in us." He also told the Philippians, "The things you have learned and received and heard and seen in me, practice these things; and the God of peace shall be with you" (4:9).

But you say, "That was Paul; that is not me! Oh, and is Paul any different or more special than you? Did God give Paul an extra portion of Himself? Not according to Paul, for he writes, "For **in Him** (*Christ*) all the fulness of Deity dwells in bodily form, and **in Him** you have been made complete . . ." (Colossians 2:9, 10). And did not Jesus say, "I in them, and Thou in Me" (John 17:23)? Of course He did! So then, seeing the Father through you is possible, isn't it?

Do you have to meditate on that? I understand. Meditate. Talk to the Father and we'll continue tomorrow. Meditate well, for it is about to get marvelously practical! Love you.

May 12

Multitudes have come to be true worshipers of Jesus Christ without ever reading a Bible or stepping inside a church building. You may say, "But how could this happen if 'faith comes from hearing, and hearing by the word of Christ' (Romans 10:17)?"

It is because they have seen the reality of God in the lives of His children and have heard the words of God from their lips. Having heard truth and having seen it, they have believed in a God whom they have never seen. Oh, they may not have read God's Word itself, but they have read it in other lives, in living epistles "known and read by all men" (2 Corinthians 3:2). They have seen and heard the Father by seeing and hearing His children.

Paul, Silvanus, and Timothy wrote to those in Thessalonica, "For our gospel did not come to you in word **only,** but also in power and in the Holy Spirit and with full conviction; just as you know what kind of men we proved to be among you for your sake" (1 Thessalonians 1:5). These men were so one with the Father that when they spoke God's truth it was not a matter of mere words, but the Word was delivered in power and in the Holy Spirit. They were so one with God that their words carried the full conviction that what they were saying was absolute truth. And their message was confirmed by their lives. People saw what kind of men they were. They were different from others. Their lives had a different dimension. They were men who lived on a higher plane—God's plane.

What about you, Beloved? What plane do you live on? Man's or God's? When you walk in the world delivering the gospel, does it go forth in more than word only? Is there a power to your life? Is the fruit of the Holy Spirit evident in your life—His love, joy, peace, patience—His kindness, goodness, faithfulness, gentleness, and self-control? When you speak of God, of His character, of His ways, of His life, are you fully convinced of the truth of it all? Of its absoluteness? What kind of a man are you? What kind of a woman? Like the world or truly different? Meditate on this and write out your insights.

May 13

Some missionaries went into New Guinea to establish a work and during their stay, a terrible drought came. The natives, seeking to appease the god of water and stop the drought, began to fast. This fasting was so stringent that they could not even swallow their own spittle but had to spit it out on the ground. The new missionaries thought that they could win the people over to the gospel by showing an appreciation for the native ways, so they joined in the fast. For days the natives watched as the missionaries fasted and spit their saliva on the ground.

The missionaries saw no harm in all this, and so, when the second part of the ceremony began, they carefully watched what the natives did and followed suit. They, too, took a pig down to the bank of the river where they slit its throat and let its blood flow into the river to appease the god of the water. They didn't believe in the god of the water, but what harm would it do? They simply wanted to relate as much as they could to the natives!

When the pagan ceremony was finished, the natives went to the government officials with this protest, "Don't let these people in here. They can't help us; they are just like us. Send us more missionaries like the Roses (Darlene and Jerry Rose); they are different from us." This, Beloved, is oneness—being like Him rather than like those in the world. The missionaries had nothing to offer because they were *just like* the natives.

In 1 Thessalonians 1:6, 7 Paul wrote, "You also became imitators of us and of the Lord, having received the word in much tribulation with the joy of the Holy Spirit, so that you became an example. . . ." The world needs so desperately to see men and women who are different from them, who are worth imitating. They need to see the Christ who is in you, who made you different. When they imitate you, they will be imitating the Lord.

Here are two questions to meditate upon. As you meditate, Precious One, write down the thoughts that come to you. It will really help. But you must not be falsely modest, or self-deprecating. That is **not** of God; it's of the flesh. Here are the questions:

What areas of your life are others able to imitate?

What would have to change before others could imitate your life fully?

May 14

So then, this is the goal of Jesus for our lives—to be one with Him so that the world might again see what God is like *in the flesh,* so that they might see that "Christ is formed in you" (Galatians 4:19) as you "put on the Lord Jesus Christ, and make no provision for the flesh in regard to its lusts" (Romans 13:14). Oneness is laying hold of Christ Jesus, of pressing toward the goal for the prize of the upward call of God in Christ Jesus (Philippians 3:12, 14). Oneness is being able to say, "Be an imitator of me as I am of Christ. Watch my pattern of life and use it for your example, for it is Christ's pattern."

This is attained by living here on this earth, for through the everyday circumstances of life's marketplace we learn and are able to achieve oneness. This is why God has left us here. It is learned through traffic jams, flat tires, spilled milk, scratched furniture, muddy carpets, broken dishes, slow people, rude people, crude people. It is learned through having to wait, through missing planes, through having orders fouled up, through all the pettiness of daily living that is enough to give a normal person an ulcer.

Oneness is learned in life's trials, in chronic illnesses, in sudden catastrophes, in financial distresses, in disasters of nature, in collapsing economies, in times of rioting and wars, in depressions of soul, in prisons of steel, in the face of ominous threats, in rumors of impending doom. Oneness is learned in life's relationships, especially those that would impinge upon our independence. And finally, God has left us on earth to learn oneness in quietness and solitude with Him.

But is it possible to attain oneness with God when we have to put up with all the pressures of living in this world? Oh yes, Beloved. As a matter of fact, there is no other way to learn oneness with Him. This is why Jesus prayed, "I do not ask Thee to take them out of the world, but to keep them from the evil one" (John 17:15). We can't be taken out of the world, because, like Jesus, we have been sent into the world.

But how do you handle it so that you don't blow it? We'll learn together in the days ahead, precept upon precept. The question is: Are you willing? Do you want it? It is yours for the believing and the doing, for the obedience of faith!

May 15

Have you ever wondered why some people are so hard to get along with? Especially those who are closest to you! And why is it, do you suppose, that we treat many outsiders, acquaintances, or friends better than we treat our family? Why do we get more upset or uptight with the people we love? Or why does there always seem to be at least one difficult person in our lives that we cannot seem to avoid?

Have you ever thought of what it must have been like for Jesus to have Judas Iscariot in His constant presence for approximately three years, knowing all the time that Judas would never believe on Him but instead would betray Him? Or have you ever wondered what it must have been like for Jesus to live with half brothers who did not recognize Him as the Messiah at the time? Brothers who instead mocked His life (John 7:2–8). It was not easy. Intimate relationships never really are easy, even when the people are nice! Why? Because at one time or another they make demands upon our independence. Yet, it is in the relationships of life that God seeks to draw us into oneness with Him, and through this oneness, into oneness with others.

God uses three major earthly relationships to achieve oneness with Him—family, marriage, and the church. Learning oneness in these relationships plays an integral part in learning oneness with God, for these relationships teach us dependence.

God has so structured our lives that, when we come into this world, we become part of a family. We are born with sinful, willful, independent spirits—spirits that need to be brought into submission to others. So what does God do? He gives us parents and with these parents come instructions. "Children, obey your parents in the Lord, for this is right. Honor your father and mother (which is the first commandment with a promise), that it may be well with you, and that you may live long on the earth" (Ephesians 6:1-3). Obeying and honoring our parents makes it well with us because it trains us and equips us for the other relationships of life, especially our relationship with God, the Heavenly Father. When children do not learn to obey and honor their parents their capacity to form worthwhile relationships with others is greatly hindered, often even ruined. The breaking down of the family unit and of discipline within the home today has created a society filled with independent misfits seemingly incapable of committing themselves to a lasting or demanding relationship.

The key word in oneness is submission, the opposite of independence. This is part of God's design for the family. If we do not learn submission here, with those we can see, how will we ever learn it with God, whom we cannot see? How is it in your family?

May 16

Marriage. You could hardly wait for it . . . but you did. You waited until "the one" came along! And in all probability when "the one" came along, some people warned you that there would be adjustments. Oh, that was fine. You listened. You were polite. You realized that they just didn't understand. They didn't realize that you two were different, your relationship was special. So you smiled, tuned them out and turned on "your" song. You became man and wife.

How long it took or when it happened, really isn't important. It was devastating enough just to have it occur. Suddenly you came face to face with disillusionment! It might have been over the toothpaste tube you shared. You rolled it from the bottom; she mutilated it. Since you were a tot you had been taught how any proper child treats his tube of toothpaste. Or maybe it happened when you told her that working in a kitchen was not a man's job. How shocked you were when she began to sob, words convulsing from her trembling body, words you couldn't believe: "You don't really love me ... I knew it was too good to be true. ... I ... I ... thought you cared." Then with a look of hysteria, she threw her last volley of words at you as she ran out of the room, "My daddy always helped my mother."

Or maybe it happened when you got upset because she bought a new dress. Or ... you fill it in yourself. It did happen, didn't it? You suddenly became aware of the fact that "the one" did not always see things the way you saw them. How could she be so blind! And if you didn't wonder whether you married the wrong one, you at least realized that marriage was going to be an adjustment! Those friends had been right after all! Marriage was going to make demands of you, demands you weren't always sure were worth it.

Oh Dear One, as compatible as Jack and I are, we still meet in petunia patches. That's what marriage is—petunia patches! But how I praise God that I am finally seeing the purpose of them. It's submission, not to Jack, but to my Lord ... and thus to Jack. Ephesians 5, after telling me in the eighteenth verse to be filled with the Spirit, points out the mutual submission of a Spirit-filled life: "submitting yourselves one to another in the fear of God" (v. 21). After saying this, Paul then tells us how this is manifested in marriage.

Marriage, as we will see tomorrow, Beloved, is one of God's major ways of bringing us into oneness with Him. That is why we are fools to walk away from it even if it seems at times more than we can bear.

May 17

Women have heard so much on submission in the last decade that they are sick of the word. "Why doesn't someone preach to the men, and tell them what their responsibility is! Why does the responsibility always fall on the woman?"

I've heard many statements like this as I have traveled teaching the Word of God. And technically, the people making them do have a point. The emphasis in much preaching on the home and marriage is on the role of the woman and really it should not be! Man is just as responsible, just as accountable. Man was born the aggressor, the initiator. He was given the role of ruler by God. He is the one who has abdicated his "throne" and woman has eagerly scrambled up its steps to sit in his place. And in doing so, she has distorted womanhood as much as man has distorted manhood, and the God-ordained institution of marriage has been so distorted as a result. I honestly do not believe you will ever know oneness with God if you willfully refuse to be what God has ordained for you as a wife or a husband. If you are married you can be sure that your marriage will be one of God's earthly means to bring you into oneness with Him.

How? Through submission to God's Spirit, being "subject to one another in the fear of Christ" (Ephesians 5:21).

How does this submission work in marriage? It works by each fulfilling his proper role. The husband submits to God and to his wife by loving her as Christ loved the church and gave Himself up for it (Ephesians 5:25). The husband is to so honor his wife in love that he will love her as he does his own body. The love that God refers to in Ephesians 5 is His *agape* love, a love that seeks another's highest good, that sacrifices, that never fails but hopes all things and endures all things. It's a First Corinthians 13 love. And in loving his wife, a husband learns and takes on the character of Jesus Christ and manifests to the world the love of the Son for the church.

The wife, in turn, learns and takes on the character of Jesus Christ through submission to her husband, for in submitting to him, she is submitting as unto the Lord (Ephesians 5:22). Christ submitted Himself to the Father, for God is the head of Christ (1 Corinthians 11:3). Therefore, when we as wives submit to our husbands, we show the world the character of Christ as He submitted to the Father. Wives are also to respect or reverence their husbands. Girls, if we want to be one even as the Father and Son are one, we must be willing to submit to that which God has ordained for women. There is no way around it. Submission to our roles in marriage is God's means to oneness with Himself.

May 18

When you sit in church and look around you, are there certain people who disgust you? Are there any whom you are quick to criticize or to "discuss" with others? Is there anyone with whom you would refuse to work? Anyone whom you avoid speaking to or sitting next to, whom you just plain do not want anything to do with? If so, where is the love of God, the character of God in you?

Remember several days ago, when I said that God works through three major earthly relationships to achieve oneness? We've looked briefly at two of those, the family and marriage. Today we will look at the third, the church. Outside of "blood" relationships, our relationship within the church is to be the most intimate ever experienced. Unfortunately, it is not usually that way today, but it was in the days of the early church. In those days, people sold what they had in order to meet the needs of their brothers and sisters in Christ. No one in the church lacked anything for they had all things in common (Acts 2:44–47; 4:34, 35).

Paul constantly reminded those in the church that although they were many members, they were part of one body with one Head. The Head was Christ. The body was the church, not a building of brick, mortar, stone, or wood—but of living stones, of flesh and blood. They were to weep with those who weep and to rejoice with those who rejoice. They were members one of another. And God's plea to His church through Paul was to keep the unity of the Spirit in the bond of peace (Ephesians 4:3), that there be no division in the body (1 Corinthians 12:25).

Jesus said, "By this all men will know that you are My disciples, if you have love for one another" (John 13:35). We are to love one another even as Christ loved us. In learning this love we are drawn into oneness with God and it is in the church that we are to learn the character of God. In Philippians 2:5 we read, "Have this attitude in yourselves which was also in Christ Jesus." What attitude was that? It was the attitude of a submissive and obedient servant who in humility regarded others as more important than Himself. . . . an attitude that caused one to be concerned not merely for his own interests but also for others. . . . that permitted no selfishness or conceit. It was a determination to be of the same mind, maintaining Christ's love, united in spirit, and intent on one purpose—God's will, His glory (Philippians 2:1–4).

O Beloved, if this does not characterize us, how can we ever consider ourselves one with God? And if the world does not see this attitude in church members, how will it ever believe that the Father sent the Son? The church is to be different—different in love. What we do or do not accomplish does not testify half as loudly as whether we really love one another! Think on it. What will oneness cost you in your relationship with those of the body, the church? Write out your answer and seeing it in black and white, deal with it in your heart.

May 19

Do you believe God's Word is true? Do you believe that it was given by God to men through His Spirit so that we who believe on the Lord

Jesus Christ might know how to live? If your answer is yes, then do you realize that, as a believer in the Lord Jesus Christ and His Word, you are a translator of the Word of God? Each of us, through his life, is continually translating God's Word into the language of the world. This is why oneness with God is our greatest, most powerful witness. If our lives do not support the words of our lips, how will the world ever see the reality of God? How accurate is your translation?

Do you realize that your relationship to God, whatever it may be, governs all your relationships **in life** and **with life.** Your relationship to your God determines how you will respond to people, no matter how they behave. It also determines how you will react to the "hardnesses" of life, to its difficulties, its trials. Conversely, your relationships in life display or expose **your relationship to God.**

Have you ever said something like, "I just couldn't help it. They provoked me!" Or "It was just too much to take . . . more than I could bear. I couldn't help getting frustrated . . . angry . . . mad . . . upset and so I just let it all hang out!"

Your response or reaction showed the depth of your relationship to God, or the lack of it. When a cup is jarred it spills whatever it contains. If you are filled with His character, His love, His words, then this is what you will spill. "But," you may say, "you are asking the impossible. We are only human!" Oh . . . are we only human? Or are we a strange but wonderful mixture of human and divine? Remember, it is God in you, Christ in you. Oneness is that life in which He increases while I decrease (John 3:30).

But can this ever be? Or is it just some theological platitude, perhaps just for a certain class or temperament? O Beloved, it is for all. It is attainable. It is yours for the submission. It is yours for the pursuing. Tomorrow we'll see how. The question is, "Will you pursue it?"

May 20

Have you ever thought, *The reason that I can't handle this is that I'm not spiritual enough. When I become more spiritual then I'll react better.*

Well, in a sense, that is right. Maturity in Christ does enable us to see more clearly the wisdom of God's ways. And experience does testify clearly that it is foolish not to walk in the obedience of faith. All this is true. But that is not the reason you can't handle things correctly or respond properly to people or to trials. Spirituality is a matter of choice regardless of your maturity in Christ. Spirituality is simply a matter of submission at any given moment to the control of the Holy

Spirit who lives in you. God's Word in 1 Corinthians 10:13 is true for all believers, "No temptation has overtaken you but such as is common to man; and God is faithful, who will not allow you to be tempted beyond what you are able, but with the temptation will provide the way of escape also, that you may be able to endure it." The word *temptation* can also be translated *trial* or *testing*. What is God saying? Simply this. He, the Sovereign God of all the universe, will not give you anything you cannot handle. If you could not handle it, then He would not permit it. God says, "I am the Lord, and there is no other, the One forming light and creating darkness, causing well-being and creating calamity; I am the Lord who does all these" (Isaiah 45:6, 7).

Why? Why would God create calamity? If He is a Sovereign God, and He is, why does He permit adversity? There are several reasons I could give you, but right now I only want to talk about one. It is very important to our study of oneness and how it is achieved. Oneness with God is developed through the physical, through the laboratory of life. It is here in the laboratory of life that we carry on our experiments until we discover and experience oneness with God. God uses the physical to teach us the spiritual. This, Beloved, is why Christ prayed **not** that we would be taken out of the world but rather that, being left in the world, we would be kept by the Father from the evil one and sanctified, made holy, through His truth.

So you can know, Beloved, that whatever adversity, calamity, or temptation comes your way the Father will keep you—if you will be kept! You can handle anything, by His Spirit, if you will but yield!

Now don't get frustrated! I have much more to say on the subject, but we must take it together, one day at a time, precept upon precept, line upon line. I love you. You are precious in His sight; that is why I write. It is His ministry, another of His ways of putting His arms around you and drawing you to Himself.

May 21

She just left. She only came for prayer. She's experiencing a little bit of hell in her marriage. Adultery, beatings, insults. This isn't what she wants; her heart pants after God, she longs for a good marriage. But she doesn't have one. And it is not that her husband does not know what is right, or where to go to get help. He knows. He has a good pastor.

How do you pray in a situation like this? What did I pray as we knelt together beside our blue couch? I prayed that no matter what happened she would walk as God would have her walk. I prayed that in all this she would learn more of God's character, more of His ways. I prayed that eternity would be ever before her eyes, and that this vision would take her beyond the plane of the temporal to the higher calling of life on His plane. I did not ask that God would remove her from trial, but that she would permit herself to be kept in the midst of it. Oh, I did pray for her husband. But he may not change. The situation may not improve. We have no definite word from God on that. But God's promise is sure that it will not be more than she can bear. God, the magnificent Redeemer of Redeemers, will see to it that this will work out to her ultimate good no matter what her husband does, for this **will be used** to make her one with Him if she will but yield, trust, obey (Romans 8:28, 29).

Every situation has a spiritual purpose, and thus God leaves us in the midst of a world of sinners to sanctify us so that we might be one with Him. But, oh, how we are missing the boat, the ship that would carry us safely across oceans of life's perplexities to the shores of a new continent where the Prince of Peace awaits with a, "Well done, My beloved servant," where we will "greatly rejoice with joy inexpressible and full of glory" (1 Peter 1:8). Instead, so many become frightened by the storms, abandon ship, and swim **back** to shore. They are missing not only the boat, but the prize of the high calling in Christ Jesus. They are shortsighted. They cannot see beyond the temporal to the eternal shores of that continent of Christlikeness. They are running from the "physical" difficulties and distresses which God would use to make them like Him. If it cannot be their way, if the ship will not take a smooth course, then they won't stay aboard. What fools they are! How blind!

May 22

The physical situations of life are meant to teach us complete dependence upon the spiritual. God uses the temporal to prepare us for the eternal. Thus Charles Haddon Spurgeon, the prince of preachers, proclaimed, "I shall welcome every storm of life that shipwrecks me on the Rock Christ Jesus."

What is it that keeps us from having this philosophy of life? Is not this viewpoint biblical? Oh, yes, it is biblical, though some naive in the Word would tell you otherwise. Some preach physical prosperity. It is wrong preaching, but hard to detect because elements of truth are woven among the threads of deception. Sadly, such teaching leads the unsuspecting astray along with those who only hear the Word of God but do not study it!

They are taught that God does not want you to suffer or lack in any way and that with enough faith you can be well, you can be rich, you can have what you confess with your mouth, and that tribulation and physical sufferings are not from Him. And many flock to hear of this physical prosperity, not realizing that, in the process, the devil may give them what they seek and thus delude them. They are ignorant of the fact that often physical ease and prosperity rob us, leaving us as spiritual paupers to wander the streets of life, separated from the oneness that comes through the difficulties of life. Many are so earth-bound, so shortsighted, so unlearned in the **whole** counsel of God, so humanistic, that they are blind to the purpose of necessities, distresses and tribulations.

"In the world you have tribulation, but take courage; I have overcome the world" (John 16:33). "I do not ask Thee to take them out of the world, but to keep them from the evil. . . . As Thou didst send Me into the world, I also have sent them into the world" (John 17:15, 18). "And if children, heirs also, heirs of God and fellow-heirs with Christ, if indeed we suffer with Him in order that we may also be glorified with Him. For I consider that the sufferings of this present time are not worthy to be compared with the glory that is to be revealed to us" (Romans 8:17, 18). "Who shall separate us from the love of Christ? Shall tribulation, or distress, or persecution, or famine, or nakedness, or peril, or sword?" (Romans 8:35).

Will they? Or will they shipwreck us on the Rock of Jesus Christ and abandon us to Christlikeness?

May 23

Have you ever really talked to someone who has suffered greatly and yet who loves the Lord dearly? I have, and do you know what I have found? An unparalleled sweetness, tenderness, gentleness, quietness, confidence. Brashness is gone! Showiness cannot be found. Striving, debating, having to prove a point has been replaced by a gentle, quiet, unshakable confidence that has been acquired in a select school of higher learning. Debate is ridiculous for they have experienced the certainty of truth. All the props of man's making and theology are removed. They have been cast onto the veracity of the Word of God alone, and it has held!

This is what I saw in Darlene Rose, a woman who has suffered such hunger that she blessed God for the maggots that provided extra nourishment in her putrid bowl of broth . . . a woman who periodically has skin cancers removed from her face, cancers that came from working in the intense heat of the sun as a malnourished prisoner of war . . . a woman whose body was badly weakened in a multitude of ways because she lived continuously on the edge of starvation . . . a woman who possesses very little materially but is so very rich spiritually.

To those who teach that prosperity is ours if only we believe and confess, I would ask, "Oh, wouldn't you like to be like her? Wouldn't it be worth it, no matter what it cost?" What will last? Material prosperity, even health, or the eternal qualities of Christlikeness?

Beloved, I want to share some Scripture with you. Do not read it lightly. Read it prayerfully. Meditate on it. "Blessed be the God and Father of our Lord Jesus Christ, who according to His great mercy has caused us to be born again to a living hope through the resurrection of Jesus Christ from the dead, to obtain an inheritance which is imperishable and undefiled and will not fade away, reserved in heaven for you, who are protected by the power of God through faith for a salvation ready to be revealed in the last time. In this you greatly rejoice, even though now for a little while, if necessary, you have been distressed by various trials, that the proof of your faith, being more precious than gold which is perishable, even though tested by fire, may be found to result in praise and glory and honor at the revelation of Jesus Christ" (1 Peter 1:3–7).

May 24

I want to share a principle with you, Beloved, that God has brought to my mind once again. As I prayed and meditated on our relationship with God and how it is developed, He showed me (as I have already shared with you) that the spiritual is developed through the physical. This, of course, is contrary to much of our thinking. We say, "I'll be spiritual **and then** I can handle the physical."

With all these thoughts carrying on a discussion in my head, suddenly 1 Corinthians 15:45, 46 came to mind. "So also it is written, 'The first man, Adam, became a living soul.' The last Adam became a life-giving spirit. However, the spiritual is not first, but the natural; then the spiritual."

I saw that in life the natural comes first, the physical, **then** the spiritual. **The spiritual is not first.** The physical is used of God to cause us to turn to the spiritual, to see our need for the spiritual. Thus the physical situations of life that every human being faces, become platforms or arenas for the Christian. It is in these arenas that we can show other

157

men and women what the last Adam, Jesus Christ, is really like. Then they can see the contrasts, the differences, between those who are in Adam and those who are in Christ (Romans 5:12–21). This is why God tells us in Romans 8, " 'For thy sake we are being put to death all day long; we were considered as sheep to be slaughtered.' But in all these things we overwhelmingly conquer **through Him** [the last Adam] who loved us' " (Romans 8:36, 37). As God's children we will never find ourselves exempt from the physical distresses of life which plague all mankind. Rather, we are allowed to go through these situations so that the world can see that we are different. In the trials of life we can overwhelmingly conquer. How? Through oneness with Him.

Now let me give you one more thing to ponder. If the natural comes before the spiritual, when you get in a "tight" situation, watch that **first** reaction. It will probably be a "natural" reaction. So hold it! Check it out! Calm down, take a deep breath, rest, and tell God you want the spiritual response not the natural reaction. Thank Him for it and accept it by faith. Then walk by His Spirit and you will not fulfill the lusts of the flesh (Galatians 5:16).

When hogs are slaughtered, they squeal like mad and make an awful noise. When sheep are slaughtered, they do not utter a sound. Meditate on that, Dear Sheep, and see that you are being put to death all day long for **His** sake. See it and conquer! The world will see it and wonder! And Jesus will see it and rejoice. His prayer is being answered.

May 25

He was huddled in the corner trying to keep warm. He had just wrapped his blanket around him when the door of his prison cell opened. As his eyes adjusted to the temporary light from the open cell door, he surveyed the condition of the new prisoner. Inwardly he shuddered. This man would never make it. He would be dead by morning. He was too emaciated, too badly beaten, in no condition to take the cold. If he had a blanket he might have a chance, but he didn't.

Having made these mental notes to himself, the first man huddled down into his blanket to sleep. Then he heard that still, small voice. There was no mistaking it . . . it was Him.

"Without a blanket, he'll be dead by morning."

"I know, Lord."

The words came ever so gently, "Give him yours."

158

"But Lord," he reasoned, "if I do, I'll be dead by morning."

"I know. Give him your blanket."

In the morning, the second prisoner looked across the narrow cell at the still form. Little by little, he realized that the man who had given him his blanket in the night was *dead.* Through one man's death, another was alive. The Word of God had been translated into a language he could understand ... "Greater love has no one than this, that one lay down his life for his friends" (John 15:13). "For while we were still helpless, at the right time Christ died for the ungodly. For one will hardly die for a righteous man; though perhaps for the good man someone would dare even to die. **But God demonstrates** His own love toward us, in that while we were yet sinners, Christ died for us" (Romans 5:6-8).

This, Beloved, is oneness demonstrated—Christ clearly seen again, in man's flesh, in an earthen vessel no different from anyone else's. Yet incomprehensibly different, unexplainably different. Unexplainable except for Jesus.

In that prison cell, the One who laid down His life almost two thousand years ago, had laid it down again! How dwelleth the love of God in us?

May 26

"But we have this treasure in earthen vessels, that the surpassing greatness of the power may be of God and not from ourselves; we are afflicted in every way, but not crushed; perplexed, but not despairing; persecuted, but not forsaken; struck down, but not destroyed; always carrying about in the body the dying of Jesus, that the life of Jesus also may be manifested in our body. For we who live are constantly being delivered over to death for Jesus' sake, that the life of Jesus also may be manifested in our mortal flesh" (2 Corinthians 4:7-11).

The treasure is God—the Father, the Son, the Holy Spirit. The vessel is you. Can you imagine it? You not only bear His name but you bear Him. Your physical body, once a slave to sin (Romans 6:16-18), has become His temple. Have you ever wondered why God makes us wait so long for our new bodies—bodies that will never sin? If He's going to give us new bodies, why doesn't He give them to us now? Why wait until the resurrection?

Why? Because He wants to use us in our earthly bodies to demonstrate to the world His grace, His power, His sufficiency. He wants to show men that sin is not a matter of "I can't help myself," but rather a matter of submission. Sin is refusal to submit to God, refusal to walk in His way, refusal to live a life of dependence upon His Spirit. Sin is a matter of man's will. Sin is refusing to become one with God. So, when God saves us He leaves us in these earthen vessels as a testimony to the world of the sufficiency of His grace for every situation.

And where is this sufficiency most often seen? In situations of life that bring us face to face with the death of our will. It is seen in situations of sacrifice that blesses rather than retaliates! Sacrifice that bears with insults, with reproaches, with distresses, with persecutions, with difficulties, with petunia patches! Sacrifice that says, "Not my will, but Thine be done!" Sacrifice that says, "Father, Your character, Your love, Your will, Your purpose, whatever the cost!" Submission and sacrifice that the life of Jesus might be visible in our mortal flesh, that others might see that Jesus did come into the world. For if He hadn't, no ordinary man would ever react the way we do! It just isn't natural!

May 27

Oneness. It all sounds so good, doesn't it? So holy, so spiritual, so Christlike, so *impossible!*

What's going to bring this oneness about? If it's so possible, then why don't you see it in more people's lives?

Oneness with God will only come in one way. And most people are ignorant of that way. Or if they are not ignorant of it, they feel it isn't worth it. It's too hard, too costly, too time consuming.

Jesus knew the way of oneness. He gave it to His disciples when He prayed for them in their presence. "I have given them Thy word. . . . I do not ask Thee to take them out of the world, but to keep them. . . . Sanctify them in the truth; Thy word is truth" (John 17:14, 15, 17). The way to oneness is through sanctification. Sanctification that comes **only** by God's Word. To be sanctified is to be holy! To be holy is to be **even as He is** for it is written, "You shall be holy, for I am holy" (1 Peter 1:16).

In the world (the physical) we have the Word (the spiritual). This Word sanctifies us. And as we are being sanctified, becoming more and more like Him, then this sanctifies Christ within the world as being the One who was distinctively God. The world can then see that He was sent to show the reality of God's love for them (John 17:21-24). We must face it. There is no sanctification apart from God's Word! This, Beloved, is why so few exhibit a true oneness of character with God, why so few are one in purpose with God, and love as God loves.

It is because they are not sanctified in truth. They do not know His Word. They do not love His Word. They do not read His Word. They do not study His Word. They do not meditate on His Word. They are too occupied with this world's passions, deceived by its philosophies, caught up in its traditions. This is why Christians today, for the most part, are anything but like Him! You can get the men and boys out for a church baseball team but not for Bible study and prayer. They don't have time for that. They'll serve on boards and committees, and run the affairs of the church, but never diligently study to show themselves approved unto God. They have time for newspapers, TV, sports, business, but not for sanctification! Women have time for craft classes, exercise salons, aerobics, beauty parlors, shopping malls, luncheons, gardens and showers, but they do not have time nor the discipline to study God's Word and meditate on His precepts.

Are you one with Him, or are you an adulteress forsaking your Bridegroom for your friendship with the world? How ashamed you would be if He ever caught you in the world's bed. What would you say to Him, when you are supposed to be one with Him? What would your excuse be? How would you explain your whoredoms?

O Beloved, Beloved, Beloved. . . .

May 28

You will never achieve oneness with another apart from communication. It is impossible. This is why so many marriages are falling apart. There is not a oneness that holds through the routineness of life, through the trials, or the temptations. Many husbands and wives simply exist together. Instead of being involved in one another's lives, they simply share the same home, paycheck, debts, bed, and children. And so one day when the boring routine of it all becomes too much, or the pressure of a trial overtakes them, or one partner finds someone of the opposite sex whom he or she can talk with—the marriage is over. You stand there thunderstruck, it's dissolved. After years together, one walks away as if those years had never existed. How can it happen?

You may say, "It is because they do not know Jesus Christ." Yet the same thing is happening to people who profess to know Christ and who even serve in the church. Many of them are walking away from their marriages. It seems we can understand when those in the world walk out of their marriages, but how can Christians do it? How can pastors, preachers, evangelists, Sunday school workers, deacons, church members do it?

Recently a friend returned home after taking care of her mother,

161

only to have her husband serve her with divorce papers. There had been no inkling of it whatever! The family had just vacationed together; their grown children had returned to their jobs. Everything seemed fine. This couple moved within a Christian circle of friends. He had held positions of leadership in the church, had led congregational prayer many times, and had sat under strong Bible teaching. Now he wanted no more of it. He would not even talk to the men who came to reason with him from the Scriptures. The "other woman" worked in his office. Even at the risk of losing the fellowship of his children, she was his choice.

It's insane, isn't it? Yet is is happening more and more. Why is it happening to Christians? Could it happen to you? To me? Is there not any way to keep it from happening? Yes, there is, and I do not believe I am being simplistic. I believe the whole key to it is communication. We'll talk about it tomorrow. However the question today is: do you want to be kept from it? At what cost?

May 29

There is a spirit of harlotry in our land as there was in the days of Hosea (Hosea 5:4). It is a spiritual harlotry that, unchecked, manifests itself in physical harlotry. The end of it all is a society of adulterers.

Unfortunately, adultery . . . spiritual and physical . . . has permeated the church until we need to put quarantine signs on our church doors. It is like an epidemic that is spreading so rapidly it cannot be contained. Even our precious young ones are being struck down.

Why? And why are so many Christian leaders divorcing their mates, and then remarrying? If the leaders are falling, what will happen to the followers?

As I told you yesterday, I believe God has shown me that a major part of the problem has to do with communication. Remember, I said there could be *no oneness without communication.* If I am going to be one with another, I must know his character, his ways, his thoughts, his goals and purposes, his heart. There has to be that absorbing of one another, that mutual sharing in common. This, Beloved, is impossible without communication. If I am going to be one with anyone, I have to spend time with him. Otherwise our relationship will only be a superficial one that I can walk away from, even forget. If two remain two, although they bear the same name, live in the same house, have the same children, it is very easy to split them in two. However, if the two become one, no one can split them apart. You would have to tear them. And even then you couldn't tear them into two separate, viable parts because the nature of oneness would make it impossible.

Marriages are being split because two have never become one. **Christians are walking away from their mates because they have never become one with God.** Oneness with God holds you in marriage, because oneness with God insures that you share His mind, His heart on the sanctity of marriage. So, Christian leaders are walking out on their marriages because they are not one with God, and they are not one with God because they have been too busy or too preoccupied or too apathetic to communicate with God, to spend time with Him. That, Beloved, is the key to oneness, not only with God, but with your mate, or with anyone with whom you would be one! It will never happen apart from time alone—sharing, listening, hearing one another. You can only learn oneness in quietness and solitude with your God. And only oneness with Him will enable you to know the commitment of oneness with another person.

But we're too busy, aren't we? Or are we? What are we doing that is more important than this? And is it worth it?

May 30

This month, Beloved, we have barely touched on oneness with our family, our spouse, and our church. We have not yet even looked at the specific things required to achieve oneness with another, be it God or your husband or your children or the members of your church. And this is where the day-by-day practicality of it all becomes reality.

Next month, we will do this, step by step, application by application. It will be like a handbook on oneness. We'll look at commitment, how it is made and what it takes. We'll consider communication, and practical ways it can be achieved, and the importance of contact and concession in relationships. We'll see how oneness is achieved step by step through the circumstances of life. We'll look at Christian dos, don'ts, and differences, and how to live with them in peace, in unity.

But today and tomorrow I want to tell you how I spend time alone with my God sharing, talking, and listening to Him.

First, if I am going to communicate with God, and I mean really communicate with Him, I must realize that it is going to take time. You can't just run into God's presence, spit out the whole ball of wax to Him in a rush of words, read your Bible for a few minutes, and then run out. To do so leaves God standing there alone, with His mouth open and His arms stretched out. You have already gone on your hurried, hectic way. There has been no communication. It has all been one-sided. You've spoken, God has listened, and then you've gone, before He has had a chance to say a word. No, Beloved, it takes time—time alone with Him, undistracted, and preferably uninterrupted. There is no substitute for time.

When will that time be? That is up to you. Just know that without it there will be **no** communication. And without communication there will be no oneness. Rather, you will find an apathy or coldness creeping in. When you turn off the heat in the house, it takes a while for the cold to settle in. When you turn on the heat, it takes a while to warm up the house. Neither is sudden. It is the same in your relationship with God.

Ask God to show you where and how to set aside time each day so you two can be alone. He'll have a way. All you have to do is agree to it and make it your number one priority.

May 31

When you fall in love, no sacrifice is too great in order to be with your lover. But being together is not enough; you also want to be alone with each other. You have to be alone. You want to talk, to share, and you have to take time to listen. You spend several hours together and you can't believe where the time has gone. You separate, but he's on your mind. You think about what you shared. And if you get a minute, you call . . . just to touch base. And it's wonderful. You love it.

But did it start out that way? No, not right at first. At first you had to make contact some way. Oh, there might have been an instant attraction. If so, you couldn't wait for a second time together. But usually even these times took scheduling, planning, commitment. But, as the relationship deepened, you wanted more and more time together. This, Beloved, is much the way it will be with God. Your desire to be with Him, to spend more time in His presence, will grow, but at first it will take careful planning and commitment. So set aside that time. Usually you will find the morning to be best, before you are caught up in the activity, pressures, and demands of the day. Or evenings might be better for you. Any time of day is adequate so long as you are certain you can be alone. Although I am a "night person," the mornings are best for me because, as a result, I find myself calling on Him during the day to continue, or to consult on what went on in our morning time together. There are days when we can't spend but just a few minutes alone, but I don't panic or feel abandoned, forsaken or unloved. After all, ours is a mutual relationship. He cares, He understands, and I know He understands. His love for me is unconditional; it is not based on performance. He knows my heart belongs to Him. He knows my commitment to Him. And the wonder of wonders is that, when I'm ready, He's always there, available, accessible. Yet I know that He does not like to hurry. I have to take time, undistracted. Thus I try to keep a set time for us.

Usually as we begin our time together, I let Him do all the talking after I tell Him that I love Him and want our time to be precious together and pleasing to Him. So, unless I am troubled or weighed down I read systematically through His Word. I read until something comes alive, speaks to me, convicts me, delights me, or puzzles me. When this happens I usually stop to think about it or to talk to Him about it. Sometimes it causes me to think of others, so I pray for them. Often I'll just stop and think. At these times, when I get really quiet, I usually hear His voice. Oh, I don't mean audibly; but rather, I hear that still, small voice that comes as a thought. Sometimes you wonder whether it is your thought or His but usually, if it is His, it will come to you again and again. It is usually in these quiet times that I get my directions from Him.

Then I usually find myself getting on the floor in a knee-chest position or flat on my face and I pour out my heart to Him. Sometimes when I am under a lot of pressure to get things done and to meet deadlines I put a pad and pen beside me. Then, when I think of something I need to do, I jot it down rather than try to remember. If the phone rings, I don't answer it. I try to avoid any distractions.

You see, this time is essential. I must have it; I must be alone with my God if we are ever to be one! There is no other way! And so must you, Precious One.

JUNE

Making Oneness Your Goal

June 1

It is not often that I am out "in the world," but in the past two weeks I have been there, and my heart has literally been broken. Generous friends loaned Jack and me their beach home for two weeks, and so we had delightful seclusion in which to write. However, from time to time as we went out, God allowed me to see the hurt and the world's rebellion in a fresh way.

As I walked the streets, watched the people, sat in restaurants and talked to waiters and clerks . . . I realized that this is where most of you are living. It seems to be a miniature version of hell, inhabited and run by people who are walking independently of God, many with no restraints whatsoever. I work with professional people who love Jesus Christ and who have given their energies and time to serving their Lord at Reach Out's thirty-two acres where I live. Here are green trees on protective hills by a quiet little stream. When I leave this place it is almost always to go somewhere to teach God's Word. Oh, once in a while, I go to the grocery store or the mall, but even the local beauty shop is owned by Christians. It is a sheltered environment. Being out in the world gives me culture shock. I have ached, I have hurt, I have wept. And I have cried out to God for forgiveness because we have made such a mess out of His creation.

And I have thought of you. Bless your hearts. I know it's hard, so hard. At times you must want to say to God, "Stop the world. I've got to get off. I can't take it anymore."

O Beloved, if I need encouragement in my sheltered environment, you must surely need it where you are. "As Thou didst send Me into the world, I also have sent them into the world" (John 17:8). He lived in this world, unsheltered, for thirty-three years, and it was just as corrupt then as it is now. He understands, and this is why He has laid this subject on my heart, to help you know how to live in a world such as ours and still be one with Him.

166

June 2

I will never forget what happened during our stay on the beach. Late one night, we stood on the second floor deck and watched the most majestic display of lightning and clouds I have ever seen. As the thunder rolled above the ocean waves and the lightning darted across the blackened sky, these words glowed in my mind: "For just as the lightning comes from the east, and flashes even to the west so shall the coming of the Son of Man be" (Matthew 24:27). My heart was full as it seemed God had turned back a corner of the veil over eternity and, for one brief moment, had allowed me to see a glimpse of His mighty power.

The next day, we walked down the beach. It was alive with people racing in cars, racing into each other's arms, racing to find a good time . . . a moment of pleasure. Then, I saw it. Several teenagers had rented a house, and there hanging from the second floor window was a bed-sheet made into an obscene sign big enough for everyone on the beach to see. It faced the ocean; it faced eternity, in puny rebellion, flapping in the face of God. With offensive rancor, it mocked the marriage union that God had declared holy. Overwhelming grief and burning indignation literally consumed me, and I felt compelled of God to speak in defense of His name. I went up to the house, knowing that I went armed with my Sovereign's sword and shield, and proclaimed His truth. I shared His hurt. I conveyed His love, and then, in grief and humility, I committed the whole situation to God who judges right-eously.

Beloved, situations like this bring me back time and time again to the determination that, no matter what the cost, we must press on to-ward the goal of Christlikeness. We must know oneness with our God so that the world will again see Jesus as He lives in us, clothed in a hu-manity so transparent that His glory radiates through it. And then, be-cause His light dispels the darkness, we will be able to show men in a corrupt world how they can live.

Until we show them how, they will never know how they can live! ". . . God is light, and in Him there is no darkness at all" (1 John 1:5).

June 3

God's ultimate goal for every one of His children is oneness with Him. The oneness that was lost through sin and gained in salvation is learned, achieved, developed, and matured only in the laboratory of life. Thus, the Son prayed to the Father on our behalf:

They themselves are in the world ... Holy Father, keep them in Thy name, the name which Thou hast given Me, that they may be one, even as We are ... I do not ask Thee to take them out of the world, but to keep them from the evil one ... And the glory which Thou hast given Me I have given to them; that they may be one, just as We are one; I in them, and Thou in Me, that they may be perfected in unity, that the world may know that Thou didst send Me, and didst love them, even as Thou didst love Me (John 17:11, 15, 22, 23).

Oneness is to be achieved in all of life's everydayness, in all its relationships, in all its trials. Everything that happens to you is permitted by a Sovereign God to draw you into oneness with Him. He permits it all and He answers His Son's prayer to keep you in the midst of it all. To keep you means that He watches over you and preserves you so that you can come through any situation as more than a conqueror. However, His keeping power is never forced upon you; it must be appropriated. The provision is yours to claim.

O Beloved, how vital it is that we realize that our response to any situation is more important even than the situation itself. If I am to be one with my God, I must do nothing on my own initiative. I must not seek my own will or my own way, but always do those things that please the Father (John 8:28).

So, Beloved, as we begin to meditate on oneness, know that it is yours for the taking in this life no matter what the circumstances—because God will keep you (see 1 Corinthians 10:13).

Do you believe that God will make a way for you regardless of the circumstances? Tell the Father. Write it out. It will be good for you.

June 4

God uses three major earthly relationships in order for you to achieve oneness with Him. They are your relationship with the members of your family, your spouse (if you are married), and the church. These are the most intimate, binding relationships in which you will ever find yourself. Except for marriage, they are not relationships of your personal choice. You don't choose your parents or your natural brothers and sisters anymore than you choose your brothers and sisters in Christ.

These relationships all limit your independence and teach you dependence. And this, Beloved, is the way oneness is achieved, for oneness only occurs when you yield yourself, blend yourself, and mold yourself into another until you become one with that person in mind, heart, and purpose, regarding others as more important than yourself (Philippians 2:3). Even as Paul wrote, "Only conduct yourself in a manner worthy of the gospel of Christ; so that whether I come and see you or remain absent, I may hear of you that you are standing firm in one spirit, with one mind striving together for the faith of the gospel" (Philippians 1:27). "Make my joy complete by being of the same mind, maintaining the same love, united in spirit, intent on one purpose" (Philippians 2:2). This, Beloved, is oneness—be it with God or with man.

This month we are going to see how this oneness is lived out on a day-to-day basis. As we begin, write out a brief evaluation of each of the earthly relationships in which you are involved.

June 5

Oneness is a sharing in common, a fellowship; and it is impossible without openness and honesty. You will never achieve oneness with God or man if you are holding anything against another. That thing must be confessed.

In his first epistle, John writes, "If we say that we have fellowship with Him and yet walk in the darkness, we lie and do not practice the truth: but if we walk in the light as He Himself is the light, we have fellowship with one another, and the blood of Jesus His Son cleanses us from all sin" (1 John 1:6, 7).

But confessing or making things right is a humbling process. It's not easy to admit that we were wrong, or that we did not behave as we should have. So we hide our failings, cover up our faults, and rationalize them. But still they are there under the blanket of our excuses.

Have you ever made a bed, pulled up the spread, and tucked in the pillows only to discover a lump near the foot of the bed? You try smoothing it, but usually you have to pull back the covers and expose the problem.

If you are ever going to be one with your God, your family, your spouse, or your church, you must expose the sin. If something is wrong it must be brought out into the open and dealt with. This is true with God, and with man.

David cried, "When I kept silent about my sin, my body wasted away through my groaning all day long. For day and night Thy hand was heavy upon me; my vitality was drained away as with the fever-heat of summer. I acknowledged my sin to Thee, and my iniquity I did not hide; I said, 'I will confess my transgressions to the Lord'; and Thou didst forgive the guilt of my sin" (Psalms 32:3–5).

Unconfessed sin, unrighted wrongs take their toll on any relationship. We are built so that we cannot keep silent about them without being affected. Confession, though painful, brings a sweet release. But what if there's no forgiveness? We'll talk about that tomorrow. Today spend time mentally walking through your relationships. See anything that needs cleansing? If so, write it down in your notebook, and then get busy.

June 6

I had just finished teaching on the necessity of forgiving others, and people were standing around waiting to talk with me. When all had finished, two women came up to tell me "how much the message had meant . . . BUT." It's the *buts* that get you!

One said that another woman had taken her husband from her and that as a result, her husband took his life. She had forgiven this woman, she said, though it had been hard. She didn't hold anything against her. But she had never talked to the woman though they lived in the same town. She knew that the woman was miserable, but she wouldn't talk to her or seek to verbally express her forgiveness.

I had to share with her that if she were ever to be one with God she would have to be willing to minister to that woman. True forgiveness behaves as if it were never offended, never hurt. This is forgiving from the heart. Without forgiveness you will never know oneness in your family, your marriage or your church. And without true forgiveness you will never know oneness with your God. What is it you pray when you say the Lord's Prayer? "And forgive us our debts, as we also have forgiven our debtors" (Matthew 6:12).

Did you notice the word *as?* Jesus followed up His model prayer with this very interesting statement, "For if you forgive men for their transgressions, your heavenly Father will also forgive you. But if you do not forgive men, then your Father will not forgive your transgression" (Matthew 6:14, 15). That's a pretty heavy statement, isn't it? Many have tried to water it down. Why? Because they say, "Surely God doesn't expect that of me. Why, look what they've done!"

Maybe I don't understand; maybe I have never been hurt like that or treated so unjustly. But Jesus understands. He suffered it all and did not in the slightest way deserve it, and yet He said "Father, forgive them."

"Yes," you may say, "but. . . ." It's the *buts* that will keep you from being one with the Father, your family, your spouse, your brothers and sisters in Christ. Is it worth it?

June 7

Confession and forgiveness are so vital that I cannot pass over the subject lightly. Without them, as I said before, you will never know oneness, no matter how hard you try. Many people are held captive in torture chambers of their own making. They thrive on their self-inflicted wounds. "He who conceals his transgressions will not prosper, but he who confesses and forsakes them will find compassion" (Proverbs 28:13). To withhold forgiveness, to harbor pain, hurt and bitterness, to refuse to extend the love and forgiveness of God to anyone is to conceal transgressions, and God cannot prosper you. Nor can your relationships prosper.

Turn in your Bible to Matthew 18:18–35 and listen carefully as you read the parable our Lord gave. Meditate upon it.

Now, let me ask one last question. Is there anyone you have not forgiven *from your heart?* If your answer is "No," then there is not one single person upon whom you could not bestow the unconditional love of God.

June 8

If you are to be one with anyone, God or man, you must be totally committed on your part. There can never be any blending of two into one without it, for commitment involves a yielding of yourself to another unconditionally. Today we know very little about this. One of the significant signs of the degradation of the last days is a lack of commitment, "For men will be lovers of self, lovers of money, boastful, arrogant, revilers, disobedient to parents, ungrateful, unholy, unloving, irreconcilable, malicious gossips, without self-control, brutal, haters of good, treacherous, reckless, conceited, lovers of pleasure rather than lovers of God" (2 Timothy 3:2–4). Examine each of these one by one and you will find that every one centers around self and the lusts of the flesh rather than the laying down of life for the good of others.

Commitments and promises are made in the passion of the moment, only to be wrenched away at the inconsistent whim of the one who spoke the words without counting the cost. And there the rejected one stands—dismayed, disarmed, disillusioned—and if not stable or secure within himself, destroyed.

As I write this, one hundred and seventeen teenagers are down in Reach Out's valley, participating in our two-week Boot Camp. Many of them bear unbelievable scars. One girl was raped by her stepfather and as a consequence was rejected by her real mother. There's a dear young man about fourteen whose dad left him and the rest of the family for a nineteen-year-old girl. I could go on and on, and I imagine you could also, telling of broken lives because of broken commitments. Maybe even you are hurting because a promise was made and then broken. How strong are your commitments to others? How secure are they?

June 9

Everyone's not bad. There are men and women of their word. Most of them, however, I believe, belong to an older generation. Right is right, wrong is wrong, and they are going to stake their lives on their convictions. They are the ones who would lay down their lives for what they believe. I love that. There's something so high, so noble, so glorious about it. When I see it, I respect it. It awakens within me the desire to lay down my life for what is right.

Many times I read of it or see it in men and women who don't even know Jesus Christ; yet I cannot help but admire such commitment. It seems so rare. And I think, "O Father, they do not even know You. They do not even have the sure hope of eternal life and I do. O Father, may I be as committed to You, to Your Word, and to Your work."

I can't help but wonder: Isn't this longing in the breasts of others? Is it not to be found somewhere deep inside the bosom of every human being? Is it not a fragment of God's image left in human flesh? For me, commitment is synonymous with God, a God who so loved, who was so committed that He gave His only begotten Son to a world which deserved to perish. A God who "demonstrates His own love toward us, in that while we were yet sinners, Christ died for us" (Romans 5:8). A God who did not spare His own Son but gave Him up for us all (Romans 8:32). A God who is the same yesterday, today, and forever (Hebrews 13:8). A God who cannot lie, whose promises are yes and Amen (2 Corinthians 1:20). A God who remains faithful, even if we are faithless, for He cannot deny Himself (2 Timothy 2:13).

If you and I are to be one with Him, will we not also have to be men and women of commitment? Will not our love for others be unconditional? Will not we seek another's highest good rather than our own? Will not right be right and wrong be wrong? Will not there be things we cannot compromise because of our commitment to our God? And will this not hold us even to death if necessary?

How committed are you . . .

to God?
to truth?
to your spouse?
to your family?
to your church?

Write out your answers, and, seeing it in black and white, deal with your commitment.

June 10

In Romans 12, God calls us to unconditional commitment. "I urge you therefore, brethren, by the mercies of God, to present your bodies a living and holy sacrifice, acceptable to God, which is your spiritual (rational) service of worship" (verse 1).

Commitment calls for commitment. God longs for, thus He beseeches or pleads for unconditional commitment from us. Whether we yield or not will have no effect on His commitment to us; that has been settled. Yet He longs for it to be returned. And if we stop to rationally consider it, how can we do any less in the light of the words of His love? This is worship, true worship!

God calls us to a commitment so total, so final that He asks us to give ourselves to Him. The verb *to present* is in the aorist tense in the Greek and indicates giving ourselves to Him once for all time. God is asking for all—our bodies, that which houses our spirit and soul to be presented to Him as a living sacrifice. And He asks this in the light of His sacrifice.

I gave My back to those who strike Me, and My cheeks to those who pluck out the beard; I did not cover My face from humiliation and spitting. . . . I have set My face like flint (Isaiah 50:6, 7). But He was pierced through for our transgressions. He was crushed for our iniquities; the chastening of our well-being fell upon Him, and by His scourging we are healed (Isaiah 53:5). And He Himself bore our sins in His body on the cross, that we might die to sin and live to righteousness; for by His wounds you were healed. For you were continually straying like sheep, but now you have returned to the Shepherd and Guardian of your souls (1 Peter 2:24, 25).

God was committed to you even at the cost of His Son. Jesus was committed to you even at the cost of His life. And all this was when you were nothing but a sinner, an enemy of God. What is God asking of you? Total commitment to One Who could not love you more; He has given His all.

June 11

In the Old Testament order of worship there were two main classes of Jewish sacrifices—those associated with reconciliation and those having to do with consecration. The three sacrifices having to do with reconciliation were the sin offering, the trespass offering, and the peace offering. The sacrifices of consecration were the burnt offering and the meal offering. Any time an animal was to be sacrificed in any one of these offerings, that animal had to be without spot or blemish.

The sacrifice for which God is calling in Romans 12:1 is of a Christian's total being to the service and worship of God. It is, therefore, a parallel to the burnt offering, a sacrifice of our bodies which house all that we are! This cannot be a plea for salvation or anything connected with our receiving Jesus Christ; for to present ourselves to God in that condition would be to offer ourselves with our spots, our blemishes, our sins. And that is unacceptable. Jesus, the Lamb of God that takes away the sin of the world, was the offering that would reconcile us to God, removing the enmity caused by our sin. You were redeemed "with precious blood as of a lamb unblemished and spotless, the blood of Christ" (1 Peter 1:19).

In Romans 12:1 the call of commitment is to the reconciled, to sinners made saints. Thus God calls us to present our bodies a living sacrifice—holy, acceptable to God. And we can come to Him as holy ones because we have been cleansed by the blood of Jesus Christ. We are now acceptable because we have been accepted in the Beloved (Ephesians 1:6 KJV). The word *holy* and the word *saints* both come from the same root word which means set apart unto God. So God's call is to those who have been set apart unto Him. He longs for those to commit themselves to Him unconditionally for His service wherever it may be, whatever it may cost.

Beloved, not all Christians have made this commitment to God. Have you?

June 12

It is my commitment to God that gives strength and stability to my other commitments.

Remember when I said that the sacrifice of Romans 12:1 parallels the burnt offering of the Old Testament sacrifices? Think with me now about the burnt offering so that you can clearly understand what God is calling for.

When some offerings were made, portions of the animal sacrifice were reserved for the priest and/or the people. However, when the burnt offering was presented, the entire animal was cut into pieces and arranged upon the wood on the altar. The priest offered up "in smoke all of it on the altar for a burnt offering, an offering by fire of a soothing aroma to the Lord" (Leviticus 1:9). Thus it was a "once for all" offering—a total dedication.

Rededication is unnecessary, when there has been a true and genuine dedication! This may blow your theology, but check your theology! You will not find rededication in the Bible. You see, Precious Ones, we call for rededication because we do not understand real commitment. Do-or-die commitment.

You may say, "But what if I can't keep my commitment to God?" O Beloved, you can for God is the keeper! When Jesus prayed in John 17 for your oneness with the Father, He asked the Father to keep you. Your God is your keeper. Paul knew this and lived in the light of it. He said, "For I know whom I have believed and I am convinced that He is able to guard what I have entrusted to Him until that day" (2 Timothy 1:12).

The priests had flesh hooks and if part of the animal started to slip off the altar of sacrifice, then they would use the flesh hooks to keep it on the altar.

You make the commitment, Beloved, and God will keep you. There will be no need for rededication after rededication, because there has been a genuine, total dedication—an unconditional commitment to your God to serve Him because you have perceived His worth, even as He perceived yours and committed Himself to you unconditionally.

June 13

When God presented Eve to Adam, it was so they might become one flesh. In speaking of this, Jesus said:

> Have you not read that He who created them from the beginning made them male and female, and said, For this cause a man shall leave his father and mother, and shall cleave to his wife; and the two shall become one flesh? Consequently they are no more two, but one flesh. What therefore God has joined together, let no man separate (Matthew 19:4–6).

God's design for marriage is oneness, and oneness involves total, unconditional commitment, "for better or for worse, for richer or for poorer, in sickness and in health, until death do us part"! God's commitment to us is like that, except that even death does not end our relationship with Him! And this is why God draws a parallel between the marriage union and His union with His bride, the church. Both are to be unions of permanence, of total commitment, of two becoming one.

So husbands ought also to love their own wives as their own bodies. He who loves his own wife loves himself; for no one ever hated his own flesh, but nourishes and cherishes it, just as Christ also does the church, because we are members of His body. For this cause a man shall leave his father and mother, and shall cleave to his wife; and the two shall become one flesh. This mystery is great; but I am speaking with reference to Christ and the church (Ephesians 5:28–32).

From the beginning, divorce has not been God's desire or His will (Matthew 19:8). God says "I hate divorce" (Malachi 2:16). To walk out on your marriage partner is to deal treacherously, because your mate "is your companion and your wife by covenant" (Malachi 2:14). A covenant is a solemn, binding agreement only to be broken by death. Therefore, a covenant is a commitment for life.

Beloved, when you break God's earthly figure of marriage you distort the heavenly reality of Christ and His unconditional, eternal commitment to His bride. This is why God hates divorce. Now I realize that many of you hate it also, and yet you are divorced. God understands. He knows every detail. But to those of you who are married I would ask, in God's stead, how committed are you to your marriage?

June 14

What would it take for you to renege on a commitment? Once you have committed yourself to another, what would cause you to draw back—to withhold yourself, your care, and your love? If commitment is based on pleasure derived from the *object* of one's commitment then age
    disfigurement
       personality flaws
          changing interests
             and fluctuating circumstances
could sever the tie. The true test of your commitment comes only in the throes of disappointments, hurts, and changing affections. Words of commitment come easily when standing at an altar amid orange blossoms with a young, lovely girl looking adoringly into your eyes. The test of your vow comes later, when that same girl is moody in her

monthly cycle, nauseated in pregnancy, unpredictable in the midst of the pressures of children and family. Will your commitment stand the test of living with her, caring for her day in and day out? Will you stand by your word even if the "for better" turns into "for worse" and "in health" becomes "in sickness"? The Lord God of the Universe made a vow to His beloved wife, Israel, who has yet to turn out "for better":

> O Israel, Fear not; for I have redeemed thee, I have called thee by thy name; thou art mine. When thou passest through the waters, I will be with thee; and through the rivers, they shall not overflow thee; when thou walkest through the fire, thou shalt not be burned; neither shall the flame kindle upon thee . . . I have loved thee . . . (Isaiah 43:2, 4 KJV).

Did you make a commitment to your mate that has somehow grown weak, or worn thin? Beloved, today can be a day of renewing, of rebuilding, of remembering. Write out in your notebook your commitment to your mate. If you are really serious about it, make a copy and give it to the one who is yours.

June 15

Dr. Ed Wheat in his outstanding book, *Love Life For Every Married Couple,* gives the most beautiful example of unconditional love that he ever had the privilege of witnessing. And I want to share it with you.

> In this case a man loved his wife tenderly and steadfastly for a total of fifteen years without any responding love on her part. There could be no response, for she had developed cerebral arteriosclerosis, the chronic brain syndrome.

> At the onset of the disease she was a pretty, vivacious lady of sixty who looked at least ten years younger. In the beginning she experienced intermittent times of confusion. For instance, she would drive to Little Rock, then find herself at an intersection without knowing where she was, or why, or how to get back home. As a former schoolteacher, she had enjoyed driving her own car for many years. But finally her husband had to take away her car keys for her safety.

> As the disease progressed, she gradually lost all her mental faculties and did not even recognize her husband. He took care of her at home by himself for the first five years. During that time he often took her for visits, she looking her prettiest although she had no idea of where she was, and he proudly displaying her as his wife, introducing her to everyone, even though her remarks were apt to be inappropriate to the con-

versation. He never made an apology for her; he never indicated that there was anything wrong with what she had just said. He always treated her with the utmost courtesy. He showered her with love and attention, no matter what she said or did.

The time came when the doctors said she had to go into a nursing home for intensive care. She lived there for ten years (part of that time bedfast with arthritis) and he was with her daily. As long as she was able to sit up, he took her for a drive each afternoon—out to their farm, or downtown, or to visit the family—never in any way embarrassed that she was so far out of touch. He never made a negative comment about her. He did not begrudge the large amount of money required to keep her in the home all those years, never even hinted that it might be a problem. In fact, he never complained about any detail of her care throughout the long illness. He always obtained the best for her.

This man was loyal, always true to his wife, even though his love had no response for fifteen years. This is agape, not in theory, but in practice!

I can speak of this case with intimate knowledge, for these people were my own wonderful parents. What my father taught me about agape love through his example I can never forget.[12]

What does your marriage teach your children about unconditional commitment? Write it out.

June 16

My mom and dad used to tell me, "Kay, we want you to know that no matter what you do, no matter whatever happens to you, you can always come home." I know that they meant it. They never kept me in line by threatening to remove their love. Their love was unconditional and I was secure because of it. I was never a winner as a child or a teenager. I was never outstanding in anything although I tried my hardest! I never ran with the popular set. Oh, I wanted to, but I just didn't have what it took. We moved a lot; I have never had the security of a lifetime friend. I went to twelve grade schools and four high schools. It seemed to me that when I was growing up I was always the kid on the outside looking in, dreaming of how I could "wow" them if I ever got inside. I never did.

Yet, despite it all I have always had a sense of well-being, of security, because I have known that Mom and Dad loved me completely and unconditionally. Talk about oneness in a family—we had it! I might get mad, frustrated, and exasperated with my parents. I might even grumble and complain, but you'd better not say anything against them or I would take you on with both fists flying! I never heard Mom or Dad disparage one another, nor did I ever hear them talk down to us! We may have had differences among ourselves but united we stood before the world! We were committed to one another.

This, Beloved, is one of the main functions of a family. A family is to provide that emotional security and well-being that every human being needs in order to function as a healthy, whole individual. Let your children be secure in the fact that they are loved not because of their performance—but because you see unique value in them as people and are unconditionally committed to them—and you will, in all probability, raise sons and daughters who are able to relax and love others freely.

Are your children secure in your love for them? _____ Do they realize your love for them is unconditional? _____ Is it? _____ How do they know? _____

June 17

What is your commitment like when you are strung tightly, when the pressure that you're under seems more than you can bear? What is your pursuit of oneness like when your anxiety level is high and your tolerance level is low?

Many times when the oneness in your relationships is fractured, it's not because the object of your love has altered or grown objectionable; rather, it's because you yourself are bound up with your own pressures.

True commitment is consistent. Depression, worry, illness, fatigue, or hormones should not affect your commitment if it is real. Your spouse and children should never have to wonder where they stand with you on a certain day. They should always know because your courtesy, kindness, and love will supersede your pressures and anxieties.

I once visited a friend in the hospital. Her head and neck were in a heavy brace. Bolts anchored her head in the contraption that looked like a device for torture. She had battled cancer for several years, and now it had hit her spinal cord. The brace and radiation were a last ditch medical effort to enable her to walk. The doctors had told her she would be in the brace at least six months. The whole time I visited with her, her face shone with sweetness, and she spoke of her husband and children with love, concern, and compassion in much the same way she would if we had been having lunch. Her circumstances, painful

179

and confining as they were, did not alter her concern and commitment to those she loved. No matter how she felt, her family knew that they were first!

The Lord Jesus, while enduring the pressure and awesome agony of the cross, had the love and compassion to see that His mother was cared for. "When Jesus, therefore, saw his mother, and the disciple standing by, whom he loved, he saith unto his mother, Woman, behold thy son!" (John 19:26 KJV).

Beloved, are you handling your pressure so that your family knows you really care? Is your desire for oneness evident in every situation? If not, then why not?

June 18

Have you ever experienced a coldness in your relationship with God? Or does that seem to be the case most of the time? Have you ever listened to others talk of their relationship with God and wondered why your heart did not burn with fervency as theirs did? You almost envied their seeming intimacy with Him, and possibly felt angry, jealous, or indignant with them! Why, they talked of God as if they had an "in" with Him! Were they putting on or was it real? You wanted to ask, but unless you were quite secure, you didn't. It might expose you. So instead you talked the talk. You agreed. Contributed enough to get by. Went home and wondered: "Why don't I have a relationship like that with God?"

Well, Beloved, a relationship like that does not come over night. No relationship does. A relationship like that takes time; it takes exposure; it takes contact.

If your heart is ever to glow with ardor for your God, you will have to spend time with Him, and the only way to spend time with Him is through His Word. Not just reading it, but hearing it, listening carefully until you hear Him explain His words to you. Then you will say, like the two on the road to Emmaus, "Were not our hearts burning within us while He was speaking to us on the road, while He was explaining the Scriptures to us?" (Luke 24:32).

As Jesus prayed for our oneness in John 17, He asked the Father to sanctify us "through thy truth. Thy word is truth." To *sanctify* means to set apart unto God. This is done through exposure to His Word, to truth. In the Word you discover that which is reality, that which is truth, that which is of God. And as you spend time with Him the embers are fanned more and more until you burn with the fervency of white heat!

Look at the relationship between God the Father and His Son and you will see how vital their time together was! Jesus was constantly praying. He took time to be alone with the Father. They were so *one* that the words Jesus spoke were not His own, but the Father's (John 14:10). This is oneness—to speak as another would speak, without contradiction. But to speak that way, you must spend time together. It only comes through contact, and contact brings warmth to a relationship.

What kind of contact do you have with your God. How much exposure do you have to Him?

June 19

The one major reason for the disintegration of the American family is that men have neglected the Word of God. I believe with all my heart that, were God to appear and judge our country, He would hold the men most accountable. Men have forfeited their God-given role and as a matter of course have upset the God-ordained order of the home.

If I had to give the second major reason for the disintegration of the American family, I would agree with Dr. James Dobson, it is overcommitment. Overcommitment to our jobs, our professions, our societies and clubs, our social responsibilities, our education, our churches. We are everywhere but at home. And when we get home we are wrung out, strung out, and don't want to be bothered. Too tired to spend time with our families, we check out in front of a television set that entertains us without demanding anything from us. We feel we've got to relax. We deserve a break. After all, we've worked hard to get our family all the luxuries of life . . . now let them enjoy them in silence. They can talk during the commercials.

"Sesame Street" has replaced the education a child once received on mother's lap as she "read" wordless books and ran her fingers through baby fine hair. "See the boat. What color is the boat? . . . That's right! It's red. Mommy's so proud!" Instead, the child sits alone watching B–O–A–T bounce all over the television screen. Then R–E–D . . . R–E–D B–O–A–T. Little legs rock back and forth on the floor, never coming into contact with the warmth of Mamma's legs and knees on the couch. No arms to cradle him; they are committed to other things. When Daddy comes home, it's late. He's tired. Too tired to wrestle, too tired to pass a ball, too tired to have a tea party, too tired to take his fifteen-year-old out for a driving lesson, Oh well, he can take Driver's

Ed at school. Besides you promised you'd buy him a car. Your dad never did that for you. What more could he ask?

What more could he . . . or she . . . or your spouse ask? Your time!!! How much time have you given your family this week? Enough to bring you into oneness with them?

Ask God to show you how you are to spend time with each one in your family. Then, write out your commitment to what He shows you.

June 20

God knew that two could not become one overnight! Oneness takes exposure and time. Thus He had Moses give the following command to the children of Israel, "When a man takes a new wife, he shall not go out with the army, nor be charged with any duty; he shall be free at home one year and shall give happiness to his wife whom he has taken" (Deuteronomy 24:5).

Oneness in the family begins with the oneness of husband and wife. That year at home was to be the bedrock foundation of the whole marriage union. It was to be a time when the husband would learn how to cheer his wife, how to brighten her up, to bring her glee; this is what the word *happiness* implies in the Hebrew language.

This first year of marriage is to be committed to establishing and strengthening the vows they have made. This is a time to learn of one another's needs, to develop activities they could mutually share and enjoy. This is a time to grow into oneness of mind, of heart, of purpose—a time for the husband to get to know his wife so that he might live with her "in an understanding way, as with a weaker vessel, since she is a woman" (1 Peter 3:7). Women are different from men. Let's admit it. They take getting used to! And since the husband is to love his wife as Christ loved the church, and nourish her and cherish her as he does his own flesh, he needs time to learn how!

If husbands would only learn that a little time spent in undistracted devotion to their wives goes a long, long way, what pressure and guilt they could rid themselves of. There needs to be contact someplace besides in the bedroom. It will make all the difference in the world for it will bring you into a oneness that would be difficult for anyone to sever!

The same is true for wives. We can become so preoccupied with our household duties or the demands of motherhood that we neglect our husbands. How surprised I was recently to hear men tell their wives that they wished their wives had more time for them. Have you ever

182

thought of taking walks together, of lingering over meals and letting the dishes go, or having an evening alone every now and then?

Today, why don't you take time to think about specific things that you can do that would draw you closer to one another, things that would please your mate. Write them out. Now, write on a sheet of paper, "Things That Would Please My Husband", and "Things That Would Please My Wife." Fill in the appropriate heading. Then under the heading that would pertain to you if your mate were filling it in, write down some things you would love to have your mate do for you.

June 21

You will never be *one* with another without communication. This is why so many relationships fail. When people feel like strangers, it is easy to say good-bye. For the next several days we are going to talk about oneness with others through communication. But first, let's think for today about knowing the will of God, something that is impossible without communication.

Oneness with God has a price. It is the discipline of one's time. God, in His plea for consecration in Romans 12:1, calls us to a "sacrifice" of time in order that we might come to know Him and, in knowing Him through His Word, to know His will. Listen to His words, spoken in the imperative: "And do not be conformed to this world, but be transformed by the renewing of your mind, that you may prove what the will of God is, that which is good and acceptable and perfect" (Romans 12:2). God gives us this command for He knows that unless we know His Word, we will never know Him or His will.

What amazes me is how many are afraid of the will of God. They feel that His will must be something horrible, painful, cruel, ugly, or at least that it will squelch their dreams, hopes, ambitions, or talents. The will of God is probably going to some far-off place, poverty, cancer, the death of a loved one . . . or prison! How diametrically opposed are such thoughts to God's description of His will. God says His will is good . . . acceptable . . . perfect. Nothing could be better or more perfect than the will of God.

Well then, how is it discerned? Through the Word of God. This is the foundation for knowing the will of God. Therefore God calls us to *saturation* in His Word for the *transformation* of a mind that until now has been squeezed into the world's mold. When God says "be transformed," the present tense in the Greek is used, meaning *keep on being transformed.*

As you saturate yourself with God's Word you will be transformed into His likeness, into oneness, and thus be able to prove or put to the test the will of God.

The will of God is difficult for people to discern only because they do not have a deep level of communication with Him. They have not developed that oneness that comes from spending time together and listening to each other's hearts. God's will comes from spiritual wisdom and understanding, and spiritual wisdom and understanding come from communication through His Word. (Read Paul's prayer in Colossians 1:9, 10.)

June 22

They seemed to have it all together. She was attractive, warm, loving—a good mother. He was attentive, affectionate, successful—a good father. When the Christmas card came, signed only with her name and the children's, I quickly read the note that explained, "It's been so hard; Frank has remarried and moved away." And there were these simple but pleading words of advice: "Don't ever lose the ability to communicate!"

Volumes have been written on how to communicate. Techniques and principles of "how to" and "how not to" have glutted the bookstores, but homes are still disintegrating for lack of communication. Even many men and women who stay together are often locked into separate, silent chambers that can't be penetrated because one or both won't communicate!

Communication is *not* unloading all of your gripes, disappointments, and frustrations on a longsuffering mate. Rather, it is the free intercourse of thoughts, ideas, and opinions between two people who are willing to be open, honest, and vulnerable and who yet remain totally committed to each other.

Communication is the compatibility of words and actions which convey a total message. When you talk to your mate you need to remember that you are a combination of personality characteristics, history, talents, shortcomings, and conflicts, and you are communicating what you think and feel to another individual who has a set of totally different characteristics. The way you speak is influenced by who you are; the way your mate hears is influenced by who he or she is. Your attempts to communicate are filtered through all sorts of extraneous material in both of you, so it is no wonder that communication is such a tough issue! The diagram below illustrates what I am saying. Study it well, and then we'll talk about it more tomorrow.

Male Expression of thoughts and feelings	**Female** Expression of thoughts and feelings
Personality	Personality
1. your flesh	1. your flesh
2. your character	2. your character
3. your talents & gifts	3. your talents & gifts
4. your past history	4. your past history
5. your conflicts	5. your conflicts

June 23

Before you can achieve oneness in a communication, you need to look at yourself and your mate and identify those characteristics that might distort communication. For instance, each of your individual personality characteristics—emotional temperaments, family, cultural, or regional backgrounds, and personal history—may make it difficult for each of you to receive and understand what the other is saying.

If a husband was rejected as a child, he may misread his wife's signals when she needs some time to be alone, or wants to have lunch with the girls. Instead of seeing this as just a time for her to have fellowship with others, he may see it as a form of rejection. This is a distortion in communication that needs to be worked out. Or maybe your dad was domineering, and so, every time your husband or wife asks you to do something, you rebel because you feel dominated or put down by any form of authority. We need to recognize and deal with these types of things in our attempts to reach oneness.

In the light of this, ask God to show you any specific characteristic or influence in your mate's life that may be hindering communication and thus, your oneness. When He shows these characteristics to you, write them in your notebook.

When you have done that, ask God to show you those characteristics in your own life that may be blocking true heart-to-heart communication. Write them out.

Now, to make it practical, ask God to show you how to adjust your communication skills in order to meet and reach your mate. Then, ask Him to show you how you can understand and work through these differences in your life that screen out what your husband or wife is trying to say to you. Beloved, this is not easy because it involves digging up and throwing away, grafting, and cultivating. But, oh, the glorious rewards! Is not oneness worth it?

June 24

There is one issue that must never be discussed between husbands and wives, and that is divorce or separation. It is not an option nor a matter for discussion. You have made your commitment, a vow never to be broken. Therefore, if the subject is ever brought up, you must refuse to discuss it. This is one time when the box needs to remain sealed. Once you open the issue, like Pandora's box, the contents may overwhelm you. Too frequently, what starts out as angry, idle threats becomes reality. If the issue had never been broached and if oneness had been the overriding concern and consuming goal, then divorce would have been impossible and the discussion of the topic unthinkable.

If you are faced with a mate who throws "divorce" and "separation" in your face all of the time, there is only one way you can communicate. Simply state the fact of your commitment—a commitment that, as far as you're concerned, can only be severed by death.

Beloved, if you have tossed around phrases like, "I'm leaving" . . . "Why don't you get out?" . . . "I want a divorce" . . . "I just want to get away for a while and see if I want to stay married," then you are guilty of crucifying the oneness principle in your relationship. It is imperative that you seek the forgiveness of your God who hates divorce, and of your mate to whom you have made a vow. Cleansing in this area can bring a renewed channel for communication and an increased potential for oneness.

Out of all the possible topics of conversation, this one you and your mate should never discuss. Your decision not to discuss it could determine whether you become *one* or whether you become a statistic of divorce.

What do you need to do?

June 25

The key word for oneness is submission. It is concession, giving in, not insisting on your ways, your rights, your dogma! This submission, I believe, only comes in proportion to our oneness with God. When you read Ephesians 5 you come to that oft-quoted command of God, "Be filled with the Spirit." What follows that command is a description of what it is like to be filled (continuously, for it is present tense in the Greek) with God's Spirit. It is not some ecstatic emotion, but rather a gut-level, practical description of how you will face the circumstances of life and how you will perform in your relationships with others.

Ephesians 5:21 gives us the principal attitude that will be ours—submitting to one another in the fear or reverence of Christ. Submission is really a matter of whom you are going to please.

We live in a society that puts such an emphasis on rights that we have been brainwashed in this area. It begins when children are told "Don't let them do that to you." "Stand up for yourself." "Don't let them walk all over you." Yet Jesus taught, "Blessed are the peacemakers, for they shall be called sons of God" (Matthew 5:9). Making peace involves concession, yet from our childhood we have been taught to stand up for our rights.

Peacemaking is the result of oneness with God—"for they shall be called sons of God." Sons of God walk as their Savior walks. "For even Christ did not please Himself; but as it is written, 'The reproaches of those who reproached Thee fell upon me'" (Romans 15:3). Jesus did not insist upon His own rights even when He was unjustly reproached by unrighteous men.

God's call to us in this matter of concession or submission is "Have this attitude in yourself which was also in Christ Jesus, who, although He existed in the form of God, did not regard equality with God a thing to be grasped, but emptied Himself, taking the form of a bond-servant, and being made in the likeness of men. And being found in appearance as a man, He humbled Himself by becoming obedient to the point of death, even death on a cross" (Philippians 2:5–8).

What does concession take? It takes humility, the laying aside of your rights for the sake of oneness. It's hard, for it is not our nature to concede, but it's worth it, Beloved. It is far better than being alone and having all your rights! Will you put aside your rights?

June 26

The church of Jesus Christ is to be the arms of God reaching out to a lost and dying world. Oh, how God longs to gather His lost sheep into His bosom that He might bestow upon them His great love and care. Thus He instructed us to "go into all the world and preach the gospel to all creation" (Mark 16:15). The church is God's only means of reaching His world. He has no other plan.

Are we one with Him in His goal? Are we caught up with Him in His one consuming passion, to bring men to Himself that they might have life and have it abundantly (John 10:10)?

I do not believe we are. Instead, we are caught up in our own brand of ecclesiastical theology, dividing the church of Jesus Christ rather than preserving the unity of the Spirit in the bond of peace as God commands (Ephesians 4:3). We are caught up in a Pharisee-Sadducee division that causes us to judge, condemn, and put burdens upon people which they cannot bear. And we have disdained other Christians and brought them to ridicule because they do not hold to our doctrinal stand right down the line.

We have forgotten that doctrinal oneness is something we grow into—"until we all attain to the unity of the faith, and of the knowledge of the Son of God, to a mature man, to the measure of the stature which belongs to the fulness of Christ" (Ephesians 4:13). Unity of the Spirit is ours by virtue of birth into God's family, but unity of faith can only come with the time it takes to grow; therefore we need to be very careful in judging and condemning.

How can arms that wrestle with each other for supremacy ever reach out to a lost and dying world? God says that it is by our love for one another that all men will know we are His disciples (John 13:35). And so in Romans 14, God calls us to concession when our opinions differ on what God says is allowable in a Christian's life. He reminds us that "the kingdom of God is not eating and drinking, but righteousness and peace and joy in the Holy Spirit . . . So then let us pursue the things which make for peace and the building up of one another" (Romans 14:17, 19). "Accept one another, just as Christ also accepted us to the glory of God" (Romans 15:7). Concede, Beloved . . . accept one another and reach out.

1. What are your do's and don'ts? List them and then next to each write in the Scripture from which this conviction comes.

2. List the things on which you judge other Christians. Then next to each, note whether these are direct, undebatable commands of God.

3. Read Romans 14. Are you a weak or strong brother? How are you to behave toward others?

June 27

If two are ever to become one, then the concession principle must be operative in their relationship. I don't mean that one must always be the underdog or that giving in is the ruling principle, but there must be a willingness within one's spirit to defer, to esteem the other's desire higher than one's own. This heart attitude of concession is a graciousness that makes oneness possible in whatever relationship God has us.

Job had the spirit of concession. When, by God's permission, Satan stripped him of his wealth and of his sons the cry of Job's heart was,

"Naked I came from my mother's womb, and naked I shall return there. The Lord gave, and the Lord has taken away. Blessed be the name of the Lord" (Job 1:21). He conceded to God. Then, in defense of the God who allowed him to be tried sorely, he boldly stated, "Though he slay me, yet will I trust in him" (Job 13:15 KJV). Deference to the wisdom, justice, and character of God brings oneness despite circumstance, trial, or sorrow.

The same goal of concession must be present in the pursuit of oneness in marriage. In Ephesians 5, God speaks of "always giving thanks *for all things* . . . to God, even the Father" (Ephesians 5:20). The mark of a heart that concedes to God is gratitude in all things. In the next breath He says, "submitting yourselves one to another in the fear of God" (Ephesians 5:21 KJV). The mark of concession in marriage is the submitting of one's self to the hopes, dreams, desires, needs, and will of one's mate.

I'm not talking now about "roles" or "position" or "order" within the family. I'm speaking of that heart attitude that says to another, whether husband or wife, "Because I love you and because I desire to be one with you, because our relationship is more important than anything I could have or attain alone, I will concede my rights. I will lay down my desire to assert my will, to claim my privileges, and I will blend with you." What is oneness anyway but the blending of two into a new entity—stronger because concession has been practiced— stronger because two have become one in thought, purpose, and deed.

Beloved, the next time you are in conflict with another, whether it's your mate or not, retreat from the heat of the battle for a moment and ask yourself, "What is my goal in this situation? Am I seeking my own way, no matter what, or am I honestly intent on the pursuit of oneness?" Truthfully answering such a question and then deciding to concede out of a desire for oneness could make a lifetime of difference.

June 28

Circumstances—those things that happen to us . . . those outside, uncontrollable forces that roll over us like the waves of the ocean . . . pushing, pulling, knocking us down . . . sometimes capturing us in the undertow . . . sometimes overwhelming us to the point that we cry for help. Circumstances, God's tool to bring us to oneness. In His eternal perspective, God uses the physical or material (our circumstances) to achieve the spiritual (oneness). In our temporal, tunnel vision we cry, "Why?" And with the tender, personal care of a nursing mother the Lord God of the Universe whispers:

"My child, my heart's desire is to bring you into oneness with Me. It was my desire when I put the first pair in the Garden. And, oh, my Beloved One, my desire has never changed. So I have put you in relationships from which I don't want you to walk away.

"The elderly I have left in your care are meant to teach you a lesson in sacrifice, mercy, and patience. I haven't forgotten them nor have I abandoned you.

"And, Beloved, those babies and toddlers that I have loaned you for a while will require constant, tender care. They will require the selfless sacrifice of your rest, your attention, your plans, your priorities.

"I want you to show this to the world, to those who are rushing to their graves, clutching their rights to their breasts only to lose them all. And the teenagers, those precious 'potentials' who live in your house and who bring you to your knees. My child, they are yours to drive you to prayer. Oneness will never be possible with them or with Me until you have allowed the circumstances to draw you into your closet, until you have bowed your heart in the inner chamber.

"And in your marriage, My child, I want you to show the world that 'submitting yourself one to another' is not My way of thwarting your individualism, but rather, it is the tool to bring you to oneness. I want the world to see such a passion for oneness in your marriage that they also see a willingness on your part to lay down your life, if need be, for another."

Beloved, are you willing to bind yourself so tightly to the mast of these irrevocable relationships that no matter the waves of circumstances, you will not be washed overboard or tempted to abandon ship?

June 29

Understanding God's goal of oneness through circumstances in your life is just half of the knowledge you need to walk in victorious oneness with Him. I believe there are five definite steps that you can take to achieve oneness with God in the circumstances of life. I pray that you will take each one to the Father and discuss it with Him, coming to some personal resolutions on how you will meet the circumstances coming your way.

When anything happens that seems senseless or is difficult to understand, you need first to realize that you are in that circumstance by divine appointment. God has placed you in a prearranged situation for His sovereign purpose. He says in Proverbs 20:24 KJV, "Man's goings are of the Lord; how can a man then understand his own way," and in Proverbs 16:9, He says "The mind of man plans his way; but the Lord directs his steps."

The second step toward oneness is to accept the circumstances as a divine appointment. It is one thing to *recognize* God's sovereignty, but another thing to *accept* it. This is especially true in those circumstances that are bothersome, wearisome, or mundane. The mark of true acceptance is when you can honestly give thanks to God. In Ephesians 5:20, we are instructed to give "Thanks always for all things unto God and the Father in the name of our Lord Jesus Christ." That simple act of giving thanks in the midst of circumstances that range from tedious to tragic is the mark of a heart that recognizes the divine appointment and sovereign power of God.

The third truth that you need to lay hold of is that God will keep you. He doesn't keep you *out* of circumstances, but rather He keeps you *in* them. In the process of refining silver, the silversmith must put the silver in the fire to achieve his purpose, to rid it of its impurities; but he *never* walks away and leaves the silver in the fire unattended, in jeopardy or in danger. He keeps it there to achieve his goal of purification not destruction. Beloved, He has said that He will *never* leave us nor forsake us! (Hebrews 13:5).

The fourth step is to realize that there is an end to every circumstance. Although it would seem some circumstances will never end, God has said our trials are "for a season." Jesus Christ is not only the Author but the Finisher. He is the Alpha and Omega, the Beginning and the End.

Beloved, the fifth and final step to oneness in *every* circumstance—whether it is physical, financial, emotional, or spiritual—is to "be anxious for nothing, but in everything by prayer and supplication with thanksgiving let your requests be made known to God. And the peace of God, which surpasses all comprehension, shall guard your hearts and minds in Christ Jesus" (Philippians 4:6, 7). Anxiety is a contradiction to oneness.

Is oneness with God your goal? Then, Beloved, recognize Him as God—in every circumstance of your life!

June 30

TLC. They are almost forgotten initials in our world punctuated with the instant, the shortened, the powered, and the concentrated. Yet TLC—tender loving care—is the fragrance that wafts from the flower of oneness. TLC is the rare and precious nectar that flows naturally in the lives of those whose goal and passion is oneness, whether oneness with God, oneness with a mate, or oneness with the church. Tender loving care is the glory of the relationship.

Oneness with God means caring as He cares. It is not the "bless you brother and be warmed" type of care, but rather, it is the tender mercy and loving compassion of a "cup of cold water" in His name. It is that extra mile to meet a need because you are His. Recently, while on our way to a dinner engagement, Jan Silvious and I passed a woman walking alone on the freeway. Not far behind her was a car with a blow-out. My first thought was that the woman looked so vulnerable, so alone, but *others would probably help.* Oneness with the Lord caused us to pull over, to give her a ride, and to be very late for our engagement. It is oneness that cares, that reaches out. And, if that care were absent, could oneness really be claimed? I think not. Care is the natural outflow of our oneness with the Father.

In our homes, care for one another is the mark of a heart's desire for oneness. Jack loves creamed peas. So, many times, even though our meal preparation may be rushed, I'll take the time to prepare creamed peas, to express my desire for oneness with Jack. It is a small thing, and yet, when Jack says, "Oh, you fixed those just for me," I know it speaks volumes of my love.

Oneness among fellow believers can be best demonstrated by the TLC among its members. No creed, no theological unity can fulfill the need that compassionate, sensitive caring can fulfill in a body of believers. Paul knew this so well when right in the middle of a discourse on spiritual gifts he wrote ". . . there should be no division in the body; but that the members should have the same care for one another. And if one member suffers, all the members suffer with it; if one member is honored, all the members rejoice with it" (1 Corinthians 12:25, 26).

Does your heart desire to beat as one with His? Then oneness must be the passion for which you are willing to live, or perhaps even to die. His desire for oneness with us caused the Father to give the Son to hang on a tree. Is oneness a worthy pursuit? O Beloved, I do believe so, I really do!

JULY

What Does It Mean to Live by Faith?

July 1

It seems that the world has put us in a pressure cooker and turned up the fire too high. In an incredibly short time, we've begun to boil and the steam is pouring out. Things usually begin to blow at the end of the day when we slide into home base. Dusty, tired, and with every ounce of energy spent, all we want is peace and quiet. Yet the family wants us; things at home need doing. The wife wants to talk; the husband wants to be left alone; the kids, for some reason or other, need our attention. So pressure, guilt, exhaustion, and responsibility toss you about in a game of four-way catch! And on top of it all, you claim to be a child of God, but where is it getting you? Where is, "silent night, holy night," "peace on earth, good will toward men"? Do you relate? I hope **you** don't; but let me tell you most of Christendom does!

So what are you going to do? You know, don't you, that you are in a Peter-walking-on-water situation? The Lord has bid you to come to Him, and you have gotten out of your boat. He has told you, "Take courage, it is I; do not be afraid." Jesus is saying, "You know it's Me. I am God. It is all under My control . . . trust Me." And Peter walked. He did well, until he looked at the things about him instead of the One Who bid him come. Then fear hit, and under pressure Peter began to sink.

O Beloved, this month God wants to teach you how to keep your eyes ever increasingly upon Him, rather than on the circumstances. He wants you to learn to trust Him more. He doesn't want you to be afraid. He doesn't want you to sink.

Just cry out, "Lord, save me." And He will. He will show you this month, and in the months to come, how to stop doubting, how to be a person of more than "little faith." But, Beloved, it will take time. It will take some evaluation of your priorities. So, in your busy schedule, determine that you are going to spend time **alone** with Him each day, just the two of you. Then discipline yourself to take that time. You will be joyfully surprised, for you will begin to experience more peace on earth and good will toward men as you have some silent times, holy times with your Christ.

July 2

Do you ever have struggles with your faith? I've been going through one, and I feel it would help me, and maybe you, just to share it. That way we can grow together. Besides, strange as it may seem, I have an incredible urge to share with you, to be open. I'm not even afraid of what you will think of me. It's funny, isn't it, because I have never seen many of you face to face? Others I have seen, yet we have not had the opportunity to talk. I think it must be like my recent trip to Portland, Oregon. I visited a Precept class of 125. There were only six people there whom I had seen before, yet the minute I walked into the church I knew they all loved me. And I felt secure. I could expose myself. They loved me not because I was perfect, but because I was His.

So this month, Beloved, will be a special month of sharing, of baring my heart and my soul, my struggles and my victories in the school of faith.

God is so good, so precious. I have been lying in bed grinning up a storm, clutching my pocket-sized New International Version to my breast and shaking my head in wonder! And yet, a few minutes earlier I was in a spiritual turmoil, outwardly calm, yet full of questions, wondering what to do and telling God that I had to have His guidance. I was thinking about other ministries and how they are allowed to do things that we are not allowed to do—things related to finances. These past four months have been months of great testing, a real trial of our faith. And in this trial God knows I have not wanted to be found lacking or failing. Living has had to be a gut-level thing with me lately—a matter of taking God at His word no matter what I saw, felt, heard, or thought.

Although we have prayed diligently, there has been no permanent relief. Day by day we have had to ask God for money and then tonight, just a few minutes ago, His word came to me when I least expected it. I know it's dumb. But we always think God speaks only after we *do* our spiritual thing. Rather, His Word came after watching a late movie intermittently as I caught up on my correspondence! Who would expect God to do something as neat as this after a late-night movie?

I chuckled. God completely disarmed me. And, oh, what He taught me about faith! This is what I will share this month so that together we might learn what God means when He says, "The just shall live by faith."

July 3

Just a year ago, as I started teaching Romans for about the eighth time, God began saying to me, "The just shall live by faith" (Romans 1:17). Throughout the year, He brought that phrase back to my heart again and again. No matter where I looked in Romans, no matter what doctrinal truth I taught, no matter what practical application I saw, there it was, "The just, *the righteous man,* shall live by faith." God's message to me was very clear. Life was to be lived simply by taking God at His Word. What He said was true. He would not alter the words that had gone out of His mouth. I was to believe what God said and live in the light of it no matter what I felt, and no matter what others said or did. There was one standard for life and that was His Word. What God said He had accomplished at Calvary, He had accomplished (Romans 3–5). What God said happened to me as a result of Christ's finished work has happened (Romans 6–8). How He said I am to live, I am to live (Romans 12–16). It is all a matter of faith.

What occurred last night was simply God's way of reminding me that I have not graduated from the school of faith. No diploma yet! There is more, much more, to be learned. Suddenly I saw how my current experiences fit into the puzzle, and more of the picture became clear! Until now, I had not associated these particular financial testings with His Word of a year ago, "The just shall live by faith."

You will never really be able to appreciate what happened to me last night until you understand the situation in which I found myself. So let me take you through it step by step. As I do, let me say that I know you must be going through struggles of your own, testings that sometimes cause you to wonder if you shouldn't just walk away, throw in the towel, and forget it all. I understand. I have been there. And, when I finish sharing my experience with you, we will talk about those pressures, those struggles of your faith, and how to handle them.

Now, let me ask you a question. Think about it and then write out your answer. Practically speaking, if a person were going to live by faith, what would he have to do?

July 4

When God began to stress Romans 1:17 to me, "The righteous man shall live by faith," I should have realized that it would have to be tested in the laboratory of my life. Please do not let this scare you. Sometimes our concept of God is so warped that we are afraid to learn anything at His feet because of what it will cost us in the way of experience. We forget so easily that the thoughts that our Heavenly Father has for us are thoughts of good and **not** of evil in order to bring us to an expected end (Jeremiah 29:11)! I would not trade what I have gone through for anything. It is all a part of the process needed to refine me so that I will not be ashamed when I see Him face to face.

The first thing that God did was to remove my sense of His special blessing as I taught. So many times last year I drove down the hill to the auditorium crying out to God that I didn't want to teach. I just wanted to stay in our house. I would teach and feel none of His usual anointing. I would look at faces and feel that somehow I had failed in letting God teach through me. Oh, people got saved, lives were touched and turned around. People learned. They grew. But I felt desperately lonely up there teaching.

Right in the midst of a lesson I would think, *You should quit. God's not speaking. You're boring them.* I would wonder, *God, how could I be so blessed in studying and preparing and then absolutely blow it?* At times I would go back to the house, go into the bathroom where no one would see me, get down on my knees, and beg God to give me another chance to teach the people, or to let them see far beyond my muddled presentation of His precious Word.

It was hard, so hard. I wanted to quit. Then His Word would come. "The just shall live by faith"—faith **not** feeling. I had studied. His words were abiding in me. I had prayed. I knew I had asked according to His will. Therefore, according to His Word in 1 John 5:14, He had to answer, whether I felt it or not, for His Word said, "And this is the confidence which we have before Him, that, if we ask anything according to His will, He hears us." I was to persevere. Yet it was wearying. The former sense of exhilaration from teaching was gone. Some nights I would cry. Some nights I would just lie in bed aching, going over and over in my mind what I "should have said." Then I would have to remind myself of all the verses I knew about controlling my thoughts and, thus, gaining the peace of God. I would have to deal with the fact that what was done was done, never to be undone or done again, and purpose fully to forget those things which were behind and press on to what lay ahead.

Can you relate to what I'm saying? Have you, in some way, found yourself in a similar situation where you felt like a failure and wanted to quit. Bless your heart. If we're honest, we have to admit it's quite a struggle, isn't it?

July 5

Teaching without feeling God's anointing was just the beginning of my lessons in God's school of faith. I have been enrolled in this intensive training program for over a year now. Even when I went on vacation during August and spoke, the feeling of failure was there; but by now the tears and the aching had gone. I knew that my gift and my ministry, no matter how I felt, were His doing (1 Corinthians 12:4–8). I was to employ my gift in serving others as a good steward of the manifold grace of God (1 Peter 4:10). Mine was to obey, to teach, no matter how I felt.

Now some of you may be thinking . . . *I bet some overt, active sin or disobedience in Kay's life has caused these feelings of failure, and that's why she doesn't sense God's anointing while she's teaching.* No, Beloved, do not be a Job's advisor. I was enrolled in His school of faith. It was part of my education. My faith needed to mature even more.

Along with a sense of God's absence as I taught came other and varied tests—in different areas of our ministry, in television, in interpersonal relationships. Then came challenges in which I had to choose to walk in obedience to God no matter what people thought of me or my ministry. Here, God was gently permitting a few people to stand faithfully by me, people who knew that my heart was right before God. It's hard, isn't it, when, at times, members of Christ's body have their own opinion of what you ought to be doing, and their opinion conflicts with what you feel you have heard from God? That's why we must be so cautious in becoming directors of those who are on God's set. We might have misinterpreted the script!

All this time, unknown to me, God wanted to perfect my love for others, for faith without love is nothing. "And if I have all faith, so as to remove mountains, but do not have love, I am nothing" (1 Corinthians 13:2). So God allowed me to be in difficult interpersonal situations where no other language but love would be understood. Reasoning was impossible, and in these situations I saw that I was to commit my way to God, to trust in Him, and allow Him to direct my paths (Psalms 37:5). I saw how love can cover a multitude of sins and how it lets the letter of the law go so that grace can be seen as it seeks the good of another.

What about you, Precious, Precious One? Has God put you in any trials or difficult situations where all you could do was love because nothing else would be accepted or received? . . . Situations you couldn't straighten out with biblical truth because no one would listen, where all you could do was allow the Holy Spirit to fill you with His fruit, even though you did not feel like it. I understand. Write out in a prayer to God your heart regarding your situation, and how you will deal with it.

July 6

I couldn't believe my eyes! A great big, long snake had stretched itself across our front door. There it hung, supporting itself on the door's decorative molding with its tail wrapped around a hinge. The night was pitch black. Everyone had gone to bed. And had it not been for the porch light which diminished the darkness, the snake and I would have had an unexpected confrontation as I approached to enter the house. Who knows what might have happened?

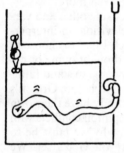 Yet, because of that light, I could see the serpent that would have kept me from the safety and security of my home. Clearly seeing its position and having some knowledge of snakes, I didn't run away in a panic, screaming my fool head off! Instead, I walked up to the snake from behind, gave it a swift kick, and entered my house. Because of that porch light, my enemy did not go undetected, and because I could clearly see the danger, I could walk as more than a conqueror.

Well, another snake had just slithered into my life, and except for God's precious light I would not have seen it either! It was pride that sought to block my walk of faith. Pride! What subtle forms it can take as we seek to serve our God! It can coil up in some of the most unusual or least expected places! Who would expect a snake on his door?!

One of the things I had rejoiced over was God's faithful provision of all our needs at Reach Out. We had covenanted with God never to ask other Christians for money. He had allowed us to tell foundations of our needs for special projects; but writing, calling, giving gifts for donations, asking or pleading with individuals to give was out! That was a no-no for Reach Out. If people asked what our needs were or wanted to know how they could help, we could tell them; but Reach Out could not solicit support or pledges. And God had been faithful. We had always paid our bills on time. We had never borrowed a penny. And I rejoiced! God was faithful! Then, just weeks ago, I began to look down at some other ministries who begged and begged for money. Why would they do that when God would provide? It was then that pride slithered in to coil at my front door. But, praise God, the porch light was on! I will tell you about it tomorrow!

But today, let me ask you: Is your porch light on? Have you ever criticized or looked down on others who were not walking the way God had told **you** to walk? Did you ever stop to think that maybe God had given them different orders?

July 7

In the summer of 1981 we were hit with a financial crisis we had never faced since we first believed God for the eighteen thousand dollar down payment needed to purchase Reach Out's property. That was ten years ago. Now we needed fifty thousand dollars if we were going to pay all of Reach Out's bills on time. Then, when that was paid, next month's bills would stare us in the face! There were several reasons for this financial bind, and, although my dear husband had anticipated the possibility of it all, it seemed he could do nothing but move forward. Oh, how we all, myself and the staff included, admire Jack, who directs all of Reach Out's activities. We never see him flustered, or angry, or in the role of an iron-fisted dictator. Rather, Jack sits behind his desk donned not in the attire of an executive, which befits his title, but rather in the attire of a servant, which befits his Christlike role. Sometimes his clothes bear grass stains from mowing, sometimes paint stains from a building project, sometimes dirt from digging . . . petunia patches. When decisions have to be made, there is that humble seeking of wisdom from our staff and the sharing with me; yet the ultimate decision is on his shoulders. And he carries it all without complaining. Unknown to many, ofttimes his light burns before dawn as he goes to his office to seek his Lord.

Suddenly it had all hit at once. It happened in summer months when our income is traditionally less.

Because of the increased demand for our *Precept Upon Precept Inductive Bible Study Courses,* we have had to engage in some heavy printing. With a selection of twelve adult courses and four children's courses, we have to keep an enormous stock. Printing costs for Precept and Prayer Guides, the salaries of over forty staff members, plus our regular operating expenses are literally faith-staggering sums. On top of this, the government threw us a whopper. Taxes! Then a foundation rightly requested a tax audit that would cost hundreds of dollars. Add to this the news that we were out of television funds.

Oh, the pressure! How do you handle it? What do you do? What can you do? Most of us, sooner or later, experience some sort of financial squeeze. And I believe it is going to get worse. Everything is going up. It seems that we are being priced right out of living. Can God's Word hold us then? Can your God, as He promises in Philippians 4:19, supply all of your needs according to His riches in glory through Christ Jesus our Lord? It is something to think about, isn't it? Why not write out your thoughts and then spend time with your Father, dealing with them in concrete terms.

July 8

Immediately we began noon prayer meetings of all the staff to seek God's face regarding our needs. Until this time, each department prayed daily at a time of its choosing, but now we felt we all had to come together for prayer. To be honest, I expected God to remedy the situation immediately with some huge gift. I forgot I was in God's school of faith and that this was not a crash course! Reach Out's need was to extend for several months without relief. During those months, for the first time, we could not meet all of our bills on time. Our printer, a godly man, told us not to be concerned. He believed in our ministry; he understood the principle of supply and demand; we could wait to pay him. Little did we realize that for him to wait, he would have to go to the bank and borrow money himself. So what I had taken pride in, always paying bills on time, became defeat. The snake had slithered to my door.

I had also boasted that we had never borrowed money. Suddenly, to avoid a six hundred dollar penalty from the government for being late with our advanced deposit of funds, we had to borrow money. The porch light came on; I saw the snake of pride. My bubble was burst. I was humbled and crushed. Then I understood the conflict of other ministries, and empathized with their pressures! On top of it all, Jack told me that unless things changed we would have to go off some of our television networks.

Then the final blow came. Because of program rescheduling and air-time expenses that we could not afford, CBN was dropping "How Can I Live?" This news fell like a ton of bricks on my wall of faith, splintering out cracks of doubt.

All this time, during these months of waiting on God day by day to meet our needs, I had been subsisting on "give us this day our daily bread." And that's the way it had come in—just enough each day for daily bread.

Once, just the day before payday, unexpected expenses took a big chunk out of the money set aside for salaries. Meeting our payroll became doubtful. Then several of our men volunteered to wait on their paychecks so that others could be paid. *But God!* How I love it! The next day's mail brought the necessary funds. God had honored their faithfulness by not requiring that sacrifice.

But the borrowing, the inability to meet the printing bill, the threat of going off the air, were still there. And it was then, in my great extremity of distress, that God met me. I will share it with you tomorrow. Just let me say, Beloved, that our extremities are always God's opportunities to show us how "the just shall live by faith."

July 9

And then in the midst of it all, relief came when I least expected it. Isn't that the way it often is? You find yourself caught, held in a state of impotency, unable to do anything to help yourself. You have called, cried, pled, and still no answer. You have searched your heart for some gross sin, some small sin, any sin that could have been the cause of your need. Yet you have found nothing.

Maybe you have even frantically turned the pages of Scripture looking for a word from God to you. And there was nothing. Perhaps the temptation then came to open your Bible and put down your finger at random. You thought, *Maybe God will speak that way.* But it's the maybe that gets you! What if your finger lands on an inappropriate statement, on the wrong verse? What if the verse doesn't mean anything? Or if you look on the same page, and there's another verse that might be the answer. Can you claim that verse? And so you wait. No earthquake comes to break the chains, flinging open the doors of your distress. You pray. You wait. No visions. No appearances. No touches. All you can do is cling to what you know of God, to His promises. Cling, clutch, and remind God over and over of what He said and Who He is!

God could not go back on His Word. That I knew. I could not go back on my word. That I knew. If I went back on what I had said, I knew I would go back on Him. These were the facts; yet deep in my heart, even though I did not like it, there was a residue of doubt. Maybe I had somehow failed to hear Him rightly! Maybe I had been deceived. Oh, how I could relate to Jeremiah. He had prophesied and prophesied, but no one believed him! He was wrong, they declared. God had not spoken to him! Even the priest, Pashhur, chief officer of the house of the Lord, wouldn't believe God had spoken to Jeremiah, so he had him beaten and put in stocks. It was hard and, even though Pashhur released him, Jeremiah cried out to God, "O Lord, Thou hast deceived me and I was deceived; Thou hast overcome me and prevailed. I have become a laughingstock all day long; everyone mocks me" (Jeremiah 20:7).

O Beloved, isn't that what often keeps us from going out on the limb of faith? We fear that God won't come through on His Word to us, and then we will become the laughingstock to many! It's less risky to live a life that does not take chances, that does not require miracles from God, a life so ordinary that divine intervention wouldn't be required. At least that way we would never be ridiculed or laughed at! But then, would we ever do anything great for God? Would we ever please Him? O Beloved, can you relate to what I'm saying?

July 10

So there I lay on my bed feeling like Jeremiah. If I said, " 'I will not remember Him or speak any more in His name,' then in my heart it becomes like a burning fire shut up in my bones; and I am weary of holding it in, and I cannot endure it" (20:9). I couldn't quit. I couldn't give up. I couldn't walk away from it all. And so I cried again, "O Father, all I want is Your will, nothing else. All I want, Father, is to be what You would have me to be. You know people respect our financial stand—not asking—but, Father!" There it was, the struggle with my faith!

Then I reached over to get my little New International Version, stuck my finger in it, opened it, and started to turn the page to where I would normally read. Suddenly my eyes fell on these words:

He who is coming will come and will not delay. But my righteous one will live by faith. And if he shrinks back, I will not be pleased with him (Hebrews 10:37, 38).

I could hardly contain myself! I clutched that New Testament to my breast and shook my head, grinning from ear to ear. "O Father, when I least expected it! What a sense of timing You have! How precious are Your ways." This is what He had been teaching me since last September, "The just shall live by faith ... don't give up, Kay; don't turn back."

Then, wanting to read it again, I saw the two verses preceding it, and I really got tickled!

So do not throw away your confidence; it will be richly rewarded. **You need to persevere** so that when you have done the will of God, you will receive what He has promised.

God had spoken. There it was. O Beloved, I understand your struggles, and your temptations to give up, to be apathetic, to go along with the stream of humanity, to do it the seemingly easy way or not at all! But, Beloved, we cannot. We are children of the King of Kings, the Sovereign God of the Universe. We cannot shrink back; if we do, He will not be pleased with us. We must believe Him. We must live by His Word. His promises, though seemingly delayed, are "yea and amen" (2 Corinthians 1:20). **"So do not throw away your confidence;** it will be richly rewarded."

July 11

Shrink back? How could I, after all God has done? No, to do so, I would have to deny the wondrous reality of these past eighteen years. As the song says, I "have come this far by faith, leaning on the Lord." Where would I go if I shrank back? Does He not have the words of eternal life (John 6:68)? I would rather die than fail Him. And even in those times when I have wrongly entertained that spirit of fear that torments me with thoughts of failure, the Spirit of God has always been at my side. He is there, my Paraclete, bringing to my remembrance the things which Jesus has spoken to my heart, truths that are unchangeable—truths which, when I have believed Him, have kept me unshakable. Oh, it is true that in this life my faith has been deluged by storms; the rain has descended, the floods have come, and the winds have blown and burst against my house of faith, but it has not fallen. It has been built on the rock of the written Word by the work of the Living Word (Matthew 7:24–27). Eighteen years ago I acted upon God's Word, and since then I have lived by it. It has not failed.

And I would not fail; I would persevere. And by His grace I have not failed; I have persevered. I, the one who was justified by faith, am learning to live by faith. I will believe no matter what! I will choose to walk by faith, not sight—by fact, not feeling. I will endure by seeing Him who is invisible (Hebrews 11:27). I will offer Him the "sacrifice of praise." No matter what my assessment of the situation, no matter how I feel, I will walk in His Spirit always giving thanks for all things in perfect trust knowing that as for God, His way is perfect, His will cannot be thwarted. I will accept by faith that these momentary, light afflictions are producing for me an eternal weight of glory far beyond all comparison. Therefore, I will look not at the things which are seen, for they are temporal; but I will look at the things which are not seen, for they are eternal (2 Corinthians 4:17, 18).

Once I was bound by my own human reasoning, by what I saw, what I heard, what I felt. But now I live by faith in the Son of God, who loved me and delivered Himself up for me (Galatians 2:20). What about you, Precious One? Will you trust Him though He slay you?

July 12

They were blind—horribly, desperately blind—groping through life, stumbling, falling, trampling over one another in their frenzy to find some light, some peace. Week after week they would make their way to the churches and close themselves in small boxes of wood where they would pour out their sins of darkness. Their confession heard, absolution received, they would make their way to Sunday Mass. Then, after receiving the bread and the wine, they knew they were safe until, of course, they sinned again. And sin they would! It seemed an unending cycle. Sin, confess, sin, confess—over and over as day followed day, month followed month, and season followed season. It was an unrelenting cycle.

And over it all hung the black threatening clouds of purgatory. The sun of hope, of deliverance from death, did not shine for them. For in those days in Germany and in other parts of Europe, it was a case of the blind leading the blind. They groped in darkness, ignorant of the light of God's Word, because they had no access to it. Little did they realize that those who stood before them as God's representatives were blind also! Fearful sermons from churches and marketplaces sent terrifying chills through hearts beating wildly at the thought of the flames of purgatory. There the incessant fire would finally purify them so that they and their loved ones might one day enter heaven. But, how long that purification would take no one really knew. Surely years of incessant burning would be needed to bring to ashes the taint of their sins.

Clergy and laity alike were held in the chains of darkness. The gangrenous putrefaction of the wounds from those chains rose to heaven! Where was the light? Where was God's Word? Where was the good news—"The just shall live by faith" (Romans 1:17)? The words were tucked away, hidden by years of dust. The gilded letters, Holy Bible, had ceased to catch the eyes of the intelligentsia who perused the shelves of university libraries. In monasteries the Bible was fastened by chains to the shelves forbidding one to take it to his bosom for prayer and meditation.

They lived in darkness and fear. They lived in impotence, without hope. The future held no prospects of release, so they lived for the immediate, which only brought pleasure for a season. Bitterness and guilt followed. All of this because they did not know God's Word. They did not know his promise of an expected end, a future and a hope (Jeremiah 29:11). That was Germany in the 1500s. Is it the same, in a sense, for you today in the 1900s, because the dust is on your Bible, because God's Word has not been clutched to your breast, because its words have not had opportunity to speak to your heart?

July 13

This was the Germany in which Martin Luther lived. And it is his story that I want to share with you these next few days. I want you to see, Beloved, how far we can stray, how blind we can become, how deceived we can be by Satan, the father of lies, **when we do not know God's Word** and do not esteem it more precious than our necessary food (Job 23:12), when we do not know that the just shall live by faith.

Faith is taking God at His Word. If the just or righteous man lives by faith, then that man must know God's Word. "So faith comes from hearing, and hearing by the word of Christ" (Romans 10:17). God's Word brings us into salvation, into life through faith. And it is the Word of God that helps us maintain that life or, to put it another way, to live by faith. This is what God means when He says in Romans 1:17, "The righteousness of God is revealed from faith to faith." In other words, you gain righteousness at salvation by faith when you believe that Jesus Christ died for all your sins. God sets you free from sin's slavery and gives you His power by placing His Holy Spirit within you (John 8:36; Romans 5:5–10, 8:15–17; Ezekiel 36:26, 27; Romans 8:1, 2; Acts 1:8). However, salvation is just the beginning of the life of faith. Once you are saved, you are to live by faith day by day. You do this by taking God at His Word. A life of faith is known only by living according to Colossians 2:6, "As you therefore have received Christ Jesus the Lord (*by faith*), so walk in Him (*by faith*)."

Yet this life is impossible, it is distorted, if we do not live by every word that proceeds out of the mouth of God (Matthew 4:4). I want you to see the twisted, distorted church of Luther's day and be warned, for it can happen even to those who profess to know God, yet who by their very lives deny Him because they do not live according to God's infallible Word. I also want you to see, Precious Ones, the power of the Word of God in a man's life, how it can work "to open their eyes so that they may turn from darkness to light and from the dominion of Satan to God, in order that they may receive forgiveness of sins and an inheritance among those who have been sanctified by faith in Me (Christ)" (Acts 26:18). You will see all of this in Luther's life. And in seeing it you will be blessed and given hope even as I have been! I pray that with hope will come a determination not to throw away your confidence, but to live by every Word that proceeds out of the mouth of God.

July 14

In the days when God was preparing Luther's heart for the Kingdom of God, He gave him a frightening and grotesque picture of what religion is like without the plumb line of the Word of God. How far we can veer off course if we do not set our compasses on His truth!

The church in Luther's day had opened a vast market. As I read about it, I could not help but think of the parallels today when so many gospel hucksters promise prosperity, healing, and blessing upon blessing to those who will enclose donations for their work and for the edifices they want to build to "the glory of God." Trinkets, Bibles, anointing oil, prayer cloths, buttons, decorations, and other memorabilia are bartered as incentives for the people to give and thus be blessed. And thousands are swayed by the testimonies of the few who seem to have been given health, wealth, and material blessings in return. And where does this leave faith? It would seem unnecessary if what I need from God can be obtained by bribery rather than belief!

The church of Luther's day also had its nets for catching silver. Listen as I quote from *The Life and Times of Martin Luther,* by J. H. Merle D'Aubigne:

A great agitation prevailed at that time among the German people. The Church had opened a vast market upon earth. From the crowds of purchasers, and the shouts and jokes of the sellers, it might have been called a fair, but a fair conducted by monks. The merchandise that they were extolling, and which they offered at a reduced price, was, said they, the salvation of souls!

These dealers traversed the country in a handsome carriage, accompanied by three horsemen, living in great state and spending freely. . . . When the procession approached a town, a deputy waited on the magistrate, and said, "The Grace of God and of the Holy Father is at your gates." Instantly everything was in motion in the place. The clergy, the priests and the nuns, the council, the schoolmasters and their pupils, the trades with their banners, men and women, young and old, went out to meet these merchants, bearing lighted tapers in their hands, and advancing to the sound of music and of all the bells, "so that they could not have received God Himself with greater honor," says a historian. . . . The pontiff's bull of grace was carried in front on a velvet cushion, or on cloth of gold. The chief of the indulgence-merchants came next, holding a large red wooden cross in his hand.[13]

The merchant of the red cross was the focus of attention for he was the one who would, for a price, grant indulgences that promised great reward for all who would pour their money into the coffer. One of these merchants was Tetzel.

A Jesuit historian, speaking of the Dominican monks whom Tetzel had taken with him, says: "Some of these preachers failed not, as usual, to go beyond the matter they were treating of, and so far to exaggerate the worth of indulgences that they gave the people cause to believe that they were assured of their salvation, and of the deliverance of souls from purgatory, so soon as they had given their money."[14]

O Beloved, what do you trust in? Your works, your giving, or God's Word?

July 15

And what were indulgences? An indulgence was a favor, a privilege, a remission of the punishment **still due after** the guilt had been forgiven. In other words, although Christ had died for sins, torment in purgatory still remained for sin's awful stains. The indulgence, given in exchange for good deeds, for meritorious works, for objects of value, or for money, if enough, would lessen or remit the punishment.

As the red cross was elevated, Tetzel would say:

"Indulgences are the most precious and the most noble of God's gifts.

"This cross (pointing to the red cross) has as much efficacy as the very cross of Jesus Christ.

"Come and I will give you letters, all properly sealed, by which even the sins that you intend to commit may be pardoned . . .

"There is no sin so great that an indulgence cannot remit. . . . Reflect then, that for every mortal sin you must, after confession and contrition, do penance for seven years, either in this life or in purgatory . . . indulgences avail not only for the living, but for the dead.

"For that, repentance is not even necessary. . . . do you not hear your parents and your other friends who are dead, and who cry from the bottom of the abyss: 'We are suffering horrible torments! a trifling alms would deliver us; you can give it, and you will not!'

"At the very instant," continued Tetzel, "that the money rattles at the bottom of the chest, the soul escapes from purgatory, and flies liberated to heaven. . . . Blessed are the eyes which see the things that ye see: for I tell you, that many prophets and kings have desired to see those things which ye see, and have not seen them; and to hear those things which ye hear, and have not heard them!" And in conclusion, pointing to the strongbox in which the money was received, he generally finished his pathetic discourse by three appeals to his auditory:

"Bring—bring—bring!"[15]

O Beloved, is this not the mentality of "religious" people today: "I'm not such a sinner; my good will outweigh my bad"? Or, of many Christians today who say, "I know I'm forgiven, but God just can't bless me, speak to me, or meet my needs because I'm not all I should be"? O Beloved, the only way you can ever please God is by faith! You can **never ever** come to Him on the basis of your own merit. You can come only by way of the finished work of Christ at Calvary. The just shall live by faith! Faith alone! Today write out a prayer of thanksgiving to your Father that your salvation is by faith, not your own works!

July 16

The words *the just shall live by faith* sparked the Reformation. They were words which were used to bring multitudes into the light of God's truth. And they can be used of God today in your life in a new and deep way to bring you into the glorious light and rest of faith.

Beloved, I believe that faith is a process much like conception and birth. A child is conceived when a sperm fertilizes an egg. There, unseen and unrealized, yet existing in all of its potential, it begins to grow. Then one day its presence is discovered. It begins to stir. Still invisible to the naked eye, we feel or see its movements. Months go by, months of progress, and then, finally, come the labor pains—and birth! It's done! We have a baby, yet it all began months before.

It was a process. Is the process complete now that the child is born? No. All that potential combined in that sperm and in that egg is not yet realized. And so, Beloved, it is with faith. It is a process whereby "you have been born again not of seed which is perishable but imperishable, that is, through the living and abiding word of God"; for "in the exercise of His will He brought us forth by the word of truth" (1 Peter 1:23;

James 1:18). Therefore, "like newborn babes, long for the pure milk of the word, that by it you may grow in respect to salvation" (1 Peter 2:2). More and more, righteousness will mature from faith to faith because all the potential is there when God's seed is sown in the soil of your heart!

And thus it was with Luther as he spent his time in the university library. One day, while opening book after book to learn the authors' names, he came to a volume that particularly attracted his attention.

> He had never until this hour seen its like. He read the title—it was a Bible, a rare book, unknown in those times. His interest was greatly excited and he was filled with astonishment at finding other matters than those fragments of the Gospels and epistles that the Church had selected to be read to the people during public worship every Sunday throughout the year. Until that day he had imagined that they composed the whole Word of God. Now he saw many pages, many chapters, many books of which he had had no idea! His heart beat fast as he held the divinely inspired Volume in his hand. With eagerness and with indescribable emotion he turned over these leaves from God.[16]

There's more. I will tell you tomorrow. But today let me ask you: is God's Word being sown in your heart? Is it growing? Has conception even taken place? Are you partaking of more than just that which you hear on Sunday? Write out your answers to these questions. Then seeing them in black and white, deal with them.

July 17

> That Book, deposited on the unknown shelves of a gloomy hall, was about to become the Book of Life to a whole nation. In that Bible the Reformation lay hidden.[17]

And in your Bible, Beloved, lies a reformation—the reformation of your life. A re-form-ing that will make you into the image of Jesus Christ. And this is what Christmas is all about. It is a Son born unto you that the government of your life might be on His shoulders as you live, by faith, with Jesus Christ as your Wonderful Counselor, your Mighty God, your Eternal Father, your Prince of Peace (Isaiah 9:6).

In the next few days we are going to unwrap God's gift of faith and examine it precept by precept. We are going to carefully read His instructions so that we will learn how to assemble it piece by piece until we see the whole. But before we proceed, I must finish the story of Luther's conversion. You might need to see how faith was born in him, a faith that would be used of God to bring reformation to the church.

Reading God's Word awakened a great thirst in Luther's heart for holiness. How "could he appear before the tribunal of a terrible God with an impure heart? He must become holy."[18] With that he left the university and, at the age of twenty, closed himself behind the gates of the convent of the hermits of St. Augustine. There, in the convent, he found "a Bible fastened by a chain, and to this chained Bible he was continually returning. . . . 'I saw that I was a great sinner in the eyes of God . . . and I did not think it possible for me to propitiate Him by my own merits.' "[19] Luther passed his life in a continual struggle, ofttimes locking himself in his cell where he afflicted his body, seeking by these wounds to tame his wretched flesh. All of this was to no avail. Then three years later, during his time as a professor, he began lectures on the Bible. On one occasion, while preparing for his studies on Romans,

> . . . having reached the seventeenth verse of the first chapter, he read this passage from the prophet Habakkuk, "The just shall live by faith." This precept struck him. There is then for the just a life different from that of other men: and this life is the gift of faith. This promise, which he received into his heart as if God Himself had placed it there, unveiled to him the mystery of the Christian life and increased this life in him. Years after, in the midst of his numerous occupations, he imagined he still heard these words: "The just shall live by faith."[20]

The seed of God's Word had found its egg, and the womb was ready to receive and nourish the life that had begun! But still there lay before him the journey to Rome!

July 18

Luther "had found the light; but the darkness was not entirely expelled from his understanding."[21] Do some of you relate? Have you found the light? Do you know about Christ and Christianity and yet you sit in the dusk of faith? Are there shadows that keep you from seeing clearly? Do you know that you believe in Jesus, that you love Jesus, yet something is missing in your Christianity? It's not as vibrant, as real, as secure as it seems to be in the lives of others! I understand. But all that can change. God's gift is a real and vital faith. And He is going to open it up to you in the days to come, even as He did for

Martin Luther. Luther's "heart was converted; his mind was not yet enlightened: he had faith and love, but without knowledge."[22] It was at Rome that the veil was withdrawn and the engrafted word cried out giving notice of its birth!

One day wishing to obtain an indulgence promised by the pope to all who should ascend on their knees what is called Pilate's Staircase, the Saxon monk was humbly creeping up those steps, which he was told had been miraculously transported from Jerusalem to Rome. While he was performing this meritorious act, he thought he heard a voice of thunder crying from the bottom of his heart, as at Wittenberg and Bologna, "The just shall live by faith." These words twice before struck him like the voice of an angel from God. They now resounded unceasingly and powerfully within him. He rose in amazement from the steps up which he was dragging his body: he shuddered at himself; he was ashamed of seeing to what a depth superstition had plunged him, therefore he fled far from the scene of his folly. . . . "When, by the Spirit of God, I understood the words—when I learned how the justification of the sinner proceeds from the free mercy of our Lord through faith . . . then I felt born again like a new man; I entered through the open door into the very paradise of God. Henceforward, also, I saw the beloved and Holy Scriptures with other eyes. I perused the Bible—I brought together a great number of passages that taught me the nature of God's work. And as previously I had detested with all my heart these words, 'the righteousness of God,' I began from that hour to value and to love them, as the sweetest and most consoling words in the Bible. In very truth, this language of St. Paul was to me the true gate of Paradise."[23]

O Beloved, I ask you, in God's stead, have you talked about Jesus without really knowing Him? Have you been born again? Have you believed God and, by faith alone, received the Lord Jesus Christ as your Savior and God? Have you turned from your own ways of reaching God and turned to His cross? Have you committed yourself to Him without reservation? Are you yours or are you His? Are you a new man, a new woman? Christ was born to save sinners from their sins! Are you saved?

July 19

Only righteous men and women will ever see God! And only the righteous will ever enter into heaven! Yet how can sinners, which is what we all are, ever hope to be made righteous? The answer, Beloved, is through faith. Faith is the means whereby we are declared righteous. It is when we come to God by faith and declare to Him our utter sin and total impotency to ever make ourselves righteous that He offers us a righteousness that comes only by faith. God so loved us that He sent His sinless Son to earth, born of a virgin, for the express purpose of becoming the sacrificial Lamb of God that would take away the sin of the world. It was God who, in love, made Jesus "who knew no sin **to be sin on our behalf,** that we might become the righteousness of God in Him" (2 Corinthians 5:21).

The Greek word for faith is *pistis,* which means a conviction based on hearing. The Greek verb to believe is *pisteuo.* So you see, to believe is to have faith! And to have faith in the Son of God is to be declared righteous, to be put into right standing with God. When you believe, you are made a partner of the life and righteousness of God. From then on, God, by His Spirit and through your faith, begins ever increasingly to produce works of righteousness in your life. The seed of faith brings forth the fruit of righteousness. There is no other way, Beloved. It is a righteousness that is reckoned to us only through faith. "For what does the Scripture say? 'And Abraham believed God, and it was reckoned to him as righteousness'" (Romans 4:3). Abraham staked his whole life on what God said. He could not point to a single work that he had done and say that because of that he was righteous before God! It was only by faith!

O Beloved, it is ours for the taking—righteousness for salvation and righteousness for daily living. When I say righteousness for daily living, I mean the ability to live according to God's standards, to do what is right at any given moment. It is yours and it is mine for the taking. And the taking comes simply by taking God at His Word, no matter what! It is yours through the obedience of faith. We will talk about it tomorrow. Meditate on these truths; they are foundational to living by faith.

July 20

If you really want to understand faith so you can live by it, then you must understand the three vital elements of faith. They are conviction (or knowledge), surrender, and obedience (or conduct). Faith is not just saying, "Yes, I believe that," and then living as if what you believed was not absolutely true. This is where we get all messed up. So many are deceived even about their salvation because they think faith is merely mental assent to some facts. These are the ones who will get the shock of their lives when they stand before God saying, "Lord, Lord, did we not prophesy in Your name, and in Your name cast out demons, and in Your name perform many miracles?" only to hear Him declare to them, "I never knew you; depart from Me, you who **practice** lawlessness" (Matthew 7:22, 23).

You see, faith is not passive; it is active. Faith is surrendering to God's truth and living accordingly! Jesus said in Matthew 7:24, 25, "Therefore every one who hears these words of Mine, and **acts** upon them, may be compared to a wise man, who built his house upon the rock. And the rain descended, and the floods came, and the winds blew, and burst against that house; and yet it did not fall, for it had been founded upon the rock." God's Word stands because it is founded on The Rock, Christ Jesus.

Thus true faith **acts on** what God says. I am utterly amazed at all of those to whom I witness who say that they believe in Jesus Christ and yet whose lives are diametrically opposed to all that such faith demands.

It is God's responsibility to speak, and thus we have **the basis of our faith,** His infallible Word. It is our responsibility to believe what God has said and to pattern our conduct after His Word, and thus we have **the behavior of true faith.** True faith then not only believes; it behaves. As it hears truth, it surrenders to the truth and conducts itself in the light of it! And when it does all of this, you see the righteousness of faith!

Is your faith genuine faith? Will it save you? Has it made . . . is it making you righteous?

July 21

What does Jesus mean when He says, "All things are possible to him who believes" (Mark 9:23)? This is a vital question, for its answer gives particular insight into what is involved in a life of faith.

A young boy possessed by a spirit that would send him convulsing to the ground, rolling about and foaming at the mouth, was brought to Jesus. And when the Lord questioned the father regarding the duration of his son's illness, the father replied with this statement, "But if You can do anything, take pity on us and help us! And Jesus said to him, 'If You can!' " (Mark 9:22, 23). I can just hear Him repeating this incredulous statement of this man, "If You can!" Of course He could. He was God! He had supreme authority over all the demonic hosts of Satan, and over Satan himself. Ability was not the issue! The issue was this man's faith. And when Jesus said, "All things are possible to him who believes," the man saw that the problem of faith lay in him, not in God's ability!

So he cried out saying, " 'I do believe; help me in my unbelief' " (v. 24). You see, as I stated yesterday, there is faith's basis and faith's behavior. One side is Godward; that's the basis of faith. The other side is manward; that's the behavior of faith. Faith has its foundation in the person of God Himself. The surety or strength of faith lies in the trustworthiness of the One Who has spoken. Remember, faith is taking another at his word. In our case, as Christians, it is taking God at His Word. The surety of our faith is found in faith's object: God and His Word. That's why Jesus incredulously repeated the father's words, "If You can!" The object of the man's faith was secure; he had the right foundation; he had come to Jesus for relief. The only problem was the man himself! He couldn't believe; he wasn't sure Jesus could do the job. He did not know Jesus well enough! He wasn't absolutely certain of Jesus' ability or His power.

Yet the ability of Jesus was not altered by the man's unbelief. Jesus' word, His power, His ability stood as sure as God is sure. The problem was the man—the activator, the behaver. It was possible for the son to be healed because of Who Jesus is, but Jesus' potential would not be experienced until the man's faith activated it.

Meditate on this. It's kind of heavy, isn't it? I pray I'm explaining it clearly. I'll share more tomorrow.

July 22

Have you ever felt blown away by the littleness of your faith, to drift like a milkweed seed caught by the wind and carried away powerless, drifting at its every whim? Have you ever felt that nothing would be possible to you because you couldn't even muster up mustard-seed faith (Matthew 17:20)? Move mountains? You couldn't even get rid of molehills! Bless your heart. But don't despair; there is hope. Let me give you that hope, a ray at a time.

First, let me review the truth we saw yesterday; and then I will begin sharing some facts of faith that I pray will enable you to move mountains. By God's grace, we'll move them together!

It is vital for us to understand that God lays the foundation of faith for us through the revelation of His character, His Word, His promises. Yet the superstructure is our responsibility! We are to build by activating what God says. Thus our Precious Lord and God says to us, "Be it done to you according to your faith." You get what you believe as long

as you believe according to God's Word, according to God's character!
Let's look for a minute at Matthew 9:27–30a:

> And as Jesus passed on from there, two blind men followed Him, crying
> out, and saying, "Have mercy on us, Son of David!" And after He had
> come into the house, the blind men came up to Him, and Jesus said to
> them, "Do you believe that I am able to do this?" They said to Him,
> "Yes, Lord." Then He touched their eyes, saying, "Be it done to you
> according to your faith." And their eyes were opened.

Did you notice the first question Jesus asked them, "Do you believe
that I am **able** to do this?" When they replied, "Yes, Lord," then the
power of God was activated: "Be it done to you **according to your
faith.**" Their blind eyes saw because of God's power **and** their faith! It
was the same with Jesus and the centurion, " 'Go your way; let it be
done to you as you have believed' " (Matthew 8:13).
So how do we learn to believe so that we can move from drifting
milkweed seeds to mustard seeds, from molehills to mountains? We'll
look at it tomorrow. I wonder if you know the love for you that's in my
heart as I write.

July 23

Faith that moves mountains finds its ability to do so not in itself, but
in God. The warrant of faith is always found in what God says, and
this in turn rests on who God is. Hebrews 11:6 says, "And without
faith it is impossible to please Him, for he who comes to God must believe that He is, and that He is a rewarder of those who seek Him." If
we are going to move mountains, we must realize that we certainly
cannot do it ourselves. It is going to take Someone far more powerful
than we. There is only One, the sovereign, omnipotent God Who says
that with Him all things are possible. That's because He is the God of
the impossible. But do we believe it? And if we have trouble believing
it, can we change our unbelief to belief? Of course! The change comes
as you get to know your God. It's difficult to trust someone you do not
know!
You begin by spending time in God's Word, shut up alone with
Him. Now, sermons, Sunday School, and Bible classes are great. I believe in all three; I listen to the former and conduct the latter two! But
these are not what I am talking about. If you are going to get to know
God, to know that He is God and that He is a rewarder of those who
diligently seek Him, then you must spend time alone with Him. You

must give yourself to reading His Word, to prayer, to meditation, and to actively listening to His voice. You must practice the art of being still and knowing He is God (Psalms 46:10). Remember Romans 10:17? "Faith comes from hearing, and hearing by the word of Christ." In this verse the word for *word* is *rhema,* not *logos. Logos* is used in John 1:1—"In the beginning was the Word (*logos*), and the Word (*logos*) was with God." *Logos* denotes the expression of thought, the embodiment of a conception or idea, and, of course, the Divine Word, Jesus Christ. *Logos* embodies all of the written Word of God. However, *rhema* "denotes that which is spoken, what is uttered in speech or writing."[24] It refers "to the individual scripture which the Spirit brings to our remembrance for use in time of need, a prerequisite being the regular storing of the mind with Scripture."[25]

And there, Beloved, is the key. It is in storing God's Word in your heart (Psalms 119:11), renewing your mind (Romans 12:2), and then being still so that God can speak it back to you as an answer, as instruction, or as a promise. We'll talk about it tomorrow. Today, go store it in your mind and heart and give Him time to talk back.

July 24

Remember when I was in such a dilemma, and then God spoke to me when I opened my Bible to Hebrews 10:37? That was a *rhema* from God. Now granted, I had not been in deep meditation or prayer for hours, but I am a woman of the Word. I do meet with my God regularly. I do spend hours alone with Him. But that night it had just been minutes. Oh, we had been talking on and off all day, but then He chose to speak. He brought those verses to me in my time of need: "He who is coming will come and will not delay. But My righteous one [that was me] will live by faith. And if *she* shrinks back, I will not be pleased with *her.* So do not throw away your confidence. You need to persevere, Kay, so that when you have done the will of God you will receive what He has promised!"

Well, what had God promised? To supply all of our needs. Was He **able** to keep His promise? Of course. The cattle on a thousand hills are His, the earth and the fulness thereof! And I knew this because I know my God. I have spent hours studying His character. And through our years together, I have learned more and more about His ways. So from that night forward I have ceased to be troubled in any way. I took that old residue of doubt and cast it totally upon Him who cares for me (1 Peter 5:7). And I kicked the snake of pride in the tail and sent it to eat more dust!

And what did God do? Well, He let us continue on a daily bread existence for awhile. Then the Precept orders started coming in, but it wasn't enough. It was September and we were short twenty-one thousand dollars for our tenth-of-the-month bills. I was working on correspondence in the office. It was 11:40 P.M. when the phone rang at our house and Jack talked with a dear, God-given friend who said, "I want to know what you need for your tenth-of-the-month bills." At 12:02 the phone was hung up. Twenty thousand dollars was on its way. It would cover our expenses and the loan that had been taken out was repaid in eleven days. It was an excited husband who embraced an excited wife at 1:30 A.M. when I came to the house. The Scripture that God had given us years ago when He first set us on this property once again had proven totally true. "Call unto Me, and I will answer thee, and shew thee great and mighty things, which thou knowest not" (Jeremiah 33:3 KJV). Tomorrow I will tell you more about *rhemas.*

July 25

It's "believed *rhemas"* that move mountains! But what are mountains? Well, obviously, when Jesus talked about faith that moves mountains, He must have directed His eyes toward the mountain and onto the sea as He said, " 'Truly I say to you, whoever says to this mountain, "Be taken up and cast into the sea," and does not doubt in his heart, but believes that what he says is going to happen, it shall be granted him' " (Mark 11:23). Yet, did He expect His disciples to go around casting mountains into seas to demonstrate their faith? Apparently not! They never did it! If they had, it would have been a spectacular of spectaculars, but I doubt it would have brought glory to God. Besides, it would have disrupted the landscape! So did His disciples have faith—faith enough to move mountains? Yes, Beloved, for mountains spoke proverbially of difficulties or great things. As a matter of fact in 1 Corinthians 13:2, Paul spoke of having "all faith, so as to remove mountains." Having our television program, "How Can I Live?" reach across the United States is a mountain. Writing these devotionals, to me, is a mountain. And it is only faith in who our God is that keeps me going—that, plus His *rhema,* which came during a time of prayer and meditation, that confirmed and established both TV and the Prayer Guide as ministries. And yet those two *rhemas* were not given in Scripture. Rather they were instructions spoken to my heart. If they were not actual verses of Scripture, how then do I know they were *rhemas?* Because *rhema* also refers to instructions and commands as is seen in Matthew 26:75 and Luke 1:37.

We will look at Luke 1:37 tomorrow; it's exciting! Today, however, let me give you something else to meditate upon. Are you faced with a mountain? Have you asked God about it? If not, take time soon— today if possible—to get alone with God. Talk to Him about it, then listen. Listen and keep on listening even if it takes weeks until He speaks. Then you will know what to do. Then you can build your superstructure of faith on the sure foundations of His Word. Hallelujah!

July 26

How do you know when God is speaking to you? How do you know it is really God so that you can believe Him? Beloved, those are not easy questions to answer. But I ask them because they are on your heart and because I have asked them myself. Let me answer them as best I can at this point in my spiritual growth. Now, remember, I have only been saved eighteen years. I am still growing; I have not attained. I am merely steadfastly pressing on "that I may lay hold of that for which also I was laid hold of by Christ Jesus" (Philippians 3:12).

"God, after He spoke long ago to the fathers in the prophets in many portions and in many ways, in these last days has spoken to us in His Son" (Hebrews 1:1, 2). I believe, because of this verse, that God speaks in these days to His children through His Son. Let me explain that. According to God's Word, Christ now dwells in me: "Christ in you, the hope of glory" (Colossians 1:27). All the fulness of Deity dwells in Christ in bodily form, and I am complete in Him (Colossians 2:9, 10). The entire Godhead has taken up residence in me (John 14:17, 23). Therefore, under this new covenant of grace, which puts the Spirit within me (Ezekiel 36:26) making my body His temple God is going to speak to me through His Son. As a child of God you have His anointing which "abides in you, and you have no need for any one to teach you; but as His anointing teaches you about all things ... abide in Him" (1 John 2:27).

So then God speaks to me or gives me *rhemas* through His Son. But how? I believe it is primarily through Scripture which He quickens to the heart or through His still, small voice that comes like thoughts to the mind, not my thoughts but His thoughts. I know of others who have had God speak to them in other ways, but even then I believe it is by His Son. And how can I tell if it is really God? If God speaks and you believe and it comes to pass, then it was God! Luke 1:37 says, "Nothing will be impossible with God," but the footnote adds: "Not any word (*rhema*) will be impossible with God." No word of God shall be void of power. So, if it is God's *rhema* and it is believed, it will happen. In prayer, the inaudible words came, " 'How Can I Live?' is to be a TV program produced by prayer. You are to write a monthly Prayer Guide for your prayer warriors. And it will become a ministry in itself." That was a *rhema.* I heard it, believed God, wrote it at His bidding, and it came to pass. But what if it hadn't? We will talk about it tomorrow.

July 27

Have you ever felt that God was telling you something or promising you something, yet it did not come to pass? Were you shattered, totally shaken in your faith? I understand, Beloved. You are not the only one to whom it has happened!

The first Prayer Guide I ever wrote was a journal of all that God taught me through my father's hospitalization, five major surgeries, and his death six weeks later. He never left the hospital; he died April 22, 1980. Yet as I wrote that Prayer Guide day by day, I said that God had given me a psalm and in that psalm I felt He was assuring me not only of my father's spiritual life but also of his physical life. As I watched him go through five major surgeries in less than a week, as I watched them amputate his leg, as I heard them tell me of his gangrenous blockages, I still believed my father would live. I clung to that psalm and read it over and over, day and night—praying it back to God, praising God through each verse. When doubt would come I would pull it out. I knew my God. It did not matter how bad or hopeless my father's condition appeared. My God could do anything, even raise the dead. But Daddy died. And how I miss him. Sometimes it's hard to imagine him gone, and at times I think my heart will convulse with pain for my mother. Yet Daddy is dead. I did not have God's *rhema,* although I thought I did!

You may say (and I have thought about it myself), "Maybe you had God's *rhema,* but your faith was lacking. Maybe it was because you doubted at times." I understand your question, Beloved, for I have wrestled with it, too. Yet as I did, I went back to the character of my God and to His sovereignty. If that supposition is true; if my times of wrestling doubt were what kept my father from living, then my doubt made God's Word void of power and altered God's perfect will. Our faith is vital. It does remove mountains. Yet does it keep God from carrying out His sovereign purpose? I do not think so. Let me cite two incidents where faith waned but God's sovereign purpose stood.

Remember when Abraham veered off God's path and had Ishmael

instead of waiting for Sarah to conceive? Remember when Sarah laughed at the angel's word about her conception at the age of ninety? Well, both demonstrated a lapse of faith and were chastened, but Abraham and Sarah still had their son, Isaac, just as God had said they would twenty-five years earlier!

O Beloved, when it all gets too hard to understand, when God does not explain, when I feel weak in my faith, I only know to run to Him and cast my insufficient self into His arms, bury my head in His all-sufficient breast and cry out with Paul, "For from Him and through Him, and to Him are all things. To Him be the glory forever" (Romans 11:36). Amen and Amen. So be it. I rest in faith in One who is greater than I!

July 28

Have you ever wondered why God keeps us waiting when we have very definite needs that seem so urgent to us? After all He is God! He is omnipotent! An all-powerful, sovereign God can really do whatever He wants to do whenever He wants to! Jeremiah prayed, "There is nothing too hard for thee" (Jeremiah 32:17 KJV). So why then does He delay?

Well, it could be that God is withholding answers to prayer because of overt sin in our lives. But, let's suppose there is no known, unconfessed sin there. Why then would God delay His answer? Psalm 84:11–12 says, "The Lord God is a sun and shield; the Lord gives grace and glory; no good thing does He withhold from those who walk uprightly. O Lord of hosts, how blessed is the man who trusts in Thee!"

What about those who trust in Him, and walk uprightly and yet have to wait for their prayers to be answered? Russ Johnston in his book, *God Can Make It Happen,* gives three possible reasons for postponing answers to prayer. The first is that postponement may be God's means of purifying our hearts. Things can creep into our lives that we are unaware of! Little subtle attitudes or insidious desires that, if left unchecked or undetected, can someday cause us great problems. Many times, Beloved, when we are forced to tarry before God in prayer for some specific need or in some particular situation, our very lingering in His presence will draw us into a closer fellowship and intimacy with Him. And it's as you draw closer to the Light in search of answers that you see dust particles of impurity floating in your soul that you had never seen before! Thus I saw the tiny particles of pride that were

220

about to settle on the table of my heart. I saw that I had taken pride in my faith, and God could not leave that unexposed. He loved me too much.

Maybe, Beloved, that is why God, too, has delayed in answering your prayers, in meeting your needs. Maybe He wants to draw you even closer into His glorious presence where there is no darkness.

July 29

A second reason why God sometimes withholds His blessing or postpones answers is that it forces us to look to the right resources. Have you ever gone to God in prayer with some great need and then found yourself thinking of all the ways God might answer that prayer? I have! It's ridiculous, isn't it? To think that we might be God's counselor or advisor! And yet isn't this what we are often guilty of? Many people would not dream of asking God for the impossible simply because they just do not see how it could possibly come to pass! *Why there's no way that God could do that!*—so they think.

How often we forget that He is the One who said of Himself, "Behold, I am the Lord, the God of all flesh; is there anything too hard for me? . . . Call unto me, and I will . . . show thee great and mighty things, which thou knowest not" (Jeremiah 32:27; 33:3 KJV).

And yet do we call? No, many times we do not because we do not see or cannot figure out any possible way that God could pull it off. I have never read the book, but I will never forget the title. *Your God Is Too Small*—that is how I would describe this thinking.

O Beloved, many times this is the reason for the postponement of our blessings. God wants to bring us to the end of our resources, the end of our reasoning until we are utterly cast on Him. He wants us to see, to know that He alone is the source of all blessing so that we will look to Him alone rather than to the arm of flesh. So often Christians have figured it all out, reasoning that if only one thousand people would give ten dollars apiece, or if they could get Mr. Got-a-lot to be on their board, or if they could have a benefit and raise so much money. No wonder there aren't more miracles; we don't need them. We have it all figured out! And thus human ingenuity or engineering replaces God.

Oh, Dear One, maybe your Father is trying to get you to simply cast yourself in utter dependence upon Him! Faith abandons itself into the all-sufficient arms of Jehovah Jireh, the God who alone can provide all we need with but a Word from His mouth. "Woe to those who go down to Egypt for help, and rely on horses, and trust in chariots because they are many, and in horsemen because they are very strong, but they do not look to the Holy One of Israel, nor seek the Lord!" (Isaiah 31:1).

July 30

A third reason God often postpones blessings is because He longs to give us so much more than we could ever think of or ask for! Oh, how He longs to have us realize that He is the God who "is able to do exceeding abundantly beyond all that we ask or think" (Ephesians 3:20).

After I was saved, I "fell in love." I had never met a Christian man like Dave before! Here seemed to be the cure for my loneliness; here seemed to be a man who could lead me and teach me about God, who could properly father my two sons. Oh, how I wanted to be married. What could be better? What was more needful? None was as ideal as Dave. Of course, I couldn't see beyond my nose. Nor did I ever in my wildest imaginations ever dream I would be doing what I am doing now. No, as far as I could see, Dave was the one; so I begged, pleaded, and wept before the Father. And poor Dave! I let loose every womanly wile that I could. Finally, we talked about marriage; yet for all my harassment God still said, "No." It didn't seem logical. In the years that followed, many of them lonely, I talked with God about several other prospects, and yet the blessing of marriage was still postponed. Sometimes I would get so lonely I would think I couldn't stand it. Why, oh why couldn't God come through?

How I love that phrase, ". . . when the fulness of the time came" or "when it pleased God . . . to" (Galatians 4:4; 1:15, 16).

You see, Beloved, when I wanted marriage then and there, I did not know about Jack. Nor did I recognize the maturing that was necessary for me before I could move into all of the responsibilities and pressures connected with marriage and ministry. Now I shudder to think of what might have happened if I had not waited for His perfect timing. How sick I would have been to have missed Jack! And who could be better for Reach Out than Jack?

Oh, for the faith to wait, to trust, to know that when the fulness of God's time comes, God will not hesitate to move heaven and earth to accomplish His will.

"Wait . . . wait, I say, on the Lord" (Psalms 27:14 KJV). Will you wait, knowing that each postponement only contains a better way or a better answer? God's timetable is so much better than ours.

July 31

Faith grows. Did you know that? I think so many times we become overwhelmed by the faith of others. We look at them, get sick inside, and talk to ourselves, "God, I'm glad that's not me. I wouldn't make it! I couldn't anymore face that . . .

> endure that . . .
> believe that . . .
> or handle that than anything."

And in all probability we couldn't, Beloved. And don't you think God knows that?! Faith must be nourished on God's Word. It must go from milk in infancy (1 Peter 2:2) to meat in maturity (Hebrews 5:14). Faith must be taught, tutored, and trained. And your Father is the perfect One to do it. He does not leave His child-training to the hands of another. No, whom the Father loves, He disciplines (Hebrews 12:6), and that discipline includes the enlarging of your faith. That is what He has been doing to Jack, to me, and to the staff. Can you imagine needing fifty-two thousand dollars right away? I remember when the thought of four hundred dollars per month as payment for Reach Out's land was almost overwhelming. It blew my mind, and I remember thinking, "Well, Father, I could always go back to nursing and pay the four hundred a month with my salary." Now I laugh the laugh of maturing faith; our electric bills are over three thousand a month. I must admit, it takes a constant rehearsing of God's promises to continue giving away free tapes on our television and radio programs. I was truly tempted to quit when everything got so tight financially. But then the Lord convicted me with several letters from people who thanked us for giving away free tapes because had we been charging they would have been unable to afford them.

O Beloved, do you see, our faith just has to keep being challenged so that it will grow? And so God permits the rocks and the hard places in order to enlarge our faith.

Precious Ones, may we say as the apostles said to the Lord, "Increase our faith" (Luke 17:5).

AUGUST

Why Are You in Despair
O My Soul?

August 1

Some people live in utter dread of the future. They are consumed with the fear of the unknown, and all their days are spent in preparation for "rainy days." Their focus is on tomorrow, and, wanting to be prepared, they imagine the worst and make provision for it. Others, for one reason or another, live with no thought of tomorrow. They are either too frightened to think about it, so they blot out the future entirely by throwing themselves into today, or they are seemingly so blasé about life that they never consider what the future might hold! Their approach is to eat, drink, and be merry (if you can), for tomorrow you die (Ecclesiastes 8:15). Both, disregarding the future for whatever reason, are determined to get all that they can when they can. And if they cannot have all they want, at least they will survive!

But not all people fall into one of these two categories. I know I don't. I think much about the future, but not with terror, dread, or panic. I know that what our near future holds is not good; difficult times are on their way. Iniquity, crime, graft, deception, and gross immorality crawl over our land like kudzu, that insidious vine that literally covers everything in sight. As that plant, fed by a giant taproot, is virtually impossible to control, so it is with evil. Planted because it looked desirable, it is now virtually impossible to stop. I know the future. I know the hearts of men. I know the desire of various nations controlled by ruthless and impetuous men who scoff at God and all that is holy. Behind these men and their governments are the unseen princes and spiritual rulers of darkness preparing their way and goading them on.

Many realize that our immediate future holds inevitable judgment; yet this knowledge does not consume us or control us. However, neither are we occupied with today. We are not to be grabbing all that we can while we can. No, we look at today as a day to be lived in the light of eternity, for our God and Father, a day to be lived in faith as He would have us live it—righteously. Some of us have chosen to live each day according to the words of Habakkuk, "The Sovereign Lord is my strength; he makes my feet like the feet of a deer, he enables me to go on the heights" (3:19 NIV).

In other words, no matter what life brings—the valleys, the ups, the downs, present or future—I can walk the heights because of the strength of my God.

Wouldn't you, too, like to walk through the rest of your life on the heights? There is a way. We shall learn together in the days to come.

August 2

As I walked rapidly down the corridor, Jan Silvious was making a beeline into one of our offices. It had been a busy Tuesday morning at Reach Out. I had just finished teaching on the role of a woman and submission. Without the slightest break in speed, Jan flipped a casual, "How are you doin'?" I had been caught! There was no disguising it; I couldn't speak without tears, so I said, "I'm crying." And without breaking pace I went into Carolyn's office. Just having to say I was crying (as you know if you're a woman) produced even more tears. By the time I stepped into my secretary's office, I was a mess! Billie, Charlotte, and Carolyn—in the middle of some discussion—all asked at the same time, "What's the matter?" Before I could answer, Jan had made a U-turn and suddenly appeared in our midst. Connie, hearing the commotion, left her layout table and joined us. I will tell you one thing . . . we are such a family at Reach Out that if you let them know you are hurting, you will never hurt alone. Pretty soon, we all had tears in our eyes. Several sets of noses squinched while eyes blinked and hands wiped away mascara-stained tears. (We cry in brown or black.) Then, after several good sniffs and with trembling lips under control, they confessed that they felt the same way I did. How was I feeling? I felt like I just couldn't do the job! No matter how much I prayed, no matter how much I searched my heart, no matter how much I studied, I still felt I was falling short. I felt that I had failed as a teacher. All I could do was throw up my hands and say, "I don't know what more to do. All I can do is keep on."

How good it was to cry, and to cry together. What release came in just verbalizing our feelings to others who cared. And how comforting it was to find out that others understood. I didn't get sympathy; I got empathy. They had been there! And until that minute we had all thought that we were the only ones going through that particular trial!

When we left that office, it was with great resolve, for we realized that we were under attack. Satan couldn't entice us, at this point, with overt sin, for the flames of consecrated lives on the altar of sacrifice shielded us from blatant temptations. So instead he sought to put out the fire of consecration with the extinguishing fluid of discouragement and defeat. We had called for help, but God hadn't rescued us—or so it seemed.

And so it seemed to the prophet Habakkuk when he cried, "How long, O Lord, must I call for help, but you do not listen?" (Habakkuk 1:2, NIV).

You understand, don't you, Beloved, for you have cried. You may be crying now. You have been there—discouraged, defeated, and maybe wondering about abandoning ship! I understand.

August 3

Remember when Satan approached Eve in the Garden of Eden? His first words were, "Indeed, has God said . . . " (Genesis 3:1).

If you and I are to live by faith, if we are to take God at His word, if we are to live by every word that proceeds out of the mouth of God, then can we not understand Satan's approach? His tactic is to make us doubt the veracity or the power of God's words. How subtly the enemy sows his seeds of doubt, and what rich harvests he gleans if we are not aware of his methods. So God warns us not to be ignorant of his schemes "in order that no advantage be taken of us by Satan" (2 Corinthians 2:11). But what are Satan's schemes? How does he work?

Years ago God allowed me to hear a message from Joseph Carroll, a dear brother in the Lord. It was a message on "The Five Deadly D's." I have shared it time and time again, and it has helped so many. Thus I want to share it with you, with the prayer that God might use it in your life in the days to come. May it become that by which He strengthens you in your walk of faith with hinds' feet on high places (Habakkuk 3:19).

One of the main principles of warfare is concentration, the massing of one's forces at a critical time and place for decisive action. The objective is to break through the opposing army's front line at a single point and then to penetrate its line of defense and secure a stronghold in its territory. Once that penetration occurs, it is easier for the enemy to forge on ahead.

This was happening to us at Reach Out. The ministry of God's Word had to be thwarted—doubt cannot abide with faith. And, since faith removes mountains and brings triumph, faith had to be destroyed. Faith comes by hearing and hearing by the Word of God;

therefore, it would only be logical for Satan to try to convince us to abandon ship as teachers and propagators of the Word. If he could bring *disappointment, discouragement, dejection,* and *despair,* then perhaps he could *demoralize* us totally.

But, praise God, we were not ignorant of Satan's devices! And neither will you be, Beloved, for with your shield of faith you will "be able to extinguish all the flaming missiles of the evil one" (Ephesians 6:16).

August 4

Satan usually spearheads his attack with disappointment. His target is your mind; his goal—to break down your line of defense.

When an army plans to break through its enemy's line of defense, the first step is to amass all the available weaponry at one particular point. Say the line of defense is thirty miles long. The goal will be to break through that line with a tip of steel (approximately five hundred tanks) a half-mile wide. Behind those five hundred tanks there will be another thousand, behind that an armored division of ten thousand, and behind that twenty thousand soldiers. Once the penetration is made by that tip of steel, the rest will move forward in an ever-widening expanse, taking over more and more of the enemy's line.

Once the initial penetration is made, it is easier to move in the rest of the troops. And so it is with Satan. He spearheads his tip of steel with disappointment, a *seemingly* common and impotent weapon! Notice I said "seemingly," for on the heels of disappointment comes a whole armored division of discouragement!

Here was where I made my mistake. I let Satan's fiery missile of disappointment break through the threshold of my mind. I failed to rest in the sovereignty of the God who causes **all** things to work together resulting in good. My service to the Lord had been done as unto the Lord. I had prayed about my lessons; I had studied diligently. Being responsible in my preparation, did not the effects belong to God "who works all things in all persons" (1 Corinthians 12:6)? Sometimes I wonder about myself. When will I learn? For over a year now, thoughts have come to mind as I have stood teaching—thoughts like *they are so bored . . . you're not reaching them . . . you have failed again . . . you might as well quit . . . they know all this already . . . God's not speaking through you . . . you should have taught something else,* and on and on.

When these thoughts came, instead of throwing up my shield of defense, I let them enter the camp, and then I called a staff meeting of me, myself, and I to try to figure out why I had messed up so badly. I failed to walk in the Spirit! Instead of exploding the missiles of disappointment with my own missiles of praise, I tried to figure out how I could have done a better job!

What about you? Do you ever get disappointed? If you have walked in obedience seeking His guidance, then the cure for disappointment is to accept it all by faith as His appointment and to rest in His faithfulness.

August 5

Discouragement and disappointment are almost twins. Open the door to disappointment, and you will find discouragement dashing in right behind. Satan's goal is to weaken you, to dishearten you, to have you lose courage. This is discouragement. And once discouragement enters your camp, it seems to be downhill all the way. That is why God was so careful in His instructions to Joshua as he prepared to enter Canaan and occupy the land that God had given them. They had missed occupying Canaan forty years earlier because of unbelief at Kadesh-barnea. Disappointment had moved in and filled them with despair. Yes, the land was as God had said, a land flowing with milk and honey. **But** there were giants in the land! What disappointment fell upon the children of Israel as they heard the report of the spies, "We went in to the land where you sent us; and it certainly does flow with milk and honey, and this is its fruit. Nevertheless, the people who live in the land are strong, and the cities are fortified and very large; and moreover, we saw the descendants of Anak there" (Numbers 13:27, 28). All courage was gone; they could never stand. In total discouragement, they lifted up their voices and cried and wept all night (14:1). All of a sudden their God had become too small to handle human giants.

Some forty years later, they were preparing to enter the same land and meet the same giants and so God said, not once but three times, "Be strong and courageous!" (Joshua 1:6, 7, 9). They were not to "tremble or be dismayed," for the Lord their God was with them.

Joshua knew the results of discouragement. He had been one of those twelve spies. He and Caleb had torn their clothes beseeching the children of Israel to walk in faith, to believe God; Caleb had said of the land and its inhabitants, "We should by all means go up and take possession of it, for we shall surely overcome it" (Numbers 13:30). Yet they would not listen. They would not believe God. They would not walk by faith. Word of the giants and the fortified cities had penetrated their line of defense, and discouragement followed bringing dejection and despair until they were totally demoralized.

And so what is God's word to you today? It is to be strong and courageous, for your Father, the Lord God Omnipotent, reigns. So stop weeping and exult in Him. Rejoice in the God of your salvation, for He is your strength and He will enable you to stand (Habakkuk 3:18, 19).

The cure for discouragement is encouragement. Encourage your heart by looking at your God and His promises.

August 6

The third deadly D is dejection. Dejection is a lowness of spirit. You feel tired, emotionally fatigued, worn out, and your ability to cope with difficult situations is at a dangerous low. This is a precarious position to be in, and, if you are at that point, you need to be aware that this is not the time to make significant decisions. If you do, they will, in all probability, be wrong. Dejection unchecked gives way to despair, our fourth deadly D.

One who is in a state of despair has lost or abandoned hope; his mind has become apathetic or numb. Thinking, decision making, or just getting through the day all seem to be impossible. How many there are that have been overcome by despair. Several precious ones have written me recently sharing that they can only make it through each day by rote, one motion at a time. The thought of coping for a whole day with even the basic routines of living is overwhelming. So they consider only the immediate and force themselves to go through the motions. Those who find themselves caught in despair usually feel abandoned by God. At such times the enemy will whisper unbelievable things in the mind—in the first person singular so they seem to be your thoughts rather than his! How clever are Satan's schemes!

Often, in times of dejection and despair, one's thoughts begin to turn to death. It seems easier to quit than to face life. "Why fight it any longer? Nothing is going to change. There's no way out." And so, in emotional fatigue, you go looking for a scrap of white material that you might use as your flag of surrender. You have called and called for help until you are too tired to call anymore. You have tried and tried until you are too tired to try anymore. So you give way to despair. In numbness and in dumbness, death seems the only cure; at least then you could rest; your struggle would cease. It is too hard to believe you could ever again be happy, out from under these circumstances and filled with joy. No, you have numbly considered the future and it is hopeless; therefore, you must abandon ship.

This is dejection, this is despair, and it is deadly. Is there any cure? Yes, for when the Psalmist asked, "Why are you in despair, O my soul?" (Psalms 42:5), he was given a cure.

August 7

I have ofttimes thought of Psalm 42 as being the longing of a consecrated heart for an even deeper walk or communion with God. And yet, after reading it carefully in its context, I saw this wasn't the case at all. Rather it is the inaudible longing that comes from the depths of a soul overcome with despair. It is the cry of a soul that feels abandoned by God. Carefully listen to the words as you read them:

> As the deer pants for the water brooks, so my soul pants for Thee, O God. My soul thirsts for God, for the living God; when shall I come and appear before God? My tears have been my food day and night, while they say to me all day long, "Where is your God?"

Here is one in desperate need of hearing from God. Ever feel this way? God seems far away, truly beyond the heavens in His domain through the north where even the stars do not inhabit His space. The gates are closed; the King is in His chambers. He is too busy or too full of disgust or displeasure to be concerned with one so disappointing as you.

Even others are saying to you, "Where is your God?" (v. 3). "Certainly if He were with you, you wouldn't be going through something like this." Then you stop and remember, "I used to go along with the throng and lead them in procession to the house of God, with the voice of joy and thanksgiving, a multitude keeping festival" (v. 4), and again you feel discouraged. "How could I have felt so good, so close to God, so joyous and now feel so empty, so alone, so full of despair?" Then Satan speaks up—in the first person singular and with a voice just like your own—"I have been abandoned by God. And if God has abandoned me, what hope is there? I might as well give up." These, Beloved, are thoughts of despair, not from the counsel chambers of heaven, but from the horror chambers of the father of lies.

You must not listen to them. You cannot listen to them. The just will live by faith (Habakkuk 2:4). Has not God Himself said, "I will never desert you, nor will I ever forsake you" (Hebrews 13:5)? In the Greek there are five negatives in that verse. Add two to the first "never" and read, "I will never, never, never desert you." Then add one more to "nor" and read it "nor never will I ever forsake you." What is God saying? "No matter how you may feel or how things may seem, I say, as sure as I am God, I will never desert you nor forsake you." You may feel abandoned, but faith answers confidently, *"The Lord is my helper, I will not be afraid. What shall man do to me?"* (Hebrews 13:6).

Are **you** in despair? Will you walk in faith or live by feeling?

August 8

Three times the Psalmist reiterates the despair of his soul. Since the mind, will, and emotions all serve as component parts of a man's soul, they are all affected. Despair has first touched the mind; he thinks he is alone, abandoned by God. He cannot reason. The emotions also are disturbed, for not only does man imagine himself alone without hope and abandoned, but every cell of his being cries out, "It's true, it's true! I feel it! I feel it in my bones!" And the will is taken in tow, dragged along by the mind and the emotions.

Is there no hope? Are these three to be held captive forever in the prison of despair? Where is the way of escape promised by the One who said, "No temptation (trial or testing) has overtaken you but such as is common to man; and God is faithful, who will not allow you to be tempted beyond what you are able, but with the temptation will provide the way of escape also, that you may be able to endure it" (1 Corinthians 10:13). And what form does this temptation take when it comes to despair? Is it not to give up, to surrender, to cease resisting, to be flushed helplessly as some captured insect down into the sewage system until it reaches the bowels of demoralization?

And what is demoralization, this fifth and final deadly D? It is a state that renders man untrustworthy in discipline of body and soul. It is to be cast into disorder, to run in circles, to be caught in cycles that throw you totally off balance so you cannot walk as God would have you walk. It is to forget that God has given you power, love, and a sound mind (2 Timothy 1:7). It is to sit in impotence, ignorant of your power. It is to tremble in fear, feeling abandoned and unloved, when in truth you could not be loved more. It is to have a mind that cannot think clearly or bring a thought to completion, when it could be a sound mind, a mind controlled by His Spirit. It is to refuse to listen to God's Spirit as He calls to you through the bars and bids you get up and at least try the cell door to see if it's locked. It is to shake your head and say, "There's no use! There's no hope!"

Demoralization is to deny the God of all hope because your mind just cannot reason, your emotions are numb, and your will is mesmerized by apathy. "Why are you in despair, O my soul? And why have you become disturbed within me?" (Psalms 42:5). It is because you **will** not hope in God and praise Him in faith.

August 9

Despair can take another form—desperation. Desperation can be energized despair that causes a frenzy of activity, ofttimes reckless activity with no thought of the consequences. Desperation agitates the soul. It has to move; it has to do something; it cannot be still. It is driven senselessly and in a wearisome way. Something must be done, but it does not know what.

And what should one do when he finds himself in the driven, senseless activity of desperation? There is only one thing to do, and that is to willfully cry out to God, to tell Him all about it, and trust Him for deliverance. Read Psalms 42:5–11 and see how the Psalmist dealt with his despair:

> Why are you in despair, O my soul? And why have you become disturbed within me? Hope in God, for I shall again praise Him for the help of His presence. O my God, my soul is in despair within me; therefore I remember Thee from the land of the Jordan, and the peaks of Hermon, from Mount Mizar. Deep calls to deep at the sound of Thy waterfalls; all Thy breakers and Thy waves have rolled over me. The Lord will command His lovingkindness in the daytime; and His song will be with me in the night, a prayer to the God of my life. I will say to God my rock, "Why hast Thou forgotten me? Why do I go mourning because of the oppression of the enemy?" As a shattering of my bones, my adversaries revile me, while they say to me all day long, "Where is your God?" Why are you in despair, O my soul? And why have you become disturbed within me? Hope in God, for I shall yet praise Him, the help of my countenance, and my God.

As you have noticed, verse 5 begins with a question that is repeated again in verse 11. It is a very needful question for one caught in the throes of despair or desperation. What is the cause of this despair? How did I get here? What brought me to this point? My daddy used to tell me, "Honey, once you know the cause of your problem, you have half the battle won." Yet so many refuse either to ask the question or even admit that there is a problem. In Psalm 42, not only does the Psalmist ask the question, but he also confesses his state to his God: "O my God, my soul is in despair within me."

And what about your soul, Beloved? Is it in despair? Is it headed that way? Has there been a penetration of disappointment? If so, ask yourself why.

August 10

What strange creatures we human beings are! How often we think we can change or alter things simply by refusing to acknowledge them. We find truth so hard to deal with! It seems unpleasant, something to avoid, and yet did God not say, "You shall know the truth, and the truth shall make you free" (John 8:32)? Somehow we think it is easier to live a lie. If we can ignore it, maybe it will go away. And so, with this twisted reasoning, we try to find our own way of coping rather than standing before the God of all truth, naked in His sight, and crying, "Help!"

And what keeps us away from Him? Is it not our own fantasizing, our own imperfect reasoning, our own concept of what this awesome and terrible God is like? Are we not really victims of the world's old wives' tales or the vain religious traditions of men? Is He a God who exists for the sole purpose of condemning us, a God whose concern for us ended after He made us? Is He a God who is too busy to care about the finite, minuscule problems of someone whose life span will be approximately threescore and ten? Is He out of reach, unattainable, unapproachable? Have we "come to a mountain ... that is burning with fire; to darkness, gloom and storm; to a trumpet blast or to such a voice speaking words, so that those who heard it begged no further word be spoken to them, because they could not bear what was commanded" (Hebrews 12:18–20 NIV)? Is this the One to whom we come when we are in despair? Oh, no, Beloved. No! We come to the God who loves us so unconditionally, so sacrificially that He gave His only begotten Son for us when we were His enemies, when we were in total despair. We come to the One who will freely give us all things.

We stand before Him without condemnation if in Christ Jesus. Or, if we stand before Him without Christ Jesus, we behold His Son at His right hand standing with outstretched, nail-pierced hands saying, "Will you not come to Me that you might have life, and have it abundantly?" So why then do we stop up our ears and say, "He doesn't care" or "It won't do any good"? Why will we not come before Him and say, "Help. Examine me, my God. Tell me what my problem is. Why am I in this state? What is the answer? Tell me, God, tell me, and I will be quick to hear Your words. I will pay attention to them. I'll trust You, God. Speak, Lord, for Your servant hears"?

O Beloved, what will your response be?

August 11

Let's begin today by reading again Psalms 42:5–11:

> Why are you in despair, O my soul? And why have you become disturbed within me? Hope in God, for I shall again praise Him for the help of His presence. O my God, my soul is in despair within me; therefore I remember Thee from the land of the Jordan, and the peaks of Hermon, from Mount Mizar. Deep calls to deep at the sound of Thy waterfalls; all Thy breakers and Thy waves have rolled over me. The Lord will command His lovingkindness in the daytime; and His song will be with me in the night, a prayer to the God of my life. I will say to God my rock, "Why hast Thou forgotten me? Why do I go mourning because of the oppression of the enemy?" As a shattering of my bones, my adversaries revile me, while they say to me all day long, "Where is your God?" Why are you in despair, O my soul? And why have you become disturbed within me? Hope in God, for I shall yet praise Him, the help of my countenance, and my God.

Faith is the only cure for despair, or for any of the deadly D's. Disappointed, discouraged, dejected, despairing, or demoralized, there is only one place to run, and that is to your God, your Rock. Cry out to Him. Say "a prayer to the God of *your* life" (v. 8). If you feel as if He has forgotten you, then ask Him if He has. If you feel as if your enemies—be they physical, emotional, or spiritual—have overwhelmed you, ask Him why. Pour out your soul to your God. Don't let your mind, your emotions, and your will cower in the corner of an unlocked cell. Rise up, O Will. Grab Mind and Emotions. Burst through that iron door and go talk to your Rock. Hope in Him, O Mind, and know, Emotions, you shall again praise Him for the help of His presence. Rehearse what you remember of your God and know that "the Lord will command His lovingkindness in the daytime; and His song will be with *you* in the night" (v. 8).

Remember the just shall live by faith. You are not abandoned. You will not live forever in this despair, for as you hope in Him, you will yet praise Him. "But we have this treasure in earthen vessels, that the surpassing greatness of the power may be of God **and not from ourselves;** we are afflicted in every way, but not crushed; perplexed, **but not** despairing" (2 Corinthians 4:7, 8).

There it is. His Word. Will you believe it? Remember that faith consists of three things: knowledge, surrender to that knowledge, and obedience to walk in the light of it. Will you live by faith?

August 12

Jesus knew that His disciples were going to face difficult times when their faith would be tested to the hilt. Thus, at every opportunity, He sought to prepare them. "These things I have spoken to you, that **in Me** you may have peace. In the world you have tribulation, but take courage; I have overcome the world" (John 16:33). Testing was inevitable; yet they were to persevere. And perseverance for the Lord Jesus Christ meant to be faithful unto death (Revelation 2:10). His concern, spoken by His own lips, was that "when the Son of Man comes, will He find faith on the earth?" (Luke 18:8). He said this after "telling them a parable to show that at all times they ought to pray and not to lose heart" (Luke 18:1).

Today we hear so much about "saving faith" which is good and vital, for it is the very beginning of life . . . "for by grace you have been saved through faith" (Ephesians 2:8). Yet sometimes I wonder if that is not all we hear. Do we not need to hear of the faith that perseveres, that not only begins life but that also is the very sustenance of this new life?

Does not God's Word teach us that true saving faith also perseveres—that it continues despite the difficulties, the trials, the testings, the challenges, the lusts of other things, and the worries of this age? Is not true faith a faith that one does not casually embrace or have an affair with? Is it not rather a faith that one *marries* "until death us do part"? Is it not to be a giving of yourself in total commitment? Is it not a faith which we believe for the benefits it brings and for which we earnestly contend, no matter what the cost (Jude 3)?

What is involved in saving faith? Can I just believe, get the assurance of a home in heaven, and then live as I please? Can I ask the Good Master for eternal life and receive it with no intention of forsaking all, taking up my cross, and following Him (Mark 8:34)? Can I call my soul my own and let my mind, emotions, and will go unaffected, uncommitted to the truths of God's Word? Can I embrace His words for my salvation from hell and yet be ashamed of my God and His Word in this sinful and adulterous generation (Mark 8:38) and still think that I have really believed and been saved? Can I? Can you?

August 13

Perilous times are not coming; they are here. Oh, you may not be aware of them yet, but they, like other fugitives, have surreptitiously crossed the borders of our nation, our age. I have talked with some Christians who are greatly burdened for our nation because they are quite aware of what is happening in high places. I have even read reports by those who know nothing of God's Word and yet who feel that the eighties may be in all probability our last decade. It's hard to perceive, isn't it? And it really isn't something that we want to think about. Do we think that maybe, if we can ignore it, this will not come to pass?

A day of judgment is coming. God's Word tells us so. You say, "People have been talking about it for almost two thousand years now, and it still hasn't happened." You are right. It hasn't happened, but it's about to! Oh, I know, people have also been saying, "You're right. It hasn't happened, but it's about to," for a long time, and it still hasn't happened!

That, Beloved, is the mentality of the world, of the pseudo-church; it is not to be the mentality of those "of saving faith." No, we are to have an alertness that results in holy conduct, godliness, and perseverance "looking for and hastening the coming of the day of God" (2 Peter 3:12).

In desperate need of a rest, I have taken a few days to be at a dear friend's home in Big Canoe. During these days, I have spent much time praying, meditating, reading, and writing and sharing these devotionals with you. Yesterday as I sat on the porch basking in the magnificence of God's world, He turned my thoughts to His coming and to Hebrews 10 which had meant so much to me at an earlier time. Now one verse in particular caught my attention: "For yet in a very little while, He who is coming will come, and will not delay" (Hebrews 10:37).

As I thought about it, God then reminded me of the days of Noah, "for the coming of the Son of Man will be just like the days of Noah. For as in those days which were before the flood they were eating and drinking, they were marrying and giving in marriage, until the day that Noah entered the ark, and **they did not understand until the flood came and took them all away**" (Matthew 24:37–39). "**They did not understand until. . . .**" They were living in perilous times and didn't even realize it! How do we know that they had no idea how perilous the times were? It is because they were occupied with everyday living— eating, drinking, marrying. When they found out, it was too late.

Are not many who profess to know Christ living the same way, occupied with the temporal without thought or due preparation for the eternal? Is this the way the just are supposed to live? And how are you living? What part does your faith play in your daily life?

August 14

Saving faith doesn't just save you and send you back to your old way of life until it's time to enter "heaven's pearly gates." No, true saving faith changes a person's life. It may not change his or her occupation or the ordinary routines of day-to-day living, but it does change man's perspective on these things. It changes his affections and the way he responds to others, for when a man is truly saved he becomes a new creature in Christ; old things are passed away and all things become new (2 Corinthians 5:17). Suddenly he becomes aware of two categories of mankind: those who belong to God and those who belong to the devil. "By this the children of God and the children of the devil are obvious; any one who does not practice righteousness is not of God, nor the one who does not love his brother" (1 John 3:10). True saving faith doesn't begin and then just fizzle out. It's not a "plop, plop, fizz, fizz, oh-what-a-relief-it-is" type of Christianity that takes care of the temporary distress of thoughts of hell fire and damnation and yet leaves you the way you used to be. No, true faith continues. It abides. It perseveres. It may falter and get perplexed, confused, shaky, but in the end, despite it all, it does persevere.

Meditate on Colossians 1:22, 23 and pray that God will show you clearly whether yours is a saving faith.

Yet He has now reconciled you in His fleshly body through death, in order to present you before Him holy and blameless and beyond reproach—if indeed you continue in the faith firmly established and steadfast, and not moved away from the hope of the gospel that you have heard.

Two insights from the Greek will help you understand what God is saying in this passage. First, the *if* is a first class conditional clause, which indicates reality and means *and it is true.* The third class condition of *if* means, *maybe it is true and maybe it is not; it is something that remains to be seen.* Therefore, what do you think God is saying about being reconciled (saved) and continuing in the faith? Why don't you meditate on it, asking God to open your eyes to His truth? Then write your insights in your notebook.

Secondly, the verb *moved* is a present participle and represents a continual or habitual shifting. Therefore, it is not referring to inter-mittent doubts that might attack you or even a short period of waning fervency or dedication to God's work.

August 15

Someday your faith will be challenged to the core. If God tested Abraham by asking him for Isaac; if He tested Joseph by letting him go into Egypt and bondage; if He tested Moses with the wrath of the king; if He tested Joshua with the walls of Jericho—and if He let His saints be stoned, sawn in two, tempted, put to death with the sword and go "about in sheepskins, in goatskins, being destitute, afflicted, ill-treated . . . wandering in deserts and mountains and caves and holes in the ground" (Hebrews 11:37, 38), do you think that your faith will go untested? If it does, then you can wonder if you are truly a child of God, for faith is not faith until it is tested!

And so, Precious One, I believe that God would have us spend yet another day naked in His sight following His admonition in 2 Corinthians 13:5: "Test yourselves [not others but yourselves] to see if you are in the faith; examine yourselves! Or do you not recognize this about yourselves, that Jesus Christ is in you—unless indeed you fail the test?"

Read what Paul says in 1 Corinthians 15:1, 2 and then I have a question for you.

Now I make known to you, brethren, the gospel which I preached to you, which also you received, in which also you stand, by which also you are saved, if you hold fast the word which I preached to you, unless you believed in vain.

The *if* in verse 2 is first class conditional. Remember, that means *and it is true.* According to these verses, what will be true if you are saved? Now then, look at 1 John 2:3–5.

And by this we know that we have come to know Him, if we keep His commandments. The one who says, "I have come to know Him," and does not keep His commandments, is a liar, and the truth is not in him; but whoever keeps His word, in him the love of God has truly been perfected. By this we know that we are in Him.

The verbs *keep* and *keeps* are all in the present tense which implies continuous action or a way of life. This does not imply perfection, but it does suggest continuance and perseverance. These verbs are also in the active voice; the subject (which is the believer) performs the action of the verb. In other words, the believer is responsible for the obedience. Believers cannot excuse themselves by saying, "The devil made me do it." O Beloved, do you keep His commandments? Are they your way of life?

August 16

> Now we have received, not the spirit of the world, but the Spirit who is from God, that we might know the things freely given to us by God, which things we also speak, not in words taught by human wisdom, but in those taught by the Spirit, combining spiritual thoughts with spiritual words. But a natural man does not accept the things of the Spirit of God; for they are foolishness to him, and he cannot understand them, because they are spiritually appraised (1 Corinthians 2:12–14).

Do you understand God's Word when you read it or does it seem like there is a veil over it, a veil that lets you see the facts clearly yet dims its spiritual meaning? Do you find God's Word hard to accept, hard to believe? Do you understand God's Word? If you cannot understand God's Word, or if it is unacceptable or even foolish to you, then, Beloved, God is showing you that you do not have His Holy Spirit living within you. And "if anyone does not have the Spirit of Christ, he does not belong to Him" (Romans 8:9). Has God's Spirit taken up His permanent residence within your body? Is your body His temple and do you realize that you **are not** your own (1 Corinthians 6:19, 20)? Does His Spirit bear (present tense) witness with your spirit that you are a child of God (Romans 8:16)?

And finally, is your life a life of righteousness? Before you answer that, let me explain righteousness, for I do not want you to confuse it with morality. Righteousness and morality are not the same. A righteous man will be moral, but being moral does not make a man righteous. Righteousness is living according to God's standard, according to His leadership. Righteousness is contrasted with sin. Sin is lawlessness (1 John 3:4), but it is also more than that. Sin is acting apart from faith for "whatever is not from faith is sin" (Romans 14:23). Sin is walking your own way. "All of us like sheep have gone astray, each of us has **turned to his own way**; but the Lord has caused the iniquity of us all to fall on Him" (Isaiah 53:6). Now then, 1 John 3:9 says, "No one who is born of God practices [present tense] sin, because His seed abides [present tense] in him; and he cannot sin [present tense], because he is born of God." A child of God can commit singular acts of sin (1 John 2:1, 2) or be disobedient in one particular area of his life, but he cannot habitually live doing his own thing, walking his own way. He must live habitually more and more according to God's standard. Are you a child of God? How do you live?

August 17

How do you convey a burden? There are times when I wonder about myself, and I know there are times when others wonder about me! Am I too extreme? Do I expect too much from Christians?

Does God expect men to be godly men who live according to the precepts of His Word—men of the Book—men who give themselves to knowing and understanding God and His ways by knowing and understanding His Word—men who are given to prayer, worship, and meditation—men who labor before God interceding for their families, their country, God's world—men who have cast themselves at the feet of God in heartfelt gratitude and utter abandonment, telling Him that above all they want to live lives pleasing to Him no matter the cost—men who are willing to discipline themselves and their appetites in order to serve Him who has called them to be good soldiers of Jesus Christ—men who are burdened for others and not ashamed of the gospel of Jesus Christ, knowing it is the power of God unto salvation to everyone who believes? Are these things too much for God to expect from those who receive the gift of eternal life through the sacrifice of His Son? Is a life-style like this too much to ask from a man who has to support his family in today's economy? Do the following Scriptures pertain to men of today, or just to women?

> If anyone comes to Me, and does not hate ... even his own life, he cannot be My disciple. Whoever does not carry his own cross and come after Me cannot be My disciple (Luke 14:26, 27). But seek first His kingdom and His righteousness; and all these things shall be added to you (Matthew 6:33). Suffer hardship with me, as a good soldier of Christ Jesus. No soldier in active service entangles himself in the affairs of everyday life, so that he may please the one who enlisted him as a soldier (2 Timothy 2:3, 4). And do not be conformed to this world, but be transformed by the renewing of your mind, that you may prove what the will of God is, that which is good and acceptable and perfect (Romans 12:2). Be diligent to present yourself approved to God as a workman who does not need to be ashamed, handling accurately the word of truth (2 Timothy 2:15).

What is my burden? My burden is that there is not any army of men who profess Jesus Christ and live as good soldiers. And why are there seemingly more women than men who live this way? Are not the men also to live according to God's Word?

August 18

Not long ago I stood sharing with a precious young wife who had recently given birth to her first child. It was after our Monday night Bible study at Reach Out. When I asked her where her husband was, her whole countenance changed. He was at home watching Monday night football. His attendance at our course on marriage ended when football got into full swing. The week before, not wanting to come alone, she, too, stayed home. But, when she started to fuss at him for putting football before learning God's Word, he told her she needed to get back to Reach Out. Her disposition was better when she sat under God's Word, he said. And it was.

So is mine. When I stay in the Word, I stay in touch with reality. I keep life in its proper perspective. But let me go on vacation and ease up on the disciplines—or let me get too busy, and I find myself more easily drawn away by the lusts of other things. Does this mean I am weak? Yes, it does. That is why I so desperately need to be careful about how I walk, being wise, making the most of my time for the days are evil (Ephesians 5:15, 16).

Have you ever evaluated how you spend your time? What do you do with the 168 hours that are in every week? If you allow yourself eight hours a day for sleep, three hours a day for eating, ten hours a day for work and travel to and from work, you still have forty-one hours unaccounted for each week. How many hours a week would you say that you give to time alone with God? Now, I am not talking about time in church or in Bible classes; rather, I mean personal prayer and Bible study. If you tithed your time like you do your income, how much time would you have to give to God each week? Would it not be over sixteen hours per week? Or say, if you did as Israel was commanded to do and kept one day of seven as holy, set aside unto the Lord, how much time would that give you for communal worship, private devotions, and study? Subtract a good night's sleep and what do you have? Is it not more than sixteen hours—a tenth of the week?

But a man needs rest and recreation, doesn't he? Doesn't he need a break from the heavy load he bears? Yes, he does. And thus Jesus Christ says, "Come to Me, all who are weary and heavy-laden, and I will give you rest. Take My yoke upon you, and learn from Me, for I am gentle and humble in heart; and **you shall find rest for your souls.** For My yoke is easy, and My load is light" (Matthew 11:28–30). Have you ever wondered if so many feel so burdened, so pressured, and in such desperate need because they have **not** taken the time to come to Him, to learn of Him, and to cast all their care upon Him? Should not times of intimate fellowship with our God be our primary means of rest and re-creation? Or should television, sports, newspapers, books and hobbies be our primary means? When do we fit God in? Is this where God should be if He is truly our God?

August 19

"Rest for your souls." That is the promise for those who take His yoke and learn of Him (Matthew 11:28–30). Remember what constitutes the soul: the mind, the will, the emotions. And what is it like in your mind? What kind of thoughts plague you? What kind of self-image do you have? What do you think about others? What are your concepts of God, of life, of Christianity, of eternity? Could you possibly be wrong? How can you tell? What is your plumb line for testing what you think, or what you think you know? Remember as a man thinks in his heart so he is (Proverbs 23:7).

And your will. Is it on target? Do you want to do the will of Him who bought you? Or is your will governed by an unrenewed mind so that you are choosing the good and missing the best? Do you have a Lord, a King, a God, and does He reign over your will? Or are you possibly your own master, governing your own will? Are you like those in the days of Judges when, because there was no king in Israel, every man did what was right in his own eyes (Judges 21:25)? What they did was wrong, horribly, destructively wrong, but they thought they were right! Have you ever really studied Judges? You ought to. You can. We have a Precept course on Judges. Of course it would take time, five hours a week, and that would mean discipline. But then out of sixteen hours—say seven for prayer and meditation, five for diligent study— that would still leave you four hours for church and Bible study. Of course all that could only be accomplished if you set your will to do it!

Then there are your emotions. Rest for your emotions? Peace, not fear. Love, not hate. Forgiveness, not bitterness. Trust, not anger. Joy, not depression. Quietness—confidence—gentleness—kindness—self-control. Can you imagine how much strife would end, how many relationships would be healed if our anxieties were cared for? Just think of the release that would come because guilt would be gone. When our emotions are off, we do so many things that bring such guilt upon us. Of course we rationalize away our wrong behavior or blame others, but even that does not remove the guilt, does it? Rest for your souls. Can you imagine it? I pray you can, so that you will long for it.

And where is it to be found? In His yoke, united to His will, learning of Him, transformed by the renewing of your mind. It will be found in discipline, in selection and rejection (choosing the best over the better), and then in concentration on the things of paramount importance, eternal things.

August 20

"All these things will I give You, if You fall down and worship me" (Matthew 4:9). When Satan said this, he was offering Jesus all the kingdoms of the world. A crown without the cross! And that is what he continues to offer every single human being—saved or lost. He parades before them the world in all its splendor, without the cross. Yet the world does not come without a cross. You cannot expect to rule and reign when Jesus is King of kings unless you are willing to bear your cross now! To think otherwise, Beloved, is to be deceived.

I am absolutely baffled by the average churchgoer's concept of true spirituality. So many are trusting in a baptism, a confession of faith, a name on the church roll, a confirmation, a life of morality and good deeds, a God who would never let anyone go to hell, a life of participation in church activities, yet their lives have never changed; they do not hunger and thirst after righteousness. (Note: I said *righteousness* not *morality*.) I wonder about all those who claim to possess Him and yet do not carry out to completion their salvation "with fear and trembling" (Philippians 2:12). I am baffled by those who claim Him as Savior, even Lord, and yet love this present world (2 Timothy 4:10). What kind of faith is this?

Remember, if you love Him, you will keep His commandments (John 14:15). And we are not to love this "world, **nor the things in the world.** If any one loves the world, the love of the Father is not in him. For all that is in the world, the lust of the flesh and the lust of the eyes and the boastful pride of life, **is not from** the Father, but is from the world. And the world is passing away, and also its lusts; but the one who does the will of God abides forever" (1 John 2:15–17). Multitudes are saving their lives only to lose them. And many who profess Christ (whether they know Him or not, I do not know—God knows) are living a pseudo-Christianity, caught up in the things of this world and only giving lip service to Jesus Christ. They use those same lips to justify their behavior with an "I am sure God understands," or "He'll forgive me," or "He certainly doesn't expect me to live that way, does He?!" There is no cross, no death to the flesh, no giving Christ the preeminence in their lives.

How about you, Beloved? Is the lure of this world more important, or will you bear your cross?

August 21

"You were running well; who hindered you from obeying the truth?" (Galatians 5:7). So wrote Paul to the churches in Galatia; some had come in and preached another gospel, and the Galatians were in danger of believing it (Galatians 1:6, 7). As a result they had been sidetracked. To put it in athletic terms, they got out of their lane. They were listening to the wrong "gospel."

Sometimes I wonder if that is not what is being proclaimed subtly today. Some refer to it as "easy believism." When Jesus and John the Baptist came proclaiming the Kingdom, their first word was "repent." When the people of Thessalonica received the Word in much affliction (a group had been following Paul from city to city persecuting him), they turned from idols to serve the true and living God. When they heard the gospel they realized that it was not only given to them to believe on the Lord Jesus Christ but also to suffer for His sake. The message of the gospel was the good news of God's love for sinful man, but it was also the good news that sinful man would be transformed from sinner to saint by yielding to God's grace. When Jesus called men to follow Him, they certainly understood His way was the way of the cross.

It was not just a case of receiving a free give-away salvation. Rather, it was a call to walk in newness of life (Romans 6:4) and to persevere in this life until the end. "For we have become partakers of Christ, if we hold fast the beginning of our assurance firm until the end" (Hebrews 3:14). Simply beginning the Christian life is not enough. It is a race to be finished in God's lane, God's way. And He is the Judge, the Giver of crowns.

Peter Gillquist, in a provocative article, "The Christian Life: A Marathon We Mean to Win?" (*Christianity Today,* Oct. 21, 1981), says, "It is remaining faithful to Christ that is essential to true spirituality, and it is of eternal importance in his sight. It is not adequate merely to have a spectacular conversion or a glowing story of deliverance. God calls us to be on our feet and in the fight at the final bell." After saying this, Mr. Gillquist then illustrates the necessity of perseverance in the Christian life, saying it is not a 100-yard dash, but a marathon.

If Paul were writing to the churches today would he write, "You were running well; **WHAT** hindered you?" What is keeping you from total consecration to Christ? Even if it is a career or a ministry, it is an idol. If it's television, sports, money, good deeds to your fellowman, home, family—if it comes before Him, it is an idol. Smash it!

August 22

If you do not plan to live the Christian life totally committed to knowing your God and to walking in obedience to Him, then don't begin, for this is what Christianity is all about. It is a change of governments. If you have no intention of letting Christ rule your life, then forget Christianity; it is not for you. Now, Beloved, lest you think I am being too hard, remember Mark 8:34–38 and remember that faith is not merely knowledge. True faith includes surrender to and obedience to that knowledge.

Let me share with you Peter Gillquist's illustration of what it is "to live the Christian life."

I went out for the high school cross-country team—a sport I consider to this day as the worst one in all the world in which to earn an athletic letter! On the first day of practice, the coach took us by bus to a course that ran up and down several hills over four miles. The prospects for those of us who were not in good shape, or who had never run distance races before, were particularly dismal on that late afternoon.

Before he fired the starting gun, that coach said something I have never forgotten: "What I am asking you to do today is to finish the race. If you don't plan to finish, then I do not want you to start. Simply stay where you are when the gun is fired. But if you start, then you *will* finish. You may slow down, or even stop for a bit, but you will not quit. Once you start, I want you to cross this finish line—no matter what."

The first mile was almost euphoric. The cool, fresh autumn air was a natural boost to my dogged determination to run a good race. But after a mile and a half or so, the joy began to fade. By two miles, whatever pleasure there had been in all of this was totally gone. From then on, it was sheer drudgery. Some of my teammates deposited the sandwiches they had eaten that noon at the school cafeteria in the tall grass and bushes at the edge of the course. Some would stop for a bit, find relief, and then fall back into the panting procession.

My legs started to cramp. I did not know thigh muscles could ever be tired. I felt my breath would leave me forever. My lungs and chest cavity were in almost unbearable pain as I approached an enormous upward hill near the 2½-mile mark.

There is one thing and one thing only that kept me going: *before I started, I had agreed to finish.* My body was spent, my mind screamed, "Quit!" But the choice had been made back when the gun went off. The issue was not open for renegotiation. There were no options, no short cuts. In inexpressible agony, I kept on running.

I can barely remember crossing the finish line. I was told I came in fifth or sixth, but even that was not of first importance. Every ounce of energy I knew had gone into finishing. I really could not believe I had made it.

Over the years, I have thought back to that experience as being an incredible picture of what it is to live the Christian life. In fact, the Scriptures more than once use a race as a metaphor of our life with Christ. And it is not a mere sprint, mind you—it is a marathon.

It is a hard and, at times, grueling marathon which will challenge the very core of your faith, Beloved. But, what a sense of victory is yours when you cross that finish line! And what defeat if you do not finish what you began. Take a few minutes and talk to God about your commitment to Him. Do you intend to finish your course, no matter what? Then record it in black and white.

August 23

Why do some Christians seem to have a greater passion for the things of God than others? Why do some seem to take their Christianity more seriously than others? What creates that gap between contentment with the status quo and a consuming passion for a greater intimacy with the Godhead? Is it because some receive a greater portion of Jesus Christ or of salvation? Do some have an extra blessing or experience with the Holy Spirit? Does God play favorites, giving more or doing more in special individuals' lives? No, according to God's Word Christ cannot be divided. Each believer is complete in Him. The same Holy Spirit dwells in each one who has been born of water and of the Spirit (John 3:5). So then what makes the difference?

I believe the answer is found in the parable of the sower as told by our Lord Jesus Christ. He wanted the people to see why, when it came to passion, some had more than others. When He finished His parable, He said: "For whoever has, to him shall more be given, and he shall have an abundance; but whoever does not have, even what he has shall be taken away from him" (Matthew 13:12). That is why just before this statement, Jesus said, "He who has ears, let him hear (9)."

He is showing them that passion for God, intimacy with God, is a matter of choice. You can be as spiritual as you want to be. Only *you* will ever limit what you are for God. If you take what you have been given, treasure it, use it for His glory, and cry to God for more, more will be given you and you will have an abundance. However, if you despise or neglect what God has given you, if you do not use it for Him, then even what you have will be taken away. It all depends on how you hear what God says to you. By hearing, God means that type of hearing which makes you a doer of the Word. This is why, in Luke 8:18, Jesus said, "Therefore take care how you listen; for whoever has, to him shall more be given; and whoever does not have, even what he thinks he has shall be taken away from him."

Since, Beloved, "nothing is hidden that shall not become evident, nor anything secret that shall not be known and come to light" (Luke 8:17), why don't you take time to examine yourself? How well do you listen to God's Word? Are you content with the status quo of modern Christianity, or do you have a consuming passion for a greater intimacy with Jesus Christ?

August 24

Why did Jesus tell His followers the parable of the sower and the other parables? The answer to that question, in part, is found in understanding the meaning of the word *parable*. It comes from the word *paraballo* which means *to place alongside for measurement or comparison like you would a yardstick*. Thus the parable of the sower and the soils was given to show men the condition of their hearts. Secondarily, it was given to prepare the disciples for the time when they would deliver God's Word. Jesus wanted His disciples to understand the differences in men's responses to His Word. When Jesus told this parable, He knew that His popularity would wane as men began to fully understand what it cost to be a true follower of His gospel. When they walked away, when they said it was too much to expect, too hard to do, He wanted His own to understand it was a matter of heart, their hearts. And so He told them this parable:

> "Listen to this! Behold, the sower went out to sow; and it came about that as he was sowing, some seed fell beside the road, and the birds

came and ate it up. And other seed fell on the rocky ground where it did not have much soil; and immediately it sprang up because it had no depth of soil. And after the sun had risen, it was scorched; and because it had no root, it withered away. And other seed fell among the thorns, and the thorns grew up and choked it, and it yielded no crop. And other seeds fell into the good soil and as they grew up and increased, they were yielding a crop and were producing thirty, sixty, and a hundred-fold." And He was saying, "He who has ears to hear, let him hear" (Mark 4:3–9).

The various soils represent the hearts of men which apparently fall into four different categories. For the next several days, we will look at each of these soils. Pray that God will reveal to you the condition of your heart. As we begin, let me ask you: do you really want to see, hear, and understand what God is saying? Or will you be like those of whom Isaiah spoke, people whose hearts have become dull, people who have purposely "closed their eyes lest they . . . see with their eyes, and hear with their ears, and understand with their heart and turn again" and God should heal them? (Matthew 13:15). The choice is yours. It is a matter of having ears to hear, and you determine that. Spiritual deafness is not clinical; it is psychological!

August 25

"The sower sows the word. And these are the ones who are beside the road where the word is sown; and when they hear, immediately Satan comes and takes away the word which has been sown in them" (Mark 4:14, 15). Why? Are they helpless victims of Satan? No, they could have heard but they didn't want to! Remember the times you could have heard but you didn't want to? You could not have cared less!

And in a similar way these are the ones on whom seed was sown on the rocky places, who, when they hear the word, immediately receive it with joy; and they have no firm root in themselves, but are only temporary; then, when affliction or persecution arises because of the word, immediately they fall away (Mark 4:16, 17).

Sixteen-year-old Hugh Makay, a Scottish covenanter, had just been sentenced to death for his faith in Jesus Christ. They could not persuade him from his faith. His trial finished, they thrust him into the street where a curious crowd had gathered. Seeing them he began to shout, "Good news! Good news! I am within four days' sight of the Kingdom." No rocky ground in this young lad's heart!

Have you ever known people who, upon hearing the good news of salvation by grace, embraced it joyfully? What more could a man or woman desire! "Who wants to burn in hell? Not me! I would be a fool not to accept Christ." And accept Christ they did, at least to all outward appearances. Everything went fine—church, Bible study, serving God. They couldn't get enough. And what a testimony! The race was on, but they didn't know it was a marathon—a hard and, at times, grueling marathon.

They were a showy plant with shallow roots. They seemingly had received Christ Jesus the Lord by faith but just didn't have or take time to become firmly rooted and built up in Him. They had been instructed to build a strong root system in the faith, but they did not listen (Colossians 2:7). Somehow, there didn't seem to be time. Besides, everything was going great. They could handle it! They had their five minutes a day, their daily devotional, their "help me, give me" prayers. Then it hit! Affliction came. Suddenly there was pain. God seemed deaf or away on vacation. He never seemed to answer and the situation only got worse. "How much can a body take?" "Why, I'm worse off than I was before I received Christ!" Or, they were persecuted. "Persecution or affliction . . . who needed it?" "If this is what it means to be a Christian, you can forget it." Their faith was only temporary— no long marathons, and they never finished.

"And by smooth words he will turn to godlessness those who act wickedly toward the covenant, **but the people who know their God will display strength and take action**" (Daniel 11:32). How is your root system? How well are you getting to know your God?

August 26

"And others are the ones on whom seed was sown among the thorns; these are the ones who have heard the word,
    and the worries of the world,
    and the deceitfulness of riches,
    and the desires for other things
enter in and choke the word, and it becomes unfruitful" (Mark 4:18, 19).

After Joshua died, and all his "generation also were gathered to their fathers and there arose another generation after them who did not know the Lord, nor yet the work which He had done for Israel

(Judges 2:10). They had not "experienced any of the wars of Canaan" (3:1). This was a generation, therefore, that did not obey God. Rather than drive out the inhabitants of Canaan as God had commanded them, they let them stay. They associated with them, married them, and went into idolatry. They simply did not listen so as to obey. God had said, "So take diligent heed to yourselves to love the Lord your God. For if you ever go back and cling to the rest of these nations, these which remain among you, and intermarry with them, so that you associate with them and they with you, know with certainty that the Lord your God will not continue to drive these nations out from before you; but they shall be a snare and a trap to you, and a whip on your sides and thorns in your eyes, until you perish from off this good land which the Lord your God has given you" (Joshua 23:11–13).

Their hearts were filled with thorns, and, as a result, we have the darkest three hundred and fifty years in the history of Israel! Here was a generation on which the sins of the fathers were truly visited down to the third and fourth generations. Why? Because the fathers did not listen to God and compromised the truth. They married whom they pleased. They permitted idols in their land, then idols in their homes. Their priests compromised and became corrupt.

The days of Judges were much like our days are. Apathy, apostasy, and anarchy reigned because there was no king in Israel. Hearts then and now are filled with thorns, caught up with the worries of the world, and the deceitfulness of riches, and the desires for other things. The Word was choked.

August 27

The worries of this world are great, aren't they? There's so much to concern you—the economy, unemployment, broken homes, crime, illness, and, on top of that, political unrest. How are we going to manage? With everything going up, how will we survive? And what if Social Security fails? Who will care for us in our old age? And what about the young newlyweds? Will they ever be able to afford a home of their own? And how will they manage with children if both of them have to work? We had better get it while we can—be as rich as we can as quickly as we can. And thus as we struggle to the top, other things are set aside, just for a while. Then we can slow down and have more time for one another, our families, our God, His Word. Besides, with all we earn, think of how we can help the work of the church!

Yet, as we struggle and climb, there are new allurements, new attainable goals. We think of them as good investments: land, jewelry, homes, stock, more insurance. Each has its demands, its payments, but, with careful budgeting, balancing, and a little more work, it'll pay off—somehow, sometime. Then, we'll have more time for one another, our families, our God, His Word.

Yet, with each year the pressures increase and so do the demands. We grow tired and need a rest. We can't keep going at this pace. But someday it has to slow down. Surely things will ease up, and then we'll have more time for one another, our families, our God, His Word.

It's a rat race, isn't it? Life becomes a maze of possibilities, one of which, if found, will surely lead us to the life of our dreams! Is this all that life is about, or is there more?

There *is* more. But so few will ever know it because of the thorns in the soil of their hearts. Their lives will never bear the fruit they were meant to bear because the eternal truths that set men free will be choked out by the worries of the world, the deceitfulness of riches, and the desire for other things. And what will they have when they come to the end of their days? Empty hands, barren lives. What will this year bring? More of the same, unless the thorns are removed.

What is the answer? The key is found, I believe, in these verses. Meditate upon them, and then we will discuss them tomorrow.

The lamp of the body is the eye; if therefore your eye is clear, your whole body will be full of light. But if your eye is bad, your whole body will be full of darkness. If therefore the light that is in you is darkness, how great is the darkness! No one can serve two masters (Matthew 6:22-24).

What are your eyes upon, honestly?

August 28

Our problem is temporal vision. We look at this life as if it is the chief aim of man. And we get caught up in it. The more we gaze upon it, the more enmeshed we become until we are unbelievably obligated to creditors, to institutions of higher learning, to professions, to religious and charitable organizations, to increased family activities. Our time is so consumed by activity that we have no suitable time to put our eyes anywhere else! We have no time to focus on "the true light which ... enlightens every man" (John 1:9).

When we keep our eyes on God and walk according to His Word, His character, and His will, we will make it through the maze of life.

We will find that one door that leads to perfect security, perfect liberty, and perfect sustenance. "I am the door; if anyone enters through Me, he shall be saved, and shall go in and out, and find pasture. The thief comes only to steal, and kill, and destroy; I came that they might have life, and might have it abundantly" (John 10:9, 10). Everything needful will be added to those who will focus their eyes upon Him and seek first His kingdom and His righteousness (Matthew 6:33). Therefore God says: "Do not be anxious then, saying, 'What shall we eat?' or 'What shall we drink?' or 'With what shall we clothe ourselves?' For all these things the Gentiles **eagerly seek;** for your heavenly Father knows that you need all these things" (Matthew 6:31, 32). Your Father "shall supply all your needs according to His riches in glory in Christ Jesus" (Philippians 4:19). Therefore, the "thorn killer" is to habitually "keep seeking the things above, where Christ is, seated at the right hand of God. Set your mind on the things above, **not on the things that are on earth"** (Colossians 3:1, 2).

As the saying goes, "Easier said than done." The pull of the world is great. Television and advertisements continually set before your eyes the temporal things of life while catchy little tunes tell you that these are the things that make life worth living! Beautiful homes, beautiful cars, beautiful clothes, beautiful possessions. And almost everyone's conversation is focused on these beautiful, temporal things. Therefore, you must have "ears to hear"; you must "take care how you listen"; you must take His yoke and learn of Him; you must constantly measure everything by the plumb line of God's Word. You can only be fruitful by enduring "as seeing Him who is unseen" (Hebrews 11:27). Do you understand? And if so, what will you do about it?

August 29

God demands holiness in His people. There is no alternative. Without holiness "no one will see the Lord" (Hebrews 12:14). Therefore, "like the Holy One who called you, be holy yourselves also in all your behavior; because it is written, 'You shall be holy, for I am holy' " (1 Peter 1:15–16). To be holy is to be godly, set apart unto Him and therefore like Him, filled with the fruit of the Spirit which is His character. Beloved, holiness, or godliness, is to be the goal of your life. "Godliness actually is a means of great gain, when accompanied by contentment" (1 Timothy 6:6).

Our problem is our lack of contentment. And this lack of contentment comes when we take our focus off of Christ and put it on the world with all its temporal riches. As I write, I cannot pass over the verses which I am about to share. They are especially needful to our particular age because it seems that we are trying to serve God and riches, and we cannot serve both. Since we brought nothing into this world and cannot take anything out of it except our godliness, then "if we have food and covering" we should be content (1 Timothy 6:7, 8).

> But those who want to get rich fall into temptation and a snare and many foolish and harmful desires which plunge men into ruin and destruction. For the love of money is a root of all sorts of evil, and some by longing for it have wandered away from the faith, and pierced themselves with many a pang. But flee from these things, you man of God; and pursue righteousness, godliness, faith, love, perseverance and gentleness. Fight the good fight of faith; take hold of the eternal life to which you were called, and you made the good confession in the presence of many witnesses (1 Timothy 6:9–12).

O Beloved, if there is even one thorn of the deceitfulness of riches in your heart, destroy it, for it could cause you to wander away from the faith. It has happened to so many and has kept many a man from holiness. Fight the good fight of faith, live by every word that proceeds out of the mouth of God. Guard carefully your time alone with your God for it will keep your life clear and your body full of light (Matthew 6:23).

The fourth kind of soil in the parable of the sower is good ground. "And those are the ones on whom seed was sown on the good ground; and they **hear** the word and **accept** it, and **bear** fruit, thirty, sixty, and a hundredfold" (Mark 4:20).

What kind of a harvest will you have this year, Beloved, and in the years to come? It all depends on what you want. You determine the harvest by what you will hear and accept. The hearing depends on you and the time you put into hearing. And what will you do with what you hear? Will you accept it all and order your life accordingly? Then you will have a hundredfold harvest. Or are you going to settle for less? Why? Will it be worth it when you see Him face to face?

August 30

The wickedness of the people was overwhelming. The burden on Habakkuk was not man-made, but rather was a load of divinely imposed concern weighing heavily on him. He could not help but cry, "How long, O Lord, will I call for help, and Thou wilt not hear? I cry out to Thee, 'Violence!' Yet Thou dost not save. Why dost Thou make me see iniquity, and cause me to look on wickedness? Yes, destruction and violence are before me; strife exists and contention arises. Therefore, the law is ignored and justice is never upheld. For the wicked surround the righteous; therefore, justice comes out perverted" (Habakkuk 1:2–4).

Sin was rife in Israel. The nation was on the brink of catastrophe, and, instead of repenting, they multiplied their sins. Habakkuk knew that God would not let them go unpunished. God Himself had told Habakkuk that He was "raising up the Chaldeans [Babylonians], that fierce and impetuous people who march throughout the earth to seize dwelling places which are not theirs" (Habakkuk 1:6). Yet it was hard for Habakkuk to understand. He knew that Israel would be judged, but why would God use such a wicked people to swallow up Judah who was more righteous than the Babylonians (Habakkuk 1:13)? All this was a challenge to Habakkuk's faith! It was hard for him to work it out in his mind. Where was God?

Can you relate? Has your faith ever had problems? And what do you do with problems that challenge your faith? How do you keep going? You can handle problems of faith the same way Habakkuk handled his.

First, openly discuss your problems with God. It is no use hiding from God for "Thou dost understand my thought from afar" (Psalms 139:2). Second, after voicing your problem, you need to keep watch to see what God will speak to you (Habakkuk 2:2). Third, as you wait to hear from God, you need to realize that you cannot be a man or woman of faith and "live in a day." In other words, faith cannot look at just the immediate situation but rather at the eternal outcome. God rules from the perspective of eternity. You must see with the eyes of faith beyond the moment, beyond the situation to your God. You must say, by faith, "Shall not the judge of all the earth do right?" (Genesis 18:25 KJV).

In that confidence you will find peace. For today, remember, faith must keep its eyes on God.

August 31

Whenever I tell the story, an incredible ache grips the very bowels of my being and I want to cry, "O Lord Jesus, come quickly. Please come . . . please. And let me be, no matter what, faithful unto death." I read the story in *Jesus To the Communist World, Inc.,* a newsletter published by Richard Wurmbrand in January, 1981.

The Russian Orthodox Priest Dudko, a kind of Soviet Billy Graham, was arrested for his faith. The Communists set before him two alternatives: either to join their evil and lying camp by withdrawing all he had said against them, or to be raped homosexually by several criminals (Welt am Sonntag, West Germany, August 30), to be photographed in this position, to be put to shame through the publication of these pictures, and to be sentenced for sexual perversity. The priest had been prepared to suffer incarceration, beatings, physical torture, or brainwashing for the Lord—he already had ten years of Soviet prison behind him—but this threat was too much. Who among us would suffer such degradation? So Dudko recanted publicly on TV and in the press. It was as if Billy Graham had denied on TV everything he had ever preached. A chain reaction followed. Other notable Christian prisoners ... recanted too and were freed, whereas those who remained faithful ... were sentenced to long years of prison.

On our final day together for this month, why would I tell you such a story? Because, Precious Ones, I believe the day is coming when your faith will be challenged to the core. And what will you do on that day? "If you have run with footmen and they have tired you out, then how can you compete with horses? If you fall down in a land of peace, how will you do in the thicket of the Jordan?" (Jeremiah 12:5).

This is the time to determine that the ground of your heart will be good soil, that you will have ears to hear, that you will listen to God's Word, that you will accept it freely, that you will live by it with the intention of bringing forth a hundredfold harvest. This is the hour to be aware of the five deadly D's so that you stand fast even against their penetration so that the enemy does not gain a stronghold in God's land. This is the time when you must realize that there is only one way to live: *by faith.*

We must put away our pride, humble ourselves under the hand of Almighty God, and live by every word that proceeds out of His mouth. We must live, not for today, but for eternity. Even though you are treated as Dudko was, you must say with Habakkuk: "Though the fig tree should not blossom, and there be no fruit on the vines, though the yield of the olive should fail, and the fields produce no food, though the flock should be cut off from the fold, and there be no cattle in the stalls, yet I will exult in the Lord, I will rejoice in the God of my salvation. The Lord God is my strength, and He has made my feet like hinds' feet and makes me walk on my high places" (Habakkuk 3:17–19). Amen and Amen!

SEPTEMBER

When the Leaders Lead, the People Follow

September 1

Times were bad; so bad that the people couldn't travel without fear. Farmhouse after farmhouse had been abandoned. Villages became ghost towns. The people were holed up behind city walls. In the evenings the men would huddle together, talking in hushed tones, making plans for their defense. The women were well aware of their danger. They knew their men had no weapons with which to defend them should the enemy attack. Their eyes caught the anger and frustration of the periodic pounding of a man's fist as he said in hushed but bitter tones, "But it's those chariots, those iron chariots!" The women did not participate in these nightly huddles. It was not their place to do so. Still they knew of Sisera and his nine hundred iron chariots (Judges 4:13).

Talk, talk, talk. Worry, worry, worry. Plan, plan, plan. It was all they had heard for almost twenty years now. It had become a national pastime. Yet what good had it done? Things only grew worse. Their city was bursting at the seams with people. All the peasantry had moved behind the security of its walls. The crowded streets, crowded markets, crowded homes were filled with the almost unbearable pressure of living under the tension of fear and an uncertain future!

And then one day it happened.

> In the days of Shamgar the son of Anath,
> In the days of Jael, the highways were deserted,
> And travelers went by roundabout ways.
> The peasantry ceased, they ceased in Israel,
> Until I, Deborah, arose,
> Until I arose, a mother in Israel (Judges 5:6, 7).

It finally happened. "The leaders led in Israel . . . the people volunteered, bless the Lord" (Judges 5:2). What were nine hundred iron chariots against the leaders of a people who cried to Jehovah God! Why even the stars fought from heaven as torrents of waters mired down Sisera's chariots of iron (Judges 5:19–22)! At last the twenty-year yoke of oppression had been broken. And why? Because the leaders led, and the people volunteered.

This month God would have us talk about leadership—the cost of leadership and the responsibilities of those who lead and those who follow. We have had enough oppression, and enough talking. It is now time for the leaders to lead and for the people to volunteer and follow.

September 2

When we think of leaders, the image that usually comes to mind is that of a man or woman who has a huge following. Yet the definition of a leader does not require a crowd. To lead simply means to guide, to show the way by going along with or in front of. To lead also means to serve, to influence, to persuade, to command, to direct. In the light of these standard dictionary definitions, can't you see how, in one sense or another, a Christian would be a leader? Because we know Jesus Christ, because we have the mind of Christ (1 Corinthians 2:16), because we are followers of Him, wouldn't we automatically be in a position to lead those who do not know Him? I think so!

As you meditate this month on leadership, please, Precious One, do not think, "This does not apply to me." Are you a parent? Then you are to lead your children. Are you an older brother or sister? Then you are to be a guide to your brothers or sisters. Are you a teen? Then you are to be one who steps out front and shows other teens God's way of life. Do you have acquaintances who do not know Christ or who are but babes in Christ? Then you are to show them the Way.

If you are a child of God, you are following Christ and in doing so you should be able to say to others, "Be imitators of me, just as I also am of Christ" (1 Corinthians 11:1).

This is what the world desperately needs! Yet leadership costs. And so few are willing to pay the price so they can honestly say to others, "Brethren, join in following my example, and observe those who walk according to the pattern you have in us" (Philippians 3:17).

Would you be willing to pay the cost? What is it? Read on, look at it objectively, and then make your commitment.

September 3

Why not just say, "God, I'll lead," and then get with it? Because to step out as a leader and then retract, turn back, or quit is very disheartening to those who have followed you and those who may only have watched you. What is worse, failure in a leader becomes an excuse for others to live life on a lower plane.

This is why our nation is in such a state of corruption. There has been corruption in high places. Surely you have heard the statement, "Everything rises or falls on leadership." Or, "As priest, so people." The Romans became corrupt because their leaders were corrupt. The leaders were corrupt because their gods were corrupt. We, as a nation, have become corrupt because our leaders have ceased to be, if not God-believing men, at least God-fearing men. "There is no fear of God before their eyes" (Romans 3:18), so they worship gods of their own choosing. In doing so, they are corrupted, so they cheat, connive, steal, lie, commit immorality, and sell their souls and their country for whatever will satiate their desires.

If you are going to lead, first count the cost of leadership. Be sure that you will not take men and women to a lower plane of life rather than to a higher plane, God's plane.

> For which one of you, when he wants to build a tower, does not first sit down and calculate the cost, to see if he has enough to complete it? Otherwise, when he has laid a foundation, and is not able to finish, all who observe it begin to ridicule him, saying, "This man began to build and was not able to finish." Or what king, when he sets out to meet another king in battle, will not first sit down and take counsel whether he is strong enough with ten thousand men to encounter the one coming against him with twenty thousand? Or else, while the other is still far away, he sends a delegation and asks terms of peace (Luke 14:28–32).

So often, the reason we fail is simply because we did not count the cost. A Christian is a disciple. And what does it cost to be a disciple? "So therefore, no one of you can be My disciple who does not give up all his own possessions" (Luke 14:33).

Think on it!

September 4

Our nation sits in bondage—the awful, oppressive bondage that comes upon a people when unbridled iniquity dashes like a crazed stallion through their land. With none to hold the reins in check, countless precious souls are being trampled mercilessly by its cruel hoofs. Shod with iron shoes, it leaves horrible scars. Its fierce snorting and wild dashing cause all to run for their very lives. And so iniquity roams and runs at will, causing untold havoc because none will risk lassoing it, jumping on its back, and bringing it under control. Many murmur, many talk, many plan, but none will move. They are all waiting for the other. Gladly would they follow if only one would take the initiative and lead. But leadership is costly. You could fail. You could make a spectacle of yourself, become an object of scorn and ridicule. Who needs it? And if you were to lead, wouldn't everyone have his own idea? Wouldn't you be open to untold suggestions, even untold criticisms? Wouldn't you constantly hear, "Why, if I were doing that, I'd . . ."? Of course you would! So why bother? No one would appreciate you anyway! Besides, why should you if no one you love has yet been trampled by the wild horse of iniquity?!!

Why bother? Why bother!! You had better bother, for if you don't, someday you will be touched in some way. Besides, touched or not, are you not your brother's keeper? Of course you are. Then awake, arise. Leaders, lead! Followers, volunteer and follow! Either lead, follow, or get out of the way! It is time for something to be done. Enough with apathy. Put away your indifference, your lack of concern. Put away your talking, your worrying, your futile planning. Awake and arise. Godliness is ceasing in our land, and we need mothers, fathers, teens, and children who will arise.

To do so will be costly; you will be opening yourself to criticism and ridicule. But God will be on your side, and you, like Paul, will be able to testify, "The Lord stood with me, and strengthened me . . . and I was delivered out of the lion's mouth" (2 Timothy 4:17). To do so will enable you to stand before your Lord God in "confidence and not shrink away from Him in shame at His coming" (1 John 2:28).

And not to do so?

September 5

And what if you do not awake? What if you do not arise? What if you, like others, continue in your apathy, indifferent to the iniquity and injustice all around you?

Martin Niemoeller, a pastor under Hitler, wrote:

> When the Nazis came after the trade unionist, I wasn't a trade unionist, so I didn't speak up.
> When the Nazis came after the Roman Catholics, I wasn't a Roman Catholic, so I didn't speak up.

When the Nazis came after the Jews, I wasn't a Jew, so I didn't speak up.

When the Nazis came after the Communists, I wasn't a Communist, so I didn't speak up.

When the Nazis came after me, there was no one left to speak up.

What will it cost you, Beloved, if you do not awake, if you do not arise, if you do not speak up?

Listen to God's Word:

"Now, gird up your loins, and arise, and speak to them all which I command you. Do not be dismayed before them, lest I dismay you before them" (Jeremiah 1:17).

Listen. And meditate. What are His thoughts toward you?

Will you lead? Will you follow? Count the cost, and then you can decide.

September 6

Like others, I am *so* concerned about the spirit of apathy that has invaded the church of Jesus Christ. You can count on this: apathy will destroy our land if it continues. By God's grace I have determined in my heart that I will arise, that I will arise a mother in our land. I will pay the price of leadership. By God's enabling, I will not permit our people to be trampled under the iron hoofs of iniquity! This leader is going to lead. I am going to be obedient to God's exhortation through the Apostle Paul, "And since we have gifts that differ according to the grace given to us, let each exercise them accordingly . . . he who leads, with diligence" (Romans 12:6, 8).

I refuse to be apathetic. I had rather die first. It is better to have died according to the will of God than to have lived apart from His will. And what about you, Beloved? Can you, will you say with Paul, "According to my earnest expectation and hope, that I shall not be put to shame in anything, but that with all boldness, Christ shall even now, as always, be exalted in my body, whether by life or by death. For to me, to live is Christ, and to die is gain" (Philippians 1:20, 21). You call yourself a Christian, a born-again child of God. You call Jesus Lord. Well, is He? Are you His? Then, if this is so, what choice do you have but to wholeheartedly follow Him?

Oh, how I wish I could say all this to you in person, so you could know how absolutely earnest I am about what I am saying. It's crucial, Beloved. It is crucial. Francis Schaeffer is saying it. Charles Stanley is saying it. President Reagan is saying it. E. V. Hill is saying it. And so are many others: "It is now or never." Time for us has run out. The leaders must lead while they can, and the people must volunteer while they can.

Will you do something for your God? Will you get on your knees right now and tell God that you will awake, that you will arise, that you will listen to what He has to say to you this month through His Word and His servant? Will you tell Him that you want to hear His voice and that you will be obedient to what **He** says?

September 7

As I write this devotional, I am currently teaching the book of *Judges Precept Upon Precept* from our inductive Bible study courses. I think it is one of the most powerful and practical Precept courses I have taught to date. God is working so mightily in the lives of many as they begin to comprehend how they can be set free from some internal enemies, from some sins which have so easily beset them.

But then, I am not surprised, for this is the book God laid upon my heart for this time. America, as does the world, needs the message of Judges. The 300–350 dark years of Judges so closely parallel our time; it was a time of apathy, apostasy and anarchy. The three go together. From the indifference of apathy comes apostasy, departure from God's Word. The Israelites were a people who did not know their God or what He had done for His people (Judges 2:10). And isn't that true of us today? We do not know the Lord nor what He has done for His people. We have so consorted with the world that we have become entangled with the affairs of everyday life (2 Timothy 2:4). We are too busy to spend time in God's book! And we have so much materially that we feel we don't need God, therefore we do not bother to know Him or to learn His ways. Is it any wonder then that we find it so easy to apostatize?

And what always follows on the heels of apostasy? Anarchy. Look around you and you will see it. Everyone is doing what is right in his own eyes because, in our day, there is no leader in our land whom we long to follow (Judges 21:25). Not even the Lord Jesus Christ. Oh, many want the benefits of heaven, but comparatively few are totally willing to heed Jesus' call of commitment: "If anyone wishes to come after Me, let him deny himself, and take up his cross, and follow Me. For whoever wishes to save his life shall lose it; and whoever loses his life for My sake and the gospel's shall save it" (Mark 8:34, 35).

Beloved, there is no apathy in following Jesus. Neither is there apostasy or anarchy! You either walk His way, according to His commandments, or you do not walk.

How would you describe your Christianity? Be honest. You cannot fool God. Write it out.

Now then, is that really what you want?

September 8

Like so many today, the children of Israel were caught in a cycle of sin.

THEY SINNED.
Then the sons of Israel did evil in the sight of the Lord, and served the Baals, and they forsook the Lord, the God of their fathers, who had brought them out of the land of Egypt, and followed other gods from among the gods of the peoples who were around them, and bowed themselves down to them; thus they provoked the Lord to anger. So they forsook the Lord and served Baal and the Astartes (Judges 2:11–13).

SO GOD SOLD THEM INTO THE HANDS OF ENEMIES.
And the anger of the Lord burned against Israel, and He gave them into the hands of plunderers who plundered them; and He sold them into the hands of their enemies around them, so that they could no longer stand before their enemies (Judges 2:14).

THEY WERE SEVERELY DISTRESSED.
Wherever they went, the hand of the Lord was against them for evil, as the Lord had spoken and as the Lord had sworn to them, so that they were severely distressed (Judges 2:15).

THEN GOD DELIVERED THEM.
Then the Lord raised up judges who delivered them from the hands of those who plundered them. . . . And when the Lord raised up judges for them, the Lord was with the judge and delivered them from the hand of their enemies all the days of the judge; for the Lord was moved to pity by their groaning because of those who oppressed and afflicted them (Judges 2:16, 18).

AND YET, DID IT DO ANY GOOD? NO!
But it came about when the judge died, that they would turn back and act more corruptly than their fathers, in following other gods to serve them and bow down to them; they did not abandon their practices or their stubborn ways (Judges 2:19).

THEY LIVED IN THAT HORRIBLE CYCLE FOR 300 YEARS.

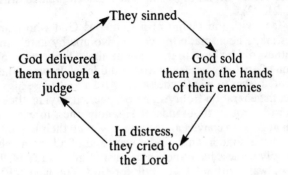

They never spun out of that cycle because they were apathetic about their sin. They never really repented.

In those 300 dark years, the only relief they ever knew from the oppression of their enemies came through a judge, a leader who led! When the leaders led, the people volunteered.

Where are the leaders who will bring the church and the nation out of its cycle of sin? And if the leaders do not arise, whose slave will we be next?

September 9

For the next few days I want to look with you at some men who stood out as leaders in certain dark periods of history. As we do, I want to share with you some things that God has taught me regarding leadership.

LEADERSHIP BEGINS WITH WALKING WITH GOD. The days following Adam's travesty in the Garden of Eden were dark days. It wasn't until Enoch that "men began to call upon the name of the Lord" (Genesis 4:26). Even then it seemed that godly men were few and far between. They were caught in a downward spiral of iniquity because, for the most part, they had chosen man's way rather than God's. The wickedness of man was becoming great in the earth, and God knew He would have to act in judgment; iniquity must always be punished.

Enoch lived sixty-five years and then he came face-to-face with a choice. A son was born to him and God named him Methuselah, meaning *when he is dead, it shall come.* God had given Enoch the word.

Judgment was coming, worldwide. "Enoch lived sixty-five years, and became the father of Methuselah. **Then Enoch walked with God"** (Genesis 5:21, 22).

Face-to-face with the reality of a righteous God who demands a righteous walk, Enoch made the choice. No apathy here! And what kind of witness did he have to those about him? Did he leave others in the oblivion of apathy where they would suddenly drown in the waters of judgment? Listen to what Jude says: "And about these also Enoch, in the seventh generation from Adam, prophesied, saying, 'Behold, the Lord came with many thousands of His holy ones, to execute judgment upon all, and to convict all the ungodly of all their ungodly deeds which they have done in an ungodly way, and of all the harsh things which ungodly sinners have spoken against Him' " (Jude 14, 15).

When you walk with God, you talk for God. You have to! You are His witness.

> For each time I speak, I cry aloud;
> I proclaim violence and destruction,
> Because for me the word of the Lord has resulted
> In reproach and derision all day long.
> But if I say, "I will not remember Him
> Or speak any more in His name,"
> Then in my heart it becomes like a burning fire
> Shut up in my bones;
> And I am weary of holding it in,
> And I cannot endure it (Jeremiah 20:8, 9).

September 10

Leadership begins with walking with God. How this pleases Him. "So all the days of Enoch were three hundred and sixty-five years. And Enoch walked with God; and he was not, for God took him" (Genesis 5:23, 24). "By faith Enoch was taken up so that he should not see death; and he was not found because God took him up; for he obtained the witness that before his being taken up he was pleasing to God. And without faith it is impossible to please Him, for he who comes to God must believe that He is, and that He is a rewarder of those who seek Him" (Hebrews 11:5, 6).

Pleasing God. That is what life is all about. And when we live for His pleasure God rewards us. What glories He has in store for us! In this life, leadership is very costly, for following Jesus will inevitably bring suffering and tribulation yet "I consider that the sufferings of this present time are not worthy to be compared with the glory that is to be revealed to us" (Romans 8:18).

What do you want, Beloved? You can have it: the world's praise for a season, or your God's, "Well done!" and His eternal reward.

I am writing this as I fly to California to speak at a military base. On this trip as I "walked with Him seeking His pleasure," He impressed upon my heart that I was to witness to the young college man who sat next to me. He was on his way to join his friends in Fort Lauderdale. I asked him if he were going to be immoral like so many would be as they hit the beaches of Florida for spring break. He was a precious young man, like the rich young ruler whom Jesus loved (Mark 10:21). I admired him, yet I knew from our conversation that although he went to church he did not know the Head of the church, the Lord Jesus Christ. The clue came when I asked him, "Tom, who do you live for?" He was living for himself—a moral life but not a godly life.

"From Him and through Him and to Him are all things" (Romans 11:36). "And for thy pleasure they are and were created" (Revelation 4:11 KJV).

Oh, One whom Jesus loves, for whose pleasure are you living? Be an Enoch; walk with God.

September 11

True leaders are men and women who are willing to stand alone. They are men and women of conviction, a conviction that ofttimes costs them greatly, a conviction that separates them from the mediocre and thus from the majority of mankind. Leadership becomes a lonely business.

And so it was with Noah. He virtually stood alone among all mankind. He made his choice. He lived in the midst of corruption and violence (Genesis 6:11). "The wickedness of man was great on the earth" and "every intent of the thoughts of his heart was only evil continually" (6:5). Mankind had so corrupted its way that "the Lord was sorry that He had made man on the earth, and He was grieved in His heart" (6:6).

He stood apart from the mainstream of life and of men, "but Noah found favor in the eyes of the Lord" (6:8). A man or woman who is willing to stand for what is right, even if it means standing alone, will always find favor in the eyes of the Lord. Don't forget it! For, although you may stand alone as far as man is concerned, God will never abandon you. Paul knew this as he wrote from prison, "At my first defense no one supported me, but all deserted me. . . . but the Lord stood with me, and strengthened me, in order that through me the proclamation might be fully accomplished, and that all the Gentiles might hear" (2 Timothy 4:16, 17).

Standing alone makes a proclamation that is more eloquent than all the sermons in the world. Man was never created to be alone; he was made for fellowship, for communion. Therefore, loneliness is one of the hardest things for man to bear. And man knows this; this is why solitary confinement was chosen as a means of punishment. Shut up from others, a man will often give in or break. That is why true godly leaders, percentagewise, are few and far between. They love the fellowship, praise, and approbation of man more than the fellowship, praise, and approbation of God. Or they fear man more than they fear God. And "the fear of man brings a snare" (Proverbs 29:25).

What about you, Beloved? Do you love your God so much that you are willing to stand alone? If not, you will never qualify for leadership.

September 12

"The fear of man brings a snare" (Proverbs 29:25). How true, how true! What an enemy fear is to leadership. In the military there are special, vital men who, in battle, serve as point men. They are the ones who step out in front to lead the way, ofttimes at the very peril of their own lives. They know that, if there is a land mine or an ambush of some sort ahead, they will be the first and probably the only ones to encounter it. That is what they are there for! Point men have to take the risks. However, in doing so they save countless lives. If they were immobilized by fear, they would be totally unable to fulfill their task. God's army requires point men too. Yet too few will rise above their fears and step out and lead with courage, willing even to lose their lives in His service.

Generally speaking, four things keep men and women from accomplishing great things for God. Let's take a brief look at each of them over the next couple of days. Maybe in doing so you will get over the hurdle that stands between you and the place God has for you. One of the things we fear is criticism. We don't want criticism; we want approval. (Please know that I am not referring to constructive criticism, but rather to complaining criticism that would tear down or destroy.) Because of the fear of being criticized, many of you will never accomplish significant things for the Kingdom of God. Isn't that sad? It makes my heart literally ache. We will always have critics, people who find it easier to criticize than to do the job themselves. If you are going to do a work for God, you must expect criticism. Jack, myself, or our staff get it in one form or another all the time. Yet if we quit there would be no Reach Out—no inductive Bible study courses, no TV or radio programs, no conferences, no Prayer Guides, no teaching tapes, nothing to further the Kingdom of God!

O Dear One, if God has laid a work upon your heart, do it.

"For am I now seeking the favor of men, or of God? Or am I striving to please men? If I were still trying to please men, I would not be a bond-servant of Christ" (Galatians 1:10).

September 13

We also fear failure. What if we don't succeed? What if our dreams, hopes, and ambitions for God do not come to pass? Everyone will know it. We will become the object of scorn and ridicule. To think this way is natural, for failure reflects on us as individuals. We forget the reason for our existence. "Thou are worthy, O Lord, to receive glory and honor and power; for thou hast created all things, and for thy pleasure they are and were created" (Revelation 4:11 KJV). You and I were created for God's pleasure, not man's approbation! And what does it matter if men judge us as failures? To whom are we accountable? If we were created by God for God, then we are accountable to Him alone, for it is God who has ordained the good works He would have us walk in (Ephesians 2:10).

Walking in faith seems risky because faith is not tangible. Rather it is "the assurance of things hoped for, the conviction of things not seen" (Hebrews 11:1). Stepping out in faith often seems tantamount to courting failure. And we cannot handle failure! Instead, we wait to see if someone else will do it. Thus people wait on people, an immobile generation living at the level of the status quo. Why? Because that is where everyone else lives and it is safe there. There is no risk of failure.

How I love and admire Noah. What it must have been like for him to be obedient to God! "By faith Noah, being warned by God about things not yet seen, in reverence prepared an ark for the salvation of his household, by which he condemned the world, and became an heir of the righteousness which is according to faith" (Hebrews 11:7).

Noah built an ark in obedience to God. He built it on dry land without a sea to sail it on! And not until one hundred and twenty years later would it sail! Was there ever a time when Noah entertained the thought of failure? I don't know, but I do know that Noah did all that God commanded him (Genesis 6:22). The ridicule and the scorn of man or the fear of failure did not keep him from living for God's pleasure. It was Noah's responsibility to obey and build the ark. It was God's responsibility to float it! Have you failed God because you feared failure?

September 14

Leadership makes you so vulnerable because it puts you out front, on display! If you have any weaknesses, they are sure to show! And how can someone lead if he is not perfect? Isn't that the way we think? And so we let fear of exposure keep us from stepping out for God. We are simply afraid to let others see that we don't always have it all together.

You probably have looked at some leaders and thought, "How did **they** ever get that job?" That thought is only confirmation of the fact that you feel leaders have to be perfect. Of course, if you are ever around any leader for an adequate period of time, you will notice imperfections. Leaders have weaknesses just like everyone else.

How you need to realize that God didn't say you had to be perfect before He could use you. Rather, He takes an imperfect you and uses the situations that expose your weaknesses to make you into a man or woman of God.

When I miss the mark of perfection, or when Jack misses the mark, it is obvious to all. Our weaknesses become glaringly obvious. And I am sure that we cause many to shake their heads in wonder because we are not perfect. Yet I have learned that if I will share my weaknesses rather than try to hide them, God will use my vulnerability to cause people to relate even more to me than if they thought I was perfect. When people see your weaknesses, and yet see God using you, they know that the power comes from God!

I am not saying we are to excuse or indulge our weaknesses. Rather, we should never draw back from serving our God for fear of exposing our weaknesses. That, Beloved, is pride, a high opinion of one's own self, worth, or possessions. Apart from Christ, I am nothing. Apart from Christ, I can do nothing (John 15:5). God warns us not to think more highly of ourselves than we ought to think (Romans 12:3).

A godly leader realizes that, if anything is accomplished through him, it has been accomplished by God. "Therefore I am well content with weaknesses ... for when I am weak, then I am strong" (2 Corinthians 12:10).

Think upon it, then write your thoughts.

September 15

What does God expect of a leader? Only one thing: total obedience. "Thus Noah did; according to all that God had commanded him" (Genesis 6:22). Leadership is doing all that God commands,

> no matter the cost
> no matter the time
> no matter the circumstances.

It cost Noah full dedication to build the ark in the middle of dry land. Can you imagine the questions and the ridicule as well?

Remember also that "the wickedness of man was great on the earth, and that every intent of the thoughts of his heart was only evil continually. . . . Now the earth was corrupt in the sight of God, and the earth was filled with violence . . . for all flesh had corrupted their way upon the earth" (Genesis 6:5, 11, 12).

Can you imagine the pressure that Noah must have felt just to go along with the crowd, not to "rock the boat," not to upset the status quo? I am sure you can, for even in many of our churches today there is a settling in to the "norm," even if the "norm" is not exactly biblical. Yet, if we are to be found pleasing to Him, we cannot settle in. We must press on to know the Lord (Hosea 6:3). And with that revelation will come the knowledge of the responsibility to be obedient to walk in the light He has given us. There will be a choosing, and the cost that goes with it. "For am I now seeking the favor of men, or of God? Or am I striving to please men? If I were still trying to please men, I would not be a bond-servant of Christ" (Galatians 1:10).

"Choose for yourself today whom you will serve" (Joshua 24:15). A leader must be totally committed to obeying God.

Will you do all that God commands, no matter the cost

> no matter the time
> no matter the circumstances?

September 16

To be a leader is to be s-t-r-e-t-c-h-e-d. You find yourself going forth into new territories, new adventures, facing new demands. And this terrifies some and causes them to turn back. They cannot handle the insecurity that comes with the unfamiliar. They forget that the Good Shepherd, "when he puts forth all his own . . . goes before them" (John 10:4). "Thou dost prepare a table before me in the presence of my enemies" (Psalms 23:5). The Lord never leads us without going before us, and, having gone before, He will lead us only to His prepared place.

Knowing this, you can lead, you can go forth, even if you have to go alone.

> Now the Lord said to Abram,
> "Go forth from your country,
> And from your relatives
> And from your father's house,
> To the land which I will show you;
> And I will make you a great nation,
> And I will bless you,
> And make your name great;
> And so you shall be a blessing;
> And I will bless those who bless you,
> And the one who curses you I will curse.
> And in you all the families of the earth shall be blessed"
> So Abram went forth as the Lord had spoken to him (Genesis 12:1–4).

It wasn't all that easy for Abraham; he was a man like you and I. He went forth, but he did not leave all his relatives behind as he was told to do. "Lot went with him" (Genesis 12:4). He went to the land to which God directed him but even then he weakened in the face of a famine and went down to Egypt apart from God's direction. God honored those first faltering steps of faith; he knew Abraham's heart and God was patient with him. God persevered with Abraham and dear Abraham persevered with God. Abraham returned to Canaan, God's land for him, separated from Lot, and then God showed him all that He had for him.

"And the Lord said to Abram, after Lot had separated from him, 'Now lift up your eyes and look from the place where you are, northward and southward and eastward and westward; for all the land which you see, I will give it to you and to your descendants forever' " (Genesis 13:14, 15).

O Beloved, wherever He leads you can follow. Will you?

September 17

"The steps of a man are established by the Lord; and He delights in his way. When he falls, he shall not be hurled headlong; because the Lord is the One who holds his hand" (Psalms 37:23, 24).

Abraham went forth according to God's word. This, Beloved, is godly leadership, going forth according to God's word.

Child of my love, fear not the unknown morrow.
Dread not the new demand life makes of thee;
Thine ignorance doth hold no cause for sorrow,
For what thou knowest not is known to me.

Thou canst not see today the hidden meaning
Of my command, but thou the light shalt gain.
Walk on in faith, upon my promise leaning,
And as thou goest, all shall be made plain.

One step thou seest: then go forward boldly;
One step is far enough for faith to see.
Take that, and thy next duty shall be told thee,
For step by step thy God is leading thee.

Stand not in fear thine adversaries counting;
Dare every peril save to disobey.
Thou shalt march on, each obstacle surmounting,
For I, the Strong, shall open up the way.

Therefore go gladly to the task assigned thee,
Having my promise; needing nothing more
Than just to know where e'er the future find thee,
In all thy journeying—I GO BEFORE.

Author Unknown

September 18

Leadership means ofttimes persevering without seeing. Many leaders never really attain their goal; rather they serve to prepare the way for others. They open up new lands, new vistas, new possibilities, new heights for others who will be the attainers. Leaders are often pioneers.
Abraham was a pioneer.

By faith Abraham, when he was called, obeyed by going out to a place which he was to receive for an inheritance; and he went out, not knowing where he was going. By faith he lived as an alien in the land of promise, as in a foreign land, dwelling in tents with Isaac and Jacob, fellow-heirs of the same promise; for he was looking for the city which has foundations, whose architect and builder is God. . . . All these died in faith, without receiving the promises, but having seen them and having welcomed them from a distance, and having confessed that they were strangers and exiles on the earth. For those who say such things make it clear that they are seeking a country of their own (Hebrews 11:8–10, 13, 14).

A person who pioneers, pressing forward yet knowing that he may never attain, is a person of deep consecration. People who step out according to what they believe is true, even though they know they may never personally see the end result of it all, are truly men and women of faith. This, Beloved, is selflessness. This is commitment—commitment to a cause because you believe in it and, attain it or not, you will give it your all. Such selfless leadership is desperately lacking today. It is leadership that brings one to sacrifice, even as "Abraham, when he was tested, offered up Isaac" (Hebrews 11:17).

Some leaders want leadership only if it brings them glory and gain, but not if it requires sacrifice. Then there are those who will pioneer, sacrificing all and persevering because they see Him who is unseen and desire only to hear His, "Well done!" What kind of leader would you be? Would you sacrifice? Would you pioneer? Would you persevere? Or do you only want glory? Write your thoughts.

September 19

As I have meditated upon the lives of biblical leaders, I have seen four basic ingredients in their lives. Let me list them for you and then we will look at them one by one. First, each leader had what I would call a sense of *destiny*. By a sense of destiny I mean a vision of what God had in store for him or an awareness that God had a specific task for him to accomplish. Next came a time of *preparation* through testing. This, then, was followed by the *performance* of his God-given goal or task. And fourth and finally, each learned who the true Leader or Deliverer was; each realized it was not him but God.

We have looked at Deborah, Enoch, and Abraham. Now I want us to turn our attention to Joseph because these four basic ingredients stand out so clearly in his life. Then, we will turn to Moses and, among other things, deal thoroughly with the fourth ingredient, that of knowing the Deliverer. How I pray that God will speak to each of you in a very special way.

Every leader has a sense of destiny. Each knows that he has been called to step out, to lead the way, to guide others. Deborah's sense of destiny is evident in her words to Barak, "Behold, the Lord, the God of Israel, has commanded, 'Go and march to Mount Tabor . . . and I will draw out to you Sisera' " (Judges 4:6, 7). Enoch's sense of destiny came through the birth and naming of Methuselah ("when he is dead, it shall come") and it changed his whole direction, for he began to walk with God. Noah gained his sense of destiny when God told him to build an ark because He was about to destroy the earth. Abraham's came when God called him to leave Ur of the Chaldees. It is evident that Moses had a sense of destiny before he ever fled from Egypt, for when he struck down the Egyptian who was unjustly treating one of his Hebrew brethren, "he supposed that his brethren understood that God was granting them deliverance through him" (Acts 7:25).

And Joseph's sense of destiny? We will look at it tomorrow. Beloved One, have you ever asked God to give you a sense of destiny? You should, for you "are His workmanship, created in Christ Jesus for good works" (Ephesians 2:10). Write out your heart's desire.

September 20

Joseph's sense of destiny came through a dream when he was only a lad of seventeen. Enoch's came through the birth of a son. Moses' came (a second time) through a burning bush, Deborah's and Abraham's came by the word of God. Each was effective although all were not alike.

God deals with each of us according to our personalities and His own purpose. God knows how He wishes to deal with each of us and what it takes, and we cannot box Him in. Of course, in saying that, we need to remember that God never acts or speaks contrary to His Word. His Word is the plumb line by which we check out our dreams, our visions, and all that we hear. Did the word you heard come from the Lord? If it did, you can be sure it will agree with His Word and you can be sure it will happen, for as He has decreed so it will be (Isaiah 14:24, 27).

Some have criticized Joseph for sharing his dreams with his brothers and father, but I cannot. God had a purpose in it all. Those dreams certainly could have been a comfort to Jacob if he had clung to them when his sons brought him Joseph's varicolored tunic stained with blood. When people have a dream, we need to listen, not wonder why God has not given us one also. We need to remember that God deals with each of us individually and that He has a unique plan for each of our lives. Remember when Peter, John, and the other disciples were with Jesus at the Sea of Tiberius after His resurrection? Jesus asked Peter three times if he loved Him. Jesus had just told Peter how he was going to die and then said to him, "Follow Me." When Peter heard this, he turned around and, seeing John, asked: " 'Lord, and what about this man?' Jesus said to him, 'If I want him to remain until I come, what is that to you? You follow Me!' " (John 21:21).

God's lesson to us as leaders is to be true to the sense of destiny He gives us. Has God spoken in some way to your heart and said, "Follow Me"? Then follow. Do not be disobedient to the heavenly vision (Acts 26:19).

September 21

A leader's sense of destiny and his knowledge of his God serve to hold him steadfastly midst the storms of testing. I don't know of any man or woman who has made a significant eternal contribution to the Kingdom of God who has not known testing or who has not had a close walk with the Lord. It is a fact. God prepares us through trials, and those trials are only endured by seeing Him who is invisible. Even our Lord Jesus Christ, "although he was a son, He learned obedience from the things which He suffered" (Hebrews 5:8). His sense of destiny, and His desire to do the will of His Father who sent Him, held Him through the agony of Gethsemane and the brutal torture of Calvary. And so God calls us to "run with endurance the race that is set before us, fixing our eyes on Jesus, the author and perfecter of faith, **who for the joy set before Him** endured the cross, despising the shame, and has sat down at the right hand of the throne of God" (Hebrews 12:1, 2).

Joseph had a dream—a dream that was of God and therefore would surely come to pass. He saw, in essence, his parents and his brothers bowing down to him. Yet the dream was for an appointed time. First, Joseph had to be prepared through testing. You know the story. His brothers "became jealous of Joseph and sold him into Egypt. And yet God was with him, and rescued him from all his afflictions" (Acts 7:9, 10). Before Joseph would ever rule Egypt under Pharaoh, before Joseph's brothers and father would ever bow before him, Joseph would first be *ruled over*. He would be sold as a slave and serve as a prisoner for two years (Genesis 41:1). Then after Joseph's release from prison there would be the performance of the task, the fulfillment of the dream that God had given him.

What held Joseph through the storms of testing? What kept him from being bitter against God, from seeking revenge against his brothers? Joseph knew the Deliverer! He knew that the Sovereign God ruled in the affairs of men. Listen as he speaks to his brothers. "And now do not be grieved or angry with yourselves, because you sold me here; for God sent me before you to preserve life. . . . And as for you, you meant evil against me, but God meant it for good in order to bring about this present result, to preserve many people alive" (Genesis 45:5, 50:20).

O Precious One, when God calls you to work for Him, you can expect testing. It is your preparation. Rest in it knowing that God will use it all "to preserve many people alive." Your anchor will hold.

September 22

Leaders must be scrupulous in their morals. Yet, unfortunately, sexual immorality has spread into the church of Jesus Christ with a more devastating effect than the bubonic plague. Very little is being done to stamp it out. If we do not declare a quarantine on this insidious disease it will lay waste the church's ministry to the world. Do we not believe God when He warns us of the danger of not dealing thoroughly with sin? "A little leaven leavens the whole lump of dough" (1 Corinthians 5:6). His clear-cut command is to "clean out the old leaven (sin), that you may be a new lump, just as you are in fact unleavened" (5:7).

Beloved, sin cannot be tolerated in the church. Thus Paul continues, "But actually, I wrote to you not to associate **with any so-called brother** if he should be an immoral person, or covetous, or an idolater, or a reviler, or a drunkard, or a swindler—not even to eat with such a one" (5:11). Yet we are not only eating with them, but we are worshiping with them every Sunday and extending to them the right hand of fellowship. Yet "the message we have heard from Him and announce to you, [is] that God is light, and in Him there is no darkness at all. If we say that we have fellowship with Him and yet walk in the darkness, we lie and do not practice the truth" (1 John 1:5, 6). To tolerate sexual immorality in the church—not to deal with it according to 1 Corinthians 5—is to walk in darkness.

In the February 5, 1982, issue of *Christianity Today,* an article by Robert J. Stout entitled "Clergy Divorce Spills Into the Aisle" told of a case that is far from being an isolated incident among Christian leaders today.

> A pastor in the Western United States recently became involved with a married woman in his congregation. Both divorced their spouses and were married in the church of which he was the minister. The congregation turned out en masse for the wedding, giving open support. The generally more tolerant attitude of society toward divorce may make it a more readily available option than in the past.

This sounds like the days of Malachi when God said to His priests, "The Lord has been a witness between you and the wife of your youth, against whom you have dealt treacherously . . . for I hate divorce" (Malachi 2:14, 16).

Mark it well and think upon it. Leaders must be scrupulous in their morals.

September 23

Like so many Christian men today, Joseph had a woman pursuing him. It's hard to handle, isn't it? Yet handle it you must, if you would be used of God, for you can mark God's Word that "marriage is honorable in all, and the bed undefiled, but whoremongers [fornicators] and adulterers God will judge" (Hebrews 13:4 KJV). "For this is the will of God, your sanctification; that is, that you abstain from sexual immorality; that each of you know how to possess his own vessel in sanctification and honor, not in lustful passion, like the Gentiles who do not know God" (1 Thessalonians 4:3–5).

Joseph, one of God's elect, found himself a slave in Egypt; yet he lived as a prince among men. Difficult circumstances never altered his commitment to his God. Although the testing was great, he would not mar God's destiny for him by having a fling with his flesh. There were to be no rationalizations, no excuses, no bitter revenges against God because things weren't going his way. Joseph would not indulge his desires just because he was in Egypt, away from home where no one knew him! No, he was God's man all the way even if it meant celibacy in the prime of manhood. Read his story carefully and then we will discuss it tomorrow. It needs discussing if you are going to be God's man or God's woman, for somewhere along life's path the enemy will see to it that you meet a "Mrs. Potiphar."

> Now Joseph was handsome in form and appearance. And it came about after these events that his master's wife looked with desire at Joseph, and she said, "Lie with me." But he refused and said to his master's wife, "Behold, with me around, my master does not concern himself with anything in the house, and he has put all that he owns in my charge. There is no one greater in this house than I, and he has withheld nothing from me except you, because you are his wife. How then could I do this great evil, and sin against God?" (Genesis 39:6–9).

Sexual immorality is a sin against God, and God's word is that "no man transgress and defraud his brother in the matter because the Lord is the avenger in all these things, just as we also told you before and solemnly warned you" (1 Thessalonians 4:6).

September 24

Potiphar's wife wouldn't take "no" for an answer. She wanted Joseph.

> And it came about as she spoke to Joseph day after day, that he did not listen to her to lie beside her, or be with her. Now it happened one day that he went into the house to do his work, and none of the men of the household was there inside. And she caught him by his garment, saying, "Lie with me!" And he left his garment in her hand and fled, and went outside. When she saw that he had left his garment in her hand, and had fled outside, she called to the men of her household, and said to them, "See, he has brought in a Hebrew to us to make sport of us; he came in to me to lie with me, and I screamed. And it came about when he heard that I raised my voice and screamed, that he left his garment beside me and fled, and went outside." So she left his garment beside her until his master came home. Then she spoke to him with these words, "The Hebrew slave, whom you brought to us, came in to me to make sport of me; and it happened as I raised my voice and screamed, that he left his garment beside me and fled outside." Now it came about when his master heard the words of his wife, which she spoke to him, saying, "This is what your slave did to me," that his anger burned. So Joseph's master took him and put him into the jail, the place where the king's prisoners were confined; and he was there in the jail (Genesis 39:10–20).

Oh, if we would only learn to "2 Timothy 2:22 it"—"to flee youthful lusts." Yet we don't. It seems we love sin's enticement when it deals with our sexuality. We want to flirt, to enjoy the flattery of it all, to have our egos built, to dream the impossible dream, and so rather than fleeing we linger close to the fire. We want the warmth of it, but, as a moth is attracted to the light only to be destroyed, so we get closer and closer until we walk right into the fire. Then, Beloved, you can know that the destiny which God so marvelously planned for you is gone. Destroyed by the temporal fires of passion. And when it's all over, how intimate can you be with your God?

No, Joseph would not exchange the eternal satisfaction of being used of God for a temporary love affair. Would you?

September 25

Before we move on, let me give some needful advice to those of you who would minister with or to members of the opposite sex.

There is so much infidelity, so many are walking out after years of marriage, that I cannot help but feel that a spirit of immorality pervades our atmosphere, luring countless men and women into troubled waters and then casting them shipwrecked on the isolated shores of lasciviousness. In Stout's article, "Clergy Divorce Spills Into the Aisle," he writes:

> Another contributing factor is infidelity. There is little doubt that there is a percentage of women who consider the sexual conquest of a pastor a goal worth pursuing. The minister may appear distant or unapproachable, above such behavior, and is thus a challenge. Pastors have relatively easy access to the homes of a vast number of people, including distraught, "helpless," and dissatisfied women. Playing on his ego over a period of time may finally succeed in the seduction. If a member of the opposite sex perceives a minister's marriage as shaky and that person is also experiencing unhappiness, there is a certain kinship. Commiseration may lead to conquest.

When men and women work together in a ministry they must at all times discipline their thought life. The minute a twinge of attraction arises, the minute you feel more drawn to each other than to your mate—wanting to spend extra time together—you **must** put to death all such thoughts and desires. They are not to be considered or entertained for even a minute. To do so is to violate Philippians 4:8. "Finally, brethren, whatever is true, whatever is honorable, whatever is right, whatever is pure, whatever is lovely, whatever is of good repute, if there is any excellence and if anything worthy of praise, let your mind dwell on these things."

Rather, you are to cast down imaginations and every high thought that exalts itself against the knowledge of the Lord and take every thought captive to the obedience of Jesus Christ (2 Corinthians 10:5). Remember, sin begins in the mind. "Keep thy heart [mind] with all diligence; for out of it are the issues of life" (Proverbs 4:23 KJV). "For out of the heart come evil thoughts, murders, adulteries, fornications ..." (Matthew 15:19).

Can you see how vital it is that you keep your mind under control? Not to do so is to court sin, and, "when lust has conceived, it gives birth to sin; and when sin is accomplished, it brings forth death" (James 1:15). Illicit sex ends in death because it is sin.

September 26

When you minister to those of the opposite sex, it is absolutely vital that, should you feel any attraction, you never verbalize it. The minute you talk about it you have opened the door to enticement. It's like breaking down a wall of defense. Suddenly your emotions are exposed. Now the one hearing the confession of attraction has to deal with all the emotions it evokes. It may evoke disgust, shock, or horror, but ofttimes it serves as a flattering enticement. Keep your mouth shut. "Let no unwholesome word proceed from your mouth, but only such a word as is good for edification according to the need of the moment, that it may give grace to those who hear. And do not grieve the Holy Spirit of God, by whom you were sealed for the day of redemption" (Ephesians 4:29, 30). Confession of an inordinate attraction does not edify; it destroys. And, oh, how it grieves God's **Holy** Spirit.

If you need help in dealing with it, confess it to God. If it still lingers, ask God what person (of your sex) He wants you to confess it to so that you might be healed. Your heart is sick; it must be healed. "Therefore, confess your sins to one another, and pray for one another, so that you may be healed. The effective prayer of a righteous man can accomplish much" (James 5:16).

Finally, and I do mean finally, I do not believe it is healthy for men to counsel women or for women to counsel men in any extensive way. I especially feel it gets dangerous when it is in the area of marital problems. Very rarely do I ever do any counseling anymore because I simply do not have the time. Yet, when I have counseled, I have been very careful in dealing with men. Our staff men and women are careful to do team counseling (a man and woman) when the situation makes it necessary to deal with members of the opposite sex. Counseling many times involves a baring of one's soul which leads to prayer. There is a drawing power in prayer, a tenderness, an intimacy. Therefore, one needs to be cautious. Many a pastor has fallen in such cases.

O Leader, "examine everything carefully; hold fast to that which is good; abstain from every form (appearance) of evil" (1 Thessalonians 5:21, 22); and say with Joseph, "How then could I do this great evil, and sin against God?" (Genesis 39:9).

September 27

As I sat in the chapel at Fort Ord, California, waiting to speak, my eyes caught the beauty of the sun illuminating a stained glass window. The window was so situated that it could only be seen from where I sat. Two figures occupied its panes, the figure of Moses and the figure of an ancient soldier. At the bottom of the window were two words: Moses, Leadership.

My heart was warmed and stirred, and we talked. "Thank You, Father." He had confirmed that which He had laid upon my heart, the message on Moses and leadership that He has given me for you and for those who would listen.

The children of Israel had been in bondage four hundred years. "And the sons of Israel sighed because of the bondage, and they cried out; and their cry for help because of their bondage rose up to God. So God heard their groaning; and God remembered His covenant with Abraham, Isaac, and Jacob. And God saw the sons of Israel, and God took notice of them" (Exodus 2:23–25).

The time had come. God's promise to Abraham was about to be fulfilled.

> And God said to Abram, "Know for certain that your descendants will be strangers in a land that is not theirs, where they will be enslaved and oppressed four hundred years. But I will also judge the nation whom they will serve; and afterward they will come out with many possessions" (Genesis 15:13, 14).

God would judge Egypt and deliver the Israelites, and in doing so He would use a man who thought he had failed, a man who had been removed from the palace of Pharaoh to the pastures of Midian, a man whom the children of Israel had disowned forty years earlier as their ruler and judge but whom God had appointed "both a ruler and a deliverer with the help of the angel who appeared to him in the thorn bush" (Acts 7:35).

Look around you, Beloved. What do you see? I see a people in bondage, a bondage worse than that of Egypt, for these people are in bondage to sin. Now look in the mirror. What do you see? Just another ordinary person? A failure? A reject? Look again and tell me what God sees?

September 28

LEADERSHIP IS KNOWING THE DELIVERER.

Moses was eighty years old when "God called to him from the midst of the bush, and said, 'Moses, Moses!'" (Exodus 3:4). The first forty years of his life had been spent in Egypt as the son of Pharaoh's daughter, the next forty years in Midian tending sheep.

> In Egypt, "Moses was educated in all the learning of the Egyptians, and he was a man of power in words and deeds. But when he was ap-

proaching the age of forty, it entered his mind to visit his brethren, the sons of Israel. And when he saw one of them being treated unjustly, he defended him and took vengeance for the oppressed by striking down the Egyptian. And he supposed that his brethren understood that God was granting them deliverance through him; but they did not understand. And on the following day he appeared to them as they were fighting together, and he tried to reconcile them in peace, saying, 'Men, you are brethren, why do you injure one another?' But the one who was injuring his neighbor pushed him away, saying, 'Who made you a ruler and judge over us? You do not mean to kill me as you killed the Egyptian yesterday, do you?' And at this remark Moses fled, and became an alien in the land of Midian, where he became the father of two sons. And after forty years had passed, an angel appeared to him in the wilderness of Mount Sinai, in the flame of a burning thorn bush" (Acts 7:22–30).

Moses listened incredulously to the words of the Lord.

And the Lord said, "I have surely seen the affliction of My people who are in Egypt, and have given heed to their cry because of their taskmasters, for I am aware of their sufferings. So I have come down to deliver them from the power of the Egyptians, and to bring them up from that land to a good and spacious land, to a land flowing with milk and honey. . . . Therefore, come now, and I will send you to Pharaoh, so that you may bring My people, the sons of Israel, out of Egypt" (Exodus 3:7, 8, 10).

It was more than Moses could handle. God was going to send him? How could *he* deliver them? He had tried once and failed! It was too late. He was eighty. And so he asked, "Who am I, that I should go?" (3:11).

As you read these devotions on leadership, do you feel like saying with Moses, "Who am I, that I should lead?" I understand. Who are you? We will look at it tomorrow. But for today, think about it? Who *are* you?

September 29

"Who am I, that I should go to Pharaoh, and that I should bring the sons of Israel out of Egypt?" (Exodus 3:11).

Moses' question was valid. What was he looking for when he asked the question? We don't know exactly, but I think it is safe to assume that he wanted God to give him some reason why he was the man for the job. I don't think Moses' question was provoked by pride. If he had had a problem with pride, that certainly must have been taken care of when he fled from Egypt only to find himself, not the deliverer of his fellow Israelites, but rather the tender of another's sheep. What Moses had gained in Egypt, he lost in Midian. Once "a man of power in words and deeds" (Acts 7:22), he now considered himself "slow of speech and slow of tongue" (Exodus 4:10). All the learning of Egypt had faded away under the hot sun of the barren plains of Midian. Moses had known at one time that God had appointed him the deliverer of his brethren but when he tried he failed. So what made God think he could succeed a second time?

Moses knew his own impotence. He had experienced a full dress rehearsal of it on stage in Egypt. It was a one-night stand, and they ran him out of town! Who was he? He was a failure. A nobody. God couldn't use him; he didn't have anything to commend himself to God!

"Who am I, that I should go?" I love God's answer! "Certainly I will be with you" (Exodus 3:12). It did not matter who Moses was; it only mattered that God would be with him! What more did Moses need? God was with him, and God never fails!

If we could only get it through our heads that God doesn't need our abilities—only our availability. All God needs is a container, something to hold Him, something to fill with His character and power, a branch to abide, a vessel to be filled. God had "come down to deliver them from the power of the Egyptians" (Exodus 3:8). God was the deliverer. All He needed was a human representative to work through!

Do you see it? If not, ask God to open your eyes.

September 30

When the Lord calls you to step out as a leader, you can know that it will never be on the basis of your courage or ability. Rather it will always be a call that is a challenge to your faith. Your only excuse for not stepping out will be that you refused to believe God and walk in "the obedience of faith" (Romans 1:5).

"But I'm afraid. I just don't have it in me." I understand how you feel but you cannot let your feelings rule you. We walk by faith not by sight (2 Corinthians 5:7). If God has called you, then you know, "faithful is He who calls you, and He also will bring it to pass" (1 Thessalonians 5:24).

When Gideon was threshing wheat in a winepress in order to hide from the Midianites, "the angel of the Lord appeared to him and said to him, 'The Lord is with you, O valiant warrior' " (Judges 6:12). At the time, Gideon was anything but a valiant warrior, and he knew it. So, when the Lord looked at him and said, "Go in this your strength and deliver Israel from the hand of Midian. Have I not sent you?" (6:14), Gideon's response was only natural. Look at how similar it is to Moses' response. "O Lord, **how shall I deliver Israel?** Behold, my family is the least in Manasseh, and I am the youngest in my father's house" (6:15).

And what was God's reply? It is the same response He gives to all those whom He calls. " 'Surely I will be with you, and you shall defeat Midian as one man' " (6:16). It was the same with Joshua when God called him to lead Israel into the promised land. "Have not I commanded you? Be strong and courageous! Do not tremble or be dismayed, for the Lord your God is with you wherever you go" (Joshua 1:9).

Whenever God sends one of His children to do a task for Him, that child never goes alone. God goes with him.

Are you not one of His children? Then, if He bids you go, to step out, to lead the way, can you not go? Faith looks not at its ability but rather at the surety of His promise, "I will be with you." And faith says, "Yes!" That kind of faith makes you into a valiant warrior!

OCTOBER

October 1

"And I searched for a man among them who should build up the wall and stand in the gap before Me for the land" (Ezekiel 22:30). The words were penned long ago by Ezekiel the prophet and yet they are for today. God is searching for men and women who will take responsibility to extend the Kingdom of Jesus Christ and who will move into positions of leadership as godly men and women that our land might not be destroyed. "For the eyes of the Lord move to and fro throughout the earth that He may strongly support those whose heart is completely His" (2 Chronicles 16:9a). "The Lord is with you when you are with Him. And if you seek Him, He will let you find Him" (2 Chronicles 15:2). This is His promise to all who will serve under their Jehovah-nissi—the Lord my banner—in positions of responsibility and leadership.

As I shared with you last month, my burden is that the leaders lead and the people follow. We need godly leaders, parents to lead their children, children to lead their schoolmates, fathers to lead their families, men to lead our churches, teachers to lead their pupils, businessmen to lead their employees. Do you see what I am saying? Leaders are in all walks of life. We also need godly followers. Don't lay these devotionals aside saying lightly, "Leadership is not for me." No, Beloved. First ask God, "Is leadership for me? What roles do I fill that put me in a position of leadership?" Remember, Moses at first turned aside from God's call, for he wondered, "Who am I, that I should go?" (Exodus 3:11). Then God showed him, "Certainly I will be with you." You can rest assured that, whenever God calls you, He will be with you. However, if leadership is not your call in any respect, learn all you can, for God has then called you to follow, and there is a godly way to follow.

Will you not take time now to bow before God and say, "Father, whatever I am to do, I will do it, be it lead or follow. I only want to do it Your way, according to Your ordinances. Teach me, for Jesus' sake. Amen."

October 2

LEADERSHIP IS KNOWING THE DELIVERER.

"But what if I go, and God goes with me, and I still fail?" There it is again, that fear of failure that would immobilize us. We are afraid that somehow we won't be able to deliver, we won't have what we need when we need it, whatever it is that we need!

Moses felt the same way. God was going to use him, but what if the people of Israel didn't cooperate? What if they didn't believe God had sent him?

It was another valid question and God respected it. Moses said:

"Behold, I am going to the sons of Israel, and I shall say to them, 'The God of your fathers has sent me to you.' Now they may say to me, 'What is His name?' What shall I say to them?" (Exodus 3:13).

How grateful I am for God's answer to Moses, for His answer to Moses is for me also. For what if I step out to do a work for Him, and it's a failure? What if I am doing what God says do, and yet I cannot deliver the goods? What if people question me or challenge me?

Listen to God's answer to Moses; it is for you as well.

And God said to Moses, "I AM WHO I AM"; and He said, "Thus you shall say to the sons of Israel, 'I AM has sent me to you.' " And God, furthermore, said to Moses, "Thus you shall say to the sons of Israel, 'The Lord, the God of your fathers, the God of Abraham, the God of Isaac, the God of Jacob, has sent me to you.' This is My name forever, and this is My memorial-name to all generations" (Exodus 3:14, 15).

I AM? That's God's name? I AM what? I AM all and everything that you will ever need! O Beloved, stop and meditate on it. Assimilate this mangificent truth into the very fiber of your being. I AM is God's name forever, His memorial-name to all generations. It is His name to you and to me. When you step out under His command, you need not fear failure no matter what the results. The results are His business not yours. He, I AM, is with you, and He is everything you will ever need. You can go, for I AM goes with you.

LEADERSHIP IS KNOWING THE DELIVERER: I AM.

October 3

"Okay. I know God is going to go with me; I know His name is I AM. But what am I going to do when I go? How am I going to know what to do as a leader?"

Have you ever had those thoughts? When I first felt God's tuggings regarding writing inductive Bible studies, these were in essence my questions. Who was I to write inductive study courses when I had never done anything like that before? When I didn't even have a college education? What would I call these studies? How would I write them? How would I set them up? How would we get them printed and to the people? Who would help lead the discussion classes? And how do you lead a discussion class? So many questions that needed answers. Besides, was God sure I was the one to do it? I was such a slow reader. I had never had any training in writing. I had never even written anything but a prayer letter. Besides, my IQ is not that high. I was afraid to have it tested. There seemed to be so many questions, so many obstacles. Yet the nudgings that had become tuggings now turned to burdens. What if people didn't accept these courses as being sent from God to help them dig deeper into His Word?

Moses had the same question:

> "What if they will not believe me, or listen to what I say? For they may say, 'The Lord has not appeared to you.' And the Lord said to him, 'What is that in your hand?' And he said, 'A staff.' " (Exodus 4:1, 2).

Moses' staff would be his weapon against Pharaoh, his source of power. And what did I have in my hand? The Bible, God's infallible, inerrant Word! I had the "sword of the Spirit, which is the word of God" (Ephesians 6:17). All I had to do was unsheath it. "For the word of God is living and active and sharper than any two-edged sword, and piercing as far as the division of soul and spirit, of both joints and marrow, and able to judge the thoughts and intentions of the heart" (Hebrews 4:12).

Moses had his staff, Kay had her Bible. But I still needed help and so did Moses. We needed specific direction. Everyone who would lead, even though he has God's Word, still needs specific direction. And who will give us specific directions?

October 4

LEADERSHIP IS BEING TAUGHT BY GOD.

Moses was to go and stand before Pharaoh! Pharaoh, who had tried to kill Moses (Exodus 2:15)!

> Then Moses said to the Lord, "Please, Lord, I have never been eloquent, neither recently nor in time past, nor since thou hast spoken to Thy servant; for I am slow of speech and slow of tongue." And the Lord said to him, "Who has made man's mouth? Or who makes him dumb or deaf, or seeing or blind? Is it not I, the Lord? Now then go, and I, even I, will be with your mouth, and teach you what you are to say." But he said, "Please, Lord, now send the message by whomever Thou wilt." Then the anger of the Lord burned against Moses, and He said, "Is there not your brother Aaron the Levite? I know that he speaks fluently. And moreover, behold, he is coming out to meet you; when he sees you, he will be glad in his heart. And you are to speak to him and put the words in his mouth; and I, even I, will be with your mouth and his mouth, and I will teach you what you are to do. Moreover, he shall speak for you to the people; and it shall come about that he shall be as a mouth for you, and you shall be as God to him. And you shall take in your hand this staff, with which you shall perform the signs" (Exodus 4:10–17).

Now, read these verses again, and look for the word *teach*. Note where the word is used along with *who* the teacher is and *what* he teaches. Write out your insights.

Beloved One who will lead, you can rest assured that if God taught Moses, He will teach you. God would not give you a task and leave you without direction. As God promised to teach Moses what to say (verse 12) and what to do (verse 15), so He promises you. This is why you have been given the Spirit of God. "When the Helper comes, whom I will send to you from the Father, that is the Spirit of truth, who proceeds from the Father, He will bear witness of Me" (John 15:26). "For it is God who is at work in you, both to will and to work for His good pleasure" (Philippians 2:13).

Meditate on that and we will talk more tomorrow. By the way, do you know how precious you are to Him?

October 5

How does God teach you? By His Spirit through His Word. And how does He lead you? By His Spirit through His Word. His Word is our plumb line of truth. Be patient and prayerful now as we seek to understand how He teaches us.

If God is going to teach you what to say and do, you are going to have to have some type of communication with Him so He can show you His truths and His ways. Knowing this, God has given you "the Helper, the Holy Spirit . . . He will teach you all things, and bring to your remembrance all that" Christ has said to you (John 14:26). "Now we have received, not the spirit of the world, but the Spirit who is from God, that we might know the things freely given to us by God, which things we also speak, not in words taught by human wisdom, but in those taught by the Spirit, combining spiritual thoughts with spiritual words" (1 Corinthians 2:12, 13). Because we are God's, because Christ is in us, "we have the mind of Christ" (1 Corinthians 2:16). We can know God because the Holy Spirit takes God's words, combines them with spiritual thoughts, and gives us His mind.

Now then, since the Spirit combines spiritual thoughts with spiritual words, it is essential that we have exposure to these words. These words, of course, constitute the Word of God, the Bible. The Bible is a supernatural book "for the word of God is living and active and sharper than any two-edged sword, and piercing as far as the division of soul and spirit, of both joints and marrow, **and able to judge the thoughts and intentions of the heart**" (Hebrews 4:12). God's Word enables me to analyze my thoughts and intentions. It instructs me in the way I should go. "Thy word is a lamp unto my feet, and a light unto my path" (Psalms 119:105 KJV). His words become my counselors or, as the literal Hebrew rendering says, "the men of my counsel" (Psalms 119:24).

You know God and His ways through His Word. This is how God leads and teaches you. Meditate on it and we will continue tomorrow.

October 6

Whether or not you are a leader, as a child of God you are to walk worthy of the vocation to which He has called you (Ephesians 4:1), accomplishing the good works which God has before ordained for you (Ephesians 2:10). This is to accomplish the will of God, to do that which pleases the Father.

But how do you determine God's will? What does God's Word say? Does the Bible give specific steps? No, it doesn't. Yet, if knowing God's will is so vital, why would God's Word obscure this truth so that only certain ones could discover the specific steps for ascertaining the will of God? From my understanding of God's Word, I would say that knowing God's will is not a matter of steps, but of relationship. Knowing God's will does not require following an intricate set of rules; rather it is a matter of desire, of commitment. "If any man is willing to do His will, he shall know of the teaching, whether it is of God" (John 7:17). Vincent writes of this, "Sympathy with the will of God is a condition of understanding it." If I want God's will, would God hide it from me? Would He make it difficult? Oh, no! He is a loving Father who longs to guide me with His eye (Psalms 32:8) and lead me in His path.

"But," you may say, "I'm afraid I won't be able to discern between my way and His way! How can I know if God is leading me or if I am trying to lead myself?" Precious One, if your heart's desire is toward God, He is not going to let you go astray. "Man's steps are ordained by the Lord, how then can man understand his way" (Proverbs 20:24).

Your responsibility, according to God's Word, is to be "transformed by the renewing of your mind, that you may prove what the will of God is, that which is good and acceptable and perfect" (Romans 12:2). A renewed mind is essential to the will of God for as a man thinks so he is. Therefore, you must saturate your mind with God's thoughts, by saturating yourself with God's Word. This, in turn, enables you to prove the will of God. To *prove* means to put to test for the sake of approving.

Think on these things, and God will give it to you precept upon precept, line upon line. I love you.

October 7

Not too long ago I found myself in conversation with some very precious children of God. Many were at a crossroads in their lives and longed to know which direction to take. As I looked at each of them I knew there wasn't a single one present who did not in his deepest heart long for God's will. Yet some of them were paralyzed. They didn't have "a definite word from God," and they didn't know what to do. They couldn't move! As we talked I shared with them Colossians 1:9, 10: "For this reason also, since the day we heard of it, we have not ceased to pray for you and to ask that you may be filled with the knowledge of His will in all spiritual wisdom and understanding, so that you may walk in a manner worthy of the Lord, to please Him in all respects, bearing fruit in every good work and increasing in the knowledge of God".

According to these verses, we are filled with the knowledge of His will not through a specific word—although God can give one—but rather through spiritual wisdom and understanding. This indicates to me that knowing God's will is more a matter of relationship, of knowing God, than of receiving a specific word for every single thing I do. (Now, there are times when decisions are so monumental that you must spend time specifically seeking His will and not move until you hear in your heart, "this is the way, walk in it" [Isaiah 30:21].)

Knowing His will is usually like in a marriage or a close friendship. Those who know me intimately can usually speak for me. They can say, "Kay would" or "wouldn't_____" not because they have a specific word from me, but because they know me. Knowing my Heavenly Father, knowing His ways, knowing of His love for me and desire for my welfare, I can walk in confidence. As long as my heart's desire is to please Him, will He not oversee my steps? And if I am going the wrong way, will He not redirect my steps? Of course. "Man's goings are of the Lord" (Proverbs 20:24). This same truth is affirmed in Philippians 3:14, 15. If your attitude (mind) is to press toward the goal for the prize of the upward call of God in Christ Jesus, God assures you that "if in anything you have a different attitude, God will reveal that also to you." Isn't that marvelous! You need not be paralyzed with the fear of being out of His will as long as Christlikeness is your goal.

October 8

"But," you may ask, "what if I make a mistake and miss the will of God because my heart is 'deceitful and desperately wicked'? What if I cannot trust my heart? How can I lead then?" Beloved, that will never be the case if you are saved by grace and are therefore under the New Covenant. Your heart is not "deceitful and desperately wicked" for the New Covenant gives you a **new** heart. Listen! "Moreover, I will give you a new heart . . . and I will put My Spirit within you and cause you to walk in My statutes, and you will be careful to observe My ordinances" (Ezekiel 36:26, 27). Hallelujah! "Our adequacy is from God, who also made us adequate as servants of a new covenant . . . of the Spirit" (2 Corinthians 3:5b–6a).

Just "trust in the Lord with all your heart, and do not lean on your own understanding. In all your ways acknowledge Him, **and He will make your paths straight**" (Proverbs 3:5, 6). That is a promise from the Father. It is a truth you can rely on.

How is it all lived out in the marketplace of life? I commit my day and my choices to God and tell Him that I will to do His will, whatever it is. Then I walk in spiritual wisdom and understanding (according to His Word), trusting God to direct my steps and show me if I stray from His will. All the time I am to stay attuned to the Spirit and His peace (Isaiah 9:6, Galatians 5:22), letting the peace of God rule (umpire) in my heart (Colossians 3:15). If that peace goes, then I need to ask God why, knowing that He will reveal this to me (James 1:5-8).

Now, back to leadership. You can lead, Precious One, because **He will lead you.** "Commit thy way unto the Lord; trust also in him; and he shall bring it to pass" (Psalms 37:5). Note, **He** shall bring it to pass. Yours is to commit, His is to bring it to pass.

Now let's review where our spiritual wisdom and understanding come from. You are transformed by the renewing of your mind and that happens through exposure to God's Word. Therefore hide God's Word in your heart so that you won't sin against Him (Psalms 119:11) and study to show yourself "approved to God as a workman who does not need to be ashamed, handling accurately the word of truth" (2 Timothy 2:15). Say to your God, "Establish Thy Word to Thy servant, as that which produces reverence for Thee. . . . I will meditate on Thy precepts, and regard Thy ways" (Psalms 119:38, 15).

"I rise before dawn and cry for help; I wait for Thy words. My eyes anticipate the night watches, that I may meditate on Thy word" (Psalms 119:147, 148).

If this is your heart, you cannot miss the will of God. He will teach you what to say and what to do, even as He did Moses.

October 9

LEADERSHIP IS EXPECTING TO BE CHALLENGED.
Work done for God will never go unchallenged. Only those who are sitting in apathy, content with the status quo, will escape the enemy's resistance. Satan doesn't need to waste time with them; he has them right where he wants them. Recently I talked with the producer of a Christian television program who told me that they had slipped into a secular format which offered very little that had anything to do with the Word of God. Producing those shows was smooth sailing all the way, but when they saw the error of their ways and returned to biblically-based programming, the seas became turbulent! It has been havoc for them ever since. You can expect to be challenged if you are doing a work for God.

I say this to prepare you, not to alarm or discourage you. Remember, you have a weapon, the Word of God, a sword as powerful as

Moses' rod, and God has said, "In all these things we are more than conquerors through him that loved us" (Romans 8:37 KJV).

God gave Moses a task to perform, to lead Israel out of Egypt into Canaan. Yet Moses knew that this task would not go unchallenged. God had prepared him, telling him that only under compulsion would Pharaoh let Israel leave Egypt (Exodus 6:1).

> But I know that the king of Egypt will not permit you to go, except under compulsion. So I will stretch out My hand, and strike Egypt with all My miracles which I shall do in the midst of it; and after that he will let you go. And I will grant this people favor in the sight of the Egyptians; and it shall be that when you go, you will not go empty-handed. But every woman shall ask of her neighbor and the woman who lives in her house, articles of silver and articles of gold, and clothing; and you will put them on your sons and daughters. Thus you will plunder the Egyptians (Exodus 3:19–22).

It is one thing to be challenged by your adversaries; being challenged "from within" can be harder to deal with. Still, you must expect it because leadership is often contested by those who follow. When the going got rough, Israel challenged Moses.

> And they said to them, "May the Lord look upon you and judge you, for you have made us odious in Pharaoh's sight and in the sight of his servants, to put a sword in their hand to kill us" (Exodus 5:21).

What is a leader to do when this happens? You are to go on with the task God has set before you. If Moses hadn't, Israel would have remained in bondage! Go forward! Lead!

October 10

When you go forth to do a work for God, never underestimate the power of the enemy, for he does have power. However, you must also never forget that "you are from God, little children, and have overcome them; because greater is He who is in you than he who is in the world" (1 John 4:4). When Moses challenged Pharaoh, and "Aaron threw his staff down before Pharaoh and his servants, and it became a serpent, then Pharaoh also called for the wise men and the sorcerers, and they also, the magicians of Egypt, did the same with their secret arts. For each one threw down his staff and they turned into serpents" (Exodus 7:10–12). Satan does have power. He is able to work miracles. Ofttimes "Satan disguises himself as an angel of light. Therefore it is not surprising if his servants also disguise themselves as servants of righteousness; whose end shall be according to their deeds" (2 Corinthians 11:14, 15). There is an "activity of Satan, with all power and signs and false wonders" (2 Thessalonians 2:9) that you need to be aware of so that you will "test the spirits to see whether they are from God" (1 John 4:1).

Once you are challenged by Satan's emissaries, you must realize that you are never to back down. Defeat is not to be in the vocabulary of those who are "more than conquerors." When Pharaoh's magicians turned their staffs into serpents, "Aaron's staff swallowed up their staffs" (Exodus 7:12b). We will have victory if we persevere. The problem, however, is that we do not persevere. When the challenge comes, we say "This is too difficult; forget it," and we give up. If we would only persevere, we would conquer! The plagues of blood and frogs brought on by Moses were duplicated by Pharaoh's magicians (Exodus 7:20–8:7). But when Moses had Aaron stretch out his staff "and strike the dust of the earth, that it may become gnats through all the land of Egypt" (8:16), Satan's power came to its end. Pharaoh's "magicians tried with their secret arts to bring forth gnats, but they could not. . . . Then the magicians said to Pharaoh, 'This is the finger of God' " (8:18, 19).

Leaders can expect to be challenged; yet they must meet that challenge head-on and go forward so that all might see "the finger of God."

October 11

LEADERSHIP IS BEING BROUGHT TO IMPASSABLE, IMPOSSIBLE WATERS.

God brought the Israelites out of Egypt just as He had promised. When the plague of death fell on the firstborn of Egypt, "the Egyptians urged the people, to send them out of the land in haste, for they said, 'We shall all be dead' " (Exodus 12:33).

It all came about just as God had said, and "the Lord was going before them in a pillar of cloud by day to lead them on the way, and in a pillar of fire by night to give them light, that they might travel by day and night" (Exodus 13:21). And where did God lead them? He led them to impassable, impossible waters—to the Red Sea at flood stage!

The best of leaders have found themselves in the same impossible, impassable situations. Why? And what does one do when he comes to a situation like this? We will see tomorrow, but first let me share with you from God's Word just how it was.

And the Lord hardened the heart of Pharaoh, king of Egypt, and he chased after the sons of Israel as the sons of Israel were going out boldly.... And as Pharaoh drew near, the sons of Israel looked, and behold, the Egyptians were marching after them, and they became very frightened; so the sons of Israel cried out to the Lord. Then they said to Moses, "Is it because there were no graves in Egypt that you have taken us away to die in the wilderness? Why have you dealt with us in this way, bringing us out of Egypt? Is this not the word that we spoke to you in Egypt, saying, 'Leave us alone that we may serve the Egyptians'? For it would have been better for us to serve the Egyptians than to die in the wilderness." But Moses said to the people, "Do not fear! Stand by and see the salvation of the Lord which He will accomplish for you today; for the Egyptians whom you have seen today, you will never see them again forever. The Lord will fight for you while you keep silent." Then the Lord said to Moses, "Why are you crying out to me? Tell the sons of Israel to go forward. And as for you, lift up your staff and stretch out your hand over the sea and divide it, and the sons of Israel shall go through the midst of the sea on dry land. And as for Me, behold, I will harden the hearts of the Egyptians so that they will go in after them; and I will be honored through Pharaoh and all his army, through his chariots and his horsemen" (Exodus 14:8, 10–17).

When God leads you to impossible, impassable waters, you must go forward.

October 12

It's *the impossible* that brings God glory. When there is no other way except God, man knows beyond a doubt that the solution, when it comes, is from Him. Man's extremity is God's opportunity. That is why God often leads you to impassable, impossible waters.

And what are we to do when we come to a situation like this? We are to cry out to God and then listen! He has a way of escape. "Do not fear! Stand by and see the salvation of the Lord which He will accomplish for you" (Exodus 14:13). "When you pass through the waters, I will be with you; and through the rivers, they will not overflow you. When you walk through the fire, you will not be scorched, nor will the flame burn you. For I am the Lord your God.... Do not fear, for I am with you" (Isaiah 43:2, 3, 5).

Yesterday, when you read Exodus 14:8–17, did you notice the "as for you" in verse 16? Moses was not to sit passively moping beside the waters; rather he was to cooperate with God. Moses was to stretch out his rod, and God would take care of the Egyptians. We are to act in faith upon God's Word, and God will do His part.

God has frequently brought us to times of great extremity in our ministry. One such time was when He showed us what was to be Reach Out's property. It cost $62,500. We didn't have any money and God had not allowed us to ask people to give. Yet we knew we were to contract for the land. Where would we ever get the $18,000 for the down payment? And how could we swing the $400 monthly payments? It was beyond us. We had just applied for status as a religious and educational nonprofit organization. We were two adults and several college students with a burden and a vision. We chuckle about it now, for our needs then were nothing compared to what they are each month now with forty-three employees and eleven buildings to care for! What did we do then? The same thing we do now. We cried to God and stretched out the sword, the Word of God, over the waters. And we saw the waters part. Right at the last moment. God satisfied that eighteen thousand dollar need by providing the final two thousand dollars on the last possible day.

Are you facing impassable, impossible waters? Did God lead you there? Go forward, stretch out your rod!

October 13

LEADERSHIP IS TAKING THE BITTER AND MAKING IT SWEET.

> Then Moses led Israel from the Red Sea, and they went out into the wilderness of Shur; and they went three days in the wilderness and found no water. And when they came to Marah, they could not drink the waters of Marah, for they were bitter; therefore it was named Marah. So the people grumbled at Moses, saying, "What shall we drink?" Then he cried out to the Lord, and the Lord showed him a tree; and he threw it into the waters, and the waters became sweet. There He made for them a statute and regulation, and there He tested them. And He said, "If you will give earnest heed to the voice of the Lord your God, and do what is right in His sight, and give ear to His commandments, and keep all His statutes, I will put none of the diseases on you which I have put on the Egyptians; for I, the Lord, am your healer." Then they came to Elim where there were twelve springs of water and seventy date palms, and they camped there beside the waters (Exodus 15:22–27).

Bitterness goes with leadership. It is part of the cost. If you are willing to lead, you must be prepared to find yourself in bitter situations. If you are a follower, know that those who lead will have to deal with enough bitterness without your adding to it.

You have heard the phrase, "bitter as gall." Well, that is exactly what it is like! A situation can become so bilious that you feel doubled over with a retching nausea, so sick that you wish you could die! Sometimes it can seem so insane that you wonder how it ever happened; yet, there you are caught in the middle of it. Is it worth it? Oh, yes, although at the time you may seriously doubt it. And how do you handle such bitter situations? Let me start my explanation today and I will finish it tomorrow.

When Israel came to Marah and could not drink because the waters of Marah were so bitter, what did Moses do? Write it out.

What made the waters drinkable?_____

Now, one more question for meditation until tomorrow: How do you personally handle bitter situations?

October 14

When God led Israel to the waters of Marah, did He know the water would be bitter and undrinkable? Of course. That, Beloved, is point one. Remember it. God knows all about the bitterness that comes with leadership. And what is His cure? A tree. Put a tree in the water and the water will become sweet. A tree?? Why? Well, let's do a little research. Listen carefully, then take it to the Holy Spirit. He's your Teacher. Remember that "whatever was written in earlier times was written for our instruction" (Romans 15:4); therefore God has a lesson for our lives in the waters of Marah.

First, look at Deuteronomy 21:22, 23: "And if a man has committed a sin worthy of death, and he is put to death, and you hang him on a tree, his corpse shall not hang all night on the tree, but you shall surely bury him on the same day (for he who is hanged is accursed of God)."

Paul was quoting Deuteronomy when he penned Galatians 3:13: "Christ redeemed us from the curse of the Law, having become a curse for us—for it is written, 'Cursed is every one who hangs on a tree.' " The literal word for *tree* in Galatians is *wood.* Peter, in preaching, said: "The God of our fathers raised up Jesus, whom you had put to death by hanging Him on a cross" (Acts 5:30). The word *cross* is also literally translated *wood.* So, we see the tree is identical with the cross. Moses made the bitter water sweet by applying the tree, the cross.

How I love to draw the parallel between Moses' experience and Jesus' words in John 7:37-39! "Now on the last day, the great day of the feast, Jesus stood and cried out, saying, 'If any man is thirsty, let

296

him come to Me and drink. He who believes in Me, as the Scripture said, "From his innermost being shall flow rivers of living water." ' But this He spoke of the Spirit, whom those who believed in Him were to receive; for the Spirit was not yet given, because Jesus was not yet glorified."

What is God's lesson? I believe it is this. The only way to handle a bitter situation is to fully apply the cross. You must declare death on normal reactions, normal responses. "Father, if Thou art willing, remove this cup from Me; yet not My will, but Thine be done" (Luke 22:42).

Calvary was bitter, yet the cross gave us the sweet water of life. In any bitter situation, leader or not, you can say only one thing to make the bitter sweet, and that is, "I have been crucified with Christ; and it is no longer I who live, but Christ lives in me; and the life which I now live in the flesh I live by faith in the Son of God, who loved me, and delivered Himself up for me" (Galatians 2:20). Will you?

October 15

LEADERSHIP IS A LIFE OF PETITION AND INTERCESSION.
No work for God can ever be accomplished apart from Him; therefore, leadership necessitates constant communion with the Father. Is this not the reason for our Lord's promise to us when He says, "You did not choose Me, but I chose you, and appointed you, that you should go and bear fruit, and that your fruit should remain, **that whatever you ask of the Father in My name, He may give to you**" (John 15:16)? Just before Jesus said this He had taught His disciples that the source of fruit is never the branch, but the vine. He was the vine, they were the branches. If they were ever to further the Kingdom of God, they had to abide. "Abide in Me, and I in you. As the branch cannot bear fruit of itself, unless it abides in the vine, so neither can you, unless you abide in Me" (John 15:4). We must constantly come to that fountain of living water for our wisdom, our power, our strength. If we fail to do so our ministries will become dry and lifeless like the drifting sands of a barren desert.

"What shall I do?" becomes the intermittent petition of those who lead. Read Moses' life and you will see him constantly falling on his face before the Lord and crying out for direction. When the children of Israel came to the wilderness of Sin and camped at Rephidim, there was no water for them to drink. The people quarreled with Moses and demanded that he give them water. They even accused him of bringing them and their animals out of Egypt to die of thirst. "So Moses cried out to the Lord . . . 'What shall I do to this people? A little more and they will stone me'" (Exodus 17:4).

Bitter water . . . no water at all! Only God could deal with situations like these. And how does one handle fainthearted followers who want to turn back, who say to one another, "Let us appoint a leader and return to Egypt" (Numbers 14:4)? What can you do? Connive, bribe, cry, plead, walk away? No, you do as Moses and Aaron did. You fall on your face in prayer. And when they challenge your leadership and accuse you of exalting yourself as Korah did Moses, there is no place to go but on your face before your God (Numbers 16:3, 4). But, oh, you learn so much there!

October 16

Where is the Author (Leader) and Finisher of your faith right now? He is at the right hand of God for He ever lives to make intercession for those who have left all to follow Him. Your Leader intercedes for you. Leaders are to be intercessors. Read Paul's epistles, and you find the record of his prayers on behalf of the churches. Read Genesis, and you find Abraham interceding for the righteous who live in Sodom and Gomorrah. Read Exodus and Numbers, and you find Moses interceding for the multitude that just left Egypt. Read the prophets, and you find them interceding for Israel and Judah. Intercession! It is the duty of every leader. How convicted I am as I write these words, for I do not intercede for others as I should. Pray for me, Beloved, that I might learn to properly intercede for others. There is a battle being fought on earth for the very souls of men. What casualties we will suffer if we do not hold up holy hands in prevailing intercession!

God had just done a marvelous thing for Israel, bringing water from the rock.

> Then Amalek came and fought against Israel at Rephidim. So Moses said to Joshua, "Choose men for us, and go out, fight against Amalek. Tomorrow I will station myself on the top of the hill with the staff of God in my hand." And Joshua did as Moses told him, and fought against Amalek; and Moses, Aaron, and Hur went up to the top of the hill. So it came about when Moses held his hand up, that Israel prevailed, and when he let his hand down, Amalek prevailed. But Moses' hands were heavy. Then they took a stone and put it under him, and he sat on it; and Aaron and Hur supported his hands, one on one side and one on the other. Thus his hands were steady until the sun set. So Joshua overwhelmed Amalek and his people with the edge of the sword (Exodus 17:8–13).

Joshua and his warriors fought the battle on the plain, but Moses—aided by Aaron and Hur—won the victory through prevailing intercession on the hill. As Moses held up his staff, so are we to hold up the Word of God, knowing with all confidence that His promises are yea and amen. Claim them in prayer, hold them before the face of God, call for others to strengthen you when you grow weary, but do not give up. "The effective prayer of a righteous man can accomplish much" (James 5:16). Did God Himself not say, "Concerning the work of my hands command ye me" (Isaiah 45:11 KJV)?

Intercede, Beloved Leader, intercede. I say it to you and to myself.

October 17

LEADERSHIP IS OFTTIMES SO BURDENSOME THAT YOU THINK IT WOULD BE EASIER TO DIE THAN TO GO ON.

Now the people became like those who complain of adversity in the hearing of the Lord; and when the Lord heard it, His anger was kindled, and the fire of the Lord burned among them and consumed some of the outskirts of the camp. The people therefore cried out to Moses, and Moses prayed to the Lord, and the fire died out. . . . And the rabble who were among them had greedy desires; and also the sons of Israel wept again and said, "Who will give us meat to eat? We remember the fish which we used to eat free in Egypt, the cucumbers and the melons and the leeks and the onions and the garlic, but now our appetite is gone. There is nothing at all to look at except this manna" (Numbers 11:1–6).

One thing a leader needs to remember is that among those who follow are some who are not totally consecrated to the cause. People can follow for a number of reasons without ever being fully committed. These become the murmurers, the grumblers, the dissenters. Nothing can be done to please them. How they can wear on a person! So it was with Moses. And so it was even with God. They made God so angry that He kindled fire on the outskirts of the camp. And if God was angry, you know it was a righteous anger!

Now Moses heard the people weeping throughout their families, each man at the doorway of his tent; and the anger of the Lord was kindled greatly, and Moses was displeased. So Moses said to the Lord, "Why hast Thou been so hard on Thy servant? And why have I not found favor in Thy sight, that Thou hast laid the burden of all this people on me? Was it I who conceived all this people? Was it I who brought them forth, that Thou shouldest say to me, 'Carry them in your bosom as a nurse carries a nursing infant, to the land which Thou didst swear to their fathers'? Where am I to get meat to give to all this people? For they weep before me, saying, 'Give us meat that we may eat!' I alone am not able to carry all this people, because it is too burdensome for me. So if Thou art going to deal thus with me, please kill me at once, if I have found favor in Thy sight, and do not let me see my wretchedness' " (Numbers 11:10–15).

When people continue to complain, and you cannot please them no matter what you do, you begin to wonder if it really is worth it all. Why bother? Why not live an ordinary life, just for yourself! Why be concerned with the furtherance of the gospel? Or the welfare of God's people? Why should you earnestly contend for the absolutes of God's Word?

Why? Think about it, and tomorrow I will share how I've felt and what God has taught me.

October 18

If leadership is burdensome, if at times you long to die just so you can escape the wretchedness of it all, then why pay the price? Why not just quit?

Love cannot quit. Love "bears all things, believes all things, hopes all things, endures all things. Love never fails" (1 Corinthians 13:7, 8a). I will never forget the time I met Haralan Popov, the godly hero of *Tortured For His Faith*. As a prisoner for thirteen years, Haralan Popov endured untold suffering at the hands of his communist captors. When we met, there was one question I wanted to ask him. "What kept you faithful?"

In broken English he said, "What do you mean?"

"I mean, what was it that enabled you to endure? Was it your knowledge of God's Word or. . . ." And then he quietly interrupted me. "When you love someone you will do anything for them," he said.

Why not quit when leadership becomes so burdensome that you want to die? You can't, even as Moses, Isaiah, Jeremiah, and others couldn't. Love won't let you quit—love of God, nor love of others. But transcending everything else is that love of God and of all that He represents. If you do not run the race, if you do not fight the good fight, if you do not finish the course, if you do not keep the faith, can you say, "I love you, Lord"? And if you fail to run the race, to keep the faith, who will?

I have thought of what it would be like to live an ordinary life. To be honest, at times I have longed for it. And there have been occasions when the going has been so rough, the complaints so many, the battles so wearying, the running so tiring, the contest so heavy that I have thought, "Lord, it would be easier just to die and go home." Sometimes I have been so sickened by my own wretchedness that I have wondered how God could ever use me, and I have thought, "You might as well quit; you are no good anyway." Can you relate, Precious One? Do you understand because, in one sense or another, you have been there?

What kept you? And what will keep you in the future when His work seems burdensome? "Greater love has no one than this, that one lay down his life for his friends" (John 15:13).

Jesus, we love You, and we love those who are Yours.

October 19

LEADERSHIP IS BEARING CRITICISM IN HUMILITY.

"Then Miriam and Aaron spoke against Moses because of the Cushite woman whom he had married . . . and they said, 'Has the Lord indeed spoken only through Moses? Has He not spoken through us as well?' And the Lord heard it. (Now the man Moses was very humble, more than any man who was on the face of the earth.)" (Numbers 12:1–3).

How it must have hurt to have his own sister and brother turn against him. Has it ever happened to you? Have you ever been wounded by those closest to you? You realized you were not perfect, but wasn't there a love which could have covered rather than exposed? If it has happened to you, I understand. It has happened to me. It will happen to anyone who ever seeks to do a work for God. Criticism is as inevitable as the seasons of the year. Thus the question is not how one can avoid criticism, but rather, how we handle criticism.

We are *not* to handle it. Meekness or humility does not handle things; instead it turns them over to God to be handled properly. And handle them He will, in His time, in His way.

And suddenly the Lord said to Moses and Aaron and to Miriam, "You three come out to the tent of meeting." So the three of them came out. Then the Lord came down in a pillar of cloud and stood at the doorway of the tent, and He called Aaron and Miriam. When they had both come forward, He said, "Hear now My words: If there is a prophet among you, I the Lord shall make Myself known to him in a vision. I shall speak with him in a dream. Not so, with My servant Moses, He is

301

faithful in all My household; with him I speak mouth to mouth, even openly, and not in dark sayings, and he beholds the form of the Lord. Why then were you not afraid to speak against My servant, against Moses?" So the anger of the Lord burned against them and He departed. But when the cloud had withdrawn from over the tent, behold, Miriam was leprous, as white as snow. As Aaron turned toward Miriam, behold, she was leprous. Then Aaron said to Moses, "Oh, my lord, I beg you, do not account this sin to us, in which we have acted foolishly and in which we have sinned. Oh do not let her be like one dead, whose flesh is half eaten away when he comes from his mother's womb!" And Moses cried out to the Lord, saying, "Oh God, heal her, I pray!" But the Lord said to Moses, "If her father had but spit in her face, would she not bear her shame for seven days? Let her be shut up for seven days outside the camp, and afterward she may be received again." So Miriam was shut up outside the camp for seven days, and the people did not move on until Miriam was received again (Numbers 12:4–15).

Do you think you can trust God to handle your critics, or can you do it better your way? Would it be done in humility and meekness?

October 20

When someone criticizes me, a part of me naturally wants to rise up in vindication, even when I know that, in a sense, the criticism might be justified. But what gets to me is being written off for not being perfect, not being allowed to fail and still be accepted. That is when I cry out, "O Father, where is the love that covers a multitude of sins?" Whether Moses was right or wrong in marrying a Cushite woman was not the issue. He could have been wrong, but did that justify Miriam and Aaron's behavior? Not if they were to walk as God walks.

Recently I heard of a man and woman who are tearing me down, along with the ministry of Reach Out. They have singled out one statement from one of my radio programs which, out of context, might appear to condone adultery in the life of a Christian. Now this couple has been to our conferences several times, and they know that adultery is one thing I am dead set against. I have said that habitual adulterers will not inherit the Kingdom of God (Galatians 5:19–21). Yet I know that the real issue with them is not adultery but a disagreement over the baptism of the Holy Spirit.

What am I to do? How am I to handle them as they slander the ministry God has called us to? I am to love them and pray for them, and that is all. Meekness receives everything as coming from the hand of God without retaliation or bitterness. Thus you can see that to be meek is not to be weak but rather to be strong in faith. God will call them to the tent of meeting. He will deal with them. He knows what is best for their ultimate good and His glory, and that is what I am to be concerned with too, their ultimate good and His glory.

Dear, dear Moses. When God made Miriam leprous, Moses did not gloat. Rather, he cried out to the Lord, "Oh God, heal her." "But I say to you, love your enemies, and pray for those who persecute you in order that you may be sons of your Father who is in heaven. . . . Blessed are the peacemakers, for they shall be called sons of God" (Matthew 5:44, 45a, 9).

Oh, Beloved, let us pray for one another that we might always bear criticism as befits sons and daughters of our Heavenly Father.

October 21

LEADERSHIP IS SOMETIMES BEING CAUGHT BETWEEN THE PROMISES OF GOD AND THE PROTESTS OF THE PEOPLE.

God had brought Israel out of Egypt with a mighty hand and outstretched arm. Now they were headed for Canaan, the land pledged to Abraham four hundred and thirty years earlier when God made His covenant with Abraham and his seed (Genesis 15:1–18; Galatians 3:16, 17).

"Now it came about when Pharaoh had let the people go, that God did not lead them by the way of the land of the Philistines, even though it was near; for God said, 'Lest the people change their minds when they see war, and they return to Egypt' " (Exodus 13:17).

At Mount Sinai, God had given the Israelites the commandments and ordinances for living as His people. Now they were ready to enter the land of promise.

Then the Lord spoke to Moses saying, "Send out for yourself men so that they may spy out the land of Canaan, which I am going to give to the sons of Israel; you shall send a man from each of their fathers' tribes, every one a leader among them. . . ." So they went up and spied out the land from the wilderness of Zin as far as Rehob, at Lebo-ha-math. . . . Thus they told him, and said, "We went in to the land where you sent us; and it certainly does flow with milk and honey, and this is its fruit. Nevertheless, the people who live in the land are strong, and the cities are fortified and very large; and moreover, we saw the descendants of Anak there. . . ." Then Caleb quieted the people before Moses, and said, "We should by all means go up and take possession of it, for we shall surely overcome it." But the men who had gone up with him said, "We are not able to go up against the people, for they are too strong for us. . . ." Then all the congregation lifted up their voices and cried, and the people wept that night. And all the sons of Israel grumbled against Moses and Aaron; and the whole congregation said to them, "Would that we had died in the land of Egypt! Or would that we had died in this wilderness!" (Numbers 13:1, 2, 21, 27, 28, 30, 31; 14:1, 2).

Out of that great multitude, only four—Moses, Aaron, Joshua, and Caleb—were willing to trust God and take the land. And what would you have done if you had been Moses, caught between the promises of God and the protests of the people?

Think about it and we will discuss it tomorrow.

October 22

If you would follow God fully then you must live by His Word rather than by popular opinion. Yet, you need to know that, if you do follow God fully, it will bring you great reproach. The congregation of Israel wanted to stone Moses, Aaron, Joshua, and Caleb because disbelief and disobedience always want to destroy trust and obedience. Truth is never popular among those who are self-centered rather than God-centered. The Israelites had spurned God; they had refused to believe Him "despite all the signs which" He had "performed in their midst" (Numbers 14:11). They wanted it their way. They had turned back from following the Lord (14:23) because their evaluation of the situation was different from God's evaluation. They saw giants in the land and cried out, "We are not able to go up against the people" (13:31). Instead they should have gone forth in faith and obedience realizing that "faithful is He who calls you, and He also will bring it to pass" (1 Thessalonians 5:24).

And what about you? Are you only willing to follow God if it all goes your way? Do you trust in God's Word or your strength? Are you like the Israelites or do you have a different spirit, like Caleb (Numbers 14:24)? Are you following God fully or living according to popular opinion?

October 23

LEADERSHIP IS DECIDING WHOSE GLORY—YOURS OR GOD'S.

When the children of Israel spurned God by refusing to enter Canaan because of the giants in the land, it really upset God.

Then the glory of the Lord appeared in the tent of meeting to all the sons of Israel. And the Lord said to Moses, "How long will this people spurn Me? And how long will they not believe in Me, despite all the signs which I have performed in their midst? I will smite them with pestilence and dispossess them, and I will make you into a nation greater and mightier than they" (Numbers 14:10b–12).

What would you have done with such an offer if you had been in Moses' place? Can you imagine how tempting God's offer was, that He would kill off all Abraham's seed and begin again with a new people from the loins of Moses? It would no longer be "the God of Abraham, Isaac, and Jacob" but rather *the God of Moses.* Moses would have his name in lights!!! Glory at last, plus no more Israelites to hassle him! No longer a servant but a star!

Yet Moses turned it down. Why? How could he? This was his big opportunity! Or was it?

But Moses said to the Lord, "Then the Egyptians will hear of it, for by Thy strength Thou didst bring up this people from their midst. . . . Now if Thou dost slay this people as one man, then the nations who have heard of Thy fame will say, 'Because the Lord could not bring this people into the land which He promised them by oath, therefore He slaughtered them in the wilderness.' But now, I pray, let the power of the Lord be great, just as Thou hast declared. . . . Pardon, I pray, the iniquity of this people according to the greatness of Thy lovingkindness, just as Thou also hast forgiven this people, from Egypt even until now" (Numbers 14:13, 15–17, 19).

Moses was more concerned for the glory of God than his own glory. This is the true glory of man, to glorify the Father. If you are ever to be truly used of God, you must realize that He says Himself, "I am the Lord, that is My name; I will not give My glory to another" (Isaiah 42:8).

This is where many a leader has fallen, only to be despised by man and disciplined by God. He must increase, we must decrease. A leader must be jealous only for the glory of God.

October 24

LEADERSHIP IS HOLDING FIRM TO YOUR GOD-ORDAINED AUTHORITY IN THE FACE OF HUMAN OPPOSITION.

Somewhere, sometime, your leadership will be contested. How will you handle it when it comes? Will you bow, step down, acquiesce? Will you assume that you are to recognize and submit to those challenging you? Will you bow to the majority or stand unbending although you may virtually stand alone? Will you surrender your role as leader because of popular opinion or will you cry to God, seeking His solution?

These are pertinent questions to which you must have answers, for your role as a leader will eventually be challenged to one degree or another. When this happens you will be so thankful that you have maintained close communication with your God. He alone can direct you. You must have His wisdom, for as a leader you are accountable to your God for your position of responsibility. If God has directed you to lead, it would be wrong to abdicate because of pressure from men.

Sometime, somewhere, someone is going to challenge what you are doing for the Lord. I do pray you *are* doing something—interceding, helping, visiting, teaching. When they challenge you, will your communion with God have been intimate enough for you to know that you are doing what He has called you to do?

Write out your thoughts and your commitment.

October 25

Finally the challenge of Moses' leadership had come. And from no small quarter! Led by Korah, a priest, two hundred and fifty leaders challenged Moses and Aaron, saying: " 'you have gone far enough, for all the congregation are holy, every one of them, and the Lord is in their midst; so why do you exalt yourselves above the assembly of the Lord?' " (Numbers 16:3).

No wonder Moses fell on his face (v. 4). The problem was evident. They were treading where they did not belong; they wanted more authority than God had given them. Moses asked them:

"Hear now, you sons of Levi, is it not enough for you that the God of Israel has separated you from the rest of the congregation of Israel, to bring you near to Himself, to do the service of the tabernacle of the

Lord, and to stand before the congregation to minister to them; and that He has brought you near, Korah, and all your brothers, sons of Levi, with you? And are you seeking for the priesthood also?" (Numbers 16:8–10).

Would Moses, under the pressure of popular opinion, relinquish his God-given place of leadership? How plentiful are these contests in the church today and how delicately they must be handled!

First, the leader must be certain that he is right with God in every area of his leadership. Moses took the matter before the Lord; "The Lord will show . . . even the one whom He will choose" (v. 5).

Second, the motives of those who challenge the leadership must be examined. The purifying fire of God's Word must be brought to bear on the situation. Everything—the motives of the heart, the attitudes of the mind, the actions of the body—must be in accord with His Word. In many church squabbles the behavior is anything but Christlike.

Third, the ungodly leaders of the rebellion must be removed. If they are not, then the contest and the conflict will only continue. However, the removal must be at God's direction and in His way. God's way with the sons of Korah, I must admit, was *a little* (I speak with tongue in cheek) dramatic and unusual. The earth opened up and swallowed all those who opposed Moses and a fire from the Lord consumed the two hundred and fifty! (*See* Numbers 16:28–35.)

Since God is not opening the earth today and swallowing leaders of rebellion, what course is a godly leader to take in removing rebellion? I think that this is something that God must show each leader, and I believe He will as each seeks God's will. One godly pastor I know simply kept his mouth shut and prayed. Although the rebellious element tried to get him to leave, he wouldn't, for God told him to stay. So he walked in the light of 1 Peter 2:21–24. The turning point came when one of his deacons hit him while he was standing in the pulpit. When the blow fell, God whispered, "That's it. It is over." The rebellious element left the church.

Let me reiterate. Leadership is having your authority challenged and not giving up when you are convinced you are right. Moses continued in his leadership. Leaders must risk the approval and/or the judgment of the onlookers and proceed as God has directed. The consequences are God's.

October 26

LEADERSHIP IS NEVER SINNING BY BECOMING SO PRO-
VOKED WITH PEOPLE THAT YOU GO AGAINST GOD'S
WORD.

For the second time the children of Israel had come to a "no water"
situation. Once again they complained and contended with Moses. For
almost forty years now, Moses had borne their hard sayings. Every
time things seemed to go wrong or every time they faced a difficulty,
they blamed Moses. Could they not remember how God had always
provided in the past?

> Then the sons of Israel, the whole congregation, came to the wilderness
> of Zin in the first month; and the people stayed at Kadesh. Now Miriam
> died there and was buried there. And there was no water for the con-
> gregation; and they assembled themselves against Moses and Aaron.
> The people thus contended with Moses and spoke, saying, "If only we
> had perished when our brothers perished before the Lord! Why then
> have you brought the Lord's assembly into this wilderness, for us and
> our beasts to die here? And why have you made us come up from Egypt,
> to bring us in to this wretched place? It is not a place of grain or figs or
> vines or pomegranates, nor is there water to drink." Then Moses and
> Aaron came in from the presence of the assembly to the doorway of the
> tent of meeting, and fell on their faces. Then the glory of the Lord ap-
> peared to them; and the Lord spoke to Moses, saying, "Take the rod;
> and you and your brother Aaron assemble the congregation and speak
> to the rock before their eyes, that it may yield its water. . . ." So Moses
> took the rod from before the Lord, just as He had commanded him; and
> Moses and Aaron gathered the assembly before the rock. And he said to
> them, "Listen now, you rebels; shall we bring forth water for you out of
> this rock?" Then Moses lifted up his hand and struck the rock twice
> with his rod; and water came forth abundantly, and the congregation
> and their beasts drank (Numbers 20:1-11).

What were God's specific instructions to Moses for obtaining water
for the children of Israel?

Did Moses follow these instructions, explicitly? Note in your notebook how Moses behaved.

Was the "no water" situation cared for?

What do you think about Moses' leadership in this instance?

October 27

What do you need from God that you do not have? Why do you not have what you need? How are you going to get it?

The children of Israel needed water—a genuine need; without it they could not survive! Yet, this was not the first time the Israelites had found themselves in a "no water" situation. Soon after their deliverance from Egypt, God had led them to Rephidim and there had been no water to drink.

> Therefore the people quarreled with Moses and said, "Give us water that we may drink." And Moses said to them, "Why do you quarrel with me? Why do you test the Lord?" But the people thirsted there for water; and they grumbled against Moses and said, "Why, now, have you brought us up from Egypt, to kill us and our children and our livestock with thirst?" So Moses cried out to the Lord, saying, "What shall I do to this people? A little more and they will stone me." Then the Lord said to Moses, "Pass before the people and take with you some of the elders of Israel; and take in your hand your staff with which you struck the Nile, and go. Behold, I will stand before you there on the rock at Horeb; and you shall strike the rock, and water will come out of it, that the people may drink." And Moses did so in the sight of the elders of Israel (Exodus 17:2–6).

They had a need. They brought it before God. And God met their need. It was as simple as that! Or was it? Not really. It took a supernatural work on God's part to meet the natural need of men. The water that would quench their thirst came forth from a rock which was struck with a rod.

O Precious Child of God, what truth there is in the striking of the rock! Learn it and you will know how God supplies "all your needs according to His riches in glory through Christ Jesus" (Philippians 4:19). Learn it and you will understand how grave a disobedience it was when Moses struck the rock a second time as the Israelites camped at Kadesh. Moses' error caused him to miss the Promised Land! He struck the rock rather than speaking to it as God had instructed, and the Lord said to him, "Because you have not believed Me, to treat Me as holy in the sight of the sons of Israel, therefore you shall not bring this assembly into the land which I have given them" (Numbers 20:12).

When you have had a need did you believe Philippians 4:19 and just speak to God about it?

"Speak," you say! "That's all? Surely it couldn't be; surely I have to do something!"

Oh, no. It was all done when the Rock was struck. We'll look at it tomorrow.

October 28

What was significant about speaking to the rock rather than smiting it a second time? To understand that, you have to understand the significance of the rock. The clue to this is found in 1 Corinthians 10:1–4; read it carefully.

> For I do not want you to be unaware, brethren, that our fathers were all under the cloud, and all passed through the sea; and all were baptized into Moses in the cloud and in the sea; and all ate the same spiritual food; and all drank the same spiritual drink, for they were drinking from a spiritual rock which followed them; and the rock was Christ.

"The Rock was Christ"—and He followed them! The rock at Rephidim, at the beginning of their journey, was the same rock that was at Kadesh near the end of their journey. The rock was a picture of Jesus Christ. Smiting the rock was a picture of His crucifixion. And what then did the water symbolize or picture as it gushed forth from the rock? Look at John 7:37–39 for the answer.

> Now on the last day, the great day of the feast, Jesus stood and cried out, saying, "If any man is thirsty, let him come to Me and drink. He who believes in Me, as the Scripture said, 'From his innermost being shall flow rivers of living water.' "

The water that came from the rock was a picture of the Holy Spirit, the One who meets our deepest need, a hunger and a thirst for righteousness.

"But," you may say, "Kay, my deepest need is not righteousness; my deepest need is _____." You can fill in the blank with a thousand different needs all determined by who you are and where you are. Yet, to do so would be wrong. Your deepest need, know it or not, believe it or not, is to be righteous before God and to live righteously in His sight. To live righteously is to live life according to God's standard. Then, and only then, will you know satisfaction.

And how can all this come about? Only one way—through the water from the rock. You have His immutable promise. "Blessed are those who hunger and thirst for righteousness, for they shall be satisfied" (Matthew 5:6). It's yours for the taking, for the faith!

310

October 29

Now let's see how all that we have learned about smiting the rock relates to our lives, first as children of God and secondly as leaders.

When Moses struck the rock the second time at Kadesh, the Lord chastened him severely because he had not treated God as holy in the sight of Israel. When he smote the rock that second time rather than speaking to it, he was in effect crucifying the Son of God again. And why did Moses do it? In order to get water to satisfy their thirst. Yet the water was there, not for the smiting, but for the speaking. You see, Precious Ones, when God took Jesus Christ to Calvary, He did it all. Everything you and I will ever need was obtained for us in that one monumental work at the crucifixion of the Son of God.

> He who did not spare His own Son, but delivered Him up for us all, how will He not also with Him freely give us all things? (Romans 8:32).

Therefore there is no need to smite the Rock again. What is it that you need? Treat God as holy, pure, undefiled and therefore true to His Word. Speak to the Rock, in faith, and your God "shall supply **all your needs** according to His riches in glory in Christ Jesus" by freely giving you all things. Do not think you've got to get it for yourself as Moses, in disgust, did when he said, "Listen now, you rebels; shall we bring forth water for you out of this rock?" (Numbers 20:10).

Whatever you need personally from God is yours for the asking. "Ask" (in Greek, "keep asking"), and it shall be given to you (Matthew 7:7a). Or James 4:2b: "You do not have because you do not ask."

And what is God's lesson to you as a leader? It is not to become so provoked in a situation that you fail to act according to God's Word. To do so is to fail to let men and women, saved or lost, see God as holy. When we do not obey God, we do not show His holiness. Moses had his instructions from God; they were very clear. The problem was that he did not follow them.

God's work must be done God's way. So stay on your knees, listen carefully to His Word, then see that you do all that He commands you. Do not turn to the right or to the left. Only then will you have success and prosper (Joshua 1:6–8).

October 30

Remember my statement yesterday, "God's work must be done God's way"? Well, I feel it would be good to elaborate on that a little bit more.

TRUE LEADERSHIP IS DOING GOD'S WORK GOD'S WAY.
When I think of Moses striking the rock a second time and failing because he did not do as God said, I always think of David when he attempted to return the ark of the covenant to its rightful place. Under Saul's reign as king over Israel, the ark of God had been greatly neglected. So, when David took the throne he called for all the leaders of Israel to join with him in bringing the ark back.

David's plan was noble and the people approved. "Then all the assembly said that they would do so, for the thing was right in the eyes of all the people. So David assembled all Israel together, from the Shihor of Egypt even to the entrance of Hamath, to bring the ark of God from Kiriath-jearim. And David and all Israel went up to Baalah, that is, to Kiriath-jearim, which belongs to Judah, to bring up from there the ark of God, the Lord who is enthroned above the cherubim, where His name is called. And they carried the ark of God on a new cart from the house of Abinadab, and Uzza and Ahio drove the cart. And David and all Israel were celebrating before God with all their might, even with songs and with lyres, harps, tambourines, cymbals, and with trumpets" (1 Chronicles 13:4–8).

What a glorious event that must have been! King and people were of one accord, all involved in a great project for the Lord. Everyone had approved, everyone except God. Suddenly excitement turned into alarm; joy was struck down by dismay. Reeling from the blow, David's joy turned to anger for "when they came to the threshing floor of Chidon, Uzza put out his hand to hold the ark, because the oxen nearly upset it. And the anger of the Lord burned against Uzza, so He struck him down because he put out his hand to the ark; and he died there before God. Then David became angry because of the Lord's outburst against Uzza" (13:9–11).

What had happened? They had not done God's work God's way.
Think about it and we'll talk about it more tomorrow.

October 31

I wonder how much of God's work in the churches and in Christian organizations is really done God's way?

David's intention was so good, but he failed because he didn't seek God the proper way. He had violated God's specific ordinances regarding the ark. The ark of the covenant was holy and was never to be touched. To do so would be death. (*See* Numbers 4:15.) Also, when the ark was moved, staves were to be put through the rings on the ark; then only the sons of the tribe of Levi were to bear it upon their shoulders. David knew this for he knew the writings of Moses. Every king was to make his own copy of the books of the Law, and then he was to live by them.

When David's anger subsided, he came to his senses. He prepared a place in Jerusalem for the ark of God and then he issued the command to bring up the ark "according to the ordinance" (1 Chronicles 15:13). "And the sons of the Levites carried the ark of God on their shoulders, with the poles thereon as Moses had commanded according to the word of the Lord" (v. 15).

According to the ordinance is a phrase that echoes in my heart. I must do God's work God's way. It is a truth that causes us at Reach Out to serve Him "with fear and trembling" (Philippians 2:12) and that is good. Moses lost his position of leadership because he failed on this crucial issue. For almost forty years he had done God's work God's way; and then he failed. It cost him Canaan, it cost him his life, even though he pleaded with God, "Let me, I pray, cross over and see the fair land that is beyond the Jordan" (Deuteronomy 3:25).

O Beloved, on this our last day together on leadership, I want to leave you with this final principle. LEADERS RECEIVE THE GREATER CONDEMNATION. The murmuring, complaining children of Israel went into Canaan, but Moses and Aaron did not, because leadership carries a tremendous responsibility. I do not say this to discourage you, but rather to exhort you.

God knows we desperately need leaders, but they must be godly leaders who will live by His word without compromise. If God has called you to be a leader will you be a godly one?

NOVEMBER

Taking the Bitter, Making It Sweet

November 1

Have you ever stood in line for a long time, patiently waiting your turn, only to have someone walk up and cut right in front of you? To use an old expression, "It gets your goat," doesn't it? How can people be so rude? So self-centered? So crass? They don't apologize! They don't excuse themselves! And, if you call their hand, they either stand there unapologetically and say nothing or they get angry!!! How dare you question their right to cut in line! I have to admit, it gets to me. When it happens in traffic where I can't get to them personally, I pray the police will get them. But, when it happens when I'm standing in line, then I want to straighten them out myself.

This past weekend we had a family outing. It was David's fifteenth birthday, and he got to choose how we would begin to celebrate it. I say "begin" for the celebration will last several weeks because all the family couldn't be together on one weekend. A drawn out celebration is far more fun anyway. We began with a trip to Opryland. Mark, our middle son, and his wife Leslie joined us for the weekend.

Opryland is entertaining for all ages, for, besides rides like the Wabash Cannonball, a wild roller coaster that literally loops the loop and turns you upside down (I laughed and screamed the whole ride), there are musical stage shows. Well, it was at one of these musicals that it happened. We had already stood in line for one musical only to be turned away at the door. Now, after a long wait in another line we dashed across the park to the Roy Acuff Theatre. The lobby was so filled with waiting patrons that the line spilled outside. We waited with anticipation, wondering if we would again be turned away at the last minute. Finally the line began to move; we were eager and hopeful. This was supposed to be the best of the musicals, one we couldn't miss! Then it happened. A couple had walked up and sat down on a nearby wall to wait in comfort. Had I realized their strategy, I would have had apoplexy sooner! When the line started to move, they glibly, with nary a pardon-me-please, walked up in front of us and got in line. We had been waiting twenty to thirty minutes! Something had to be done! It was more than I could take—or was it? Later, when I got quiet, the

Lord would say, "Blessed are the meek; for they shall inherit the earth" (Matthew 5:5 KJV). And I would have to confess my sin, for sin I did.

November 2

I don't know what your temperament is, but mine is the type that just cannot stand injustice. There is nothing naturally meek about me. If something is wrong I want to straighten it out. If it's unjust, let's go to war! If I recall correctly, there was a battalion during the Revolutionary War that carried a flag with the slogan, "Don't Tread On Me." It bore the symbol of a snake. Well, that summarizes my personality apart from the Spirit of God, "Don't Tread On Me." Like that serpent of old, the "I" is very strong in my flesh. I'm just not the complacent type, and, if you're not either, then you understand exactly how I felt and what I had to deal with when that couple cut in line. If you are the peace-at-any-price type, then a shrug of the shoulders would have suited you. Yet, for either type, there was only one Christlike thing to do. Obviously, because I had to confess, I didn't do it! Rather, I simply told the couple how wrong they were. Another man, obviously of like temperament, joined me and really got into it!

The line kept moving and soon the intruders were out of my sight. The crush got tighter as we entered the door. Whew! We had made it! We were inside! My chicks in front of me, the mother hen in me wanted to cackle until suddenly I missed the closeness of the protective wings of my rooster. As I turned around, what should I see but the guide at the door holding out her arm forbidding entrance to any more. My rooster was outside! And who was standing in line **in front of him** but that same foxy couple! That was it! Scratching the ground, feathers ruffled, red wattle* shaking, I turned back to the door. There I complained to the establishment, pointing out the offenders, while Mr. Peace-At-Any-Price just shook his patient head and silently mouthed words that told me not to fret. Finally the arm came down, and my beloved husband, along with others, was admitted—after the couple that had cut in. Oh, I didn't say a word to them, but I must admit that if looks could have killed they would be dead. I glared at them, the way I used to look at people before I came to know Jesus Christ!

What happened? Why did I act just like I used to act in bitter situa-

---

I had to look this one up in the encyclopedia. A wattle is the red thing that hangs on the neck below the beak! Stick with me—we'll learn about chickens! I love you.

tions like this? It was because I forgot how to take the bitter and make it sweet. I forgot about God's tree. I forgot that, like Paul, I, too, was "crucified with Christ." I forgot to live "by faith in the Son of God, who loved me, and delivered Himself up for me" (Galatians 2:20). Can you relate?

November 3

This month we are going to talk about life at the cross or taking the bitter and making it sweet. How my heart was smitten by the Lord the next morning as, in my quiet time, He brought that Opryland situation to my mind. I had reacted as any lost person with my type of temperament would have reacted! How sad! How would I ever make it in the face of *real* injustice? I honestly think it would be easier for me to handle a grave injustice such as being persecuted for being a Christian than to cope with someone breaking into line in front of me. Why? Because of the difference in the gravity of the situation. Have you ever heard that verse that says *it's the little foxes that spoil the vines* (Song of Solomon 2:15)? I think I was caught off guard because of the inaneness of it all. I wasn't walking circumspectly as the King James Version puts it in Ephesians 5:15. Plus, that morning I had not quieted my heart before Him before I began my day.

However, whether our situations are grave or inane, we need to learn how to take the bitter and make it sweet, for each of us will face bitter situations as we go about this business of day-by-day living. The world needs to see Jesus living in these temples made of flesh. That is why we have Jesus Christ, "this treasure in earthen vessels, that the surpassing greatness of the power may be of God and not from ourselves" (2 Corinthians 4:7). There's a little chorus that goes, "You're a pot, you're a vessel, made to hold Someone special." My pot sure got in the way, didn't it? There was nothing special about my behavior at all. Jesus' longsuffering love certainly was not radiated through my mean eyes. They say that the eyes are the windows of the soul. Whew! What dark things were in my soul.

I was angry! Now, anger is not always wrong. Read the Old and New Testaments, and you find God the Father and God the Son both getting angry. Therefore, all anger is not sin. God cannot sin, for He is a holy God, righteous in all His ways. There is a righteous anger, and I believe mine was a righteous anger. However, God does say, "Be angry, and yet do not sin; do not let the sun go down on your anger" (Ephesians 4:26).

I was angry, righteously so, but I sinned because I did not act in righteousness. My anger rather than God's Holy Spirit controlled me.

"But, Kay," I can just hear some of you say, "how do you handle it?"

O Dear One, as you have read I am not an expert. I have failed, but I do have the answer, and I intend to learn to live accordingly. So hang in there. We will learn together.

November 4

It had been three days since their glorious triumph. They had found themselves caught between the Red Sea and the Egyptian army, and God had worked a miracle. With great gusto Moses and the sons of Israel sang their song. The first four lines gave God all the credit. "I will sing to the Lord, for He is highly exalted; the horse and its rider he has hurled into the sea. The Lord is my strength and song, and He has become my salvation; this is my God, and I will praise Him; my father's God, and I will extol Him. The Lord is a warrior; the Lord is His name" (Exodus 15:1–3).

The pillar of cloud that had stood between the Egyptians and the children of Israel now led them "into the wilderness of Shur; and they went three days in the wilderness and found no water. And when they came to Marah, they could not drink the waters of Marah, for they were bitter; therefore it was named Marah. So the people grumbled at Moses, saying, 'What shall we drink?' Then he cried out to the Lord, and the Lord showed him a tree; and he threw it into the waters, and the waters became sweet. There He made for them a statute and regulation, and there He tested them" (Exodus 15:22–25).

The bitter water was a test. God wanted to teach them another lesson, how to take the bitter and make it sweet. He did it by using a tree to make the waters drinkable. And what is God's lesson to us? Some theologians would say, "There is no lesson for the Christian today. It is merely a historical account of a miraculous event performed by God for the children of Israel."

Yet, in this case, I would disagree. I believe that God has hidden spiritual truths for His church in many of these events in Israel's history. When God does this, I believe, He then uncovers these "hidden treasures" of truth for us by paralleling them in the New Testament. If an Old Testament event is specifically paralleled in the New Testament, then there can be no doubt that God has a lesson for us in it. However, if the New Testament does not clearly show us what the Old Testament foreshadowed, then we must be careful not to read in something which is not there.

For instance, the Passover is an example of what is called an Old Testament type or foreshadowing of truth. The Passover lamb (Exodus 12) was a picture of the Lord Jesus Christ, "the Lamb of God who takes away the sin of the world" (John 1:29), "for Christ our Passover also has been sacrificed" (1 Corinthians 5:7). In 1 Corinthians 5:8, we are specifically told that, as the Jews celebrated the Passover, we are to "celebrate the feast, not with old leaven, nor with the leaven of malice and wickedness, but with the unleavened bread of sincerity and truth."

Tomorrow we will talk more about this and share a wonderful biblical application, but for now, Beloved, rest assured that there is no bitter situation that Jesus cannot make sweet.

November 5

For you to really appreciate what I want to teach you about the bitter waters of Marah and the tree that made them sweet, I believe I should first give you a little teaching on typology. Now, don't shy away from learning. Doctrine, which is another word for teaching, is invaluable, for one's life-style is based upon that which he believes. Unfortunately, we don't know God's book, so we are loose in our living, doing what is right in our own eyes rather than living by every word that proceeds from the mouth of God. As a result, we are following man's traditions, vain philosophies, and worldly wisdom.

In biblical interpretation, a "type" is an Old Testament foreshadowing of a New Testament truth or spiritual reality. The word *type* comes from the Greek word *tupos,* meaning a mark formed by a blow, an impression or an image. For example, Adam was a figure of type of Christ who was to come. Romans 5:14 says, "Nevertheless death reigned from Adam . . . who is a type of Him who was to come." In 1 Corinthians 15:45, Christ is referred to as "the last Adam." The parallel is clear and specific and cannot be denied. (Let me add a word of caution. Typology is a beautiful study, but it can easily get out of hand. For further study, you will find an excellent chapter on types in T. Norton Sterret's book, *How to Understand Your Bible,* InterVarsity Press.)

A beautiful example of a type is given to us in John 3:14, 15: "And as Moses lifted up the serpent in the wilderness, even so must the Son of Man be lifted up; that whoever believes may in Him have eternal life." Jesus likens His death on the cross to Moses lifting up the serpent in the wilderness as recorded in Numbers 21. Israel had sinned and as a result many had died from the poisonous bites of fiery serpents sent by God as just punishment. The people confessed, Moses interceded, and God commanded Moses to "make a fiery serpent, and set it on a standard; and it shall come about, that everyone who is bitten, when he looks at it, he shall live" (21:8). Jesus, in John 3, shows that this historical event was a foreshadowing of His death on the cross. As men were saved from physical death by looking to the brass serpent on the pole, so men would be saved from spiritual death by believing in Him, for He was made sin for us, and hung on a tree. The act of faith, looking unto Christ to save you from your deserved death as a sinner, gives you eternal life.

Now that you understand types, can you see how, "beginning with Moses [the first five books of the Old Testament] and with all the prophets, He [Jesus] explained to them the things concerning Himself in all the Scriptures" (Luke 24:27)? Blessed, isn't it? Oh, what riches there are in God's Word! If we would only take the time to discover them, how wealthy we would be!

November 6

One of the clearest passages in the New Testament that shows the purpose of types for our lives is 1 Corinthians 10:1–13. As you read this passage, there are two things I want you to note. First, notice the two uses of the word "example." The Greek word *tupoi*, "types," is here translated "examples." Second, note how God uses the incidents in the lives of the Israelites as a means of instructing us. Now then, let's carefully read the Scripture.

> For I do not want you to be unaware, brethren, that our fathers were all under the cloud, and all passed through the sea; and all were baptized into Moses in the cloud and in the sea; and all ate the same spiritual food; and all drank the same spiritual drink, for they were drinking from a spiritual rock which followed them; and the rock was Christ. Nevertheless, with most of them God was not well-pleased; for they were laid low in the wilderness. Now these things happened as examples for us, that we should not crave evil things, as they also craved. And do not be idolaters, as some of them were; as it is written, "The people sat down to eat and drink, and stood up to play." Nor let us act immorally, as some of them did, and twenty-three thousand fell in one day. Nor let us try the Lord, as some of them did, and were destroyed by the serpents. Nor grumble, as some of them did, and were destroyed by the destroyer. Now these things happened to them as an example, and they were written for our instruction, upon whom the ends of the ages have come. Therefore let him who thinks he stands take heed lest he fall. No

temptation has overtaken you but such as is common to man; and God is faithful, who will not allow you to be tempted beyond what you are able, but with the temptation will provide the way of escape also, that you may be able to endure it.

What was a type of Christ in this passage? And what are God's lessons to you, Dear Believer? Write out your thoughts.

November 7

Now let's return to Exodus 15 and see what lessons God has in this Old Testament event for His church.

And when they came to Marah, they could not drink the waters of Marah, for they were bitter; therefore it was named Marah. So the people grumbled at Moses, saying, "What shall we drink?" Then he cried out to the Lord, and the Lord showed him a tree; and he threw it into the waters, and the waters became sweet. There He made for them a statute and regulation, and there He tested them. And He said, "If you will give earnest heed to the voice of the Lord your God, and do what is right in His sight, and give ear to His commandments, and keep all His statutes, I will put none of the diseases on you which I have put on the Egyptians; for I, the Lord, am your healer' (Exodus 15:23–26).

It was the tree applied to the waters of Marah that turned the waters from bitter to sweet and made them drinkable. And what is God's picture, God's truth, God's instruction for those upon whom the end of the ages has come?

Was the tree a picture of something? I believe so. In Galatians 3:13, Paul writes, "Christ redeemed us from the curse of the Law, having become a curse for us—for it is written, 'Cursed is every one who hangs on a tree'—." Paul was quoting from Deuteronomy 21:22, 23.

And what tree did Christ hang on? A cross. The Greek word translated "tree" in Galatians 3:13 is the word for wood. The same word is translated "cross" in Acts 5:30—"The God of our Fathers raised up Jesus, whom you had put to death by hanging Him on a cross [wood]." Do you think that God intended, by having Moses place the tree in the waters of Marah, to teach us to apply the cross to the bitter situations in our lives?

Tomorrow we will look at the timing of this event in Israel's history. But what is God's lesson for you today? Ask Him, and then write it out in your own words.

November 8

The bitter waters of Marah followed the Passover, which was truly a symbol of salvation. Under the cruel bondage of Pharaoh, the children of Israel had lived as slaves in Egypt for four hundred years. Egypt serves as a type of the world; Pharaoh as a picture of Satan. Through the plague of death upon the firstborn males Pharaoh finally released the children of Israel from bondage. As God's angel of death moved throughout Egypt visiting every home and killing the firstborn male, he passed over every dwelling where he saw the blood of the lamb on the doorposts. And so we have a picture of our salvation: living in the world, in bondage to sin, under the dominion of Satan, we only find freedom through the blood of Jesus Christ applied in faith to the doorposts of our heart. Thus we pass from death to life (John 5:24), for "every one who commits sin is the slave of sin" (John 8:34), however, "if . . . the Son shall make you free, you shall be free indeed" (8:36).

Since the waters of Marah came after the Passover, the tree could not symbolize the cross as it brings salvation. Yet if not salvation, then what? If the tree represented the cross, then we should look at the significance of the cross in the life of a believer. What place does the cross have at that point? The place of preeminence, for it is there that every believer is to live. This is what Jesus meant when He said, "If anyone wishes to come after Me, let him deny himself, and take up his cross **daily,** and follow Me. For whoever wishes to save his life shall lose it, but whoever loses his life for My sake, he is the one who will save it" (Luke 9:23, 24). The cross must be a place of daily crucifixion so that you do not live independently of Him.

What is the lesson of Marah? Is it not that, even as a child of God, I will face bitter situations? The bitter situations are meant to test me. However, the bitter can be made sweet and palatable through the tree, the place of crucifixion. There I am to let the cross have its effect in my daily life as I die to my way and follow Him.

It was the cross that was needed at Opryland. The bitter could have been sweet had I stopped and said in faith, "Lord, although what they are doing is wrong and hard to take, I will not react in my own way. I choose to take up my cross, to follow You . . . to walk as You would walk."

Oh, the sweetness of obedience! It so outweighs belching the gall of disobedience. How distasteful my behavior appeared when, in my quiet time, I went to sit in His presence.

November 9

A Gallup poll in the early eighties showed that more Americans are attending church now than at any time in history. The percentage is higher than in colonial America. George Gallup was impressed with the following:

1. The high percentage of people who claimed that the Bible is the Word of God and authoritative for their lives.
2. The high percentage who believed in a literal heaven and a literal hell.
3. The large percentage who believed that a born-again experience is essential for entrance into heaven.

The results were really quite impressive until one read Gallup's conclusion, **"Never before in the history of the United States has the Gospel of Jesus Christ made such inroads—while at the same time making so little difference in the way people live."**

When you read things like that do you ever ask, "Why?"

I believe it all centers around the cross. Believing in it, in its purpose and its work is far different from embracing it as a way of life. I can acknowledge the cross's existence, agree with its necessity, and yet still not take it up daily and live accordingly. And this is exactly where the greater majority of professing Christendom is! Note I said "professing." We say we believe in God's Word, in the necessity of a born-again experience, in the reality of heaven and hell, and yet how do we live? Can we honestly say with Paul, "I have been crucified with Christ; and it is no longer I who live, but Christ lives in me; and the life which I now live in the flesh I live by faith in the Son of God, who loved me, and delivered Himself up for me" (Galatians 2:20). Does Christ live in us? Do we live by faith in the Son of God or do we live as pleases us? Surely if we lived crucified lives, if we lived by faith in our Lord, we would have a greater impact on the world!

What is the problem? Let me answer that by asking you how many sermons or messages you have heard on the cross in the past few years. How many Christian books have you read lately that deal with the crucified life? What is the thrust of the messages that you are hearing? Are they centered around man, his needs, and how God can supply them or are they centered around holiness, purity, and denial of self?

What do you want to hear? What do you need to hear?

November 10

In the Gospels there are seventeen references to the cross. Of these, six refer to the cross as the identification mark of all who would follow Jesus as disciples. The question that students of God's Word have debated is whether one can be a Christian without taking up his cross and becoming a disciple. It is interesting to me that, as you read the Gospels, you find Jesus addressing the multitudes with the message of the cross. An example of this is found in Luke 14:25–27,

> Now great multitudes were going along with Him; and He turned and said to them, "If anyone comes to Me, and does not hate his own father and mother and wife and children and brothers and sisters, yes, and even his own life, he cannot be My disciple. Whoever does not carry his own cross and come after Me cannot be My disciple."

One thing is for sure. Apart from taking up the cross and following after Him, you **cannot** be His disciple. Now then, let me ask this. Do you think it is right or equitable to receive God's free gift of eternal life and yet refuse to love Him above all others or to take up your cross and follow Him? To me it is not right or equitable or even possible! I personally believe that discipleship is synonymous with salvation. If you should disagree with me, then tell me how you or anyone could bear to enter heaven's portals and stand before the One who, in doing the will of the Father, denied Himself and took up His cross.

At the end of His discourse on discipleship in Luke, Jesus concludes with an analogy to salt: "So therefore, no one of you can be My disciple who does not give up all his own possessions. Therefore, salt is good; but if even salt has become tasteless, with what will it be seasoned? It is useless either for the soil or for the manure pile; it is thrown out. He who has ears to hear, let him hear" (14:33–35). Matthew 5:13 says we are to be the salt of the earth, but, if salt loses its savor, with what will it be salted? "It is good for nothing any more, except to be thrown out and trampled under foot by men." As I considered this and the use of salt in biblical times, a thought came to me. Salty salt acts as a preservative which stops the spread of corruption. Used in this way, salt loses its life, disappearing into what it seasons. You only know it has been there because of its effect. Yet when salt loses its savor it retains its identity. In the days of the Bible, when salt lost its savor and was therefore not even good for the soil or manure pile, it was used for sidewalks so to speak—men trampled on it. Is this not so with our brand of Christianity today? We have lost our savor because we are not willing to lose our lives, and so we have little impact on a corrupt society.

How salty are you, Beloved? And would you call yourself a disciple of the Lord Jesus Christ?

November 11

What place does the cross have in the life of a believer? It is twofold. At Calvary's tree we are crucified with Jesus Christ once for all. And at the cross we are to live as we take up our cross daily.

Today we will look at the first aspect of the cross where we are crucified with Christ. It is stated for us so magnificently in Romans 6:1–7. Let's read it carefully and then we will discuss it. (Now, I know this may seem a little heavy to you, full of doctrine but lacking in practicality, but it is vital. Be patient, Precious One, it will get practical. First things first. This is where we are lacking. We are so used to being entertained rather than taught!)

> What shall we say then? Are we to continue in sin that grace might increase? May it never be! How shall we who died to sin still live in it? Or do you not know that all of us who have been baptized into Christ Jesus have been baptized into His death? Therefore we have been buried with Him through baptism into death, in order that as Christ was raised from the dead through the glory of the Father, so we too might walk in newness of life. For if we have become united with Him in the likeness of His death, certainly we shall be also in the likeness of His resurrection, knowing this, that our old self was crucified with Him, that [purpose clause meaning "in order that"] our body of sin might be done away with, that we should no longer be slaves to sin; for he who has died is freed from sin.

The "baptism" that is referred to means to be united with, identified with. If you have been united with Christ, then you have been united into all that happened to Him. You have died with Him, been buried with Him and are raised with Him. And what has this union wrought for you? It has freed you from sin's power to reign over you! How did it do that?

Well, when you died with Christ your old *self* or, to put it into King James English, your old *man* was crucified. "Was crucified" is in the aorist tense which is a punctiliar verb meaning at one point in time. The old man was all that you were "in Adam" (Romans 5). When that old man died it rendered your body of sin powerless so that you were no longer a slave to sin. The phrase "done away with" is used in reference to the body of sin and is *katargeo*. It is also used in Hebrews 2:14. It does not mean "annihilated" but rather "made inoperative" or "powerless." When the old man was put to death, your body, as an instrument of sin, was rendered inoperative, thereby freeing your body from sin's slavery. The old man who ruled your flesh is dead. Therefore, no true Christian has to sin; rather a Christian only sins because he chooses to sin. The cross of Christ sets him free from sin's dominion by crucifying the old man.

November 12

In God's economy, crucifixion always brings resurrection. We are going to see that over and over in the next few days, and what a blessing it will be! How I pray, Precious One, that you are hanging in there with me. I so long to be used of God to root and ground you, always establishing you in the truth, so that you will not be "tossed here and there by waves, and carried about by every wind of doctrine, by the trickery of men, by craftiness in deceitful scheming" (Ephesians 4:14). We live in days when many "will not endure sound doctrine; but wanting to have their ears tickled, they . . . accumulate for themselves teachers in accordance to their own desires; and . . . turn away their ears from the truth" (2 Timothy 4:3, 4). Crucifixion never has been popular; it goes against the flesh. Yet, Beloved, there is no real life apart from it; no resurrection power.

In Romans 6 the whole purpose of death is life—death to sin's power "so we too might walk in newness of life" (v. 4). Thus Paul writes to the Corinthians, "Therefore if any man is in Christ, he is a new creature; the old things passed away; behold, new things have come" (2 Corinthians 5:17). "Passed away" is in the aorist tense; it took place at one point in time. The verb "have come" is in the perfect tense, denoting a past completed action with a present or continuous result. This is how effective Calvary was for all who truly believe; there **is** newness of life.

What makes us new creations? It is the death of the old man and the new indwelling of the Holy Spirit. "For the law [principle] of the Spirit of life in Christ Jesus has set you free from the law [principle] of sin and of death" (Romans 8:2). But is this to be the only work of the cross in the life of the believer? No, yet this work is a sure work in the life of every single believer, without exception.

Remember I said, in essence, that life always follows death. In Galatians 2:20 Paul wrote, "I have been crucified with Christ; and it is no longer I who live, but Christ lives in me; and the life which I now live in the flesh I live by faith in the Son of God, who loved me, and delivered Himself up for me." The crucifixion is a thing of the past: "I have been crucified." Yet does that mean we have no more need of the cross? Did Christ not talk about taking up our cross daily? What did He mean by that? We will look at it tomorrow. The question for today is, "Who is living your life—you or Christ?"

November 13

Andrew Murray, a mighty man of God who walked in the Spirit, wrote, "The cross leads to the Spirit and the Spirit to the cross." What did he mean by that? Simply that it is through our identification in the death, burial, and resurrection of Jesus Christ that we are given the gift of God's Holy Spirit. Thus the cross leads us to the Spirit. Yet, when the Holy Spirit comes to indwell us, where does He lead us? To the cross! A personal cross. Why? Because the cross works death—to self, to our ways, to our desires—death to our own life. And through this death, Christ is manifested in our flesh. That is why, Beloved, God does not redeem our bodies immediately when we are saved. Rather He puts His spirit in our mortal bodies of flesh in order that men might see the surpassing greatness of the power of His Holy Spirit. When other mortals watch us living lives that are different than theirs although we live in bodies just like theirs and experience the same trials and testings, then they see the reality of "Christ in you, the hope of glory" (Colossians 1:27). It is through the hard or difficult situations of life that the reality of God's presence in us is best seen. "Just as it is written, 'For thy sake we are being put to death all day long; we were considered as sheep to be slaughtered.' But in all these things we overwhelmingly conquer through Him who loved us" (Romans 8:36, 37). Slaughter hogs and the screaming is horrible; slaughter sheep and you do not hear a sound. "As a sheep before her shearers is dumb, so he openeth not his mouth" (Isaiah 53:7 KJV). Death worked in our Lord that life might work for us.

Let me repeat Andrew Murray's statement, "The cross leads to the Spirit and the Spirit to the cross." These are two different crosses. The cross that leads to the Spirit is Calvary's cross which is common to every believer, but the cross that the Spirit leads us to is unique to each believer. Oh, granted, it is the same in that it is a place of death; yet it is unique in that it takes all different forms. Thus Jesus said, "If anyone wishes to come after Me, let him deny himself, and take up **his** cross, and follow Me" (Mark 8:34). In Luke 14:27 the cross is personalized even more, "Whoever does not carry his own cross. . . ." Taking up your own cross is synonymous with losing your life for Christ's sake and the gospel's (Mark 8:35).

Have you, Precious One, found yourself in a difficult or trying situation? Have you seen it as an opportunity for His life to be seen in you? Remember you are accounted as sheep to be slaughtered; you are being put to death. Accept it, that the reality of Christ might be seen in you.

November 14

It was hard to hold back the tears. Her anguished lips trembled; she wanted to scream. Periodically her eyes would dart down at the wasted form of her mother. As the stretcher moved through the hospital corridors down to the dingy X-ray department, she wondered if her face reflected the anguish of her heart. She tried to smile but couldn't. How can you smile when your mother is suffering so? Why didn't God just take her? Why did He let her linger? What purpose was all this pain? The referred pain from mother to daughter was too much. Tears welled up. Suddenly she squinched her eyes, but it was too late. The tears spilled out, and her lips gave way to a whimper. As she looked down to see if her mother had heard her, their eyes locked. Her mother smiled weakly as she formed a kiss with her lips.

Finally they were alone outside X ray. Looking away, gazing at nothing, still fighting tears, she suddenly felt her mother's hand in hers. Then her instructions came. Once more she was a little girl, listening to mother's wonderful words of wisdom. "Smile, Darling, smile. God has us on stage and all the world is watching. His grace is sufficient."

> But we have this treasure in earthen vessels, that the surpassing greatness of the power may be of God and not from ourselves; we are afflicted in every way, but not crushed; perplexed, but not despairing; persecuted, but not forsaken; struck down, but not destroyed; always carrying about in the body the dying of Jesus, that the life of Jesus also may be manifested in our body. For we who live are constantly being delivered over to death for Jesus' sake, that the life of Jesus also may be manifested in our mortal flesh (2 Corinthians 4:7–11).

Who can smile in the face of death? Or who can be willing to live in difficult situations? Only those who are willing to take up their cross and follow Him, saying, "Not my will but Thine be done." Only those,

Beloved, who know that "to live is Christ, and to die is gain" (Philippians 1:21). Only those who know that they are considered as sheep to be slaughtered (Romans 8:36). Only those who "are convinced that neither death, nor life, nor angels, nor principalities, nor things present, nor things to come, nor powers, nor height, nor depth, nor any other created thing, shall be able to separate us from the love of God, which is in Christ Jesus our Lord" (Romans 8:38, 39).

November 15

Now, Beloved, if you have read yesterday's devotional and are upset because you are a proponent of this new doctrine that says, with enough faith and a positive confession, you can be healed or never know sickness, please do not write me. I love you, but it grieves me to hear this unbalanced teaching that has wrested God's Word out of context and distorted it to the point of saying that Job and Paul ended up in their respective states because of a lack of faith or a negative confession. I would challenge you to search the Scriptures inductively rather than to base your doctrines on the experiences and interpretations of men. What grave harm this teaching is doing. Yes, I believe God can and does heal. I have seen Him do it. Yet I know there are times when He does not heal (1 Timothy 5:23; Galatians 4:13–15). If God's children are always healed of physical illnesses, why are they not also always healed of physical deformities? Why do they need glasses, false teeth, or hearing aids? Is it because of a lack of faith or a negative confession? And what about those who believe and make positive confessions and are still not healed? Do you doubt their faith? Do you judge your brother's walk with Christ? Or is it possible that at times God lets His children experience the same illnesses the world experiences so that the world might see the sufficiency of Christ?

Where, Beloved, is the teaching on holiness, on purity, on suffering for Christ's sake in the arena of His choosing, on a cross of His sovereign design? Our current theology today lays emphasis on obtaining blessings rather than on attaining holiness which comes through trials, testings, and sufferings. "Death works in us, but life in you" (2 Corinthians 4:12). A situation of death can take all sorts of forms, but whatever form it takes it will be seen as a death situation. By that I mean a hard situation, a difficult situation, a situation one would not choose nor remain in except for one purpose only—"that the life of Jesus also may be manifested in our body. For we who live are constantly being delivered over to death for Jesus' sake, that the life

328

of Jesus also may be manifested in our mortal flesh" (2 Corinthians 4:10, 11).

"Therefore we do not lose heart, but though our outer man is decaying, yet our inner man is being renewed day by day. For momentary, light affliction is producing for us an eternal weight of glory far beyond all comparison, while we look not at the things which are seen, but at the things which are not seen; for the things which are seen are temporal, but the things which are not seen are eternal" (2 Corinthians 4:16–18). Note, Paul says the "outer man is decaying." The Greek word for decaying (perish, KJV) is *diaphtheiro* and is in the passive voice which means "is being destroyed."

Let us look unto God. "See now that I, I am He, and there is no god besides Me; it is I who put to death and give life. I have wounded, and it is I who heal; and there is no one who can deliver from My hand" (Deuteronomy 32:39).

November 16

"Death works in us, but life in you" (2 Corinthians 4:12). How imperative it is that we know what this means, for here is the key to the Christlike life! Here is the bitter made sweet! If men are again to see Jesus, it will only be as we bear the dying of Jesus in our bodies so that the life of Jesus also may be manifested in our bodies (2 Corinthians 4:10). Although I have said it before, let me repeat it: in God's economy resurrection always follows crucifixion.

Calvary, Calvary! At times we speak of it so lightly, and yet it was a bitter and horrible experience. The flaying and mutilation, the contortions of pain, the agony of an unquenchable thirst. These were nothing compared to the sheer horror of absolute holiness being made sin and then forsaken by the Father (Psalms 22:1, 2). All this awaited our Jesus, and He knew it full well, thus the pleading with the Father in Gethsemane.

Then Jesus came with them to a place called Gethsemane, and said to His disciples, "Sit here while I go over there and pray." And He took with Him Peter and the two sons of Zebedee, and began to be grieved and distressed. Then he said to them, "My soul is deeply grieved, to the point of death; remain here and keep watch with Me." And He went a little beyond them, and fell on His face and prayed, saying, "My Father, if it is possible, let this cup pass from Me; yet not as I will, but as Thou wilt." And He came to the disciples and found them sleeping, and said to Peter, "So, you men could not keep watch with me for one hour? Keep watching and praying, that you may not enter into temptation; the spirit is willing, but the flesh is weak." He went away again a **second** time and prayed, saying, "My Father, if this cannot pass away unless I drink it, Thy will be done." And He came back and found them sleeping, for their eyes were heavy. And He left them again, and went away and prayed a **third** time, saying the same thing once more (Matthew 26:36–44).

What was the cup that Jesus wanted to pass from Him? John 18:11 states it clearly. After Jesus had wrestled in prayer, they came to arrest Him. When Simon Peter drew his sword and cut off the ear of the high priest's slave, his intention was to save Jesus from arrest and death. "Jesus therefore said to Peter, 'Put the sword into the sheath; the cup which the Father has given Me, shall I not drink it?' "

It was a bitter cup—yet He would drink it, the cup of death, for it was the Father's will. Death would work in Him, but life in us. Except He drink it we would die, not live.

November 17

The tree made the waters sweet. God's people could drink . . . and be satisfied. Life is hard, bitter, cruel. It is marred, distorted, disfigured. Sin has done it. And whether your life be hard or not, you are still a member of the human race which has experienced untold suffering because of man's sin. We reach, grasp, and pursue dreams which somehow never quite satisfy the yearnings deep down inside. Even the pleasures of life seem to have a hint of bitterness about them. There is a purity missing. Thus your thirst is never quite satisfied.

Jesus knew this. He was man, and as man He knew that only one thing would ever really fill that God-shaped vacuum in everyone, and that is God. Fellowship with the Father. Communion with the Father. Submission to the Father. Therefore, "on the last day, the great day of the feast, Jesus stood and cried out, saying, 'If any man is thirsty, let him come to Me and drink. He who believes in Me, as the Scripture said, "From his innermost being shall flow rivers of living water." ' But this He spoke of the Spirit, whom those who believed in Him were to receive; for the Spirit was not yet given, because Jesus was not yet glorified" (John 7:37–39).

The sweet water that would satisfy, and take away life's bitterness, would come from His death on the tree. "The soldiers therefore came, and broke the legs of the first man, and of the other man who was crucified with Him; but coming to Jesus, when they saw that He was already dead, they did not break His legs; but one of the soldiers pierced His side with a spear, and immediately there came out blood and water" (John 19:32–34).

They mourned, they wept, they grieved, for they did not yet realize that resurrection would follow death, that the death worked in Him would be life for them. It was so then, and it is so today.

November 18

It would have been hard to believe that George Mueller, the handsome Prussian playboy, would become a man totally consecrated to God—a man who would live a life of such import that even after his death in 1898, he would continue to minister clear into the twentieth century. When I was still but a babe in Christ, God used the biography of this man to set some of the financial principles of my life and later of Reach Out's ministry. Through Mueller's life and ministry we learned that God could supply all our needs without the direct solicitation of funds from individuals.

George Mueller did not become a Christian until he was twenty-one. Those first years of his life were entirely devoted to the world. At sixteen, his life-style was set. Drinking, gambling, lying, forging, stealing, partying were all an integral part of his life, even through his first year at seminary.

In 1826, when George was twenty-one, the turning point in his life came. George saw a young man go to his knees in prayer; he had never seen anyone on his knees nor had he himself ever knelt to pray! Within a few days he was saved; six or seven weeks later he decided he ought to be a missionary. It was then that George had his first experience with taking up his cross to fully follow his Lord. His father was vehemently opposed to his becoming a missionary.

Do not think that I came to bring peace on the earth; I did not come to bring peace, but a sword. For I came to set a man against his father, and a daughter against her mother, and a daughter-in-law against her mother-in-law; and a man's enemies will be the members of his household. He who loves father or mother more than Me is not worthy of Me; and he who loves son or daughter more than Me is not worthy of Me. And he who does not take his cross and follow after Me is not worthy of Me. He who has found his life shall lose it, and he who has lost his life for My sake shall find it (Matthew 10:34–39).

At twenty-one, George Mueller had a choice to make. Yet it was only one of many that would come in the months and years to follow.

Following Jesus costs. It costs you your life—but then it gives you His!

What do you want? At what cost? You need to decide. This is your month of decision.

November 19

The cross is the pivotal point of history, of man's destiny, of every situation in life. Study the diagram below and you will see what I mean. Look up the Scriptures and meditate on them.

OF HISTORY

B.C.	A.D.

OF MAN'S DESTINY

B.C.	A.D.
Death (Ephesians 2:1)	Life (1 John 5:11, 12)
Sin (John 8:34)	Salvation (Forgiveness) (Ephesians 2:8, 9)
Old Man (Colossians 3:9)	New Man (Have Holy Spirit) (Colossians 3:10, Ezekiel 36:27)
Heart of Stone (2 Corinthians 3:3)	New Heart of Flesh (Ezekiel 36:26)

OF EVERY SITUATION OF LIFE

B.C.	A.D.
Live by Flesh (Galatians 5:16–17)	Live by Spirit (Galatians 5:24–25)

Not only does all of mankind's history pivot around Jesus Christ, but so does the history of your life. There were those B.C. days—before Christ came into your life, and now you have Anno Domini, the years of our Lord.

And what was your destiny, your condition, before you came to Him? Christ's cross was your only way to life, to God. And yet there is another cross—your cross, a cross that determines the outcome of every situation of life, the cross that works death in you, the cross that deals with the self life and in doing so manifests His life.

Think about it. Where are you?

November 20

George Mueller once made this statement about himself:

There was a day when I died,

   utterly died,

died to George Mueller and his opinions,

   preferences,

   tastes,

   and will,

died to the world, its approval

   or censure,

died to the approval

   or blame of even my brethren,

   and friends

and since then

   I have studied only to

show myself approved unto God.

In April 1874, when he was almost sixty-nine, George Mueller wrote, "Delight thyself also in the Lord; and he shall give thee the desires of thine heart (Psalms 37:4). 'I know what a lovely, gracious, bountiful Being God is, from the revelation which He has been pleased to make of Himself in His Holy Word; I believe this revelation; I also know from my own experience the truth of it; and therefore I was satisfied with God, I delighted myself in God; and so it came, that He gave me the desire of my heart. . . .' "[26]

"But may it never be that I should boast, except in the cross of our Lord Jesus Christ, through which the world has been crucified to me, and I to the world" (Galatians 6:14).

Can you imagine the ramifications of such a life? Think upon it, Beloved.

November 21

"Save Yourself, and come down from the cross!" (Mark 15:30). They shouted it at Jesus. They will shout it at you.

Listen to their voices. Close your eyes and imagine what it must have been like. Get a good grasp on it. He was hanging there for them, yet they wanted Him to come down from the cross! They didn't understand; they didn't know what they were saying. And so it will be with you, Beloved; they will taunt you with their words, "Save yourself and come down from the cross." The same words will be said to you as were said to Jesus but, in a sense, for a different reason. Maybe they won't understand your sacrifice. Maybe it will seem stupid to them, a waste or a judgment from God. "Why be a martyr?" they will probably reason. But in all probability their motive for trying to get you off that cross will be more self-centered. Your Christianity convicts them—not by your preaching but rather by your eloquent silence in following your Lord's example when He laid down His life for us. "I am the good shepherd; the good shepherd lays down His life for the sheep. . . . even as the Father knows Me and I know the Father; and I lay down My life for the sheep" (John 10:11, 15).

We, too, can lay down our lives, following in His footsteps because we know the Father, and knowing Him we know His heart for His sheep. And, in love's obedience, we will stay on the cross we have taken up as we have sought to follow Him.

"If You are the Son of God, come down from the cross." In the same way the chief priests, along with the scribes and elders, were mocking Him, and saying, "He saved others; He cannot save Himself" (Matthew 27:40b–42).

O Beloved, if Christ had come down off that cross, if He had saved Himself, He never could have saved us. He would have lived, and we would have died. "Death works in us, life in you" if reversed would rightly read, "If life works in us, death will work in you."

It is in dying that we live. Stay on that cross. For His sake and the sake of others do not come down from your cross.

November 22

What distinguishes Christians from non-Christians? The cross. **The cross is the identification mark of a Christian,** first because of what it effects in our lives and second because of our constant identification with its work. Note, I said effects, not affects. Not that lives and situations of life are not affected, yet the essential and fundamental thing is what the cross works within a Christian. That is what we will talk about for the next several days. Then we will see its outworking. **The**

cross works deliverance—from sin's dominion, from sin's penalty, and from Satan's power. Today we will look at each one briefly.

Remember on the eleventh day when we discussed Romans 6? Our identification in Christ's death, burial and resurrection set us free from sin's dominion. "For he who has died is freed from sin. . . . For sin shall not be master over you, for you are not under law, but under grace" (Romans 6:7, 14).

And what about sin's penalty? It is one thing to be free from sin's dominion, but what does one then do with the awful wages of sin which is death, eternal separation from God (Romans 6:23). Praise God, the cross not only took care of sin's dominion; it also wrought deliverance from sin's penalty! At Calvary, God "made Him who knew no sin to be sin on our behalf, that we might become the righteousness of God in Him" (2 Corinthians 5:21), causing Jesus to cry out "MY GOD, MY GOD, WHY HAST THOU FORSAKEN ME?" (Mark 15:34). Because He was forsaken we will never be (Hebrews 13:5)! Those who come to Calvary and bow the knee, confessing the Lord Jesus Christ wait, not for sin's awful penalty but "for His Son from heaven, whom He raised from the dead, that is Jesus, who delivers us from the wrath to come" (1 Thessalonians 1:10). Hallelujah! I just had to say it! O Father, thank You for so great a salvation that delivers us from sin's penalty and sin's dominion. No longer condemned, no longer a slave, all because of Calvary!

But what about that enemy of our soul who for so long dominated our lives, the prince of the power of the air, that devil Satan who blinded our eyes, desiring our destruction? The cross delivers us from Satan's power. "Since then the children share in flesh and blood, He Himself [the Lord Jesus Christ] likewise also partook of the same, that through death He might render powerless him who had the power of death" (Hebrews 2:14). Now, greater is Jesus who is in us than Satan who is in the world (1 John 4:4). Because of Calvary, we can overcome him by the blood of the Lamb and the word of our testimony (Revelation 12:11). Want to say it again? I do. Hallelujah!

O Beloved, is this deliverance yours? And what will you give back to God for Calvary? Is the cross too much to ask?

November 23

What gives you the more pressure, your self or the world? It's a toss-up, isn't it, for one appeals to the other and it seems to be a vicious circle, first dealing with one and then with the other? Is there no relief?

Will it continue until you die? Yes, it will. But you can die early! You can strike a death blow at the root of the problem. You can take up your cross. **The cross works separation—separation from self and separation from the world.** Listen to Paul's words again in Galatians 2:20, "I am crucified with Christ nevertheless I live; yet not I." *I* am not to live; it is no longer *my* life but His, no longer *my* body but His. "You belong to Christ" (1 Corinthians 3:23). The cross not only separates us unto God. It separates us from the world.

"But may it never be that I should boast, except in the cross of our Lord Jesus Christ, through which the world has been crucified to me, and I to the world" (Galatians 6:14). Therefore when self or pride would insist upon its own way or when the world would try to squeeze me into its mold, I must remember the cross.

> Even so consider yourselves to be dead to sin, but alive to God in Christ Jesus. Therefore do not let sin reign in your mortal body that you should obey its lusts, and do not go on presenting the members of your body to sin as instruments of unrighteousness; but present yourselves to God as those alive from the dead, and your members as instruments of righteousness to God (Romans 6:11–13).

Did we not choose to follow Him? Then follow Him we must, His way! The cross is an instrument of death separating me from myself and from the world. "For the love of Christ controls us, having concluded this, that one died for all, therefore all died; and He died for all, that they who live should no longer live for themselves, but for Him who died and rose again on their behalf" (2 Corinthians 5:14, 15).

November 24

The Cross of Calvary not only effected our deliverance and our separation, but it also brought us life. One can only pass from death to life through the cross of Calvary. Eternal life, the fruit of Calvary, came when that precious and priceless grain of wheat died.

> Truly, truly, I say to you, unless a grain of wheat falls into the earth and dies, it remains by itself alone; but if it dies, it bears much fruit. He who loves his life loses it; and he who hates his life in this world shall keep it to life eternal. If any one serves Me, let him follow Me; and where I am, there shall My servant also be; if any one serves Me, the Father will honor him. Now My soul has become troubled; and what shall I say, "Father, save Me from this hour"? But for this purpose I came to this hour (John 12:24–27).

He was born to die that we might live; that was His purpose. Without His death there would be no life for us.

The same truth carries over into our own lives. When we are willing to die, to lose our lives for His sake and the gospel's, it brings life to others. All of life's power radiates from the cross. Oh, that we would be willing to be poured out for others even as Paul, "But even if I am being poured out as a drink offering upon the sacrifice and service of your faith, I rejoice" (Philippians 2:17).

You have heard the statement that the blood of the martyrs is the seed of the church. It is true, and yet I do not believe that it is only physical death in martyrdom that brings forth a harvest of souls, but also simply the willingness to lay aside one's own life, to die to all but the will of God. From martyrs such as these the church is built, living stone by living stone. Billy and Ruth Graham (Billy Graham Evangelistic Association), the late "Uncle Cam" and Elaine Townsend (Wycliffe Bible Translators), Bill and Vonette Bright (Campus Crusade for Christ) are but three modern-day couples who have literally poured out their lives in sacrifice and service for the faith of others and, in doing so, have wrought a great harvest of souls. They chose death, the cross, because so many needed life.

"Oh, but look how glamorous it is to be in the limelight and be the head of such big and great organizations," some may say. Yet little do they realize that the glamour, the notoriety, the excitement is not even a consideration, for in ministries such as these it is but tinsel in comparison to the long hours of labor, the agonizing in prayer, the godly fear of doing His work His way, the rigid discipline, the total occupation with the task before you, the awesome responsibility of leadership, the life that is never your own because it belongs to Him and thus to others. In any ministry that is being used of God to transform lives, you can rest assured they have lost their lives for the sake of the gospel. And they labor as Paul did to the point of exhaustion. Why? Because the harvest is plentiful, but the laborers few!

November 25

All that you and I will ever need, or should ever want, will be found in the fruit of Calvary. Since God gave you His all, His Son; since Jesus gave you His all, His life; since the Holy Spirit gives you His all, His indwelling presence, is it too much for Him to ask your all in return? Where would you be if it were not for Calvary? How I shudder when I think upon it! I look at the women "of this world," scantily clothed, moving from one husband to another or from one affair to another. I see them pushing, shoving, demanding, crying out for fulfillment as they abandon their God-ordained roles. I see their guilt, their frustration, their depression, and I understand. The pleasures of sin only endure for a season; there is always "a morning after the night before" that one must awaken to! I ache as they live with the "if onlys" of their past. I see it all, I feel it all, I've known it all, for before Calvary I was there. But now, because of Calvary, it seems as if I have lived two totally different lives in two different bodies. Because I have become His temple, my body behaves so differently. It has been released from its slavery as an instrument of sin, and, although it still has its fleshly appetites, it has taken on robes and deeds of righteousness. It has become my means of ministering life rather than death. Truly I am a new creation in Christ Jesus. The old things have passed away; all things have become new (2 Corinthians 5:17).

I will never forget the day I discovered 2 Corinthians 5:17. I was a brand-new Christian, so hungry for truth that I couldn't get enough. At that time I was a divorcee with two sons, trying to make ends meet, take care of my children and still have time to be alone with God so I could grow! It was hard! Yet I devised ways. One, which I would not recommend, was to read while I drove to work! One day, with my book propped up in my lap against the steering wheel, I nearly came unglued. I couldn't believe what I read! It said that if any man be in Christ he is a new creature, old things have passed away. . . ! Why, that was an exact description of me! I shook my head! In my naiveté I thought God had put it into His Word just to describe what happened to me! Now I know that it's God's work for all who come to Calvary.

New! Oh it is so good to be new—and to be free, free to be what He wants me to be.

November 26

Free! Free from sin, free from guilt, but most of all free from me! Oh, how we need the message of Calvary not just from the lips of men, but from their very lives. Will it not be easier for others to believe in Him who laid down His life for us if they see us lay down our lives also? Oh, that we would learn to glory in the cross.

How true are F. J. Huegel's words in his book, *The Cross of Christ, The Throne of God.*

A great cry went up from the jeering, reviling Jews who surged about the Crucified Redeemer. "If he be the King of Israel let him now come down from the cross and we will believe on him." We read that "the thieves also, which were crucified with him, cast the same in his teeth."

In recent years a great cry, an echo of that ancient clamour, has gone up from the Church. If Christ would only come down from the Cross! We want the Christ of the Mount, we believe on the Christ of the healing ministry, we love the Christ of the sublime example, we preach the Christ of the Social Gospel—but the Christ of the Cross is an offense. "Let him now come down from the cross and we will believe on him."

But the King did not come down. His right to Kingship was never more Divine than in that awful Hour. It was from the Accursed Tree that He would reign. It was *here* that He wrought redemption. It was when from *here* He cried, "It is finished," that "the rocks were rent and the graves were opened." It was when *here* He tasted death for every man, that the veil of the temple was rent, symbolic of the clearing of the way for immediate access into the Presence of God for all the children of men. It was *then* that God's Hour struck—the dawn of the Christian Age. It was *then* that the shackles of an enslaved humanity were broken. It was from *this* Ignominious Tree, however galling the offense of the Cross, that the King still reigns. *From no other throne will He establish His Kingdom.*

Christians do not enter into the unutterable glories of the Christian Life, in union with Christ, until they learn to glory, as did Paul, in this Cross, offensive as it is to the natural man. The Cross is *still* the only way to God. The Christ of the Cross is *still* humanity's only hope. Calvary's amazing consummation is *still* the Alpha and the Omega of the Church's life and message.[27]

Is this your message?

November 27

"Take the world but give me Jesus." Oh, that this were the heart cry of every Christian! And if not, let it at least be my heart's cry. Will it be yours? Oh, that it would be, so that at every moment, in every place where we find ourselves, He would abide as our everlasting portion. To be satisfied with Him alone! Jesus, our all in all.

And where is such a passion schooled? How can one be so disciplined as to attain such a measure of life? Paul can tell us, for the passion of his life was that Christ would be exalted in his body whether by life or by death. His commitment was such that for him to live was Christ and to die was gain (Philippians 1:20, 21).

Listen to the price that Paul was willing to pay: "But whatever

things were gain to me, those things I have counted as loss for the sake of Christ. More than that, I count all things to be loss in view of the surpassing value of knowing Christ Jesus my Lord, for whom I have suffered the loss of all things, and count them but rubbish" (Philippians 3:7, 8a).

And now listen as Paul describes that one thing which is of such unequalled value that he was willing to give his all for it: "That I may gain Christ, and may be found in Him, not having a righteousness of my own derived from the Law, but that which is through faith in Christ, the righteousness which comes from God on the basis of faith, that I may know Him, and the power of His resurrection and the fellowship of His sufferings, being conformed to His death; in order that I may attain to the resurrection from the dead" (Philippians 3:8b–11).

Being conformed to His death! There it is again. Death! But death followed by resurrection—"that I might attain to the resurrection from the dead"! What does this mean? It means that you will lay hold of His life only to the degree that you lay hold of His death. You simply cannot have the world and have Jesus too! The two are incompatible. The world hates Jesus. You cannot cooperate with Jesus in becoming what He wants you to become and simultaneously be what the world desires to make you. If you would say, "Take the world but give me Jesus," then you must deny yourself and take up your cross. The simple truth is that your "self" must be put to death in order for you to get to the point that for you to live is Christ.

What will it be? The world and you or Jesus and you? You do have a choice to make. God is setting it before you as you read these pages.

November 28

Yesterday, I told you that you had a decision to make—your way or His cross. When you read that did you say in your heart, *Later, I'll decide later?* Or *Maybe?* Or perhaps you said, *I will, but first I must. . . .*

And as they were going along the road, someone said to Him, "I will follow You wherever You go." And Jesus said to him, "The foxes have holes, and the birds of the air have nests, but the Son of Man has nowhere to lay His head" (Luke 9:57, 58).

Do you want to follow Him? Then first you must know the path He trods. If it is to have any holding power, your decision to follow Jesus cannot be based on your emotions. It must be based on knowledge and conviction. And so Jesus says that if a person wants to follow Him, he must be prepared to leave the comforts of home. How hard that is! Often we love our homes so much that we are unwilling to count all things loss. So we hold on to things and lose the joy of companionship, the deep satisfaction of His, "Well done, my good and faithful servant."

"Peter began to say to Him, 'Behold, we have left everything and followed You.' Jesus said, 'Truly I say to you, there is no one who has left house or brothers or sisters or mother or father or children or farms, for My sake and for the gospel's sake, but that he shall receive a hundred times as much now in the present age, houses and brothers and sisters and mothers and children and farms, along with persecutions; and in the world to come, eternal life' " (Mark 10:28–30). If we would but let go, we will gain one hundred fold. Yet with it (and I so love His honesty) will come persecution! But then would you enter heaven on flowery beds of ease and casually stand before the One despised and rejected of men? I pray not.

He is saying to you just as He said to another centuries ago, "Follow Me." That man's response was, "Permit me first to go and bury my father." And Jesus replied, "Allow the dead to bury their own dead; but as for you, go and proclaim everywhere the kingdom of God" (Luke 9:59, 60). The man's father was not actually dead. What he was really saying was that he wanted to follow Jesus at a later time, after his father died. Are relationships keeping you from following Him? Remember you cannot love others more than Jesus and be His disciple (Luke 14:26).

Or did you start to follow Him but somehow get waylaid? Have you kept saying, "As soon as I _____, then I'm going to fully serve the Lord"?

> And another also said, "I will follow You, Lord; but first permit me to say goodbye to those at home." But Jesus said to him, "No one, after putting his hand to the plow and looking back, is fit for the kingdom of God" (Luke 9:61, 62).

November 29

The Cross: Endurance in the face of misunderstanding! Endurance like that of the Lamb of God, "Who committed no sin, nor was any deceit found in His mouth; and while being reviled, He did not revile in return; while suffering, He uttered no threats, but kept entrusting Himself to Him who judges righteously" (1 Peter 2:22, 23).

The Cross is a voluntary place of sacrifice. The choice is yours, and you must choose. Be assured that it will be a place of laying down your life for others. You will have to sacrifice yourself **even as your Lord did** in order to be used of God to save others. To live at the cross is to pour out your life for those who have misjudged, scorned, rejected or deserted you. And then to say, "Father forgive them; for they do not know what they are doing" (Luke 23:34). How do you do it? It is not easy and many times I fail, yet those failures are getting less frequent. Usually, when I am tempted to react in my flesh, I stop and remember that they will never see Christ **if they see me.** And the world is still saying, "We would see Jesus." If we remember this, then we will say with Paul, "For all things are for your sakes." This is the heart of Calvary. We are not to lose heart, for "though our outer man is decaying, yet our inner man is being renewed day by day. For momentary, light affliction is producing for us an eternal weight of glory far beyond all comparison, while we look not at the things which are seen, but at the things which are not seen; for the things which are seen are temporal, but the things which are not seen are eternal" (2 Corinthians 4:16–18).

Let me give you an illustration from the life of Heinrich Suso.

He had suffered much, so much that he was quite at home with the Cross. So at home that he once said to a friend, "I guess the Lord has forgotten me, He has not sent me any great trial for a long time." Then it was that the Lord used a circumstance to bring him to a participation in the deepest forces of Calvary. A woman of evil character came to his door and left a babe in his arms, saying, "Here you have the fruits of your sin." Suso was innocent. He had never seen the woman before. He felt it keenly. . . . A great storm of reproach and of gossip arose. . . . So great was Suso's shame and pain that he fled to a mountain retreat where he could groan out before the Lord in unrestrained fashion his complaint. "What," he cried, "am I to do?" "What are you to do?" came the Divine reply, "Do as I did. Suffer for the sins of others and say nothing." Suso went back home, took the child and reared it in silent resignation. Years later the woman in question returned for her child, publishing to the four winds the saint's innocence. Thus was the Lambhood nature of Christ wrought into the great Suso. Verily we are the partakers of the Cross of our Redeemer.[28]

November 30

Everything that is natural in you is repulsed by turning the other cheek, going the extra mile, giving away your cloak, blessing those that curse you, praying for those that despitefully use you! I understand. As

I shared at the beginning of this month, my flesh rose in indignation at the inconsiderate behavior of those people who cut right in front of us. Enduring all the things I have just mentioned seems like such weakness. It seems like giving in, like complying with what is wrong in people. Yet what did our Lord say?

"You have heard that it was said, 'An eye for an eye, and a tooth for a tooth.' But I say to you, do not resist him who is evil; but whoever slaps you on your right cheek, turn to him the other also. And if any one wants to sue you, and take your shirt, let him have your coat also. And whoever shall force you to go one mile, go with him two. Give to him who asks of you, and do not turn away from him who wants to borrow from you. You have heard that it was said, 'You shall love your neighbor, and hate your enemy.' But I say to you, love your enemies, and pray for those who persecute you in order that you may be sons of your Father who is in heaven; for He causes His sun to rise on the evil and the good, and sends rain on the righteous and the unrighteous. For if you love those who love you, what reward have you? Do not even the tax-gatherers do the same? And if you greet your brothers only, what do you do more than others? Do not even the Gentiles do the same? Therefore you are to be perfect, as your heavenly Father is perfect" (Matthew 5:38–48).

As you read this did you notice that Jesus was covering insults and misuses of our person, our possessions, and our privileges as members of the human race? Why can't we behave as "the Gentiles"? Why can others react "normally" and yet we cannot?

Because, Precious Ones, we are not normal! We are not just ordinary human beings. We are soldiers of the cross of Jesus Christ. To turn the other cheek, to give to him who asks, to pray, to love those who are your enemies is not natural. It is divine. It is sacrifice. It is death to the natural and thus resurrection of the supernatural.

"Therefore Jesus also, that He might sanctify the people through His own blood, suffered outside the gate. Hence, let us go out to Him outside the camp, bearing His reproach. For here we do not have a lasting city, but we are seeking the city which is to come" (Hebrews 13:12–14).

DECEMBER

Following in His Steps

December 1

The Cross must come before the Crown. Christianity is more than, "I am saved. I am healed. I am happy!" Beware of any gospel which does not tell you that "to you it has been granted for Christ's sake, not only to believe in Him, but also to suffer for His sake" (Philippians 1:29). "Indeed, all who desire to live godly in Christ Jesus will be persecuted" (2 Timothy 3:12). Satan offered Jesus the world and its temporal crown without the cross; he will seek you out with the same offer. And if that does not work, then he will seek to strip and afflict you as he did Jesus, as he did Job. His desire is to get you to turn back, to spare your life. "Skin for skin!" Satan said to God, "Yes, all that a man has he will give for his life" (Job 2:4). Yet Satan is wrong, for anyone who has truly taken up his cross to follow his Lord has already died.

The story is told of a man who was being threatened in all sorts of ways because he would not deny Christ. When they finally threatened to take his life, he said, "You cannot take my life, I am already dead"—already dead because his life was hidden with Christ in God! Oh, that we would realize that! What fearlessness, what boldness it would bring!

Yet, boldness in the face of adversity does not always come immediately. Sometimes it must be wrestled out at the foot of the cross. " 'Dr. J. G. Fleming tells how, in the days of the Boxer uprising in China, Boxers captured a Mission school, blocked all gates but one, placed a cross before it, and sent in word that any one who trampled on that cross would go free, but that any one who stepped around it would be killed. The first seven, we are told, trampled on the cross and were allowed to go free. The eighth, a girl, knelt before the cross, and was shot. All the rest in a line of a hundred students followed her example' (*Sunday School Times*)."[29]

As sheep for the slaughter, we are put to death all day long! Beloved, beware of teaching that centers around man and concentrates on the gifts of God rather than on the cross of Christ. Many want crowns without the cross and so teachers tickle their ears with an unbalanced theology which lays emphasis on obtaining blessings rather than on attaining holiness, a holiness wrought on the anvil of trials, testings, and sufferings. So much of our witnessing, our preaching, and even our literature stresses what God can do for us rather than what we are to be and what we are to do for God. We are more concerned with our pleasure than with His!

And what is His pleasure? That you realize that your Sovereign God permitted the bitter waters and that with the cross they will be made sweet and palatable. So do not turn away; take up your cross and follow Him.

December 2

Have you ever found yourself in a situation that was so horribly bitter that you wondered how you could bear it, how you could go on? Or have you ever looked at others and wondered how they could possibly retain their sanity in the midst of such inhumane atrocities? I have. I've been in bitter situations, situations that I never dreamed I would ever face. And yet, there have been moments when I have looked at the excruciatingly painful lives of others and realized that I have never really tasted bitterness. Not compared to some!

I remember one night when I sat on my bed and, as is my custom many evenings, took out a file folder of correspondence to work on. In that file folder was a transcript of a man's confession to a grotesque crime. Matter of factly, in words void of emotion, he told how he had raped a little girl. As he forced himself on her in the back seat of a car, she quietly said, in essence, "You shouldn't do this. Jesus says it's wrong." With that, in anger, he proceeded to kill her. My account is brief. His was not. It seemed as if he did not miss one horrible detail. As I read the transcript, my body contorted in pain, my lips could not hold back the groans. It seemed as if I could see the whole grotesque scene. As I inwardly screamed, the words resounded back and forth through the corridors of my mind, *Oh, God! . . . Why? . . . How?* The torment was too great. It could not continue. No longer could I let this murderer's words paint such vivid pictures in my imagination. It seemed too unjust, too cruel, too distorted, too ungodly to be allowed. My mind had turned into a chamber of horrors. Mentally I ran out of it and slammed the door to my thoughts. "Father, I cannot think about it. I cannot understand it. Oh God, it's too much for me . . . too difficult." And with that I buried my head in the bosom of my El Shaddai. I clung to the One I knew, the God of Calvary.

I would not, I could not permit myself to think of anything else but

Him, the One who died, the One who so bore the atrocities of men that He "was marred more than any man" (Isaiah 52:14) and yet, in the midst of it all, cried out, "Father, forgive them; for they do not know what they are doing" (Luke 23:34). There are many things, many situations I could not handle if I did not know how to put the tree, the cross, into the bitter waters of life. That, Beloved, is what we will continue to talk about this month, taking the bitter and making it sweet, palatable, drinkable ... bearable!

December 3

When the children of Israel came to the bitter waters of Marah, the Lord showed Moses "a tree; and he threw it into the waters, and the waters became sweet" (Exodus 15:25). And so the Lord showed us last month that our tree, the cross (Galatians 3:13), when applied to the bitter situations of life, can make them sweet ... drinkable. As the waters of Marah were a test and the tree was the solution, so are the bitter situations in our lives a test for which we have a cross, His or ours. And you can know, Beloved, with every test that "no temptation has overtaken you but such as is common to man; and God is faithful, who will not allow you to be tempted beyond what you are able, but with the temptation will provide the way of escape also, that you may be able to endure it" (1 Corinthians 10:13).

And yet, although we know the truth of 1 Corinthians 10:13, don't we wonder deep in our hearts if life's situations are not sometimes really more than we can bear? That is what caused me such agony when I read the transcript of that little girl's death. I wondered, "How could she bear it, God?" And yet I was not there. I do not know how God met that precious girl's need. But I do know God's Word, and so, when I start to wonder, I cling to the God of the tree, the God of Calvary. Because of who He is, "we know that God causes all things to work together for good to those who love God, to those who are called according to His purpose" (Romans 8:28). "For from Him and through Him and to Him are all things. To Him be the glory forever. Amen" (Romans 11:36).

Knowing the God of Calvary will enable you to apply the cross to any bitter situation of life. Therefore, in the next days we are going to look at the God who conceived and permitted Calvary. Then we will look at how these truths can be applied to any of life's bitter situations. Our devotions this month should then become, Beloved, a manual of how-to's in applying God's precepts. Give yourself time to meditate each day upon what you read. Examine what I share very carefully in the light of His Word, and, if you find my words to be truth, then live accordingly. We shall move together step by step, precept upon precept, line upon line, trusting God's Spirit to guide us into all truth.

Bitter days are ahead; the last days are coming to a close. We must be prepared. I love you.

December 4

Who is the God of Calvary? If we are called to live crucified lives, to deny ourselves and take up our cross and follow Him (Mark 8:34, 35), then we need to know the character of the One who sanctioned Calvary. Or did He? Did God have anything to do with it at all or was His Son nailed to that cross despite all God could do? Was the cross an accident, a whim of ungodly men, or was it part of God's predetermined plan? And, if God knew about Jesus' cross with all its bitterness, does He know about mine? If He permitted Jesus' cross, does He permit mine?

Before Adam and Eve ever sinned and acted independently of God, *there was the cross,* older than man's sin. Jesus, the Lamb of God, was slain before the foundation of the world (Revelation 13:8). Therefore, when God confronted Adam, Eve, and the serpent in the Garden of Eden, He knew what was to be! There would be a righteous pardon for their sin. Thus to the serpent He said, "I will put enmity between you and the woman, and between your seed and her seed; He shall bruise you on the head, and you shall bruise him on the heel" (Genesis 3:15). Crucifixion is the only death whereby the heel is bruised! The God of Calvary not only knew His lamb would someday die, He also knew how He would die! Before man ever conceived the horrible means of crucifixion, it was already in the plan of the God who rules over all, supremely ordering the time of each event. Nothing escapes His notice, not even the sparrows sold for mere farthings nor the hairs of your head, which are numbered by Him.

Jesus' apostles knew this. God had announced beforehand through the prophets that His Christ would suffer (Acts 3:18). Thus, when they experienced the suffering that came from taking up that cross and following Jesus, they cried to the God of Calvary, "O Lord, it is Thou who didst make the heaven and the earth and the sea, and all that is in them, who by the Holy Spirit, through the mouth of our father David Thy servant, didst say, 'Why did the Gentiles rage, and the peoples devise futile things? The kings of the earth took their stand, and the rulers were gathered together against the Lord, and against His Christ.' For truly in this city there were gathered together against Thy holy servant Jesus, whom Thou didst anoint, both Herod and Pontius Pilate, along with the Gentiles and the peoples of Israel, **to do whatever Thy hand and Thy purpose predestined to occur.** And now, Lord, take note of their threats, and grant that Thy bond-servants may speak Thy word with all confidence" (Acts 4:24–29).

The bitterness that came from following Jesus was made sweet because they knew the God of Calvary. What about you? Do you know your God?

December 5

Have you ever felt helpless? A victim of circumstances, circumstances beyond your control, circumstances that seemingly could alter the course of your life? Have you wondered what would become of you? How you could go on? Whether it was worth going on? O Beloved, have you not seen your Father, the Sovereign God, standing in the shadows behind the curtain as you have lived out those events. Look! He has been there all along! Look to His cross and drink the sweetness of the waters that flow because of Calvary.

> Pilate therefore said to Him, "You do not speak to me? Do You not know that I have authority to release You, and I have authority to crucify You?" Jesus answered, **"You would have no authority over Me, unless it had been given you from above;** for this reason he who delivered Me up to you has the greater sin." As a result of this Pilate made efforts to release Him, but the Jews cried out, saying, "If you release this Man, you are no friend of Caesar; every one who makes himself out to be a king opposes Caesar" (John 19:10–12).

Jesus was neither in the hands of Pilate nor that angry mob of Jews. His Father was in control, the Sovereign God of Calvary, and Calvary was His plan. It had a purpose, man's redemption. Your cross, Beloved, comes from God. It is that which effects your death. As we learned last month, it is a death that works life in others.

> Always carrying about in the body the dying of Jesus, that the life of Jesus also may be manifested in our body. For we who live are constantly being delivered over to death for Jesus' sake, that the life of Jesus also may be manifested in our mortal flesh. So death works in us, but life in you (2 Corinthians 4:10–12).

And what is God's lesson to us? I'm sure you already know without my saying it. In any trial, in any bitter situation, you are not alone, you are not helpless, you are not a victim. You have a tree, a cross shown to you by the Sovereign God of Calvary. Whatever the trial or temptation, it is not more than you can bear. It is bearable. It can be handled. You can know as Joseph knew, "You meant evil against me, but God meant it for good in order to bring about this present result, to preserve many people alive" (Genesis 50:20). Therefore "consider it all joy, my brethren, when you encounter various trials, knowing that the testing of your faith produces endurance" (James 1:2, 3). You count it all joy by putting the cross into the trial and bringing death to your evaluation, to your expectations.

December 6

Remember, I said that knowing the God of Calvary enables us to take the bitter and make it sweet. Look at Calvary and what do you see besides a Sovereign God? You see that the One who is in control is a God of grace, a God of love. Only love would cause Him to give His Son to die in our stead, to bear the just judgment for our sins. "But God demonstrates **His own love** toward us, in that while we were yet sinners, Christ died for us" (Romans 5:8). The God who bids me put the tree into the bitter situations of life is a God of love. He can never act apart from that love—a love that desires my highest good, that never fails, that never ceases no matter how I respond.

God's love is incomprehensible; we can never fully plumb its depths. Yet, isn't it in the face of bitter situations that we question that love? Haven't you heard people say, "If God is a God of love, how could He ever permit this?" When people ask questions like these, they forget that the God of Calvary is not only a God of love, but also a God of grace. Usually when we speak of God's grace we refer to that unmerited favor that is bestowed upon us when we deserve otherwise. And this is true. Yet grace has a more comprehensive definition which I like even better than "unmerited favor." The grace of God is all that Christ is and has made available to us. This marvelous grace is available to all who would come to God through the Lord Jesus Christ. When one is justified by faith, put in right standing before God because he has acknowledged that Jesus is the Christ and has surrendered to Him as God and walks in the obedience of faith, then he has access to the grace of God. Listen to Romans 5:1, 2: "Therefore having been justified by faith, we have peace with God through our Lord

Jesus Christ, through whom also we have obtained our introduction by faith into this grace in which we stand."

Since as a child of God you stand forever in the grace of God, you can rest secure in the knowledge that everything, including life's bitter situations, comes to you filtered through His fingers of love. And you can face them because His grace is sufficient to cover the bitterness of the past, even those years before you knew Christ, and sufficient for anything the future may hold.

December 7

Some live with the bitter gall of what might have been, "If only. . . ." The sickness of their past long gone, their minds still have periodic attacks of the dry heaves. A sight, a sound, a word, a look, a face—or even a mind with nothing to occupy it—brings on the nausea. There seems to be no cure. It was too horrible, too unfair, too much for any human being to bear! "No wonder I am what I am! Wouldn't you be too if the same thing had happened to you?" And for many there really is no cure, no solution—at least not one that men could devise. They are victims, and what does it matter who is at fault; a victim is still a victim! The question is are they to remain victimized for life? Is there never to be a way of escape? A new beginning? A life with purpose? Hope? Peace? Must they drink bitter waters forever or can the bitter be made sweet, palatable, satisfying?

There is only one real solution. The cross—and the grace of the God of Calvary. Paul called himself the chief of sinners (1 Timothy 1:15). Formerly a blasphemer, a persecutor, a violent aggressor, he could have been distressed forever because he had given consent to Stephen's death and to the death of other Christians. Yet Paul would not waste the grace of God. He knew that where sin did abound the grace of God abounded far more. There was one cure and only one and that was to choose to believe in the grace of God and say, "But by the grace of God I am what I am, and His grace toward me did not prove vain" (1 Corinthians 15:10). God's grace was not empty, void of power or useless in respect to Paul's situation because Paul appropriated it!

O Beloved, Beloved, where are you? Regretting or resting? You cannot tell me there is no cure, no hope, no way to mend the wounds. To say so is to say that the grace of God is not sufficient, and to say that is to contradict His Word. Whatever the past, whatever the present, whatever the future, the God who bids you to take up your cross and follow Him says, "My grace is sufficient for you" (2 Corinthians 12:9). Do not let it prove vain in your life.

December 8

Have you ever ridden the waves on some ocean beach? I'm not much of a swimmer so I never go out beyond where my feet can touch solid ground. Plus, I can't stand to get water up my nose. It makes me choke, cough, and sputter like a whale with hiccups! Yet I enjoy riding the waves if I can stay in control of the situation. Watching for that big wave to come along, catching it at its crest and allowing it to propel me toward the shore is grand fun.

But have you ever been picked up by a wave, pitched head first into the surf, and held there by the relentless force of the water? I have, and I can tell you I was terrified. I tried desperately to regain my footing, and my throat burned from all the salt water I was swallowing. All dignity gone, crawling on all fours, I clawed the sand frantically trying to get up only to feel the undertow dragging me farther from the safety of the shore. Fighting with all the energy of one who has been terrorized, I finally made it to my feet. Choking violently I stumbled toward shore only to be knocked down again as I was hit by a second wave and dragged back toward death. Engulfed in the water, I couldn't even cry for help but I pleaded inwardly, *O God, don't let me drown.* Head over heels I turned until I hit the bottom. Finally getting to my feet, weak, belching, and choking, I was caught for the third time and taken under. With all that was in me I fought the waters and cried to God. I didn't give up. I didn't want to surrender to the waters. I wanted to live.

Those who have never been so overwhelmed or caught so helplessly in such an undertow could never understand my panic and my desperate effort to survive. They would only laugh, kid or condescendingly say they were sorry. But those who have been where I was would know how I felt. They could relate. They would understand my struggle to survive and they could shake their heads and say with empathy, "I know the feeling. You survived because you were determined you weren't going to give up." And it is true; the survivors are those who "fight the good fight," those who persevere. If you do not persevere, you have surrendered!

A life lived for Jesus, a life lived at the cross, a life that follows Him fully will always be a life that is contested on every hand in one way or another. Waves and undertows may knock the breath out of you, pulling you under, leaving you gasping and choking. Men may not hear your cries, but God will—"O God, don't let me drown."

"The cords of death encompassed me, and the terrors of Sheol came upon me; I found distress and sorrow. Then I called upon the name of the Lord: 'O Lord, I beseech Thee, save my life!' " (Psalms 116:3, 4).

December 9

The Psalmist asked: "What shall I render the Lord for all His benefits toward me?" (Psalms 116:12). What is the answer? Would it not be to live at the cross, letting the bitter be made sweet rather than making me bitter? Would it not be to drink the cup by taking up my cross, even as Jesus took up His cross, saying, "Father . . . not my will, but Thine be done; if it pleases Thee, it pleases me"?

I read of such a woman, to me a heroine of the faith, whose story will probably never be in print except here and in *The President's Letter,* where I read it. *The President's Letter* is a publication sent out by Robertson McQuilkin, president of Columbia Bible College, a man Jack and I love and admire. In April, 1982, he told the story of Mae Louise Westervelt. When I read her story I remembered my experience at the beach. Mae Louise was a survivor. She knew the God of Calvary, and, because of this, the bitter was palatable.

The child of missionary parents, Mae Louise's dream was to provide a home for missionary children. Her husband shared that dream. "She was carrying her firstborn when her husband was crippled in body and spirit in a terrible automobile accident. Partially recovered, he carried on valiantly, but little Mae Louise was destined to carry the spiritual thrust of the family."

While recovering from the first wave, they were hit by a second—their newborn son was born helplessly handicapped. The third wave came years later when at the age of eleven their son drowned. But life went on—without bitterness. "For Thy sake we are being put to death all day long; we were considered as sheep to be slaughtered" (Romans 8:36). A fourth wave was to hit when their daughter, a few weeks away from graduation from the University of South Carolina, was killed in an automobile accident. "But in all these things we overwhelmingly conquer through Him who loved us" (Romans 8:37). Undaunted, Mae Louise did not give up; she kept on leading the missions program in her little Baptist church, teaching the teenage girls, and shepherding the children of the neighborhood. A fifth wave, a sixth would come, again she would say, "The Lord preserves the simple; I was brought low, and He saved me" (Psalms 116:6). You can say the same, if you will. He saves you. He preserves you at Calvary. Don't give up. Fight the good fight of faith.

December 10

Although Mae Louise Westervelt and her husband never attained their dream of providing a home for missionary children, God did allow them to secure several low-cost homes in Denny Terrace, a community near Columbia Bible College. These were rented to students and to missionaries home on furlough. With a sensitive heart, Mae Louise prayed, wrote, and gave sacrificially to those serving God on foreign fields. Then, unexpectedly, she was hit for the fifth time. "One day as her husband changed a tire by the roadside, he was killed by a drunken driver."

> But we have this treasure in earthen vessels, that the surpassing greatness of the power may be of God and not from ourselves; we are afflicted in every way, but not crushed; perplexed, but not despairing; persecuted, but not forsaken; struck down, but not destroyed; always carrying about in the body the dying of Jesus, that the life of Jesus also may be manifested in our body (2 Corinthians 4:7-10).

"Undaunted, Mae Louise walked the streets of Denny Terrace, selling Avon products to support her adopted son, and sharing the good news of life in Christ. On Fridays she visited the sick in the hospital. On Thursdays there was an evangelistic home visitation, at other times there were Bible studies with the unsaved." "As unknown yet well-known . . . as sorrowful yet always rejoicing, as poor yet making many rich, as having nothing yet possessing all things" (2 Corinthins 6:9, 10).

Then came the sixth wave. "A pacemaker extended her fragile life, but she just kept pressing on. Sunday morning she would gather a load of little boys in her rattly old Plymouth, bring them to Sunday School and sit with them as they wiggled their way through the worship service." At Christmastime Dr. McQuilkin told her, "You are one of my true heroes!" A hero she was, a soldier of the cross. Mae Louise had lived at Calvary, making the bitter sweet, and her God had not let her drown. Nor had she let Him down. She endured as seeing Him who is invisible (Hebrews 11:27). Then one day, having been "poured out as a drink offering upon the sacrifice and service of *others'* faith" (Philippians 2:17), while sipping tea as she sat on her living room sofa, she heard her Lord say, "Come home, and we'll dine together at My table."

Someday, Beloved, He will call you home. How comfortable will you be when you see Him face to face, the God of Calvary? How well have you fought the good fight? How well have you kept the faith?

December 11

The God of Calvary is a merciful God. You can trust His mercy in any bitter situation because at the cross He granted you your own High Priest, the one and only mediator between God and man, the man Christ Jesus (1 Timothy 2:5), that you might always find mercy and grace to help in time of need (Hebrews 4:16).

How quick we are to cry for justice! How slow to realize that what we need is not justice but mercy! And what is the difference? Justice is that which is fair or correct in treatment, in reward, or in punishment. When we find ourselves in seemingly unjust circumstances, we need to remember God's words from Lamentations. "Why should any living mortal, or any man, offer complaint in view of his sins? Let us examine and probe our ways, and let us return to the Lord" (Lamentations 3:39, 40). And when we return, what will we find? Justice? Yes, justice, but justice in mercy poured out in righteous wrath, not upon us but upon the One who, voluntarily, was made to be sin for us. At Calvary, we see God as "just and the justifier" that we might obtain mercy, for "his mercies are over all His works" (Psalms 145:9). Mercy goes beyond justice; it is kindness or compassion over and above what can be expected or even claimed. And how does mercy differ from grace? "Grace is concerned for man as he is guilty; mercy, as he is miserable."[30]

In the misery of the bitter situations of life, we need to remember that each situation has been sovereignly permitted by a merciful God. Enthroned at His right hand is our High Priest who can sympathize with our weaknesses because, although without sin, He was "tempted in all things as we are" (Hebrews 4:15). Therefore, we can hold fast to our confession. We need not give in nor give up.

> The Lord's lovingkindnesses indeed never cease, for His compassions never fail. They are new every morning; great is Thy faithfulness. "The Lord is my portion," says my soul, "therefore I have hope in Him." The Lord is good to those who wait for Him, to the person who seeks Him. It is good that he waits silently for the salvation of the Lord. . . . For if He causes grief, then He will have compassion according to His abundant lovingkindness (Lamentations 3:22–26, 32).

Mercy—it is yours for the appropriation—new every morning. You may not say, "I cannot have it because I don't deserve it." You can only say, "I do not have it because I will not take it."

December 12

Does the call to take up your cross and follow Jesus strike terror in your heart? I can understand, yet you need not fear. Let me explain. The cross was an instrument of death, and man is bent on life. Yet, even more than death, the cross was an instrument of inexorable torture. It was the place of the cursed, not only to the Jews (Galatians 3:13) but also to the Romans. Cicero wrote, "Let the very name of the cross be far away not only from the body of a Roman citizen, but even from his thoughts, his eyes, his ears" (Cicero, *Pro Rabirio 5*).

Yes, natural men were to shun the cross, to keep it from their thoughts, their eyes, their ears; yet, to those who would be God's men and women, came the call of Jesus to keep the cross ever before them. Why? Because the cross is where the natural dies and the supernatural takes over. "I have been crucified with Christ; and it is no longer I who live, but Christ lives in me; and the life which I now live in the flesh I live by faith in the Son of God, who loved me, and delivered Himself up for me" (Galatians 2:20).

We who love God are never to fear the cross. Rather we are to fear its absence. Therefore, when you want to run, to escape, to save yourself from the call to forsake all and take up your cross and follow Him, you can be certain that that fear is not from God. Fear would cause you to doubt the character of the God of Calvary. God is a God of love. He would never allow you in any situation that would destroy you without always making clear a way of escape (1 Corinthians 10:13). No, the fear that would keep you from the cross comes only from the one who would offer you a crown without a cross, the devil himself. Satan fears the cross, for there men are set free from bondage to death.

At Calvary, perfect love casts out all fear, for fear has torment, and the one who fears is not perfected in love (1 John 4:18). "He who did not spare His own Son, but delivered Him up for us all, how will He not also with Him freely give us all things?" (Romans 8:32).

O Beloved, you can rest secure in His love—be it in taking up your cross daily or in applying the cross to each of life's bitter situations. We will talk more about it tomorrow, but for today let me leave you with this thought. If you will permit yourself to be secure in God's love, then that security will become the foundation for dealing with all other fears. Never let the cross out of your thoughts, your hearing, or your sight, for it is God's eternal testimony of His immutable love. It is your release from the natural to the supernatural.

December 13

We need to talk about fear for two more days, Dear One, for we live in times when men's hearts will fail them for fear. In any bitter situation, you need not fear. See that cross? What does it tell you? It tells you that your Sovereign Father God loves you with a perfect love. Remember this. Never forget it. Fear is to Satan what faith is to God. Satan operates on the basis of fear, and that immobilizes you. He will parade before you the fear of death, the fear of failure, the fear of man with his criticism or his rejection, the fear of having your weaknesses exposed for all to see. And where does fear of failure, of man, of your weaknesses find its root? Is it not in pride? And what is the answer to pride? Death. The cross. There all pride is stripped away. When Jesus hung on the cross, He hung there at almost eye level, stark naked, to be gaped upon by dogs and bands of evildoers (Psalms 22:16, 17).

Let me say it again: Fear is to Satan what faith is to God.

God never operates on the basis of anything but faith. "Without faith it is impossible to please Him" (Hebrews 11:6). "According to your faith be it unto you" (Matthew 9:29). While fear immobilizes, faith energizes. Therefore, in every bitter or difficult situation, if you apply the cross, you will drink the sweetness of power, love, and a sound mind that belongs to every believer. "For God hath not given us the spirit of fear; but of power, and of love, and of a sound mind" (2 Timothy 1:7 KJV). That power is resurrection power. Remember, last month I shared that, in God's economy, resurrection always follows crucifixion. Thus Paul prayed for us that the eyes of our understanding would be enlightened that we might know "the surpassing greatness of His power toward us who believe ... which He brought about in Christ, when He raised Him from the dead, and seated Him at His right hand in the heavenly places, far above all rule and authority and power and dominion, and every name that is named, not only in this age, but also in the one to come" (Ephesians 1:19–21).

Fear is always held in check by power, love, and a sound mind.

December 14

God has given you power, love, and a sound mind. It is yours for the believing. Faith unlocks the door to God's treasure house. To fear is to forget God and to live like a pauper when you really are a prince.

"I, even I, am He who comforts you. Who are you that you are afraid of man who dies, and of the son of man who is made like grass; that you have forgotten the Lord your Maker, who stretched out the heavens, and laid the foundations of the earth; that you fear continually all day long because of the fury of the oppressor" (Isaiah 51:12, 13).

Note it carefully, fear of man causes us to forget God. And who is man in comparison with God? Is not the Sovereign God of Calvary in control? Of course!

> The king is not saved by a mighty army; a warrior is not delivered by great strength. A horse is a false hope for victory; nor does it deliver anyone by its great strength. Behold, the eye of the Lord is on those who fear Him, on those who hope for His lovingkindness, to deliver their soul from death, and to keep them alive in famine. Our soul waits for the Lord; He is our help and our shield. For our heart rejoices in Him, because we trust in His holy name. Let Thy lovingkindness, O Lord, be upon us, according as we have hoped in Thee (Psalms 33:16–22).

When fear hits, remember you have been given a sound mind. A sound mind is a mind under control, not one given to vain imaginations or thoughts that exalt themselves against the knowledge of God (2 Corinthians 10:5). You don't have to throw a tizzy, lose touch with reality, check out or go bananas (that's a fruit that does not belong to the Spirit)! The Holy Spirit is there with His fruit basket (Galatians 5:22, 23). Partake! There's self-control in there! Bring your thoughts, every one of them, captive to His obedience. Remember, His Word is truth. "When I am afraid, I will put my trust in Thee. In God, whose word I praise, in God I have put my trust; I shall not be afraid" (Psalms 56:3, 4). "I will cry to God Most High, to God who accomplishes all things for me" (Psalms 57:2).

That's right, cry to Him and know that love provides all you need (Romans 8:32). "For I am convinced that neither death, nor life, nor angels, nor principalities, nor things present, nor things to come, nor powers, nor height, nor depth, nor any other created thing, shall be able to separate us from the love of God, which is in Christ Jesus our Lord" (8:38, 39).

Sweet, isn't it? Drink deep and be satisfied. It is all yours because of the cross.

December 15

We have learned how to take the bitter and make it sweet by looking unto the God of Calvary. But is there anything more we can learn about how one responds or behaves when he is being crucified by another? Or to put it another way, how does one bear up under sorrows when suffering unjustly? This is what I mean when I say, "crucified by another."

Peter and the Gospels have the answer and I believe that as we examine them together God is going to give us some invaluable insights. Some of you are suffering so unjustly, and I ache for you. I hurt with you. There is a mental anguish that can even exceed physical pain. And you may suffer more emotionally than you do physically. Yet even emotional pain takes its toll on the body, doesn't it? We are psychosomatic beings. What affects the body affects the soul, and vice versa.

Or maybe you are not hurting right now; maybe all is sweet. Then what is going on with you? Is God not working with you? No, God has given you a time of rest, a time to prepare, a time to grow in the easy progression of the seasons rather than in a forced hothouse environment. The early church had this rest and uncontested time to grow; then the tide turned with the stoning of Stephen, and they all fled Jerusalem. Please let me share a word of admonition. Watch carefully during these times of rest, for one can become lax in spiritual exercises and drift away only to be caught in a weakened condition, unprepared for the trials of faith that must come if he is ever to be fully prepared to be glorified with Him. Since* "indeed we suffer with Him in order that we may also be glorified with Him" (Romans 8:17). Suffering . . . suffering unjustly . . . teaches us obedience and matures us even as it did Jesus. Listen carefully to Hebrews 5:7–9.

> In the days of His flesh, He offered up both prayers and supplications with loud crying and tears to him who was able to save Him from death, and who was heard because of His piety, although He was a Son, He learned obedience from the things which He suffered; and having been made perfect, He became to all those who obey Him the source of eternal salvation.

We have been called to suffer; therefore, let's learn how by looking unto Jesus, "the author and perfecter of faith, who for the joy set before Him endured the cross" (Hebrews 12:2).

*I have used the word since here for clarity's sake because the if in Romans 8:17 is a first class condition and therefore denotes reality.

December 16

Unjust suffering is hard. It goes against the flesh. And we are all made of flesh! When He saved us, God crucified the old man, setting us free from slavery to sin (see November 11 for an explanation of this). He gave us a new heart, and put His Spirit within us. Our bodies became His temple. Yet, with all that, God left us in a body of flesh—"we have this treasure in earthen vessels" (2 Corinthians 4:7). Because of this you are going to suffer just as any other human being would suffer. It does not hurt less to be railed against or to be scorned. Rejection, abuse, contempt, defamation or any other cruel thing that man can do to man does not hurt less simply because you are a child of God. Note now, that I am talking about the reality of pain **not** the mentality of acceptance which can ease pain's intensity! Two people undergo an operation or experience the pain of cancer. One does not hurt less than the other simply because he or she is a child of God. No, suffering is suffering because we live in bodies of flesh. As Christians we still sorrow, we still grieve, but not as others who have no hope (1 Thessalonians 4:13).

As Christians, we are not of this world but are strangers and pilgrims because our citizenship is in heaven (Philippians 3:20). As a result, we are not only called upon to suffer the normal distresses of life in a world under bondage to sin, but also to face, as Christ faced, the hostility of sinners (Hebrews 12:3). And how do Christians deal with all the suffering—much of which will come simply because they are living in a world that cannot understand their righteous life-style and even hates them for it? How do we behave when others crucify us? How do we respond in such a way as to let the life of Jesus Christ be manifested in our **mortal** flesh?

We will answer that question step by step in the days to come as we look at God's Word precept upon precept. Today though, Precious One, I want you to remember one thing. Being a Christian does not mean you hurt any less. So, if at times you have felt as if your heart would literally break, do not despair. You are not any less "spiritual"! If Jesus cried, shedding tears (Hebrews 5:7), shall we not also cry? It is not the pain of suffering that reflects your Christlikeness; rather it is how you handle it!

December 17

Today I want us to concentrate on one passage of Scripture. To many of you, it will be a very familiar one, yet I pray that as you read it you will ask God for a fresh insight into what He is saying. Why don't you read it, and then we will do a little digging together. Have your notebook handy and, on a fresh page, put the heading: **When You Suffer Unjustly.**

1 Peter 2:18–3:2

18 Servants, be submissive to your masters with all respect, not only to those who are good and gentle, but also to those who are unreasonable.

19 For this finds favor, if for the sake of conscience toward God a man bears up under sorrows when suffering unjustly.

20 For what credit is there if, when you sin and are harshly treated, you endure it with patience? But if when you do what is right and suffer for it you patiently endure it, this finds favor with God.

21 For you have been called for this purpose, since Christ also suffered for you, leaving you an example for you to follow in His steps,

22 Who committed no sin, nor was any deceit found in His mouth;

23 and while being reviled, He did not revile in return; while suffering, He uttered no threats, but kept entrusting Himself to Him who judges righteously;

24 and He Himself bore our sins in His body on the cross, that we might die to sin and live to righteousness; for by His wounds you were healed.

25 For you were continually straying like sheep, but now you have returned to the Shepherd and Guardian of your souls.

3:1 In the same way, you wives, be submissive to your own husbands so that even if any of them are disobedient to the word, they may be won without a word by the behavior of their wives,

2 as they observe your chaste and respectful behavior.

I. Now that you have read the passage, go back and draw a around each use of the word "suffer" or "suffering."

II. Verse 21 says "You have been called for this purpose."
   a. To whom is Peter speaking? Write it in your notebook.
   b. Do you think this applies to Christians in general or only to servants (slaves)? Why?

III. The word *example* in verse 21 in the Greek is *hupogrammos*. It is only used here in the New Testament. It refers to an outline drawing or copybook of letters to be used by a pupil.
   a. Who is to be our example in suffering?
   b. What steps did He go through that we are to follow when we suffer unjustly? List them.

IV. Mark each use of the word *submissive* with a ⬜ . What role does submission play in unjust suffering? Look at 1 Peter 2:20 in conjunction with this.

V. What does the phrase, "In the same way" (3:1), refer to?

VI. What is the key in this passage when it comes to suffering: my pain, the equity of it all, my behavior, Christ's toughness in enduring, or God's judgment? Underline one and write out why you chose the answer you did.

Now, Beloved, meditate on all you've read today.

December 18

Favor with God. Beloved, there is nothing on this earth, absolutely nothing greater or more satisfying than knowing that what you have done has found favor with God. Conversely, there is nothing worth the loss of His favor, for, when this world and all it contains pass away and you stand naked before God, nothing else will matter except that you have found favor in the eyes of the One who created you for His pleasure.

When "for the sake of conscience toward God a man bears up under sorrows when suffering unjustly" (1 Peter 2:19), "when you do what is right and suffer for it [and] you patiently endure" (1 Peter 2:20), then you find favor with God. Why? Because, you have been called for this purpose. Precious One, if you can only see it as having a purpose, suffering is so much easier to take. It is not for nought that men crucify you or unjustly treat you. You are not a doormat to be trampled upon by the feet of wicked man. Rather you are a platform to be used to give them a closer glimpse of God. And you just may be that box, that step, that boost that causes them to see over the world's fence into the realities of life as it is to be played according to God's rules in the Kingdom of God.

You are not alone. Jesus has gone before you, suffering unjustly, becoming to all either a stepping-stone into heaven or a stone of stumbling into the depths of hell. He did His part. In God's eyes, He achieved His purpose at Calvary. The choice then became man's. God asks no more and no less of you than that you follow in His steps according to His example (1 Peter 2:21).

And what is His example, His *hupogrammos* to be used by you, His disciple? Well, I know you saw it for yourself yesterday, but let me state it again and elaborate on each step just a little so we won't miss what God wants us to know and to do.

The first thing we see is that when Jesus suffered unjustly, He did not sin. What does God mean when He says that Jesus did not sin?

Well, sin has a number of definitions from God's Word, such as being a transgression of the law (1 John 3:4) or knowing to do good and doing it not (James 4:17). However, the root of sin is independence from God. It is "each one turning to his own way" (Isaiah 53:6). When Jesus suffered unjustly, he did not act or react independently of God. Instead He did what pleased the Father. Therefore, when we are suffering unjustly, we must run to God and say, "O Father dear, what would You have me to do? I will to do Your will."

December 19

Never forget, Beloved, that it was Christ's purpose to suffer, the just for the unjust that unjust men might be made just before God. And, Beloved, don't forget your purpose. It is a high and noble one, a godly one, one that the world will scoff at, one that the world may trample under foot, calling you a fool while they seek to crush out your life-blood. Just remember, they know not what they do. The blood of the martyrs is the seed of the church—the church, bone of His bone, flesh of His flesh, His glorious virgin bride who shall someday reign with Him who is King of kings and Lord of lords! Oh, do not listen to the taunts of blind, ignorant, deceived sinners who shout, "Come down off that cross." Do not believe them when they say, "If God delighted in you, He would deliver you!" They know not what they say. "For the word of the cross is to those who are perishing foolishness, but to us who are being saved it is the power of God. For it is written, 'I will destroy the wisdom of the wise, and the cleverness of the clever I will set aside' " (1 Corinthians 1:18, 19).

Remember as they crucify you that "the foolishness of God is wiser than men, and the weakness of God is stronger than men" (1 Corinthians 1:25). Therefore, follow Christ's example, "who committed no sin, **nor was any deceit found in His mouth; and while being reviled, He did not revile in return; while suffering He uttered no threats**" (1 Peter 2:22, 23).

What was the second thing Christ did in leaving us an example? He kept His mouth shut. No battle with words. No, "You'll be sorry," or "You'll get yours." As a lamb before his shearers was dumb He opened not His mouth (Isaiah 53:7). To me, this is the hardest of all. All my life I have fought with my tongue. This has been my weapon. I was always too weak to overcome physically, so I fought and defended with my tongue. My flesh is adept in verbal battles. Remember how we used to taunt as children? "Sticks and stones will break my bones, but names will never hurt me!" And that was usually followed by sticking out your tongue! How childish we were, and how wrong! It is easier to mend bones than it is psyches that have been wounded by cruel tongues. Many wounds never show, but except for God's balm of Gilead, they would leave irreparable damage.

What have you said when you've suffered unjustly? What good did it do?

December 20

So far we have seen two things that we are to do when someone treats us unjustly. **First,** we are not to sin, not to act independently from God. We are to continually seek God's wisdom, remembering that God will never lead us contrary to His Word.

Secondly, we are to keep our mouths shut; by this I mean, no verbal battles. This does not mean that you give them the "silent treatment." Jesus did talk while they crucified Him, but He did not retaliate by reviling or uttering threats. His speech was not abusive. Controlled by God's Spirit, He never acted apart from love. Love "does not seek its own, is not provoked, does not take into account a wrong suffered" (1 Corinthians 13:5). That was Love hanging on that tree, remember? And, because you too are being crucified, the same God of Calvary is present with you when you take up your cross to follow Him. Please, Precious One, do not carry what I am saying to an extreme that God never intended. The key is Christianity in balance—balance that comes from knowing the whole counsel of God rather than going off on tangents. To avoid this let me cite an incident from the Gospels when Jesus did answer Pilate.

John 18:33–38

33 Pilate therefore entered again into the Praetorium, and summoned Jesus, and said to Him, "You are the King of the Jews?"

34 Jesus answered, "Are you saying this on your own initiative, or did others tell you about Me?"

35 Pilate answered, "I am not a Jew, am I? Your own nation and the chief priests delivered You up to me; what have You done?"

36 Jesus answered, "My kingdom is not of this world. If My kingdom were of this world, then My servants would be fighting, that I might not be delivered up to the Jews; but as it is, My kingdom is not of this realm."

37 Pilate therefore said to Him, "So You are a king?" Jesus answered, "You say correctly that I am a king. For this I have been born, and

for this I have come into the world, to bear witness to the truth.
Every one who is of the truth hears My voice."
38 Pilate said to Him, "What is truth?"

You might also want to read John 19:9–11. The example Jesus left us is a tongue under God's control, gracious speech seasoned with salt (Colossians 4:6), wisdom from above which is "pure, then peaceable, gentle, reasonable, full of mercy and good fruits, unwavering, without hypocrisy" (James 3:17).

December 21

The **third** thing that Jesus did that we are also to do was to pray, entrusting Himself to God. You cannot survive in such a way as to find favor with God without communicating with Him. The whole ordeal of the cross was wrestled out in Gethsemane and then sustained on Calvary. God does not expect you to go it alone because, Beloved, to do so is more than you can bear. Paul wrote in 2 Timothy 4:16, 17: "At my first defense no one supported me, but all deserted me; may it not be counted against them. **But the Lord stood with me,** and strengthened me, in order that through me the proclamation might be fully accomplished, and that all the Gentiles might hear; and I was delivered out of the lion's mouth."

Jesus, as He walked through the Kidron Valley to Gethsemane, said, "Behold, an hour is coming, and has already come, for you to be scattered, each to his own home, and to leave Me alone; and yet **I am not alone, because the Father is with Me**" (John 16:32).

God's promise to us is as true as He is unchangeable. "For He Himself has said, 'I will never desert you, nor will I ever forsake you,' so that we confidently say, 'The Lord is my helper, I will not be afraid. What shall man do to me?' " (Hebrews 13:5, 6).

His promise is good. You can trust Him. But remember all that He said is ineffectual if you do not appropriate it by faith. God is waiting for faith's call. His ear is not deaf that it cannot hear, nor is His arm short that it cannot help (Isaiah 59:1), but you must call to Him in the day of trouble (Psalms 50:15). "I sought the Lord, and He answered me, and delivered me from all my fears. They looked to Him and were radiant, and their faces shall never be ashamed. This poor man cried and the Lord heard him; and saved him out of all his troubles. The angel of the Lord encamps around those who fear Him, and rescues them" (Psalms 34:4–7).

Peter says that Jesus "kept entrusting Himself to Him who judges righteously" (1 Peter 2:23). "Entrusting" ("committed" KJV) is an imperfect active indicative verb. The imperfect tense indicates continuous action in the past, the active voice indicates that the subject did the entrusting, the indicative mood is the mood of reality. All of this means that Jesus kept on entrusting Himself to God during His unjust suffering. He stayed in constant communion with the Father. O Beloved, you may not feel like praying, but do not quit. You cannot survive without it—and still find favor with God.

December 22

You cannot pray effectively to someone you really do not trust. And this, Beloved, is the grabber. It stirs our soul to hear of becoming soldiers of the cross, but, when it gets down to the time when we are to take up our cross and follow Him, what is our response? Let's put it bluntly. Can we trust Him? Can we really trust God, give Him our all and leave the results with Him? Can we handle life's situations God's way, according to His Word, rather than our way?

Our counseling department at Reach Out and many of our dedicated Precept coordinators and leaders are finding that, under the guise of Christianity, many are being counseled to flee from the suffering that obedience would bring. In many counseling instances, human philosophy has usurped the authority of God's Word.

When Jesus suffered unjustly, the example that He left was not only that of not sinning, of keeping His tongue under control, of praying, but also of complete trust in the will and sovereignty of God. The Bible says Jesus "kept entrusting Himself to Him **who judges righteously**" (1 Peter 2:23). Note: "Who judges righteously." The suffering was unjust. Jesus was the innocent victim. Yet He knew God was in control. In God's time and in God's way, He would be vindicated. You will be too, Beloved, if you follow Christ's example. Some of you have unjustly lost homes, monies, children, lands, prestige, possessions, even credibility. It has seemed almost unbearable, hasn't it? You dare not even let your thoughts dwell on it, for to do so would throw you into depression or worse. So how do you handle it? There is only one way. Complete trust and constant communion. It is not all over yet. There is a payday someday, a day of retribution.

Just think! Jesus could have called a legion of angels to come to His defense, but He didn't. It wasn't God's time, so instead He entrusted Himself to Him who judges righteously.

O Beloved, do you find yourself in the same straits? I know it's hard. In all probability, try as I may, I cannot even begin to imagine how hard it is for you. Yet I do know that, because He promised, it is not more than you can bear (1 Corinthians 10:13). Will you follow His example?

December 23

Finally, 1 Peter tells us of one last thing that Jesus did that we, too, must do if we are going to follow in His steps when we suffer unjustly. I have taught this passage in 1 Peter for some time and until recently I missed this last step. It's a hard step, and God is patiently teaching me the reality of it in my own life. It so goes against my flesh. I must admit it is quite a struggle. What is it? It is that **"He Himself bore our sins in His body on the cross."** This, I believe, was also the hardest part of Calvary for Jesus. Harder for Him than it would ever be for anyone of us, for two reasons. First, He bore the sins of every human being who ever lived. Secondly, and I believe far worse, was the fact that Jesus Himself knew no sin. He was the total epitome of holiness, therefore sin was much more repulsive to Him than it would ever be to me or to you.

No invisible shield went up to protect Jesus from the full impact of sin's despicable awfulness. I want to say more, to describe it better, but I cannot find words atrocious enough. To me bearing another's sins in your own body must be the epitome of "turning the other cheek"—being willing to be wounded, to be hurt, if it will heal the one who is hurting you. Strange isn't it? I told you it would go against the flesh! It goes against human reasoning also, doesn't it? But does bearing another's sin, letting that sin hit you full force, make us passive or masochistic? No, neither of these has anything to do with what Jesus is saying. We are not talking about the passive reaction of quietly "taking it" because you don't have the courage to do otherwise. We are talking about exercising that amazing kind of strength which is able to receive unjust, personal suffering for the purpose of healing. Neither are we talking about finding masochistic pleasure at the hands of a sadist. No, the only delight here is in finding favor with God for Christlike suffering. Read 1 Peter 2:24, 25 again so you can see the purpose for bearing another's sins in our body. As you read, mark and think about the use of the words "that," "for," and "but now." "And He Himself bore our sins in His body on the cross, that we might die to sin and live to righteousness; for by His wounds you were healed. For you were continually straying like sheep, but now you have returned to the Shepherd and Guardian of your souls."

Whenever I have been hurt unjustly, my tendency has been to fight back, to hurt back, rather than just to take it and keep on loving in return. Now, though, God has opened my eyes and by His grace, I'm learning, opportunity by opportunity, to look beyond my hurt to their healing. Jesus won me that way! Amazing grace!

December 24

I want us to go one step further in looking at the cross so that we might gain an even deeper insight into how we are to behave when we are "being crucified" by another. In these last days together we need to go to Calvary and there behold the Lamb of God whom the Lord was pleased to crush as Jesus poured Himself out unto death (Isaiah 53:7, 10, 12). How did Jesus handle it? What did He do that we might also follow in His steps?

Luke 23:34 tells us the first of the seven statements that Jesus made during those awesome dark hours of crucifixion. "Father, forgive them; for they do not know what they are doing" (Luke 23:34).

The cross is a demonstration of love and forgiveness. It is at Calvary that love and forgiveness marry, becoming inseparably one. You cannot have one without the other. Jesus said, "For if you forgive men for their transgressions, your heavenly Father will also forgive you. But if you do not forgive men, then your Father will not forgive your transgressions" (Matthew 6:14, 15).

Therefore, the work of the cross begins with, "Father, forgive them." No bitterness. Bitterness is incompatible with the character of God. What about anger? Can you be angry? Yes! There can be righteous anger at sin, but no bitterness. There is a difference! Look at Calvary, and you see the wrath of God poured out on sin as you hear Jesus cry, "My God, My God, why hast Thou forsaken Me?" (Matthew 27:46). But, before wrath, did you not first hear His pardon to sinners? Calvary shows you the love of God, the wrath of God, the forgiveness of God, but never do you see bitterness in God, because bitterness contradicts the character of God!

If you are bitter, Beloved, it is because you have not put the tree into the waters. Forgive them and you will find the situation palatable. Now don't say, "I can't." If you are a child of God it is not that you cannot, it is that you will not! Forgive them; it will be the beginning, and from there you can move forward. You must by faith utter those words, "Father, forgive them—him, her, whoever—for they do not know what they are doing." And believe me, they do not know! They are blind, living in darkness. Yet your light may pierce that darkness. You may be their only human hope.

May they hear the gospel through your words, "Father, forgive them . . . ," so that their blood will not be upon your hands.

December 25

Today is Christmas and here we are studying His crucifixion! Yet this is what Christmas is all about; Jesus Christ born to die for you.

What follows crucifixion? Paradise! Fellowship with the faithful of God, with those who have believed, who have persevered, who have held "fast the beginning of our assurance firm until the end" (Hebrews 3:14). Jesus' second statement from that cross was the promise of Paradise to one of the malefactors being crucified with Him.

> And one of the criminals who were hanged there was hurling abuse at Him, saying, "Are You not the Christ? Save Yourself and us!" But the other answered, and rebuking him said, "Do you not even fear God, since you are under the same sentence of condemnation? And we indeed justly, for we are receiving what we deserve for our deeds; but this man has done nothing wrong." And he was saying, "Jesus, remember me when You come in Your kingdom!" And He said to him, "Truly I say to you, today you shall be with Me in Paradise" (Luke 23:39–43).

All suffering has an end. To those who believe on Jesus, it has a beginning and it has an end. It will not go on forever because it is controlled by the Alpha and the Omega. The end for every believer is Paradise and Paradise belongs to God. It was the place where the righteous dead longingly awaited the resurrection of Jesus Christ, the first begotten from the dead. Then Paradise was taken into the third heaven where Paul, caught up, heard inexpressible things, things man is not permitted to tell (2 Corinthians 12:3, 4). Paradise is where that blessed tree of life is—once shut away from man, but now again made accessible. It is the reward of those who overcome. Listen, it's beautiful. "To him who overcomes, I will grant to eat of the tree of life, which is in the Paradise of God" (Revelation 2:7).

What does one need in the midst of crucifixion? The hope of glory, of life, of fellowship with Jesus and fellowship with others who through believing have overcome! And what does one need to convey to others as he hangs there suffering? He needs to convey the reality and glory of the sure hope of heaven, "for I consider that the sufferings of this present time are not worthy to be compared with the glory that is to be revealed to us" (Romans 8:18).

And what does such certainty say to those who still persist in crucifying us? When we suffer and are "in no way alarmed by our opponents" because Paradise is before us, then our confidence becomes "a sign of destruction for them, but of salvation for you, and that too, from God" (Philippians 1:28).

The bitter is made sweet if we will but keep looking to the reward, enduring as seeing Him who is invisible, and remembering His promise, "You shall be **with Me** in Paradise."

This, Beloved, is God's gift to you, the promise of heaven for all those who receive God's Christmas gift, the Lord Jesus Christ.

Have you ever truly received Jesus Christ as your Lord and Savior? If not, then it is no wonder you feel like something is missing. It is! It's Jesus! It's life—eternal and abundant.

Turn from all else to Him. Give yourself to Him without reservation and He will give you Jesus the Christ.

December 26

Jesus' first three statements from the cross reveal our Lord's primary focus, and what a marvelous lesson there is in them for us. It really is a key, Beloved, and, if heard with your heart so that it is truly believed and acted upon, it can become one of the most potent cures for the cancer of misery that consumes the lives of many of God's children.

Jesus' third statement, like His first two, dealt with His concern for others.

> Therefore the soldiers did these things. But there were standing by the cross of Jesus His mother, and His mother's sister, Mary the wife of Clopas, and Mary Magdalene. When Jesus therefore saw His mother, and the disciple whom He loved standing nearby, He said to His mother, "Woman, behold, your son!" Then He said to the disciple, "Behold, your mother!" And from that hour the disciple took her into his own household (John 19:25–27).

Recently I have read two books, *Chosen to Live* and *Run for the West,* both of which are autobiographies of Jews who became Christians and lived under the terror of Hitler's holocaust. A pall has hung over me as I have witnessed a thousand deaths and heard the cry of millions mourning for their dead. I have tried as best I could to imagine the fellowship of their sufferings that I might not live at ease in my Christian Zion with no thought for those who, especially in distant lands, are "filling up that which is lacking in Christ's afflictions" (Colossians 1:24). As I read, over and over I was challenged by those who would say, as did Sandor in *Run for the West*, "I will take his beating for him," or do as a Jewish girl did when she gave herself over to be raped in order to spare the lives of the other women hidden behind coal boxes in a cellar.

You see, the cross assumes our death, the surrender of our life that others might live. And yet what do we do? We cling to what is not ours! "Do you not know that ... you are not your own? For you have been bought with a price: therefore glorify God in your body" (1 Corinthians 6:19, 20). And how do we glorify Him? By doing as He did when he gave His life a ransom for many!

If we would only learn to get our eyes off ourselves and on others. "Woman, behold your son. Behold your mother." Many a counselor's office could be cleared, many a depression cured if we would not merely look out for our own personal interests, but also for the interests of others (Philippians 2:4).

December 27

One of the horrendous things about unjust suffering that everyone has to deal with at one time or another is that devastating premonition that you have been abandoned, forsaken by God. It happens to the godliest of saints. It happened to Jesus, only His was real. God did forsake Him. But because His was real, yours will never be.

Suddenly about noon a darkness came over the whole land, the sun's light failing. "And at the ninth hour Jesus cried out with a loud voice, 'ELOI, ELOI, LAMA SABACHTHANI?' which is translated, 'My God, My God, why hast Thou forsaken Me?' " (Mark 15:34).

God had forsaken Jesus. It was not His imagination! God had actually abandoned His Son leaving Him in the throes of sin's awful death, separation from God and man. Jesus had no recourse; He had no aide. In that one inexplicably horrendous moment, the Father and the Holy Spirit were estranged from the Son. Thus, abandoned by both, He cried twice, "My God, My God," or literally, "God of Me, God of Me, why hast Thou forsaken Me?"

The cry had been recorded a thousand years earlier, when his agony was prophetically penned by the Psalmist in God's Holy Writ (Psalm 22). Written by the Word and read countless times by the Word who had become flesh! Now it was fulfilled and screamed into the ears of the Holy God who had to punish sin, for He who knew no sin was at that moment made to be sin for us.

Who suffered the greater agony, the Father who was made impotent by His own righteous justice, or the Son, who foreseeing this had pled, "Father, if thou be willing, remove this cup from me: nevertheless, not my will, but thine, be done" (Luke 22:42 KJV)? The hour had come, the eternal hour of destiny. Never before, never again would there be a time like it when God the Father and God the Spirit would forsake God the Son for the sake of mankind, who for the most part couldn't care less! Yet He did it that we, who were dead, estranged from God, might live, never to be forsaken by Him.

O my God . . . "what shall I render to the Lord for all His benefits toward me? I shall lift up the cup of salvation, and call upon the name of the Lord. . . . O Lord, surely I am Thy servant, I am Thy servant, the son of Thy handmaid, Thou hast loosed my bonds" (Psalms 116:12, 13, 16). **"He shall see of the travail of his soul, and shall be satisfied"** (Isaiah 53:11 KJV).

December 28

Jesus was forsaken by God so that the immutable God could say to you, "I will never, no, never, forsake you nor ever leave you, that you, my child, might not fear what man would do to you." That is God's word to every believer in Hebrews 13:5. Yet, at times we wonder, don't we? At times the thought insidiously creeps in that God has abandoned us. And then, rather than reason through God's Word, we begin to reason within ourselves, "God must have forsaken me. Surely He would not let me suffer so! Surely His justice could not tolerate such iniquity to triumph, surely!" Deep within we know God cannot lie; yet dazed by pain, tormented by men who have no fear of God, crying to God yet seemingly not heard, we **feel** forsaken.

Beloved, when you suffer unjustly, when you are being crucified by another and you want to cry, "My God, my God, why have You forsaken me?" He understands. He does not want you to feel forsaken because you are not! Know it or not, feel it or not, it does not change the reality that He is there. Silent though He may be at the time, He is an ever present help in the time of need (Psalm 46:1). Remember the trial is not without purpose, His eternal purpose. God has a plan.

In *Run for the West,* on a grueling march toward the camp where he was to be exterminated, Sandor, a Christian Jew, came across a detachment of Jews working outside a city. He stared at them, envy gnawing at his heart.

Their cheeks were full and their arms strong and muscular. It was obvious that they were getting enough food. I was more jealous of that group than I had ever been of anyone in my entire life.

It would be nice to be able to work and to eat when I was hungry. Why could I not stay with them? I asked myself bitterly. Why would God allow me to be treated so cruelly? Why was I being taken to a place that would mean certain death?

I cried out to God, but there was no answer. I felt deserted by him. It seemed as though He had turned his back on me. Deep within, I knew that was not true, but my pain was so fierce I could not reason. [There it is, the cry of the crucified, "Why have You deserted me?" And how do you handle it? The cross, Beloved, the cross! Listen to Sandor's words.]

As I walked, I began to consider the suffering of Jesus Christ on the cross. He did not have to die there. He did it for me, Sandor Berger, so I could have victory over death and spend eternity with him. Who was I to expect to be treated differently than any other Jew? God would not allow me to suffer any more pain than I was able to bear.

The day before Sandor was to be killed, the Americans liberated his death camp. Sandor walked back across the land to his home. When he approached the city of Wells, he remembered the large detachment of Jews that he had envied so.

I supposed that they had been released and were back with their families again. I was so sure of that, I was surprised to hear myself asking a farmer about them.

"Them?" the bent, gray-haired farmer echoed, a strange tone in his voice. "When the Nazis decided to pull out, they shot and killed the whole lot."

I stared incredulously at him. That could not be true, I told myself.

Reading the doubt in my face he added, "It's the truth. I saw the bodies myself, after it was over."

How jealous I had been of those Jews because they were getting enough to eat and were being fairly well treated. I had complained bitterly to God because I and those with me were being singled out for torture when that group of Jews had much to make them comfortable. Now those I had envied were dead, and I was alive.

Tears streamed down my gaunt cheeks as I asked God to forgive me. I had learned again the truth of the Bible verse, "All things work together for good to them that love the Lord." God had shown his marvelous lovingkindness and care to me, something I did not deserve.[31]

O Beloved, you can imagine yourself forsaken of God—but it's a lie. He is there in His all-sufficient grace.

December 29

> Reproach has broken my heart, and I am so sick. And I looked for sympathy, but there was none, and for comforters, but I found none. They also gave me gall for my food, and for my thirst they gave me vinegar to drink (Psalms 69:20, 21).

"Jesus . . . saith, 'I thirst' " (John 19:28 KJV). It was His fifth statement from the cross.

There's an agony of heart and of soul that leaves one weak and broken of body. At times like that, when the pain is so intense, it's almost impossible to talk. Torturously swollen, your tongue cleaves to the roof of your mouth. The pain causes you to pant for breath. The hysteria of emotion can bring on a hyperventilation that leaves you parched. Your heart aches so that you feel it will burst. You need relief. You thirst. The cup or wet washrag is lifted to your lips; you choke and turn away. Why can't you just die?

Crucifixion hurts. Don't deny it and do not make others deny it and play the hero while you, immune to their pain, watch and testify, exclaiming, "See, God is sufficient. They didn't even cry! They smiled the whole time. What a testimony! Praise the Lord."

No, Beloved, no! Crucifixion hurts. Let them weep! Let them tell you that they hurt, that they thirst! Succor them. Weep with them!

How different it is for me now since Daddy died. There's a new compassion, an empathy, no more pious platitudes when others are suffering. They thirst. And all I want to do is to be there and minister to their needs. The bitter is bitter. Oh, it is made bearable by the cross, but, if it were not bitter, it would not be a test. When a person is taking an exam from God, you don't cheat and give them the answers. God never would have taken them through that exam without first preparing them. No, instead of showing answers you sit, wait, pray, and when they look up with a face beaded with perspiration, you hand them your handkerchief, and say, "I know it's hard, awfully hard, but you'll make it. I'm pulling for you with the Father." You are there to affirm, to confirm not to lecture. Meet their need.

"I thirst." Of course you do, insufferably. And I will not make you deny it. I will suffer with you.

December 30

> A jar full of sour wine was standing there; so they put a sponge full of the sour wine upon a branch of hyssop, and brought it up to His mouth. When Jesus therefore had received the sour wine, He said, "It is finished!" (John 19:29, 30).

Jesus' purpose was to give His life a ransom for many; that He had done. Now He could say, *Tetelestai. Tetelestai* comes from the Greek word *teleo,* which means to bring to an end. *Tetelestai* was also used as a legal term to denote the fact that a debt had been paid in full. Man's debt of sin had been paid in full by Christ's death on the cross. Jesus could say, "It is finished," with full assurance for there was not a thing that He had left undone. He could say to the Father, "I glorified Thee on the earth, having accomplished the work which Thou hast given Me to do" (John 17:4). Jesus had been "obedient to the point of death, even death on a cross" (Philippians 2:8). Jesus' unjust suffering had come to an end because its purpose was accomplished.

And so it is with you, Beloved. No suffering is without purpose in God's economy. Therefore, throughout the Epistles the believer is told, in one form or another, to rejoice in trials. James 1:2–4 puts it this way: "My brethren, count it all joy when ye fall into divers temptations; knowing this, that the trying of your faith worketh patience. But let patience have her perfect work, that ye may be perfect and entire, wanting nothing" (KJV).

The word "perfect" in James 2:4 has the same root as does "it is finished." What does it mean? It means, Precious One, that all trials, including unjust suffering, have as their purpose to bring you to a specific end, a specific state of maturity or completion. When that has been accomplished, then the trial or suffering comes to an end and you can say, "It is finished." God's perfect purpose has been accomplished.

And what does it mean practically? How will it help you to endure the cross, although you, like Jesus, despise its shame? Whenever someone is crucifying you, whenever you are suffering unjustly, you can rest assured that the time is coming when you can say, "It is finished."

Yet, Beloved, know this. You are not to bring it to an end; not in any form, including suicide. To do so is to fall short, to fail to persevere, never to be able to say to God, "It is finished." You will not be shut out of Paradise, but I'm sure that, in a way, heaven will not be as joyous, at first, for the shame of not enduring.

Persevere, Beloved, persevere. The end shall come, and you, too, can say to your Father, "I have glorified You on earth."

December 31

Jesus' last and final word from the cross was uttered with a loud cry—a cry of trust, a cry of committal, the cry of a son to a father.

"And Jesus, crying out with a loud voice, said, 'Father, into Thy hands I commit My Spirit.' And having said this, He breathed His last" (Luke 23:46). It is evident from Jesus' words, that the darkness was gone, the light of the Father's face had been restored, the serenity had returned. No longer is it "my God," but instead, "Father." It is to His Father that He commits His spirit.

Matthew tells us that Jesus "yielded up His spirit" (Matthew 27:50). His spirit was not taken from Him in death, rather it was surrendered. This was in keeping with Jesus' statement in John 10:17, 18: "For this reason the Father loves Me, because I lay down My life that I may take it again. No one has taken it away from Me, but I lay it down on My own initiative. I have authority to lay it down, and I have authority to take it up again. This commandment I received from My Father." Jesus laid His life into the loving hands of His Father, who would do no wrong, the God He could trust. His last words were a direct quote from Psalm 31. Their content shows the security that can come when one knows the character and ways of his God. Read the Psalmist's words carefully and meditate upon them:

In Thee, O Lord, I have taken refuge; let me never be ashamed; in Thy righteousness deliver me. Incline Thine ear to me, rescue me quickly; be Thou to me a rock of strength, a stronghold to save me. For Thou art my rock and my fortress; for Thy name's sake Thou wilt lead me and guide me. Thou wilt pull me out of the net which they have secretly laid for me; for Thou art my strength. Into Thy hand I commit my spirit; Thou hast ransomed me, O Lord, God of truth (Psalms 31:1-5).

How secure are you, Beloved, with your God? It will show when the test of bitter waters comes your way.

Let me share with you a true story I once heard that illustrates the reality of the bitter being made sweet. A young traveler was mesmerized by the countenance of a woman sitting across the aisle from him on the train. There was such joy in her face. *How could one with a hook for a hand be so radiant?* he mused. Finally, overcome with curiosity, he asked her if he might sit beside her. As the train rhythmically clattered over miles of track, he learned her story. She had been a missionary when an illness forced her to leave the people and the land she had intended to serve the rest of her days. Broken in health, without family, she returned to her homeland and a little plot of ground. As her health became somewhat restored, she began to farm the land in order to eke out her existence. Then one day as she was working in the fields, her hand was caught in a threshing machine of some sort. "As I stood in the field, my hand torn from my arm I looked to heaven and said, 'Father, what is it now You would have me to do since I have lost my hand?' I did not question His ways. I trusted Him. I only wanted to know what was next!" What was next? Collecting clothing and taking it over the border to Christians in Russia who were in need.

O Beloved, you will never be able to take the bitter and make it sweet until you trust the God of Calvary and can say to Him, "Father, I trust You; into Thy hands I commit my spirit. Do as You would with me. You are my God. My times are in Your hand."

NOTES

1. Baxter, J. Sidlow, *Explore The Book Vol. IV* (Grand Rapids: Zondervan, 1967), p. 261.
2. Jensen, Irving, *Jensen's Survey of the Old Testament* (Chicago: Moody Press, 1978), p. 467.
3. Ibid., p. 468.
4. Morgan, G. Campbell, *The Minor Prophets* (Old Tappan: Fleming H. Revell, 1960), p. 154.
5. Vine, W. E., *An Expository Dictionary of New Testament Words* (Nashville: Thomas Nelson, 1978), p. 688.
6. Ibid.
7. Lambert, Lance, *Battle for Israel* (Eastbourne, Great Britain: Kingsway Publications Ltd., 1976), p. 21.
8. Feinberg, Charles L., *The Minor Prophets* (Chicago: Moody Press, 1978), p. 260.
9. Wright, H. Norman, *The Christian Use of Emotional Power* (Old Tappan: Fleming H. Revell, 1974), p. 135.
10. Ibid., p. 142.
11. Ibid.
12. Wheat, Ed, *Love Life for Every Married Couple* (Grand Rapids: Zondervan, 1980), pp. 120, 121.
13. D'Aubigne, J. H. Merle, *The Life and Times of Martin Luther* (Chicago: Moody Press, 1978), p. 90.
14. Ibid., p. 92.
15. Ibid., pp. 92–94.
16. Ibid., p. 20.
17. Ibid., p. 21.
18. Ibid., p. 24.
19. Ibid., pp. 30, 32.
20. Ibid., p. 46.
21. Ibid., p. 52.
22. Ibid.
23. Ibid., pp. 54–56.

24. Vine, W. E., *Vine's Expository Dictionary of Old Testament and New Testament Words* (Old Tappan: Fleming H. Revell, 1981), p. 230.
25. Ibid.
26. Steer, Roger, *George Mueller: Delighted in God!* (Wheaton: Harold Shaw, 1975).
27. Huegel, F. J., *The Cross of Christ, The Throne of God* (Minneapolis: Bethany House, 1965), pp. 9, 10.
28. Ibid., p. 78.
29. Ibid., p. 79.
30. Trench, R. C., *Synonyms of the New Testament* (Grand Rapids: Wm. B. Eerdmans, 1948).
31. Palmer, Bernard, *Run for the West* (Elgin: David C. Cook, 1979), pp. 82, 121.